CALIFORNIA
SLAVIC
STUDIES

VOLUME 14

CALIFORNIA SLAVIC STUDIES

—

VOLUME 14

HENRIK BIRNBAUM,
THOMAS EEKMAN,
HUGH McLEAN, and
NICHOLAS RIASANOVSKY,
EDITORS

UNIVERSITY OF CALIFORNIA PRESS
Berkeley • Los Angeles • Oxford

University of California Press
Berkeley and Los Angeles, California

University of California Press, Ltd.
Oxford, England

Library of Congress Cataloging-in-Publication Data

California Slavic studies : volume XIV / edited by Henrik Birnbaum . . .
  [et al.]

     p.   cm. — (California Slavic studies ; vol. 14)

  Includes bibliographical references.

  ISBN 0–520–07025–9 (alk. paper)

  1. Slavic philology. 2. Soviet Union—History. I. Birnbaum, Henrik.
II. Series.

DK4.C33 vol. 14

[PG13]

947 s—dc20

[891.8]   90-37039
                                                   CIP

Printed in the United States of America

1 2 3 4 5 6 7 8 9

CONTENTS

PREFACE

This is a good time to write and publish in the Slavic and East European field. Recent political developments in that vast area are both permitting and inspiring new and more extensive scholarship, a process of revival which is still at an early and confusing stage but possesses great potential. Indeed a single universe of study and discourse might finally become a reality for all of us. Closer to home, *California Slavic Studies,* always much in demand in the Soviet Union and repeatedly favorably reviewed in Poland, might fully assume its legitimate place in the Eastern as well as in the Western world.

Our publication, which began to come out in 1960, relying in the main on the University of California and its Press, is now presenting its fourteenth volume. Not a periodical in the usual sense and not tied to a calendar, it has the capacity to include some longer pieces as well as articles of regular size. The editors and the Press have in recent years decided to concentrate on thematic tomes, as exemplified by our recent or forthcoming volumes on medieval Russian culture, Tolstoy, and the Silver Age, with only occasional miscellaneous ones. This is such a miscellaneous volume.

The volume contains twelve contributions. Henrik Birnbaum, the most active Western specialist on Novgorod, offers a state-of-the-art account of his favored subject and of the international scholarship devoted to it. Thomas Eekman writes on Muscovite international relations in the late seventeenth century in terms of the observations of Johan van Keller. A distinct contribution to knowledge, the piece combines Muscovite and Dutch expertise and exemplifies the increased recent scholarly interest in the West in the immediately pre-Petrine period. Terence Emmons deals, brilliantly as well as informatively, in our opinion, with "Kliuchevskii's Pupils," the major Russian historians of our century. Starting the part of the volume devoted to Russian literature, Leighton Brett Cooke applies modern psychology, more precisely sociobiology, and the concept of the *femme fatale* to Pushkin's *Cygany*. The point of Paul A. Karpuk's study of Gogol, in this case Gogol's *Strašnaja mest',* is the restoration of the historical framework on which Gogol relied in his writings and which has been neglected and even denied by scholars: these histories were important to Gogol, although they may be faulty in the eyes of present-day specialists. Bernice Rosenthal treats in a forceful manner the difficult topic of Vyacheslav Ivanov's version of *Sobornost'*. Next, and to quote an anonymous reader for the Press: "Jerry

Heil's essay about the film *Poručik Kiže* (script by Tynjanov) is excellent in every respect: original, well researched, perceptive in analysis, and yet written in a lively and accessible style. With deceptive ease, Heil brings off the difficult trick of getting the reader to visualize cinematographic effects without the benefit of seeing the film." Immediately following Heil's article, John M. Kopper explores in a stimulating manner a still more recent topic, namely that of mythopoetic thinking in Aleshkovsky's *Smert' v Moskve.*

  California Slavic Studies remain interested in Eastern Europe outside Russia, or the ex-Soviet Union, as well as inside. The present volume includes Walter Schamschula's meticulous tracing of "Pan Twardowski: The Polish Variant of the Faust Legend in Slavic Literatures." And it encompasses three contributions dealing with the South Slavs. Zlatan Čolaković examines expertly "South Slavic Muslim Epic Songs: Problems of Collecting, Editing and Publishing." A veteran scholar in the South Slavic field, Ante Kadić offers "A Literary and Spiritual Profile of Ruger J. Bošković." Kadić's essay is accompanied by a long note written by Roger Hahn, a historian of science and the scholar most responsible for bringing the Bošković papers to the Bancroft Library of the University of California in Berkeley. Finally, Marc L. Greenberg writes on the prosodic possibilities of modern standard Slovene and its dialects. Neither of us can claim competence in regard to the last item, but we were cheered by the following opinion of an outside reader: "Far more technical than any of the other papers, Marc Greenberg's on the prosodic possibilities of Slovene is a substantial contribution in its field of linguistics. It is based mostly on unpublished materials and applies an innovative mathematical approach. The method is clearly set forth, the thesis is articulated, and the exposition is carried through with precision. Not only are the results illuminating for Slovene, but there may be broader applications. Altogether a fine piece of work from this young linguist."

  This time we accepted either the international scientific system of transliteration or that of the Library of Congress, at the discretion of the author. This pleased the writers; as to the readers, all of us are surely by now accustomed to both.

N.V.R.
H.Mc.

MEDIEVAL NOVGOROD

Political, Social, and Cultural Life
in an Old Russian Urban Community*

HENRIK BIRNBAUM

I

The story to be told here will take the reader to a remarkable place in the Slavic world during a period when its potentials, though they were to remain unrealized, could conceivably have changed the course of world history. This was a time and a community of manifold and impressive cultural achievements, some of which have survived to this day. The medieval city of Novgorod was favorably situated on the banks of the Volkhov, just as that river forms a stream flowing out of Lake Ilmen. The Old Russian city could thus be reached by ship from the Baltic Sea, or more specifically from the Gulf of Finland, following the water route of the Neva, sailing along the southern shore of Lake Ladoga, and then entering the Volkhov. By the high Middle Ages, Lord Novgorod the Great—*Gospodin Velikij Novgorod,* as the city's proud people had come to refer to it—had gradually grown from modest beginnings in the ninth century, shrouded in a mist of legend and lore, into an urban community of considerable size even by contemporary European standards. It has been estimated on fairly reliable grounds that Old Novgorod, at its fullest flowering in the fourteenth and fifteenth centuries, had an urban population of 25,000 to 30,000 people. Kiev, the first capital of Old Rus', had 35,000 to 40,000 inhabitants toward the end of the pre-Mongol period, i.e., in the early thirteenth century, while Moscow probably did not pass 20,000 until the early fifteenth century. In comparison, Paris is believed to have had a population of about 80,000 in the first half of the fourteenth century, and London no more than 35,000 to 40,000

---

*A shorter version of this essay (without bibliographic references) was presented as the UCLA Sixtieth Annual Faculty Research Lecture on 7 March 1985, and published as a separate illustrated booklet titled *Lord Novgorod the Great: Sociopolitical Experiment and Cultural Achievement* (Los Angeles, 1985). I am indebted to Professor Andrzej Poppe, Warsaw, who read an earlier version of this study and suggested a number of improvements.

residents in the second half of the same century. Of Italy's cities, Milan, Venice, Florence, and Naples had a population in excess of 50,000 as early as the fourteenth century, as did the two commercial centers of Flanders, Ghent and Bruges. Of the German cities, only Cologne, with 30,000 to 40,000 citizens, seems to have surpassed Novgorod numerically in the fifteenth century, whereas Nuremberg, Augsburg, Vienna, and Strasbourg, each with about 20,000 inhabitants, did not, in terms of numbers, quite match the population of Novgorod. Lübeck, long-time trading partner of Novgorod; Prague, in the mid-fourteenth century briefly the capital of the Holy Roman Empire; and, on the Iberian Peninsula, Valencia, Saragossa, and Lisbon appear to have been roughly of Novgorod's size by the fifteenth century.[1] Medieval Novgorod was thus the scene of a pulsating urban life, complex sociopolitical activities and tensions, and a booming, productive economy. It was the hub of a far-flung, largely international trade and the center of a flourishing, many-faceted culture. Among the cities of the East Slavic lands, only Kiev and Moscow were, as indicated, comparable in size and significance to Novgorod during medieval times. While Novgorod reached the height of its importance during the high Middle Ages (using here the slightly adjusted chronological scale applicable to Russian history), the period of Kiev's greatness came in the early Middle Ages, and that of Moscow only began toward the later medieval period.[2] The latter city's importance was, as is well known, eclipsed during the two centuries—the eighteenth and the nineteenth—when imperial St. Petersburg, its Western flair in many ways reminiscent of Novgorod's earlier Western outlook, outshone the glitter and pomp of the ancient capital in the heart of Russia.

Though long regarded as older than the southern metropolis on the Dnieper,[3] based on the legend of its origin (a claim, incidentally, not borne out by archeological finds of the last few decades), and aspiring to rival the capital of the earliest East Slavic state—Kievan Rus'—from the middle of the eleventh century onward, Novgorod did not reach the peak of its glory, wealth and splendor until after the invasion of the Tatars in the late 1230s and the victories, under Prince Alexander Nevskij, over the invading Swedish forces and the Teutonic-Livonian Knights in the early 1240s. It has recently been contended that Alexander's much-glorified role as a warlord has been greatly exaggerated in Russian biographical writing and historiography and that his successful battles against the Swedes on the banks of the Neva (earning him his epithet) and against the Knights of the German Order and their Estonian allies on the ice of Lake Peipus did not in actuality amount to much more than relatively minor defensive skirmishes.[4] Rather, it was his skillful diplomatic maneuvering and subsequent shrewd collaboration with the Khanate of the Golden Horde that preserved and, at least for the time being, saved Novgorod's autonomy. Thus he was able to turn its relationship with the invaders into a mere tributary dependence on the Mongol rulers (comparable to that entered into, more than a century later, by another Slavic commercial and cultural center, the city-republic of Dubrovnik on the Adriatic coast, acknowledging the formal supremacy of the Ottoman Sultanate). From 1249 until his death in 1263, Alexander's diplomatic skill even brought him the coveted title of grand prince of Vladimir-Suzdal', a mostly nominal distinction granted with the explicit approval of Russia's Tatar overlord residing at Saraj on the lower Volga. By then, of course, Kiev had long ceased to count as a viable competitor, and Muscovy had barely entered upon the historic course that would lead to its subsequent unchallenged dominance of Russia and, ultimately, world-power status. Novgorod's cherished liberty and political autonomy came to a tragic, but not entirely unexpected, end in 1478 with the conquest and incorporation of the North Russian city-state, with its widespread dominions, into the Grand Duchy of Moscow (thus virtually doubling the latter's territory). Yet it is worth noting that some aspects of Novgorod's urban life, particularly in the spheres of intellectual, religious, and artistic activities, continued to thrive even after the Volkhov city's subjugation. A few of these actually reached their full development only after the collapse of what in historiography, though not in contemporary sources, is occasionally referred to as the Republic, or Realm, of St. Sophia. The House of St. Sophia (*Dom sv. Sofii*) was, however, used not only as a designation of the archiepiscopal palace and court but also with reference to the city-state as a whole formally headed by Novgorod's archbishop.

These appellations allude not only to the form of government practiced in Novgorod and the territories it controlled, but also to the significance attributed to its famous cathedral, located within the citadel known as *Detinec,* and from 1165 onward, to the office of the city's archbishop, or *vladyka.* This latter term, a calque from Greek *despotēs,* literally means ruler, but among various Slavic peoples was and still is used to refer to a bishop or archbishop of the Eastern Church. However, in Novgorod, as well as in the South Slavic principality of Montenegro, it designated the holder of combined spiritual and temporal powers (cf. also German *Fürstbischof, Fürsterzbischof*). Until the very end of Novgorod's independence, then, its archbishop acted as its formal head of state. Popular sayings such as "One does not fight against God and Novgorod," "To stand and die for St. Sophia," or "Where St. Sophia stands, there too stands Novgorod" echo both the pride the townspeople took in their cathedral and the genuine political power that the Church as an institution commanded; the latter was symbolized by the archbishop's presiding over the Council of Lords (*Sovet gospod* or *Gospody,* used as a collective noun). This as well as the other ruling bodies and high offices of Novgorod will be discussed below.

It was in this city, in the second half of the thirteenth century, that a man wrote what is considered to be the earliest extant love letter in the Old Russian vernacular. This was only a few decades after the Tatars had entered and overrun most of the Russian lands but miraculously, as it were, spared Novgorod and its territories—or, possibly as a result of a deal struck with the Volkhov city and its prince, after having captured the town of Toržok, halfway between Moscow and Novgorod, did not continue their advance toward the northwest. To be sure, it is quite possible that the sender himself was illiterate and thus did not personally write this letter. Instead, a professional but perhaps only semi-literate scribe or poorly educated, low-ranking cleric may well have written his love declaration and marriage proposal for him. It is brief and to the point, and reads in translation: "From Nikita to Uljanica. Come join me. I want you, and you me. Ignat is (or will be) a witness to this."[5] The stark tone and terse phrasing of this highly personal communication should not surprise us. For not only were the people of Novgorod usually very straightforward and down-to-earth; they were, as a rule, also thrifty and no great spenders where little would do. Thus the message just quoted was not written on expensive parchment; instead it was incised on birch bark, a cheap and abundant commodity, and therefore a widely utilized writing surface in medieval Novgorod. The birch, with its smooth, white bark which easily peels off in thin sheets, was—and still is—among the most common trees in northern Russia. Up to the present, about seven hundred such private letters and legal or paralegal documents on birch bark have been unearthed in Novgorod and published, many of them quite short or incomplete, but some longer ones as well. They have been recovered at certain levels of permanently moist ground beneath the old city; for a specific degree of moisture is a necessary condition for the preservation of these unique records. Thus, in the dry or insufficiently moist uppermost as well as in the deepest strata of archeological deposits, no such inscribed or legible birchbark texts have been found. While the vast majority of them has been discovered inside the bounds of the medieval city, a few birchbark documents have also been excavated elsewhere in North Russia, notably in the smaller town of Staraja Russa, in medieval times known simply as Rusa, south of Lake Ilmen. It was on 26 July 1951 that among the many uninscribed scraps of birchbark the first birchbark letter was accidentally discovered by a woman worker employed by the Novgorod Archeological Expedition, which began regular and systematic excavations more than half a century ago. Since that day more and more such records have come to light and still continue to do so.[6]

Another frequently cited birchbark letter, written (and perhaps commissioned) probably as early as the beginning of the twelfth century or even shortly before that, reads as follows: "From Gostjata to Vasilij. What my father gave me and my relatives left me, that he has taken possession of (or possibly: that he may keep). But now he has taken himself a new wife and has left me with nothing. Having broken his commitment, he has abandoned me and taken another one. Come and set things straight." Several of the words and phrases occurring in this particular text remain controversial as to their precise meaning and stylistic value. Some may well echo the legal parlance of the day. As a matter of fact, not even the crucial sex of the letter writer is beyond doubt. For Gostjata is either the abandoned wife, as the contents of the message would seem to suggest, or, as has also been argued, the name of a male relative writing on her behalf or in his own interest.[7] Along with much additional evidence, this letter indicates, not surprisingly, that the status of women, including some female members of well-to-do and privileged families, was not equal to that of men. As a recent study on the subject aptly concludes: "For all their exclusive property rights, women were not the equal of their male counterparts, because they had to rely upon men to defend their claims if any question arose. Equality and independence, however, are anachronistic concepts for medieval Russia, just as they are for medieval Western Europe."[8]

One set of birchbark artifacts, consisting largely of some first writing exercises and awkward drawings, as well as some mindless scribblings, seems to have been the work of a six- or seven-year-old boy named Onfim. They are thought to date from the early thirteenth century, since it has been established that they were all discarded on one and the same occasion, sometime between 1224 and 1238.[9]

It is on the strength of data contained in several birchbark documents, and by collating that data with evidence from other sources, that we can now tentatively identify the name and some aspects of the checkered biography of the hitherto anonymous master painter (and perhaps head of the team of artists) responsible for the magnificent frescoes which once decorated the Church of the Savior on Neredica Hill southeast of Old Novgorod (which, unfortunately, were completely destroyed during the Second World War).[10]

Two general conclusions, controversial to be sure, have been drawn by scholars concerning this treasure of predominantly vernacular epigraphic material from medieval Novgorod. First, it has been suggested that the birchbark texts are proof of widespread literacy among the ordinary people of the Volkhov city. However, these records are frequently of only a semi-literate character and, more important, it is probable that many, if not most, of them were written not by the person indicated as the sender, but on his or her behalf by a professional scribe or barely literate cleric. For this reason, only limited significance can be attached to the admittedly large number of these documents recovered from medieval Novgorod. They are more revealing about social conditions than about the level of literacy attained by the majority of the citizens. Second, and from a linguistic-historical point of view of considerable interest, a highly regarded Russian scholar, A. A. Zaliznjak, has recently stated that the language of the birch-bark letters, thought to reflect with some accuracy and consistency the patois of Novgorod's urban population, is in fact less flawed and faulty than has previously usually been claimed. Moreover, it is said to reflect not so much a particular early variety of spoken East Slavic, but rather a late Common Slavic dialect—thus a local form of the last phase of the ancestral language of all the ancient Slavs. This dialect would be characterized by a blending of what was to become early East Slavic with other, primarily northern West Slavic, linguistic elements. If proven correct, this view, expressed by a renowned linguist, would support the hypothesis advanced on other grounds that Novgorod's earliest Slavic population was not made up entirely of one or two East Slavic (i.e., Old Russian) tribes—namely the *Slověne* and, possibly, the *Kriviči*—but that, from an early date on, it also included some West Slavic ethnic group, traceable to the region of the Pomeranian Wends on the southern shores of the Baltic. More surprisingly, the language of the birchbark texts is also claimed to exhibit some charac-teristics otherwise found only in South Slavic, more specifically, Slovenian. While I personally remain somewhat skeptical of this whole line of reasoning (though I certainly concede the possibility of a later West Slavic influx into Novgorod, resulting largely from the German conquest of Slavic Pomerania a few centuries later), I nonetheless feel that the purely linguistic argument in favor of a mixed origin of Novgorod's Slavic population deserves further exploration.[11]

Undoubtedly, however, these and other archeological finds not only tell us something about the earliest settlements in Novgorod, but they also shed light on the city's social stratification and topography. In addition, they supplement our knowledge of the crafts and commerce which provided the main source of income for most of Novgorod's population.[12]

Novgorod's name, meaning New Town (cf. the synonymous designations for Carthage founded on the coast of North Africa by the Phoenicians or Naples and Nablus, both going back to Greek *Nea-polis,* not to mention the frequent English place-name Newton), has long been a puzzle to scholarship. Did this name imply that the new town was the successor to an earlier settlement of some size? If so, where are we to look for it? Among the candidates first considered by archeologists was the small hill-fort known as Gorodišče located a good mile south of Novgorod overlooking Lake Ilmen and by legend associated with Rjurik, leader of the Varangians. These Northmen had begun infiltrating Rus' from southern Finland and Estonia, as well as, mainly, "from beyond the sea" (that is, Sweden) no later than the early ninth century. Subsequently, Gorodišče was used by the princes of Novgorod or their lieutenants as their official residence, especially after 1137, when they were banned from permanently dwelling within the city limits; perhaps this is the source of the alleged association with Rjurik, the founder of the first ruling house of Rus'-Russia (note also the later-used name, Rjurikovo gorodišče). Other places considered as possible predecessors of Novgorod were the previously mentioned Rusa, across Lake Ilmen and a few miles up the Lovat' River, which fairly recent archeological finds have shown to be of considerable antiquity as well, or (and perhaps more likely) the town of Ladoga (now Staraja Ladoga) close to the entry of the Volkhov into Lake Ladoga. This early settlement—the Aldeigjuborg of the Old Norse sagas—is known to have been the first major stronghold of the Varangians.

In recent years, however, another hypothesis, supported by much archeological evidence, has won fairly wide acceptance. According to this theory (associated primarily with the Russian historian and archeologist V. L. Janin), we do not have to look for another location at some distance from Novgorod as its predecessor. Instead, the name Novgorod would have been introduced in connection with the fusion of the city's original three districts, or "ends" (*koncy*). These were Slavno, on the right bank of the upper Volkhov (the earliest purely Slavic settlement in the area, at least until the arrival of the Varangians, who also settled in that district), and Nerev and Ljudin, on the left bank of the river, the former further to the north, the latter more to the south. Originally, when they were no more than small trade posts, these two left-bank settlements very likely had an indigenous Finnic-speaking population which only gradually became Slavicized but was eventually entirely absorbed by Slavs. Nerev and Ljudin were separated by a tract of land that was at first vacant and probably served as a place of pagan worship and public gatherings. Given its slight elevation, it may also have been used as a place of refuge, a haven for the local population in times of war and unrest (in German referred to as *Fluchtburg*). In the course of merging the three separate settlements into one unified town, this previously uninhabited but defensible district was incorporated and became the New Town's fortified center, from then on referred to as *gorod* (subsequently, of course, the Russian word for city or town, but initially merely designating an enclosed or stockaded area; cf. English *yard* and *garden,* German *Garten,* Swedish *gård,* 'courtyard, farmhouse', Latin *hortus*). Another name for it was, as already indicated, *Detinec,* a term of controversial provenance usually translated as 'citadel' or 'kremlin.' It was here, then, that most of the centralized administrative and public activities of the former three townships, now united into one larger communal entity called Novgorod, were relocated. It was also here that the worship of pagan deities was succeeded, in the late tenth century, by the establishment of the Christian Church in its Byzantine, or Greek Orthodox, observance. Christianity in all likelihood came to the North Russian city from the capital, Kiev, which, in turn, it had reached via the Byzantine outpost at Cherson in the Crimea. However, some scholars—on insufficient grounds, I believe—have been inclined to think that Christianity was brought to Novgorod from the Czech lands of Bohemia and Moravia, with their particular brand of Slavic ecclesiastic tradition, blending eastern and western elements.[13] In any event, the new faith had to overcome considerable resistance, as we learn from reading the pertinent passages of the local town chronicle as well as the more succinct account in the *Primary Chronicle,* embracing all of Rus' and compiled in the late eleventh and early twelfth centuries in the Kievan Caves Monastery. Thus it was probably only in the second half of the eleventh century—or, to be precise, after a last pagan-inspired riot in 1071—that Christianity won general and final acceptance in Novgorod. St. Sophia Cathedral, located inside the *Detinec,* was originally a thirteen-domed oak building, erected probably in 989 under the supervision of Novgorod's semi-legendary first bishop Joachim (Jakim, Akim) from Cherson (*Korsunjanin*), but that burned down in 1049 (or perhaps already in 1045) during one of the many devastating fires which periodically ravaged the city. It was replaced near the same location in 1045–50, by the imposing, yet austere, stone structure which remains to this day. The cathedral was certainly Christendom's chief symbol in Novgorod (cf. above). With its gilded dome and whitewashed walls, it was visible from far away across the surrounding marshy flatlands. It was only natural, therefore, that the left bank of the Volkhov came later to be referred to as the city's Sophia Side (*Sofijskaja storona*), while the opposite bank, with its teeming commercial activity on and around the main market square (*torg*) and down at the piers where the foreign merchant vessels were moored became known as the Commercial, or Market, Side (*Torgovaja storona*) of town. Subsequently, in the

1160s and 1260s, respectively, two more boroughs, or ends, were added to the original settlements in this growing urban community. One, on the right bank of the river just north of Slavno and across the brook entering the Volkhov from the east, was called Carpenters' End (*Plotnickij konec*), apparently because members of that particular craft made up a substantial portion of the population. The other was a previously unincorporated area referred to as *Zagorod'e*, subsequently *Zagorodskij konec*, which literally means "the district beyond the *gorod*" (i.e., the *Detinec*) and can thus be roughly translated as "Trans-Citadel End." The depth of the cultural layer ascertained in various parts of the ancient city as a result of extensive (and continuing) excavations seems to confirm this general chronology of its gradual emergence and growth.[14]

Old Novgorod's topography in many ways reflects its demography and social stratification. We thus have a fairly accurate notion of the various social classes residing in the medieval city. At the top of the scale were the feudal lords, or boyars. These were the hereditary nobles who derived their wealth, and the power that came with it, from their vast possessions throughout the Novgorod Land (*Novgorodskaja zemlja*), the feudal republic extending as far as the gulfs of the Arctic Ocean in the north and the foothills of the Ural Mountains in the east. The propertied patriciate would compete in this role only with the local prince and the Church, including the ecclesiastic establishment's numerous monasteries; for the sovereign and the Church were themselves major landowners. Novgorod's privileged boyars resided in the city in their well-protected mansion complexes (*usad'by*)— veritable compounds, connected by a network of roadways consisting of half-logs joined to form deckings. It is by counting the number of such superimposed roadway deckings, which in Nerev and Ljudin amount to as many as twenty-eight, and by applying dendrochronological dating techniques to them, and stratigraphic dating to the objects surrounding them at roughly the same depth, that we can gain some insight into the absolute age of the archeological deposits of medieval Novgorod. On Sophia Side they range (at this writing) from the tenth to the fifteenth century, and on Market Side from the same time and up at least to the mid-fourteenth century. In addition to serving as homes for the feudal lords and their families, the boyars' mansions also provided living quarters for a number of servants and, possibly, some artisans and members of other professions. Most of these residential complexes were clustered in certain districts of the city. Many lined major thoroughfares, especially on Sophia Side, in Nerev and Ljudin Ends; one of these, Prussian Street (*Prusskaja ulica*), marked the border between Ljudin and Trans-Citadel End.

The boyars were obviously not the only well-to-do citizens of medieval Novgorod. Aside from these "greater men" (*vjatšie muži*), as the hereditary aristocracy was sometimes referred to in local sources, the "lesser men" (*men'šie muži*, also known as *žit'i ljudi*) would likewise occasionally acquire large estates. However, their major source of income was the wholesale, long-distance trade which they controlled. Novgorod was, in fact, a major commercial center, with strong links not only to the far-flung Russian market and, beyond it, to the countries of the Middle East, but also to the merchant cities of northern and western Europe. By the high Middle Ages Novgorod's western trade was handled primarily through the agency of the Hanseatic League, the network of German merchant towns, which had established its own trade station, the German Yard (*Nemeckij dvor*), or *St. Petershof*, on the city's Commercial (Market) Side. The German Yard in due course came to franchise an earlier foreign trade station, the Gotland Yard (*Gotskij dvor*), which originally handled Novgorod's commerce with the Baltic island of Gotland. There, both German merchants (of the city of Visby) and seasonal Swedish peasant traders (Swedish *farmannabönder*) participated in trade with Novgorod. The center of the essentially North German Hansa was, as is well known, the city of Lübeck at the southwestern end of the Baltic Sea. Other important Hanseatic centers directly involved in trade with Novgorod were from the fourteenth century on, in addition to Visby, the towns of the Baltic regions of Livonia and Estonia—Riga, Dorpat (now Tartu), and Reval (now Tallinn).[15]

The numerous and multilayered clergy of medieval Novgorod, both "black" and "white" (i.e., the clerics proper of various ranks and the male and female members of the monastic community), could, in principle, come from any stratum of society. They thus did not constitute a separate social class, notwithstanding their considerable spiritual influence and political power. But in the course of medieval Novgorod's history, the Church was mostly allied with the boyar class and was deeply involved with the city-republic's internal and external affairs.[16]

The city's common people, usually referred to as "black folk" (*černye ljudi*), no doubt made up the vast majority of the urban population. Most members of this numerous social class busied themselves with various crafts and other manual work; but they could also be active as shopkeepers and petty traders or street peddlers, occasionally combining the manufacture and the sale of their products. However, the prestigious designation of merchant (*kupec* and, particularly, *gost'*) was reserved for the better-situated commercial entrepreneurs, especially those engaged in large-scale, often international and overseas, trade. As was already indicated, they belonged mostly to the non-aristocratic but propertied class of "lesser men."

On the outskirts of the urban community also presumably resided some peasant farmers (*smerdy*), otherwise encountered mostly in the countryside. And, at the bottom of the social scale, finally, were the slaves (*xolopy*), whose numerical share in the overall population of the city is difficult to estimate, as they are recorded, for the most part, only in connection with some transgression or crime, or in the context of some legal transaction. For example, runaway slaves are mentioned in several of the birchbark texts, and specific penalties are set for certain misdemeanors or felonies involving slaves in various legal documents. Among the latter is the earliest Russian law code, the *Russkaja Pravda* (or *Pravda Russkaja* of the sources), the original core sections of which were presumably drafted in Novgorod during the eleventh century. In any event, slaves must have been present in Novgorod in considerable numbers, given, among other things, the fact that a whole street in one of its districts, Nerev End, was called Slave Street (*Xolop'ja ulica*), which may either reflect the original settling or otherwise concentration of slaves here or possibly could indicate the earlier location of a slave market (*Xolopij torg*) somewhere along this route.

In addition to the Slavic population of Novgorod, elements of other ethnic backgrounds were present at various times in the Volkhov city. As already mentioned, two of Novgorod's earliest boroughs, Nerev and Ljudin, were at first in all likelihood populated by Finnic-speaking settlers. It should be noted in this connection that the city emerged in what had once been Finnic territory, conquered and colonized in the second half of the first millennium A.D. by the rapidly expanding Slavs. Further, the Varangian Northmen, mostly coming from Sweden or from areas previously settled by Swedes —southern Finland, the Åland archipelago, parts of Estonia, with the islands of Dagö (Hiiumaa) and Ösel (Saaremaa)—constituted an important and, at times, quite unruly foreign element in the urban panorama. They had arrived—for the second time, if we are to believe the folklorically-colored chronicle account—with Rjurik and his two brothers in the mid-ninth century. Originally traders (and soon enough rulers), they had their own military guard to protect them. Subsequently, they were also used in large numbers as mercenary troops stationed in a separate garrison near— but originally not forming part of—Slavno End. (We may also note in this context that a special mercenary Varangian Guard, recruited from Rus' or through East Slavic territory from Sweden, at one time shielded the life and safety of the Byzantine emperors and was subsequently used by the emperor as his special crack troops.) As Novgorod's trade with the merchant towns of the southern and eastern coastlands of the Baltic developed and increased, West Slavic (primarily Pomeranian-Wendish), Baltic (apparently mostly Prussian), and particularly North German (Low German, Hanseatic) merchants with their support personnel—the Germans in Novgorod being confined to residence on the premises of their own spacious trade station—also were part of the urban population on the banks of the Volkhov, thus lending the North Russian metropolis an international atmosphere.[17]

What, then, was the form of government, and which were the various policy-making bodies and administrative offices which ran the day-to-day affairs and planned the long-range policies of Novgorod and the vast territories over which the city held sway? The history of medieval Novgorod is marked by a shifting balance of power between the local ruler and the town assembly. Up to the Mongol invasion and final collapse of the Kievan state in 1238/40, the local prince or his lieutenant was, at least in name, the representative of the grand prince of Kiev. For as a rule, it was the prince of Novgorod who was to succeed his father or older brother on the Kievan throne. This made the North Russian polity a stepping-stone to the position of supreme power in Old Rus'. Yet at the same time it kept the nominal ruler of Novgorod less than fully committed to, or prepared to identify himself with, the separatist spirit which pervaded the Volkhov metropolis. It is worth noting, though, that the rule of succession assigning Novgorod the second place among the principalities of the Kievan state was broken more than once in the course of the three-hundred-year history of Kievan Rus'. The general town assembly, or *veče*, was in principle open to all free men of Novgorod, though wealthy citizens, and in particular the boyars, seem increasingly to have dominated the decision-making process. Meetings were held outside St. Sophia Cathedral (which also served as the city-state's official depository and treasury) or on the opposite bank, on the premises of Jaroslav's Court, i.e., the site of what had once been Prince Jaroslav's residential palace. The powers of the prince, essentially military and judiciary (in addition to his substantial economic privileges), were soon drastically curtailed, so that Novgorod—and later, after it had seceded from the Realm of St. Sophia, also its former subordinate town (*prigorod*) of Pskov—formed the exception to the general trend in medieval Russia, where any balance of power initially shared by the sovereign and the town assembly soon shifted in favor of the former. Too much significance has perhaps been attached to the Novgorod uprising of 1136, since, on the one hand, the prince's powers had, as a matter of fact, been unequivocally circumscribed also before that date, and, on the other, he continued to exert some influence after it as well.

Yet this revolt did mark a definite tuning point in the distribution of governmental responsibilities between the prince and the *veče,* the latter at the time clearly dominated by the boyars. Henceforth, the prince was to be elected (or invited) by the free men of the Volkhov city, and his permanent residence was, as previously mentioned, relocated outside the city, at Gorodišče. During the last two centuries of independence, there were even times when no one held the title of prince of Novgorod, or when that title, bestowed upon the ruler of a neighboring principality, was purely honorific. The successful military exploits of Alexander Nevskij may have temporarily restored some of the political power of the prince.

The Tatar invasion and the final collapse of the Kievan state put an end to Novgorod's by then only formal subordination to the southern capital. It was replaced by a mostly economic dependence on the distant foreign ruler residing on the lower Volga. Novgorod was thus spared the worst consequences of Mongol rule, and the financial hardship this tributary relationship brought was more than offset by the considerable revenues derived from Novgorod's widespread dominions (yielding agricultural and mining products), its own variegated and highly productive manufacture, and its flourishing international trade. Increasingly, then, it was in the town assembly, the *veče,* that political power came to reside. As has been noted, this body was dominated by wealthy boyars and possibly some members of the equally well-off commoner class of free men, engaged primarily in foreign trade. The office of lord mayor, or *posadnik*—originally appointed by the prince, but soon turned elective—became itself restricted to a relatively small number of boyar clans. It would thus be a mistake to regard the form of government practiced in the Novgorod Republic from the mid-thirteenth century onward as truly democratic. Yet precisely that has been claimed by some scholars, particularly in Russia during the nineteenth century (as a way of protesting against the autocratic rule of the tsars) and, more recently, also in some quarters in the West. Instead, what we find in medieval Novgorod, as in so many other more or less autonomous urban communes and city-states during the later Middle Ages and the Renaissance (as well as, for that matter, in ancient Greece), is an oligarchic form of government. It is conceivable, though, that had this kind of rule been allowed to develop freely, it might at some point have approached and ultimately turned into genuine democracy. This would therefore allow us to view oligarchy as a predemocratic form of government, at least in contrast to its opposite—autocracy and absolutism. The latter, as we know, came to prevail in Russia from Ivan IV (if not earlier) through at least the dictatorship of Stalin.[18]

The ever-increasing power of the boyar-dominated Novgorod *veče* and the *de facto* delegation of the decision-making process to a select group of nobles within the legislative assembly, necessitated not only the establishment or redesign of a number of executive offices invested with the responsibility of carrying out the decisions of the *veče,* but also the creation of a formal body of legislators and policy-makers to whom much, if not most, of the *veče*'s functions could be entrusted. The chief executive officer, or lord mayor, of Novgorod was the aforementioned *posadnik*. He was assisted by the *tysjackij*—literally, "chiliarch"—who was originally the commander of the town levy, but soon also was given a judiciary function. His title derives from his erstwhile role as head of the Novgorod militia, numbering one thousand men, which in turn may have been subdivided into groups of one hundred, each led by a *sockij*—literally "centurion." (To be sure, these makeshift literal renditions evoke associations of Greco-Roman antiquity which, naturally, are out of place in this context.) While the *posadnik* acted as the chief spokesman of the landed nobility, the *tysjackij* was supposed to represent the rest of the free men of the city; however, his office too was soon appropriated by the boyars. The policy-making organ of the *veče,* admitting only members of boyar families, was the previously mentioned Council of Lords, or *Sovet gospod* (also referred to simply as *Gospody*), on record since the thirteenth century. By the fourteenth century, the office of *posadnik* was itself converted into a multimembered leadership group, the *posadničestvo,* headed by a chief lord mayor (*stepennyj posadnik*). This expanded office was at first made up of six members, one representing each of the city's five ends in addition to the presiding lord mayor; a century later it already numbered dozens of simultaneous office-holders, each with a short term of tenure. While the *vladyka* was the head of Novgorod's Church and at the same time, in his political role, chaired the Council of Lords (that is, the republic's *de facto* government), the monastic community of Novgorod and its vicinity, though part of the overall ecclesiastic establishment, had, at least since the beginning of the thirteenth century, its own chief representative in the person of the archimandrite residing in the majestic St. George's Monastery (*Jur'ev monastyr'*), located outside the city, south of Ljudin End.[19]

The steady increase in the number and subdivision of administrative offices and decision-making bodies, largely in the hands of the boyar class, was undoubtedly a factor contributing to the decline of the Novgorod Republic as a viable political entity. It was further exacerbated by the fact that, by the fifteenth century, feuding factions within the city-republic's boyar class would seek the support of one of the two major powers threatening Novgorod's survival as an autonomous state—the ever stronger Muscovite state and Novgorod's mighty neighbor to the southwest, the combined Kingdom of Poland and Grand Duchy of Lithuania.[20] Still, despite the fact that current Russian historical scholarship is bent on emphasizing the socially conditioned decay of Novgorod's political life in the final phase of its independence, the last word has not yet been spoken in attempting fully and fairly to assess both the decline and, at the same time, the considerable degree of sophistication in the political process of Lord Novgorod the Great during the decades before its fall. In fact, there may be some justification, as I have proposed elsewhere, for viewing the statecraft practiced by the political leadership of the republic, no matter how corrupt, as a measure of the level of civic awareness and civilization in general that Novgorod had attained by that time. Jacob Burckhardt's dictum of "the state as a work of art," coined with the polities of Renaissance Italy in mind, may indeed, albeit with some qualification, be applicable also to medieval Novgorod in the period of its political decline.[21] The North Russian city-state thus provides yet another telling example of the simultaneous disintegration of political power and the flowering of creative imagination and culture in general.

It is to this cultural achievement that we shall now turn. Before doing so, let us note, though, that Novgorod's loss of independence—which marks Muscovy's decisive victory over her Russian competitors—not only weakened Russia's ties with the West, never to be fully and permanently restored, but may also have set back her own cultural evolution by at least two centuries, until the times of Tsar Alexis and his son, Peter the Great, or perhaps even until the subsequent enlightened age of the Empresses Elizabeth and Catherine the Great.[22] Yet the immediate result of Novgorod's annexation by the Grand Duchy of Moscow was that the latter, by assuming control over Novgorod's Western connections, temporarily was able to intensify its own contacts with the West.

II

In discussing the arts in medieval Novgorod, it is useful at the outset to distinguish between verbal and visual art forms.[23] Among the various expressions of verbal art, it is perhaps appropriate to begin with the oral tradition and, specifically, with the particular type of epic poetry known as heroic songs or *byliny*. These songs have been recorded only in modern times but date back, in many instances, to the period of Old Rus'. The *byliny* may have originated, in part at least, in the circles of the higher social strata, in that segment of Old Russian society where the prototypes of their heroes were to be found. Subsequently, though, they not only traveled across the land, to be preserved primarily in Russia's peripheral northern regions, but also descended, as it were, from their presumed former elevated position to the level of the common folk. The *byliny* thus constitute a classic example of what in German parlance is referred to as *gesunkenes Kulturgut*. Medieval Russia's vagrant minstrels and professional entertainers, known as *skomoroxi*, certainly played some part, though it is not clear how large, in the transmission and preservation of these historical songs through time and space.[24] Two groups of *byliny* stand out as particularly ancient: on the one hand, the so-called Kiev cycle, with the figures of Il'ja Muromec, Dobrynja Nikitič and Aleša Popovič as their chief protagonists, but also featuring such mythological anthropomorphizations as Svjatogor and Dunaj; and, on the other hand, the epic poems which can be traced to Novgorod. Of the latter, there are three main cycles, which deal with the legendary long-lived giant Vasilij Buslaevič, the rich and widely traveled merchant Sadko, and the only superficially "Kievized" Xoten Bludovič. In addition, a few of the Novgorod *byliny* treat *skomoroxi*, thus suggesting their direct involvement with this genre of oral creativity.[25] It is not possible here to enter into a detailed discussion of the poetics of the Novgorod *byliny,* with their peculiar syntax, phraseology, and meter, though these considerations also bear on their origin and age. Let us merely note that in many cases these *byliny* seem to reflect a highly fictionalized and imaginatively embellished historical reality, echoing the social tensions peculiar to the urban community on the Volkhov. In addition, they tell of, and obviously embroider on, the distant journeys undertaken by some of Novgorod's merchants. Thus, for example, Sadko appears to have had his historically attested prototype in a wealthy merchant, Sotko Sytinič, who in 1167 is known to have laid the foundations of a stone church dedicated to the first Russian martyr-saints, Boris and Gleb (not counting the martyred Christian Varangians in as-yet-pagan Kiev), inside the Novgorod *Detinec*. Generally, it can be said that the Novgorod *byliny,* although recorded only much later, testify to the vivid imagination and sense for the fantastic so typical of much of the medieval Novgorodians' artistic expression, starkly contrasting with, and generously compensating for, their otherwise sober and pragmatic, not to say dry, approach to the exigencies of everyday life.

This dual, even split, attitude toward reality and its imaginative transformation is characteristic also of much of the writing produced in Old Novgorod. Thus, while the question of where and how to draw the line between artistic prose and plain, noncreative writing in medieval Russia is generally one of considerable intricacy and controversy, it is much less of a problem in the case of texts which originated in the Volkhov city. In other words, the criteria separating nonartistic and ordinary from artistic, poetically-shaped writing in Novgorod are often more sharply defined than elsewhere in Old Rus'. For this reason, we may safely disregard any attempt to ascribe artistic formulation or intent to the Novgorod birchbark letters, though some scholars (N. A. Meščerskij, A. I. Efimov) once regarded them as displaying a specific "epistolary style." Chronicle writing as well was not motivated by any particular aesthetic ambitions (though such was often the case in some other parts of the country, as evinced by many passages in such Old Russian chronicles as the *Primary Chronicle* or one of its local sequels, the *Galician-Volhynian Chronicle*). In the North Russian city-republic, the annalistic entries were, on the whole, purely factographic, and if they had any edifying or entertaining purpose, this was clearly secondary. The most important of the Novgorod annals, historiographically and linguistically, was the earliest town chronicle known as the *First Novgorod Chronicle,* extant in two basic versions and a number of manuscript copies.

Yet some of Old Rus's most fanciful tales and adventure stories, occasionally tinged by a very specific political or theological ideology, originated in Novgorod, mostly in the later medieval period. Among these are such works as the *Epistle of the Novgorod Archbishop Vasilij to the Bishop of Tver', Fedor, about Paradise* (from the mid-fourteenth century), or the *Tale about the Travel of John of Novgorod to Jerusalem on a Demon* (recorded in the early fifteenth century and deriving from a legend containing elements of fairy-tale–type folklore), the *Tale about the Novgorod Posadnik Ščii* (late fifteenth century), and the politically-colored *Tale of the White Cowl.* This last work has usually been associated with the political-theological doctrine of Moscow as the Third Rome (following the conquest of Constantinople by the Muslims in 1453), propounded by the Pskov elder Filofej at the beginning of the sixteenth century. In all probability, however, the theme of this tale originated in Novgorod a century or so earlier, as part of a tradition focusing on the political leadership ambitions of the Volkhov metropolis. Another biographical—or rather hagiographical—story composed in or around Novgorod is the *Life of Mixail Klopskij* (in oral form from the late fifteenth century; the extant version, written in Moscow, dates from 1537). This story tells of the eccentric behavior of an influential, saintly man, by some considered one of the "holy fools" (*jurodivye*) swarming about Russia in the Middle Ages and later. The phenomenon of the "holy fools" grew out of and exemplifies that counterculture (surfacing here and there in Old Rus') also identified as the "world of laughter"—and tears, one might add—which rebelled against, and poked fun at, the increasingly stifling cultural rigor and official etiquette pervading Muscovite Russia, particularly after the subjugation of the more free-thinking, nonautocratic Novgorod.[26]

Still, summing up these remarks on Novgorod's literature, it must be said that, notwithstanding the strong imaginative component in some of its artistic expression, Old Novgorodian society, with its pluralism and relative freedom as well as its receptiveness to impulses coming from the outside, did not produce any truly great works of verbal art. The Volkhov city thus has nothing that could match such masterpieces of Old Russian letters as the *Igor Tale* (assuming its authenticity or, at any rate, medieval origin), the *Supplication of Daniel the Exile* (traceable to the Russian North and probably, as D. S. Lixačev has persuasively argued, to a *skomorox* milieu), or even the brief but highly poetic *Discourse about the Destruction of the Land of Rus'*, the latter preceding, in the manuscript tradition, the *Life of Alexander Nevskij* (and thus perhaps, at least loosely, associated with Novgorod). To be sure, the biography of the Novgorod prince (in the last decade of his life, also grand-prince of Vladimir) was most likely authored by some Galician bookman displaced to the northeastern, Vladimir-Suzdal' region of Old Rus'. It is usually considered transitional between the well-established genre of hagiography (imported from Byzantium) and that of secular biography, notably the kind that is sometimes referred to as princely lives (*knjažeskie žitija*). As a genre in medieval Russian literature, secular biography thus cannot easily be distinguished from hagiography proper. This is noteworthy in view of the clear distinction between hagiographic and nonhagiographic biography as we know it from medieval Serbia, where the autonomous secular type, however, also goes back to purely hagiographic origins.[27] Moreover, the straightforward style of the undogmatic sermons written by the early Novgorod bishop Luka Židjata (eleventh century) appears dry and fairly simple by comparison with the flowery homiletic rhetoric of an Ilarion, metropolitan of Kiev (eleventh century), Kliment Smoljatič, elevated to the same dignity, or Kirill, bishop of Turov (the latter two active in the twelfth century). The writings of these three prelates are now considered to have been trend-setting for the subsequent, late medieval mannerism of "word-weaving" (*pletenie* or *izvitie sloves*). This literary technique has been shown to emulate Serbian, to a lesser degree Bulgarian, and ultimately Byzantine stylistic models. A highly ornate, opaque style was alien to the more down-to-earth taste and perception of the readership of Old Novgorod.[28]

Before we leave the subject of writing in medieval Novgorod, mention should be made of another kind of activity which only in part found its expression in written form. Moreover, even of that which actually was put in writing, little has survived. I am referring here, on the one hand, to certain religious movements, viewed as heretical by official Orthodoxy and therefore suppressed, and, on the other, to the learned facet of the relentless, indeed brutal, response to one of them. More specifically, I have in mind two sects which initially developed in the fold of the Russian Church, but which were soon condemned and eventually eradicated by the ecclesiastic establishment and its chief representative in the Volkhov city. The earlier one, which arose in Novgorod and its former satellite town Pskov in the second half of the fourteenth century, was primarily directed against the power and amassed wealth of the Church. Known by the somewhat opaque name of *strigol'niki* (presumed to be derived from the Old Russian verb for cutting or shearing, *strići*), which originally referred either to the newly tonsured members of the clergy or, perhaps, to the trade of the cloth-cutters, the movement seems to have been embraced primarily by low-ranking clerics, notably deacons, as well as a number of the "black folk," mostly simple craftsmen. Clearly, then, this earlier heretical movement was essentially social in nature, opposed, as it was, to the Church as the largest single owner of immense feudatories. Though comparatively little is known about the activities of the *strigol'niki* (other than some details of the persecution they endured), there is reason to believe that this was a genuine grass-roots movement, advocating, among other things, independent—i.e., nonsupervised—reading of the Bible. We further know that members of this sect advocated certain forms of devout behavior, for example the seemingly outlandish requirement of "confessing to the earth" (*zemli kajatisja*), which may have had some deep folkloric, presumably pagan, roots and certainly was at variance with the official emphasis on the strictly conventionalized ritual of the Orthodox liturgy. The "shorn ones" or "shearers" were thus not merely one of several socially motivated, anti-feudal movements within the Russian Church of the premodern period. (The most influential of these was that of the later Nonpossessors, *nestjažatel'nye,* including, in particular, the hermits usually referred to as Trans-Volga Elders, *zavolžskie starcy*). The *strigol'niki* have parallels elsewhere in medieval Europe, for example in the Bogomils of the Balkans (initially in Bulgaria and later notably in Bosnia) and in the Cathars and Waldensians of northern Italy and southern France.[29]

The other—political and ideologically more significant—heresy, centered in Novgorod but spreading to Moscow as well, was that of the so-called Judaizers (*židovstvujušćie,* also *židovstvujušćaja eres'*). This designation, or its equivalent, *Judaizantes*—common also in other parts of Europe where Christian converts from Judaism were suspected of having changed faith in name only, or where originally-Christian groups were thought to toy with the idea of apostasy in favor of Judaism—was given to them by their detractors, needless to say. Though there may have been a tenuous link with the earlier *strigol'niki*, the "Judaizing" heresy, which surfaced at the end of the fifteenth century, after the Novgorod Republic had been annexed by Muscovy, was largely different in character. Again, our knowledge of the views and practices of the Judaizers is scant and distorted, so that much regarding them remains guesswork at best. This includes what we can gather about their origin, which some scholars—on uncertain grounds, it must be emphasized— trace to Lithuanian-held Kiev and ultimately to the Genoese enclave on the Crimea and possibly other parts of the northern shores of the Black Sea. Most of our meager information about them can only be distilled from the strongly biased and hostile accounts by their adversaries, notably the polemic tract by Iosif Volockij (Joseph of Volok Lamskij) commonly known as the "Enlightener" (*Prosvětitel'*). Two basic facts seem certain, however. First, while the *strigol'niki* had encouraged Bible-reading without the guidance of the Church, the Judaizers went a step further. Some of them seem to have studied, in an early humanist vein, the biblical books in the original, and more specifically the Old Testament in Hebrew, probably relying on the proficiency of Jewish men of letters settled in the East Slavic region under Lithuanian rule. Quite probably they even translated some of the Hebrew texts into the East Slavic (or more precisely, "Ruthenian," i.e., western East Slavic) variety of Church Slavonic.[30] This, as well as their explicit deemphasizing (or even outright denial) of Jesus' divine nature and some of their other beliefs and practices which were not consonant with the teachings of the Orthodox Church, earned them the indictment of being apostates to Judaism or, at least, of "pondering things Jewish." Second, the social strata affected by this heresy were not, as in the case of the *strigol'- niki*, primarily the lowest ranks of the clergy or the lower classes of the free townspeople. Rather, it had its adherents in the middle and higher ranks of the ecclesiastic hierarchy, and among its followers and sympathizers, there seem to have been some highly placed people close to the Muscovite court. One of these was Fedor Kuricyn, at one time concerned with, or even in charge of, Muscovy's foreign relations, and most likely the author or trans- lator of one of the few preserved genuine "Judaizing" literary pieces, known in scholarship as the "Laodicean Epistle" (*Laodikijskoe poslanie*). There is, further, at least some indication that there might have existed some ideologi- cal—and perhaps even personal—ties between the Judaizers and the radical (Taborite) faction of the Hussites displaced to Transylvania and Moldavia, regions visited by Kuricyn. There may also have been contacts between the

Russian sect and the Bosnian Bogomils (or the separate, as yet not fully understood Bosnian Church).

This learned and socially prestigious religious movement of Novgorod and Moscow was resolutely persecuted and brutally suppressed, particularly by the (in some respects) equally learned archbishop of Novgorod, Gennadij. It was he who introduced means of torture worthy of the Spanish Inquisition, which latter he greatly admired. Surrounded by a circle of humanists and scientists, several of them from the West (Lübeck, Croatia, and some other places), Novgorod's archiepiscopal palace, known as the House of St. Sophia, was in a way not unlike the learned, art-promoting courts of some princes and high-ranking prelates in Central and Western Europe during the age of the Renaissance. Gennadij too was a generous patron of the arts and lent his vigorous support to renewed church building. These activities were in keeping with those of his great predecessor in the see of St. Sophia, Evfimij II, who also had a strong Western orientation. Among Gennadij's most important cultural accomplishments was the commissioning of the first translation of the complete text of the Bible into Russian Church Slavonic. This rendition is therefore usually referred to as Gennadij's Bible. The task was accomplished by a group of scholars, assembled by the archbishop and headed by the Croatian Dominican Benjamin. The primary source for this translation was therefore not the Greek original of the New Testament (not yet available in Erasmus' first critical edition) nor, for that matter, the Greek version of the Old Testament known as the Septuagint. Instead, it was the received Latin translation of the entire Bible, the Vulgate, attributed to St. Jerome and used throughout the Roman Catholic world. This, then, was but one of the many influences of the "Latin" West felt in Novgorod during the incumbency of Gennadij, who, understandably, soon became suspect for his Catholic leanings in the eyes of the Orthodox Muscovite leadership of Church and state. In its overt beginnings, this opening towards Catholicism in Novgorod dates back to the times shortly after the Council of Ferrara and Florence (1438/39), which strove—though apparently without much sincerity—for a restoration of the unity of the Eastern and Western Churches. Locally, one of the consequences was the sudden, if temporary, appearance in Novgorod of several Catholic priests who were allowed to preach publicly in some of the city's churches. In addition to using the Latin Vulgate for their translation, the team that produced Gennadij's Bible of 1499 also had access to some earlier Church Slavonic versions of portions of the Bible, as well as possibly to some newly translated sections of the Old Testament (which thus might point to a milieu of Judaizers or their informants knowledgeable in Hebrew). Although not, strictly speaking, a manifestation of verbal art, this learned prehumanist or early humanist activity of the Gennadij circle and its victims, the Judaizers, also forms part of the cultural legacy of medieval Novgorod.[31]

Finally, one more remark ought to be made concerning writing as practiced in the Volkhov city. It should be noted that the type of early chancery language used for official and legal documentation in Novgorod, though far from being smooth and consistent, had a certain impact in Moscow after the collapse of the republic.[32] This applies particularly to treaties with foreign powers (including the Hanseatic towns) and with other Russian territories and principalities drawn up by the office of the Novgorodian archbishop in his capacity of head of state and previously by the chancery of the prince of Novgorod. In Moscow, the Novgorodian manner of phrasing such documents served as a model for the shaping of the grand duchy's own chancery language (later known as *prikaznyj jazyk*). In turn, the Muscovite chancery language was one of the several components, along with the colloquial speech of the capital, Church Slavonic, and, above all, foreign—notably Polish and (considerably later) French—borrowings, from which the modern Russian literary language was ultimately forged. Admittedly, this occurred only after a long period of relatively stable Church Slavonic/East Slavic linguistic coexistence, or diglossia, in Old Rus', followed by a briefer period of instability, marked by mutual interference (so, at least, B. A. Uspenskij's argument runs).[33] Eventually, as is well known, this written language crystallized, at the end of the eighteenth and in the beginning of the nineteenth century, in the polished and coherent style created by Karamzin and the poetic language perfected by Puškin. Though remote, Novgorod's official and legal language was thus one of its ultimate, indirect sources.

Turning now to art and architecture in medieval Novgorod, we should note at the outset that it is in this area, more than in any other, that the lasting cultural achievement of the North Russian metropolis lies. As was the case throughout medieval Europe, it was religion—in this instance, Christianity in its Eastern observance—that was the main source of inspiration for the artists, domestic as well as foreign, who were active in Novgorod. It is also predominantly Christian motifs that we find depicted in the works of art which the wealthy and mighty citizens of Novgorod acquired and brought to their city. Compared to the abundance and variety of Novgorod's Christian art, the share of art objects lacking a clear religious theme or connotation—mostly in the domain of the minor and applied arts—does not weigh heavily, though some interesting specimens of such work, too, have been recovered. Generally speaking, the Christian thematics of Novgorodian art combine a naive immediacy with realistic intimacy, sometimes supplemented by imaginative expressiveness. All of this lends to this local variety of Old Russian art its peculiar stamp and, in part at least, can also be found in some of the works of art imported—and obviously cherished—by the people of Novgorod. As the ranking expert on Novgorodian art, V. N. Lazarev, once put it succinctly: "Novgorodian religiosity is marked by a warm, intimate faith and a certain personal note in the attitude toward the dogmas of the Church. Yet, by the same token, this religiosity impresses us with its sober, absolutely nonmetaphysical spirit. From it, a bridge readily spans to practical life: it has organically absorbed a variety of folk traits; profound sincerity and impulsiveness are its hallmark. That is why the religious art of Novgorod captures us with its naive immediacy. Its clear and simple images are to such a degree concrete and peculiarly democratic that they are perceived as the product of the living imagination of the people."[34]

When discussing the art of Old Novgorod in any of its manifold forms and manifestations, it is important to distinguish, whenever possible, between local accomplishments, for which domestic Russian artists are to be credited, and such works found in the Volkhov city for which foreign masters, some of them even invited to work in Novgorod, can be considered responsible. Moreover, various external influences, primarily Byzantine, but soon also from the West, the Slavic Balkans, and the Middle East, need to be considered in any detailed study of Novgorodian art. As was just indicated, there are some works of art which were either entirely or in part manufactured abroad and only later brought to Novgorod, sometimes to be completed or supplemented there. Though not to be counted among Novgorod's own artistic accomplishments (except partially, in some rare instances), they nonetheless reflect the artistic taste and preferences of some influential Novgorodians and thus convey a certain impression of their level of sophistication and refinement in matters pertaining to the visual arts. Naturally, while there are certain overall characteristics peculiar to much of Old Novgorodian art throughout the centuries, chronological considerations, reflecting changes in style and influence, must always be taken into account as well.

For practical purposes, it may be helpful to classify Novgorodian art treasures into three main groups—architecture, painting, and handicrafts—or, to categorize them more specifically under several rubrics: architectural monuments, secular and ecclesiastic; frescoes, icons, and book illumination, as well as other manuscript ornamentation; and minor and applied arts, ranging from sculpture to small decorated practical objects and beadwork (often found in the course of archeological excavations). This latter group of artifacts can be further subdivided on the basis of such criteria as the material used, the particular technique employed, specific function fulfilled, etc.[35] In this overview only some, but not all, of the above categories can be exemplified by some of their more conspicuous specimens.

Moreover, there are a few impressive secular buildings extant in Novgorod from medieval times which deserve closer scrutiny. These include the imposing walls of the *Detinec* with its towers (partly dating from the late fifteenth century) and the central portion of the archiepiscopal palace, with St. Nikita's Chambers and an added wing, the Palace of Facets (*Granovitaja palata*), constructed in 1433 by German and Novgorodian master builders commissioned by Archbishop Evfimij II, which served, among other things, as the meeting place of the Council of Lords.

Still, Novgorod's architecture is dominated by the city's numerous churches. Of course, only those built of stone had much chance of survival. The erstwhile density of Novgorod's ecclesiastic topography (including a great number of no longer existing wooden parish churches and chapels) will become clear when we recall that at one time the concentration of church structures per square mile within the bounds of the Volkhov city is thought to have been higher than anywhere else in Europe east of the Elbe and north of the Danube. But perhaps this is merely an impression based on the more ample data available from Novgorod as compared to the records pertaining to towns such as Vladimir, Polock, or Pskov. In addition to the many churches inside the old city, Novgorod was virtually encircled by monasteries, situated at varying distances from the center of town and serving, in addition to their spiritual and educational role, as an outer defense line, or at least as outposts in an "early-warning system," so to speak. These monasteries had their own church or churches. Further, some smaller, private churches, not connected with any monastery or convent, were located in the countryside in the immediate vicinity of Novgorod.

This is not the place to discuss even in bare outline the details of the basically traditionalist style encountered in Novgorod's church architecture. Suffice it to say that practically all ecclesiastic structures of Old Novgorod, except the truly large ones, are based on the Byzantine principle of the cruciform floor plan with just a few variations. It was the overall size, the number and distribution of the supporting pillars, the fashioning and decoration of the façades, the addition or lack of separate porches and apses, the height and shape of the dome (or domes) and of the drum on which the dome rests, and the particular form of the roof that gave each church its peculiar appearance.[36] Still, there are certain architectural and decorative features that set apart the earlier (eleventh and twelfth century) from the later (fourteenth and fifteenth century) churches of the Volkhov city, suggesting a far-reaching modification in masonry technique sometime during the thirteenth century, the time of the Tatar invasion.

Even today we can surmise how crowded Novgorod's ecclesiastic cityscape must have been from the several remaining stone churches within what was once Market Square and the adjoining Jaroslav's Court. Here we find, almost one next to the other, St. Nicholas' Cathedral (founded by Prince Mstislav in 1113 to challenge the boyar-dominated Novgorod Cathedral of St. Sophia facing it on the opposite bank), the Church of St. Procopius, the Church of the Myrrh-Bearing Women, the Church of St. Parasceve-Pjatnica (founded in 1207 by the overseas merchants and reconstructed in the four-teenth-sixteenth centuries), the Church of the Assumption (built in 1135), the Church of St. George, and the Church of St. John the Baptist at Opoki (constructed 1127–30); it was in this latter church that the commercial court, chaired by the *tysjackij*, was convened. Some important later churches on Market Side were the Church of the Savior of the Transfiguration in Elijah (*Il'ina*) Street, erected in 1374 and decorated with the priceless frescoes of Theophanes the Greek (Feofan Grek), and the Church of St. Theodore Stratelates on the Brook (i.e. the small stream separating Slavno and Carpenters' End). South of Novgorod, on the left bank of the Volkhov and facing the hill-fort of Gorodišče, in 1119 Prince Vsevolod built the Cathedral of St. George inside the monastery bearing that saint's name (*Jur'ev monas-tyr'*). This plain but nonetheless imposing edifice was—at least in some scholars' view—intended as yet another princely challenge to the boyars' more than just symbolic hold on St. Sophia. The listing of major and minor stone churches inside and outside the city, extant as well as destroyed, could go on and on. However, we shall not pursue such an enumeration here, but shall return to some of these churches in connection with what is probably Novgorod's single greatest contribution to the visual arts—its frescoes. (Parenthetically, it should be mentioned that the term "cathedral" is used here throughout to render the Russian *sobor*, although, strictly speaking, the English expression applies only to St. Sophia Cathedral while the other "cathedrals" were in fact merely "main churches.")

The art of the mosaic, so characteristic of Byzantine pictorial creativity, in Old Rus' did not extend beyond the early capital city of Kiev (and possibly the nearby Kiev Caves Monastery). Instead, the less costly, while technically and thus aesthetically less constrained, art form of mural painting reached one of its absolute peaks in East Slavic territory, especially in and around Novgorod. Again, we will be able to dwell here only on a few exquisite examples of Novgorodian fresco-painting.

Among the early and, at the same time, most magnificent murals in or near Novgorod is—or, alas, was—the cycle of frescoes which once adorned the small Church of the Savior on Neredica Hill. Painted toward the end of the twelfth century by a team of artists until recently considered entirely anonymous, the Neredica frescoes, in the subtle manner of their execution and the overwhelming power of their expression, remind us of some of the most grandiose mural paintings known from Byzantium. Unfortunately, they were totally destroyed in the shelling of World War II. As for the painter or painters to be credited with this chef-d'œuvre, it has recently been suggested that the twelfth-century master who headed or, at any rate, was a member of the Neredica group of artists, can in fact be tentatively identified. His epithet, "the Greek" (cf. above, with n. 10), would seem to point to his—or perhaps only his ancestors'—Byzantine origin. It is not entirely certain that Olisej Petrovič Grečin had actually immigrated from Byzantium, since he is on record as having actively participated in the affairs of the city; at one point he was a candidate for archbishop of Novgorod, which, however, would by no means exclude the possibility of his having, in fact, been a Greek. But even if he himself was Greek, this should not lead us to believe that the whole Neredica cycle was necessarily painted by invited Greek masters only.

At least two more sets of frescoes, this time from the late fourteenth century are—or rather, were—to be found in small churches just outside Novgorod. One is the Church of the Dormition at Volotovo Pole, whose frescoes seem to have been completed around 1380. This church, unfortunately, shared the fate of that at Neredica: during World War II it was completely destroyed. However, preserved photographs of these exquisite paintings give us a fairly accurate notion of their sublime style and the masterful touch of the artist's brush. Their earlier attribution to Theophanes the Greek, who indeed resided in Novgorod up to approximately that time, is now generally rejected and only some vague conjectures have been advanced as to the anonymous painter's identity.[37] The other church is that of the Savior of the Transfiguration at Kovalevo; it too was razed to the ground in the military actions of 1941–43. Strongly reminiscent of some of the most beautiful murals of medieval Serbia, the Kovalevo frescoes are assumed by many scholars (among them such authorities as V. N. Lazarev and D. S. Lixačev) to be indeed the work of a Serbian painter (or even several Serbian masters) brought to the North Russian boyar and merchant republic by wealthy patrons of the arts. As shown by an entry in one of the local chronicles, these frescoes were painted in the year 1380 and are thus contemporary with those of Volotovo. A partial devastation soon thereafter, in 1383, ruined some of the Kovalevo murals, but their total destruction did not, as indicated, occur until the twentieth century.[38]

Inside Novgorod, the most famous murals are undoubtedly those produced in 1378 in the Church of the Savior of the Transfiguration in Elijah Street (on the right bank of the Volkhov) by the great icon and fresco painter Theophanes the Greek, an immigrant from Byzantium. Many of Theophanes' marvelous pictures, showing the serene Christ Pantocrator, monumentally portrayed forefathers, the Old Testament Trinity, expressionistic stylites and other saints, and playful seraphim as well as other Christian motifs, have fortunately been preserved. Yet the extant frescoes represent only a small fraction of the former interior mural decoration of that church. Theophanes, who subsequently moved on to Muscovite Rus', leaving traces of his activity in Moscow, Nižnij Novgorod, and Kolomna, is rightly considered one of the truly great painters of the Middle Ages, inspired by the Hesychast ideology and lifestyle he himself may well have embraced.[39]

These few remarks about fresco painting in Novgorod should suffice to convey at least a general impression of the wealth and beauty of that art form as it was developed and cultivated in and around the Volkhov city. Needless to say, many more examples—among them the monumental stylized wall paintings in St. Sophia (eleventh and twelfth centuries)—would have very much deserved to be discussed here, were it not for considerations of space.

The Russian icon—perhaps the most typical form of Orthodox art, with its own specific functions and intricate semiotic code[40]—also had its peculiar Novgorodian variety, or rather, several successive varieties.[41] Icon painting flourished in Novgorod particularly from the late thirteenth through the fifteenth centuries. Even before that time, though, and also afterwards, particularly in the sixteenth century, when Novgorod was merely part of the Muscovite state, easel painting in the Volkhov city yielded impressive accomplishments. The earliest known Russian icons are in fact those from Novgorod, dating back to the twelfth century, by which time Novgorodian art had already achieved its own individuality. In a few instances, such icons go back even further in time. Thus, what is probably the earliest known Russian icon altogether, depicting the apostles Peter and Paul, is believed to date from as early as the mid-eleventh century. It hangs on a wall in St. Sophia Cathedral and appears to be roughly contemporaneous with the erection of that monumental structure. Since, as is well known, the Tatars never captured and occupied Novgorod and its "younger brother," Pskov, the tradition of icon painting was kept alive in these two cities, which were spared the fate of other Russian communities. They thus became the chief centers of the local Russian schools of painting, before Moscow could claim such distinction. In addition to being displayed on the walls and pillars of Novgorod's churches and monasteries, icons presumably adorned the homes —primarily the large town estates—of the wealthy boyar families. Particularly, however, they formed part of the iconostasis—the inner screen of the Orthodox church separating the congregation from the altar and from the sacred portion of the house of worship accessible only to the clergy. Indeed, some of the most beautiful Novgorod icons, though not always necessarily painted with that purpose in mind, were once or are still to be found in one of the strictly ordered ranges, or tiers, of the iconostasis, notably in St. Sophia Cathedral.[42] Still other icons, picturing specific motifs of the Christian calendar, were kept in monthly succession on the shelves of the lecterns in front of the altar covered by artfully embroidered altar-cloths.[43]

The finest works of the Novgorod school of icon painting belong to the period from the turn of the fourteenth through the end of the fifteenth century. By this time, the traces of Byzantine influence, though still felt, had begun to fade as the artistic vocabulary increasingly acquired exclusively Russian traits, to which were now added local, specifically Novgorodian qualities. As already indicated, Novgorod art—in particular painting—bears the imprint of a vital, popular taste. Its colors are bright and unmixed, and its general character is that of conciseness, often combined with a high degree of expressiveness. The Novgorod masters avoided the deeper symbolism which soon became fashionable, especially in the perfectly balanced icons of the Moscow school. By contrast, the themes found in icons from Novgorod were usually simple and did not require any particular commentary. Biblical figures and saints, such as the Prophet Elijah, St. George, or St. Nicholas, had their well-known, generally understood functions, sometimes transferred from previous pagan deities. Even when the Novgorod painters would portray more than one figure on an icon, their compositions were sufficiently clear and sharply delineated so that their messages could be immediately grasped without any obscuring details or secondary episodes. The intense, vibrant tones, with flaming red often predominant, were less harmonious and subtle than those of the art of the Moscow masters, foremost among the latter Andrej Rublev, but they possessed a virile, dynamic quality with their own chromatic tension and unique brilliance. The purity and contrast of colors which expressed the artistic taste of the Novgorod school and its clientele, the stylized figures, restrained gestures, and illusion of slow movement, as well as the barely suggested background objects, such as a hill or a building, in turn strongly influenced the provincial icons of what has occasionally been referred to as the Northern school, while other local painting styles, for example, those of Pskov and Tver', but particularly the refined Moscow icons, used a different range of colors and a technique unlike that employed by the Novgorod painters. Though remaining essentially in the service of religion, some Novgorod icons, mostly of the second half of the fifteenth century, also depict secular or semi-secular subjects or events, though usually with a religious message or connotation. These include, for example, the famous battle scene of the Novgorodians and Suzdalians (the victory of the Novgorodians was attributed to a miracle) and the praying Novgorodians shown standing below a Christ enthroned and flanked by saints and angels.

The third variety of painting practiced in medieval Novgorod, book illumination—or miniature painting and manuscript decoration—also yielded some highly attractive specimens. It is very likely, though not absolutely certain, that the oldest dated manuscript known from Russia, the sumptuously illustrated *Ostromir Gospel-Book* of 1056/57, a lectionary commissioned by the Novgorod *posadnik* after whom it is called, was actually copied in the northern metropolis. Another similar manuscript, the *Mstislav Lectionary* from the early twelfth century, copied for Prince Mstislav of Novgorod (son of the famed Kievan grand prince Vladimir Monomax), was undoubtedly written in the Volkhov city by a scribe named Aleksa. Its miniatures, headpieces, and illuminated initials are in several colors and gold, the latter here used much more lavishly than in otherwise comparable Byzantine manuscripts of the period. Yet another lectionary, that of a certain Tošnič (the scribe who executed it), or of Pantoleon (the Novgorodian citizen who commissioned the book), dates from the late twelfth or early thirteenth century and contains only a single illumination, portraying the martyrs St. Pantoleon—the wealthy Novgorodian's namesake and patron of physicians —and St. Catherine. Though not in the best state of preservation, this miniature, dominated by red, blue, and white, with the symbolic divine light radiating from the robes of the saints, bears a striking resemblance to some of the early frescoes found in churches near Novgorod, especially those of Neredica, Staraja Ladoga, and Arkaži. Two further illuminated manuscripts, the *Simon Lectionary* and the *Simon Psalter,* were commissioned by a monk, Simon, of the St. George Monastery in the second half of the thirteenth century. They contain images of Christ and portraits of saints as well as scenes from the life of David. Several Novgorod lectionaries date from the fourteenth century, as does the *Anthology of Sylvester,* decorated with seventeen miniatures depicting episodes from the lives of Boris and Gleb and five illuminations from the apocryphal life of Abraham. From the late fourteenth century we have the highly decorative, perfectly interlaced and calligraphic psalter known as that of Ivan the Terrible. Another Novgorodian manuscript, a Russian Church Slavonic version of St. John Climacus' famed *Ladder of Divine Ascent,* is from the fifteenth century, as can be gathered both from the younger, semi-uncial (*poluustav*) script and the material used—paper, not the more costly parchment. Yet it too is richly illuminated with colored miniatures, one of them representing St. John Climacus.

The Novgorod scriptoria continued to produce decorated manuscripts long after the Volkhov city had been degraded to the status of a mere provincial town in the Muscovite realm. It should be noted, however, that whereas Novgorodian fresco and icon painting were marked by their very own, specific style, the same does not hold true for book illumination; here Novgorod was merely one of the main centers of that art form, but did not elaborate any peculiar, unique character. One might argue that in addition to the Byzantine, or Byzantinesque, element perceivable in the Novgorod manuscripts (as in those produced elsewhere in Old Rus'), occasional Western influences, from Germany, Italy, France, and the British Isles, can also be discerned in the art of the Novgorod miniature painters and master scribes.[44]

We cannot survey here the items of the minor and applied arts that the skilled artisans of Novgorod manufactured or its prosperous boyars and merchants imported. Let us merely mention that archeological excavations over the last half century within the perimeter of what was once Old Novgorod have yielded remarkable remnants of magnificent treasures, supplementing the previously known artifacts and art objects preserved in Novgorod's numerous stone churches and elsewhere (now on display primarily in the Novgorod Museum of History, Architecture, and Art). Ranging from tastefully arranged glass beads and jewelry to embroidered shrouds as well as other textile fabrics; from simple ceramics to exquisite enamel work (partly imported from Byzantium and France, but also skillfully emulated by local masters) and superb specimens of gold- and silverware; from minor plastic art objects and massive metal bindings set with precious stones to ivory and other bone staffs; from sophisticated mitres and ornamental plates to censers and costly vessels used in mass—all of these artifacts testify to the level of refined taste and great wealth in the upper strata of Novgorodian society and its ecclesiastic and monastic hierarchy. They also bear witness to the skill and imagination of a segment of the city's lower classes—the craftsmen at work in medieval Novgorod. While it is not always easy to determine whether a specific item was manufactured in the Volkhov city or imported from abroad, the numerous artisans' workshops that have been excavated (and in a few instances restored) suggest that a substantial share of these artistically fashioned objects were indeed produced locally. In some cases it has even been possible to identify an individual master craftsman by name. In other instances we can assume, or demonstrate, that some portion of a specific work of art was first brought to Novgorod, but that subsequently local masters completed or supplemented it with added features or decorations.[45]

In closing these remarks on Novgorodian art—undoubtedly the city's greatest contribution to European culture—let us dwell briefly on one such stunning and complex piece which, in the form we know it, is by most experts thought to be the result of the combined efforts of foreign and local artisans. I am referring here to the famous Magdeburg bronze doors, erroneously known also as the Sigtuna or Cherson gates—thus incorrectly identifying their assumed place of origin—in the western entrance to St. Sophia Cathedral. The major portion of these doors, executed in a purely Romanesque style, was cast by German foundry masters in the city of Magdeburg sometime in the early 1150s. Having traveled a route that can no longer be charted with certainty, but possibly by way of Poland (as it was the bishop of Płock on the Vistula who had initially commissioned them), they probably did not arrive in Novgorod until the mid-fifteenth century. Here the bronze doors were supposedly further embellished with local artwork, tastefully adding to that which was already in place, before they were installed in the cathedral's main entrance. As a harmonious ensemble they are certainly on a par with the dozen or so other magnificent medieval bronze church doors in Europe, notably in Germany, Italy, and Poland.[46]

With this we have come to the end of our imaginary visit to the ancient city on the Volkhov River, glowing in its distant splendor through the centuries and across thousands of miles. This was indeed an urban community which combined pragmatic realism in its everyday dealings and business transactions with a high degree of imaginative power and exquisite taste. It was thus the genuine equal of some of the other, often self-ruled cities of late medieval and Renaissance Europe. Similar to them, Novgorod was a major center of crafts and commerce as well as a focal point of creative writing, learning, and splendid art and architecture. Contrary to the, no doubt, intriguing view held by D. S. Lixačev, who in some of Novgorod's cultural and artistic manifestations of the late fourteenth and early fifteenth centuries perceives the expression of a distinct pre- or proto-Renaissance spirit (admittedly not followed by a full-blown Renaissance civilization on Russian soil),[47] I would rather consider all of independent Novgorod's cultural achievement genuinely medieval, while allowing for a fair amount of change and renewal within the broad framework of medieval civilization. A possible exception is the second of the Novgorod heresies and the learned response to it by its adversaries, just heralding—but not yet truly signaling—the advent of humanism.

The oligarchic form of government practiced in the Novgorod Republic at the height of its power in the fourteenth and fifteenth centuries might well—had it been allowed to develop freely—have marked but a way station on the road to genuine democracy. Moreover, the ties which Novgorod had established with the West—had they been allowed to continue—might have prevented the tragic isolation, overcome only temporarily in the eighteenth century, that Russia's rulers, in the name of shifting ideologies, have imposed on her people.

Notes

1. See C. Goehrke, "Einwohnerzahl und Bevölkerungsdichte altrussischer Städte. Methodische Möglichkeiten und vorläufige Ergebnisse," *Forschungen zur osteuropäischen Geschichte* 18 (Osteuropa-Institut an der Freien Universität Berlin, *Historische Veröffentlichungen*) (Berlin and Wiesbaden, 1973), 25–53, esp. 44–45. For further data and references, see H. Birnbaum, *Lord Novgorod the Great: Essays in the History and Culture of a Medieval City-State,* 1: *The Historical Background, UCLA Slavic Studies* 2 (Columbus, Ohio, 1981) (hereafter, *LNG*), 124, n. 10. Generally on medieval Novgorod, with bibliography up to the mid-60s, cf. also the entry "Nowogród Wielki" (in two sections, authored by A. Poppe and W. Molè), in *Słownik starożytności słowiańskich,* ed. G. Labuda and Z. Stieber, vol. 3 (Wrocław-Warsaw-Cracow, 1968), 421–30; C. Goehrke, "Gross-Novgorod und Pskov/Pleskau," in *Handbuch der Geschichte Russlands,* ed. M. Hellmann et al., vol. 2 (Stuttgart, 1976–80), 431–83.

2. For a general comparison of the three major urban centers of Old Rus', see my essay "Kiev, Novgorod, Moscow: Three Varieties of Urban Society in East Slavic Territory," in *Urban Society of Eastern Europe in Premodern Times,* ed. B. Krekić (Berkeley-Los Angeles-London, 1987), 1–62.

3. The belief that Novgorod is in fact older than Kiev is based on the legend of its origin. However, this claim has not been corroborated by recent archeological finds which have brought to light traces of prehistoric settlement on the site of Old Kiev earlier than the first human dwellings identified at Novgorod. Cf. P. P. Toločko, *Drevnij Kiev* (Kiev, 1983), esp. 18–29 ("Pis'mennye i arxeologičeskie istočniki o vozniknovenii Kieva"); id. et al., eds., *Novoe v arxeologii Kieva* (Kiev, 1981); Ja. E. Borovs'kyj, *Poxodžennja*

Kyjeva. Istoriohrafyčnyj narys (Kiev, 1981); M. Ju. Brajčevskij, *Kogda i kak voznik Kiev?* (Kiev, 1964); I. I. Artemenko et al., *Istorija Kieva*, I: *Drevnij i srednevekovyj Kiev* (Kiev, 1982), esp. ch. I: "Territorija Kieva v èpoxu pervo-bytnoobščinnogo stroja" (19–37) and ch. II: "Drevnie slavjane i vozniknovenie Kieva" (38–67). For references regarding Novgorod's beginnings, see the relevant titles cited in n. 6.

4. See J. Fennell, *The Crisis of Medieval Russia* (*Longman History of Russia* 2) (London and New York, 1983), 103–6.

5. The Old Russian message reads (in slightly normalized form): *Ot Mikiti k Uliaanic. Poidi za mьne. Jazъ tьbe xocju a ty mene. A na to posluxo Ignato;* cf. A. V. Arcixovskij, *Novgorodskie gramoty na bereste (Iz raskopok 1958–1961 gg.)* (Moscow, 1963), 76–77 (*gramota* no. 377). See further H. W. Dewey and A. M. Kleimola, "Muted Eulogy: Women Who Inspired Men in Medieval Rus'," *Russian History* 10: 2 (1983), 188–200 esp. 189.

6. For relatively recent progress reports on the archeological findings in Old Novgorod, see in particular *Arxeologičeskoe izučenie Novgoroda,* eds. B. A. Kolčin and V. L. Janin (Moscow, 1978), and *Novgorodskij sbornik. 50 let raskopok Novgoroda,* eds. B. A. Kolčin and V. L. Janin (Moscow, 1982), esp. pp. 3–137 (the essay "Arxeologii Novgoroda 50 let," jointly authored by the editors). For semi-popular surveys of the Novgorod birchbark texts and an assessment of their significance, see, e.g., V. L. Janin, *Ja poslal tebe berestu . . .* , 2nd rev. ed. (Moscow, 1975); id., *Berestjanaja počta stoletij* (Moscow, 1979). For an early evaluation of these documents as historical source material, cf. L. V. Čerepnin, *Novgorodskie berestjanye gramoty kak istoričeskij istočnik* (Moscow, 1969). The most recent publication of Novgorodian birchbark documents, with commentary, is V. L. Janin, A. A. Zaliznjak, *Novgorodskie gramoty na bereste (iz raskopok 1977–1983 gg.). Kommentarii i slovoukazatel' k berestjanym gramotam (iz raskopok 1951–1983 gg.)* (Moscow, 1986). According to the most recent data reported in this volume, birchbark documents have been found in a total of eighteen building strata ("horizons") ranging from the mid-eleventh century to 1419 and later in the fifteenth century. So far a total of 614 birchbark texts from Novgorod and fourteen from Staraja Russa have been published in this series; however, at this writing c. 700 such texts have come to light and been made available to scholarship. An additional seventeen birchbark texts have been found at other places (ten in Smolensk, four in Pskov, and one each in Vitebsk, Mstislavl' near Smolensk, and Tver').

7. The Old Russian texts reads (in slightly normalized form): *Ot Gostjaty k Vasilьvi. Eže mi otьc dajal i rodi sъdajali, a to za nim. A nyne vodja novuju*

ženu, a mne ne vьdastъ ničьto že. Izbiv ruky, pustil že mja, a inuju pojal. Doedi, dobro sotvorja. Much scholarly effort has gone into the proper reading of this text without, however, leading to any consensus or unequivocal results. For some of the relevant problems of interpretation, see A. Issatschenko, *Geschichte der russichen Sprache,* vol. 1 (Heidelberg, 1980), 118–19; see further, e.g., V. L. Janin, *Ja poslal tebe berestu . . .* , 162–63; and, of earlier treatments, W. Kuraszkiewicz, *Gramoty nowogrodzkie na brzozowej korze,* Zeszyt A: *Opracowanie językowe* (Warsaw, 1957), 51–54.

8. See E. Levine, "Women and Property in Medieval Novgorod: Dependence and Independence," *Russian History* 10:2 (1983), 154–69, esp. 169.

9. See A. V. Arcixovskij and V. I. Borkovskij, *Novgorodskie gramoty na bereste (Iz raskopok 1956–1957 gg.)* (Moscow, 1963), 17–32 (texts nos. 199 through 210, with drawings A to D).

10. See B. A. Kolčin, A. S. Xorošev, and V. L. Janin, *Usad'ba Novgorodskogo xudožnika XII v.* (Moscow, 1981). The relevant birchbark texts are nos. 502, 505, 531, 546–49, 552, 556, and 558; cf. passim in A. V. Arcixovskij and V. L. Janin, *Novgorodskie gramoty na bereste (iz raskopok 1962–1976 gg.)* (Moscow, 1978). See also V. L. Janin, "Otkrytie masterskoj xudožnika XII veka v Novgorode," in *Drevnij Novgorod* (for full bibliographic data, see n. 23 below), 82–110. In addition to being, most likely, a fresco painter, the same artist is also believed to have been a major icon painter.

11. The linguistic observations referred to were made by A. A. Zaliznjak in his study "Nabljudenija nad berestjanymi gramotami," in *Istorija russkogo jazyka v drevnejšij period,* ed. K. V. Gorškova (*Voprosy russkogo jazykoznanija* 5) (Moscow, 1984), 36–153; and, more recently, in the same scholar's essay "Novgorodskie berestjanye gramoty s lingvističeskoj točki zrenija," in V. L. Janin and A. A. Zaliznjak, *Novgorodskie gramoty* (see n. 6 above), pp. 88–219 (cf. also 89, n. 1, for two further relevant studies by Zaliznjak). See now also "Tekstovaja struktura drevnerusskix pisem na bereste" in *Issledovanija po strukture teksta* (Moscow, 1987), 147–82; and "O jazykovoj situacii v drevnem Novgorode," *Russian Linguistics* 11 (1987, Festschrift B. A. Uspenskij), 115–32. Concerning the controversy about a possible early West Slavic component among Novgorod's population, and my reservations, see H. Birnbaum, *LNG,* 27–33. Regarding a recent theory according to which the *Slověne,* settled on or around Lake Ilmen, may have originated as far away as the Balkans, see H. Kunstmann, "Wie die *Slověne* an den Ilmensee kamen," *Die Welt der Slaven* 30 (1985), 387–401. On the *Kriviči* and their origin see esp. Z. Gołąb, "The Origin and Etymology of Old Russian *Kriviči,*" *International Journal of Slavic Linguistics and Poetics* 31/32 (1985, Festschrift H. Birnbaum), 167–74. Generally on the level of literacy in Old

Rus' and for some related cultural-historical and sociological observations, cf. A. Poppe, "Kultura piśmiennicza dawnej Rusi," *Slavia Orientalis* 21 (1972), 365–82, and H. Birnbaum, "Orality, Literacy, and Literature in Old Rus'," *Die Welt der Slaven* 30 (1985) 161–96. On the Slavs settled and settling on the southern and eastern shores of the Baltic Sea, cf. also the entry "Słowianie na Bałtyku (authored by L. Leciejewicz) in *Słownik staro-żytności słowiańskich,* eds. G. Labuda and Z. Stieber, vol. 5 (Wrocław-Warsaw-Cracow, 1975), 292–94, with further references.

12. See, in general, the titles indicated in n. 6 above. Of the archeological evidence of Novgorod's far-flung trade, cf. in particular also E. A. Rybina, *Arxeologičeskie očerki istorii novgorodskoj torgovli* (Moscow, 1978). On earlier work on Novgorod's western trade connections in the later Middle Ages, see also A. L. Xoroškevič, *Torgovlja Velikogo Novgoroda s Pribaltikoj i Zapadnoj Evropoj v XIV–XV vekax* (Moscow, 1963).

13. For some reasoning along these lines, see A. Issatschenko, *Geschichte der russischen Sprache* 1 (see n. 7 above) 35–36, with references to earlier suggestions (by N. K. Nikol'skij and G. Y. Shevelov); cf. further H. Birnbaum, *LNG,* 119 (n. 9). See now also H. Birnbaum, "When and How Was Novgorod Converted to Christianity?" *Harvard Ukrainian Studies* 12/13 (1989): *Proceedings of the International Congress Commemorating the Millennium of Rus'-Ukraine,* 505–30.

14. For a general discussion of these matters, see H. Birnbaum, *LNG,* 13–39, esp. 17–20 and 37–39, as well as 101–16 (notes with bibliography). For a somewhat far-fetched hypothesis according to which Novgorod corresponds to a Starigrad, as a Slavic designation of Epidaurum (Civitas antiqua or Civitas vetus Ragusina) on the Adriatic coast, see H. Kunstmann, *Die Welt der Slaven* 31 (1986), 112–13 (in the section "Warum *Novgorod?*" in his article "Woher die *Russen* ihren Namen haben," ibid., 100–120).

15. On the foreign trade stations in Novgorod, see the recent comprehensive treatment by E. A. Rybina, *Inozemnye dvory v Novgorode XII–XVII vv.* (Moscow, 1986).

16. On the role of the Church in Novgorod's sociopolitical system, see A. S. Xorošev, *Cerkov' v social'no-političeskoj sisteme Novgorodskoj feodal'noj respubliki* (Moscow, 1980).

17. For a survey of Novgorod's social structure and ethnic makeup, see H. Birnbaum, *LNG,* 27–37 and 55–81 (as well as 106–15 and 123–27, for references). Cf. in particular also J. Leuschner, *Novgorod. Untersuchungen zu einigen Fragen seiner Verfassungs- und Bevölkerungsstruktur* (Berlin, 1980) (*Giessener Abhandlungen zur Agrar- und Wirtschaftsforschung des europäischen Ostens* 107), 32–44. Specifically on the Varangians, see the now

somewhat dated but still significant contributions in A. Stender-Petersen, *Varangica* (Århus, 1953); further S. Bløndal and B. S. Benedikz, *The Varangians of Byzantium* (Cambridge, 1978); H. R. Ellis Davidson, *The Viking Road to Byzantium* (London, 1976); *Varangian Problems* (*Scando-Slavica, Supplementum* 1) (Copenhagen, 1970); and, the popularized but valuable survey by R. P. Jordan, "*Viking* Trail East," *National Geographic Magazine* 167:3, March 1985, 278–317. Generally on Rus' and Scandinavia, cf. also E. A. Rydzevskaja, *Drevnjaja Rus' i Skandinavija IX–XIV vv.* (Moscow, 1978).

18. For an attempt at tracing the roots of Russian autocracy to the rule of Ivan IV and its treatment in Russian historiography, see the controversial book by A. Yanov, *The Origins of Autocracy: Ivan the Terrible in Russian History* (Berkeley, Los Angeles, and London, 1981).

19. For a general discussion of medieval Novgorod's political-administrative structure, see H. Birnbaum, *LNG,* 82–100 and 128–30 (notes). For a more thorough analysis, cf. J. Leuschner, *Novgorod,* (see n. 17 above), 44–132. On the role of the Novgorod *veče,* see in particular K. Zernack, *Die burgstädtischen Volksversammlungen bei den Ost- und Westslaven. Studien zur verfassungsgeschichtlichen Bedeutung des Veče* (Wiesbaden, 1967) (*Giessener Abhandlungen zur Agrar- und Wirtschaftsforschung des europäischen Ostens* 33), 126–97; id., "Fürst und Volk in der ostslavischen Frühzeit," *Forschungen zur osteuropäischen Geschichte* 18 (cf. n. 1 above), 9-23. On the office of the Novgorod *posadnik* and its individual incumbents, cf. V. L. Janin, *Novgorodskie posadniki* (Moscow, 1962). For some comparative aspects of the Novgorod and Pskov *posadničestvo,* see L. N. Langer, "The *posadničestvo* of Pskov: Some Aspects of Urban Administration in Medieval Russia," *Slavic Review* 43:1 (1984), 46–62. On the Church in Novgorod and Old Rus' in general, see, in addition to the study by Xorošev (cf. n. 16), also A. Poppe, *Państwo i kościół na Rusi w XI wieku* (Warsaw, 1968), esp. 160–64; id. *The Rise of Christian Russia* (London, 1982), esp. chs. I, III, VIII, and IX. On the Novgorod archimandrites see esp. V. L. Janin, "Iz istorii vysšix gosudarstvennyx dolžnostej v Novgorode," in his book *Očerki kompleksnogo istočnikovedenija. Srednevekovyj Novgorod* (Moscow, 1977), 136–49.

20. For a discussion of the political groupings in the last decade before Novgorod's fall, see, e.g., J. Leuschner, *Novgorod* (cf. n. 17 above), 133–252.

21. See J. Burckhardt, *The Civilization of the Renaissance in Italy,* trans. S. G. C. Middlemore (Vienna and New York, 1937), 1–69 ("The State as a Work of Art"; German original: J. Burckhardt, *Die Kultur der Renaissance in Italien. Ein Versuch,* 13. Aufl. [Neudruck der Urausgabe] (Stuttgart, 1922), 1–95 ("Der Staadt als Kunstwerk"). For an extensive modern treatment of

the interaction between politics and culture in late medieval and Renaissance Italy, see L. Martines, *Power and Imagination: City-States in Renaissance Italy* (New York, 1979).

22. Naturally, this is not a particularly popular view with present-day scholarship in Russia, nor, for that matter, is it consonant with convictions held in some Russian émigré quarters. Yet just such an idea (primarily with respect to the linguistic evolution in Russia but also, by implication, to Russian civilization as a whole) was proposed by A. Issatschenko (A. V. Isačenko) in his provocative, much assailed paper "Esli by v konce XV veka Novgorod oderžal pobedu nad Moskvoj (Ob odnom nesostojavšemsja variante istorii russkogo jazyka)," *Wiener Slavistisches Jahrbuch* 18 (1973), 48–55; cf. also id., *Geschichte der russischen Sprache* 1 (see n. 7 above), 212–13. Earlier, similar ideas were set forth by the liberal Russian emigrant writer A. Herzen (Gercen); for reference, see A. V. Isačenko, ibid., and H. Birnbaum, *LNG*, [7].

23. For recent assessments of the overall impact of Novgorodian culture, see the two introductory essays by D. S. Likhachev (Lixačev), "The European Significance of Novgorodian Culture," in *Novgorod Icons: 12th–17th Century* (Leningrad, 1980), 7–19; and id., "The Culture of Novgorod," in *Novgorod Art Treasures, Architectural Monuments, 11th–18th Centuries. Architecture, Frescoes, Archaeological Artefacts, Minor Arts, Icons, Illuminated MSS* (Leningrad, 1984) (hereafter: *Novgorod Art Treasures*), 5–23. Cf. also the same scholar's earlier study, *Novgorod Velikij. Očerki istorii kul'tury Novgoroda XI–XVII vv.* (Moscow, 1959). Of previous general treatments, see in particular N. G. Porfiridov, *Drevnij Novgorod. Očerki iz istorii kul'tury XI–XV vv.* (Moscow and Leningrad, 1947); and K. Onasch, *Gross-Nowgorod. Aufstieg und Niedergang einer russischen Stadtrepublik* (Leipzig/Vienna and Munich, 1969), 131–90 ("Kulturgeschichte Nowgorods"). See also S. Jamščikov, "Gorod-muzej," in *Drevnij Novgorod: Istorija, iskusstvo, arxeologija. Novye issledovanija,* ed. S. Jamščikov (Moscow, 1983), 5–81.

24. For more about the oral tradition and its relation to literacy and literature proper in medieval Russia, see H. Birnbaum, "Orality, Literacy, and Literature in Old Rus'" (cf. n. 11 above), with further references. On the Russian *skomoroxi,* see the uneven treatment by A. A. Belkin, *Russkie skomoroxi* (Moscow, 1975), and the more reliable and objective monograph by R. Zguta, *Russian Minstrels: A History of the Skomorokhi,* (Philidelphia, 1978).

25. On the Kiev and Novgorod *byliny,* see esp. *Byliny. Kievskij cikl,* ed. I. P. Berezovskij (Kiev, 1982); and *Novgorodskie byliny,* ed. Ju. I. Smirnov and V. G. Smolickij (Moscow, 1978).

26. Concerning oral creativity and the demarcation between mere writing (literacy) and artful literature in Old Rus', cf. my essay cited above (in n. 11). For further discussion and references, see also H. Birnbaum, "The Subcultures of Medieval Russia: Chronology, Regional Distribution, Internal Links, and External Influences," *Viator* 15 (1984), 181–222, especially 203–4 and 214–15. On the "world of laughter" of Old Rus', see particularly D. S. Lixačev, A. M. Pančenko, N. V. Ponyrko, *Smex v Drevnej Rusi* (Leningrad, 1984) (on the phenomenon of *jurodstvo*, the essay by A. M. Pančenko, "Smex kak zrelišče," 72–153). For a detailed assessment of an earlier edition of this work (without the contribution by Ponyrko), see Ju. M. Lotman, B. A. Uspenskij, "New Aspects in the Study of Early Russian Culture," in their *The Semiotics of Russian Culture,* ed. A. Shukman (Ann Arbor, 1984) (*Michigan Slavic Studies* 11), 36–52. Here the authors briefly sketch some new directions for future research, implicit or only hinted at in Lixačev's and Pančenko's work. For a suggestive, albeit in certain respects questionable, treatment of the dynamic bipolarity in the evolution of early Russian culture, cf. the same scholars' essay "The Role of Dual Models in the Dynamics of Russian Culture (Up to the End of the Eighteenth Century)," ibid., 3–35. On the *jurodivye,* the *skomoroxi,* and other representatives of the "world of laughter" as well as phenomena of the counterculture in premodern Russia in general, see, more recently, also my forthcoming contributions to the Festschrift for D. Ward, "Laughter, Play, and Carnival in Old Rus'," in *Words and Images,* (Festschrift D. Ward), ed. M. Falchikov et al. (Nottingham, 1988), 21–39; and "The World of Laughter, Play, and Carnival: Facets of the Counter-Culture in Old Rus'," *The Semiotic Bridge: Trends from California* (Berlin–New York, 1987), 207–25.

27. For a novel approach to the highly controversial issue of defining the literary genres of medieval Russia, see the well-argued points in G. Lenhoff's recent essay "Toward a Theory of Protogenres in Medieval Russian Letters," *The Russian Review* 43 (1984), 31–54. A wide-ranging discussion of problems of genre assignation in medieval Slavic literatures can be found in the papers contained in the volumes *Gattungsprobleme der älteren slavischen Literaturen (Berliner Fachtagung 1981),* ed. W. H. Schmidt (Berlin and Wiesbaden, 1984) (*Veröffentlichungen der Abteilung für slavische Sprachen und Literaturen des Osteuropa-Instituts [Slavisches Seminar] an der Freien Universität Berlin,* vol.55) and *Gattung und Narration in den älteren slavischen Literaturen,* ed. K.-D. Seemann (Wiesbaden, 1987) (in the same series, vol. 64). See now also "Forum; The Problem of Old Russian Genres," guest ed. N. W. Ingham, *Slavic and East European Journal* 31 (1987), 234–79, with contributions by N. W. Ingham, K.-D. Seemann, and G. Lenhoff.

28. On early Russian hagiography (of the Kievan period), see e.g., G. Podskalsky, *Christentum und theologische Literatur in der Kiever Rus' (988–1237)* (Munich, 1982), 106–45. Concerning the stylistic device of *pletenie sloves* and the as yet somewhat controversial complexities of its appearance in Old Russian letters, see my remarks in "The Balkan Slavic Component of Medieval Russian Culture," in *Medieval Russian Culture,* eds. H. Birnbaum and M. S. Flier (Berkeley, Los Angeles, and London, 1984) (*California Slavic Studies* 12), 3–30, esp. 19–24, with references.

29. For a general discussion of heresy in medieval Europe, cf. e.g., M. Lambert, *Medieval Heresy: Popular Movements from Bogomil to Hus* (New York, 1977), passim.

30. On the various recensions of Church Slavonic, among them Ruthenian Middle Church Slavonic, see R. Mathiesen, "The Church Slavonic Language Question: An Overview (IX–XX Centuries)," in *Aspects of the Slavic Language Question,* ed. R. Picchio and H. Goldblatt, vol. I: *Church Slavonic— South Slavic—West Slavic* (New Haven, 1984), 45–65; for an assessment of this contribution, see H. Birnbaum, "Die Sprachfrage bei den Slaven in neuer Beleuchtung," *Die Welt der Slaven* 30 (1985), 119–45, esp. 126–28.

31. For further discussion of the *strigol'niki* and the Judaizers, as well as their Orthodox adversaries, see K. Onasch, *Gross-Nowgorod,* 150–57 and 179–85; and, in particular, N. A. Kazakova and Ja. S. Lur'e *Antifeodal'- nye eretičeskie dviženija na Rusi XIV–načala XVI veka* (Moscow, 1955); E. Hösch, *Orthodoxie und Häresie im alten Russland* (Wiesbaden, 1975) (*Schriften zur Geistegeschichte des östlichen Europa* 7), with further references. On the term *strigol'niki,* see also A. Poppe, "Ešče raz o nazvanii novgorodsko-pskovskix eretikov strigol'nikami," in *Kul'tura Drevnej Rusi* (Festschrift N. N. Voronin) (Moscow, 1966), 204–8. For a recent contribution to the debate about the Judaizers and related problems, see also J. S. Luria, "Unresolved Issues in the History of the Ideological Movements of the Late Fifteenth Century," in *Medieval Russian Culture* (see n. 28 above), 150–71. For some philological aspects of the Gennadij Bible, cf. G. Freidhof, *Vergleichende sprachliche Studien zur Gennadius-Bibel (1499) und Ostroger Bibel (1580/81)* (Frankfurt am Main, 1972) (*Frankfurter Abhandlungen zur Slavistik* 21); id., "Problems of Glossality in Newly Translated Parts of the Gennadius and Ostrog Bibles of 1499 and 1580–81," in *Medieval Russian Culture,* 343–64, with bibliography. For an assessment of Archbishop Evfimij II, see J. Raba, "Evfimij II., Erzbischof von Gross-Novgorod und Pskov. Ein Kirchenfürst als Leiter einer weltlichen Republik," *Jahrbücher für Geschichte Osteuropas,* N. F., 25 (1977), 161–73. Considerable research on Early West Russian (Ruthenian) translations from the Hebrew has been done

by M. Altbauer and some of his disciples, notably M. Taube; for bibliographic information, see *Slavica Hierosolymitana* 7 (1985, Festschrift M. Altbauer), 273–79 (especially titles under the years 1960, 1966, 1967, 1968, 1971, 1972, 1978, 1983, 1984); cf. further also ibid., 203–9: M. Taube, "On Two Related Slavic Translations of the Song of Songs."

32. Cf. A. Issatschenko, *Geschichte der russischen Sprache* 1 (see n. 7. above), 203–4 and 236–39. Most of the relevant documents are published in *Gramoty Velikogo Novgoroda i Pskova,* ed. S. N. Valk (Moscow and Leningrad, 1949).

33. Cf. B. A. Uspenskij, "Diglossija i dvujazyčie v istorii russkogo literaturnogo jazyka," *International Journal of Slavic Linguistics and Poetics* 27 (1983), 81–126. See now also id. *Istorija russkogo literaturnogo jazyka (XI–XVII vv.)* (Munich, 1987), 14–21.

34. Cf. V. N. Lazarev, *Iskusstvo Novgoroda* (Moscow and Leningrad, 1947), 10; see further È. A. Gordienko, "Osnovnye napravlenija v xudožestvennoj kul'ture Novgoroda XIV v.," in *Drevnerusskoe iskusstvo XIV–XV vv.,* ed. O. I. Podobedova (Moscow, 1984), 156–67.

35. The suggested classification corresponds largely (though in a different order) to that used in *Novgorod Art Treasures* (see n. 23 above).

36. For a more detailed discussion of the architecture of Old Novgorod, see V. N. Lazarev, *Iskusstvo Novgoroda* (cf. n. 34 above), 52–62, 98–105, 132–37; I. I. Kušmir, *Arxitektura Novgoroda* (Leningrad, 1982), 3–30 ("Gospodin Velikij Novgorod"); further, the reprinted and updated version of I. Grabar's 1910 essay "Arxitektura Novgoroda i Pskova" in his volume *O russkoj arxitekture. Issledovanija. Oxrana pamjatnikov* (Moscow, 1969), 98–164 (and 391–400). Cf. also M. K. Karger's popular English-language introductions, *Novgorod the Great: Architectural Guidebook* (Moscow, 1973); and *Novgorod: Architectural Monuments* (Leningrad, 1975). For a recent general survey of Novgorod's early (eleventh–twelfth-century) ecclesiastic architecture, with further references, see N. Dejevsky, "The Churches of Novgorod : The Overall Pattern," in *Medieval Russian Culture* (cf. n. 28 above), 206–23. For a discussion of some foreign influences in Novgorod's (and Pskov's) architecture, cf. P. N. Maksimov, "Zarubežnye svjazi v arxitekture Novgoroda i Pskova XI–načala XVI vekov," *Arxitekturnoe nasledstvo* 12 (1960), 23–44.

37. Cf. the detailed analysis in M. V. Alpatov et al., *Freski cerkvi Uspenija na Volotovom Pole / Frescoes of the Church of the Assumption at Volotovo Polye* (Moscow, 1977); see also G. S. Kilpakova, "O kompozicionnyx osobennostjax rospisi xrama na Volotovom Pole," in *Drevnerusskoe iskusstvo* (cf. n. 34 above), 179–95.

38. Over the last twenty years (since 1965, when the church building itself was restored), an artist and professional restorer, A. P. Grekov, assisted by his wife and a dedicated team of co-workers, has been busy getting these frescoes together again by assembling tediously and systematically the many thousands of small pieces secured after the destruction of the church and tastefully filling in the relatively few empty spaces which remain. This giant jigsaw puzzle is now virtually complete, and it must be considered a triumph of sustained, devoted and selfless labor, as well as technical know-how. Perhaps it is not unreasonable to hope that the Volotovo frescoes (but not the irretrievably lost murals of Neredica) may also one day be similarly restored. For an earlier progress report and some background, see H. Birnbaum, "Ancient Russian Art—Its Destruction and Restoration," in my volume *Essays in Early Slavic Civilization / Studien zur Frühkultur der Slaven* (Munich, 1981), 298–304.

39. On Theophanes' Novgorod frescoes, see in particular G. I. Vzdornov, *Freski Feofana Greka v cerkvi Spasa Preobraženija v Novgorode. K 600–letiju suščestvovanija fresok, 1378–1978* (Moscow, 1976). For a recent general discussion of the life and art of Theophanes, see id., *Feofan Grek. Tvorčeskoe nasledie* (Moscow, 1983).

40. On the semiotics of Russian icon painting, see B. Uspensky (Uspenskij), *The Semiotics of the Russian Icon,* ed. S. Rudy (Lisse, 1976). For a general discussion of the art of the icon, its theological function and formal aesthetics, technique and sociology, as well as the relationship of text and image, cf. K. Onasch, *Die Ikonenmalerei. Grundzüge einer systematischen Darstellung* (Leipzig, 1968). See further also L. Ouspensky, *Theology of the Icon* (Crestwood, N. Y., 1978).

41. On Novgorodian icon painting, see in particular V. N. Lazarev, *Novgorodskaja ikonopis' / Novgorodian Icon-Painting* (Moscow, 1976); id., *Russkaja ikonopis'. Ot istokov do načala XVI veka* (Moscow, 1983), esp. 48–71 in the introductory text volume and the separately issued "Novgorodskaja škola i 'severnye pis'ma';" D. S. Lixačev, V. K. Laurina, V. A. Puškarev, *Novgorodskaja ikona XII–XVII vekov* (Leningrad, 1983) (English edition *Novgorod icons, 12th–17th century* (Leningrad, 1980). Of specialized literature, cf. further E. S. Smirnova, *Živopis' Velikogo Novgoroda. Seredina XIII–načala XV veka* (Moscow, 1976); E. S. Smirnova, V. K. Laurina, È. A. Gordienko, *Živopis' Velikogo Novgoroda. XV vek* (Moscow, 1982). On some of the differences between Novgorodian and Muscovite icon painting in the crucial early fourteenth century and its ties with Byzantine art (of the Palaeologan era), see O. S. Popova, *Iskusstvo Novgoroda i Moskvy pervoj poloviny četyrnadcatogo veka. Ego svjazi s Vizantiej* (Moscow, 1980).

42. Cf. e.g. V. Filatov, *Prazdničnyj rjad Sofii Novgorodskoj. Drevnejšaja čast' glavnogo ikonostasa Sofijskogo sobora / Church Feasts Range at St. Sophia's Cathedral: The Oldest Section of the Main Iconostasis at the Novgorod Cathedral of St. Sophia* (Leningrad, 1974).

43. See V. M. Lazarev, *Stranicy istorii novgorodskoj živopisi. Dvustoronnye tabletki iz sobora sv. Sofii v Novgorode / Pages from the History of Novgorod Painting: The Double-Faced Tablets from the St. Sophia Cathedral in Novgorod* (Moscow, 1983). Cf. further id., "The Bipartite Tablets of St. Sophia in Novgorod" in *Studies in Memory of David Talbot Rice*, eds., G. Robertson and G. Henderson (Edinburgh, 1975), 68–82.

44. For further exemplification of Novgorod book illumination and decoration, see, e.g., *Novgorod Art Treasures*, plates 199–212; and O. Popova, *Russian Illuminated Manuscripts* (New York; Russian edition, Leningrad, 1984), passim. For general discussions of Old Russian book illumination, decoration, and calligraphy, see further the monographic studies in *Drevnerusskoe iskusstvo. Rukopisnaja kniga*, 3 vols. (to date) (Moscow, 1972/1974/1983). Specifically on book decoration in Novgorod (and Pskov), cf. also T. V. Il'ina, *Dekorativnoe oformlenie drevnerusskix knig. Novgorod i Pskov* (Leningrad, 1978).

45. For a discussion and some exemplification of archeological artifacts and otherwise preserved minor art objects from Novgorod, see B. Kolčin, V. Janin, S. Jamščikov, *Drevnij Novgorod. Prikladnoe iskusstvo i arxeologija* (Moscow, 1985). Cf. further, e.g., *Novgorod Art Treasures*, plates 114–56. See also G. N. Bočarev, *Prikladnoe iskusstvo Novgoroda Velikogo* (Moscow, 1969); A. V. Ryndin, *Drevnerusskaja melkaja plastika. Novgorod i central'naja Rus' XIV–XV vekov* (Moscow, 1978); N. A. Majasova, *Drevnerusskoe šit'e / La broderie russe ancienne* (Moscow, 1971), passim; M. V. Sedova, *Juvelirnye izdelija drevnego Novgoroda X–XV vv.* (Moscow, 1981).

46. For details on the Magdeburg doors, see in particular A. Goldschmidt, *Die Bronzetüren von Nowgorod und Gnesen* (Marburg, 1932) (*Die frühmittelalterlichen Bronzetüren* 2), 7–26 and 39–41; *Die Bronzetür von Nowgorod*, ed. W. Sauerländer (Munich, 1963); *Die Bronzetür der Sophienkathedrale in Nowgorod*, eds. H. J. Krause and E. Schubert (Leipzig, 1976); U. Mende, *Die Bronzetüren des Mittelalters. 800–1200.* Aufnahmen A. Hirmer und I. Ernstmeier-Hirmer (Munich, 1983), 74–83; Tafeln 100–21; 154–61 (with further references). For discussion of specific issues, see further, A. Poppe, "K istorii romanskix dverej Sofii Novgorodskoj," in *Srednevekovaja Rus'* (N. N. Voronin commemorative volume) (Moscow, 1976), 191–200; id., "Die Magdeburger Frage. Versuch einer Neubewertung," in *Europa Slavica—Europa Orientalis* (Festschrift H. Ludat) (Berlin, 1980) (*Giessener*

Abhandlungen zur Agrar- und Wirtschaftsgeschichte des europäischen Ostens 100), 297–340, esp. 297–300; id., "The 'Chersonian Doors' from Magdeburg," in *Medieval Russian Culture,* 85–92 (a section of the author's essay "On the So-Called Chersonian Antiquities"). It is surprising, incidentally, that an authority of the stature of D. S. Lixačev repeats the claim, long since disproven, that "the Sigtuna gates . . . apparently were brought from the Swedish town of Sigtuna" (*Novgorod Icons,* 9); the claim is repeated in the more recent Russian edition, *Novgorodskaja ikona,* 9 (see n. 41 above). A. Poppe's most recent thinking on the subject is that the Magdeburg gates were probably manufactured in their entirety in Magdeburg and then for some time were actually located at their original destination, the cathedral in Płock, before, for some unexplained (and perhaps forever inexplicable) reason, being transported to Novgorod—probably only in the fifteenth century—where merely some Cyrillic inscriptions were added. This view, in essence already expressed in some of his earlier writing on the subject, especially in "The 'Chersonian Doors' from Magdeburg," has been further elaborated by the Polish medievalist in some of his subsequent studies.

47. Cf. e.g., *Novgorod icons,* 12–17; *Novgorod Art Treasures,* 14–15. On some forms of humanism in the western parts of the East Slavic lands, see, e.g., I. N. Goleniščev-Kutuzov, *Gumanizm u vostočnyx slavjan (Ukraina i Belorussija)* (Moscow, 1963) (*Doklady sovetskoj delegacii, V Meždunarodnyj s"ezd slavistov* [Sofia, sentjabr' 1963]). It should, incidentally, be noted that in his broadly conceived monographic treatment of Italian Renaissance civilization and the Slavic literatures of the fifteenth and sixteenth centuries, published in the same year as his study of Ukrainian and Belorussian humanists (*Ital'janskoe Vozroždenie i slavjanskie literatury XV–XVI vekov,* Moscow, 1963), Goleniščev-Kutuzov did not include any East Slavic writer or poet in his analysis. For a discussion of Renaissance civilization, its spread and flowering and virtual absence, respectively, in various Slavic countries, see also my earlier essay "Some Aspects of the Slavonic Renaissance," first published in *The Slavonic and East European Review* 47: 108 (1969), 37–56, and reprinted (and updated) in my volume *On Medieval and Renaissance Slavic Writing. Selected Essays* (The Hague and Paris, 1974), 41–61 (and 365).

MUSCOVY'S INTERNATIONAL RELATIONS IN THE LATE SEVENTEENTH CENTURY

Johan van Keller's Observations

THOMAS EEKMAN

The late seventeenth century was truly a climactic period in Russian foreign policy.

C. Bickford O'Brien

During the first three quarters of the seventeenth century, the States General of the United Netherlands Republic did not appoint a permanent representative to the Muscovite court. Holland had less frequent contacts with the Russian authorities than England, whence every few years a delegation was sent to Moscow, even though Dutch trade with Russia soon equalled and then far surpassed the trade volume of the English Muscovy Company.[1] The Dutch, who had established their first commercial contacts toward the end of Ivan the Terrible's reign, were attracted in increasing numbers to the White Sea in the early seventeenth century; however, each entrepreneur operated independently, although there were voices advocating the foundation of a company, after the model of the English company and of the Dutch East Indies and West Indies Companies. For a long period the Amsterdam-based Dutch merchants preferred to conduct their business individually.

The States General (up to 1648 still involved in the "Eighty Years War" with Spain) were only beginning to establish themselves as the official government of a sovereign state with international diplomatic relations and representatives; they often lacked appropriate, trained cadres to fill diplomatic posts and were hesitant to appoint more than a minimum number of permanent agents abroad (they did have constant representatives at the courts of London, Paris, Vienna, Constantinople, Copenhagen, and Stockholm). As early as 1614, Isaac Massa, one of the first Dutchmen to write extensively about Muscovite Russia and advocate closer ties, argued for a permanent "resident" of the Netherlands Republic at the Kremlin, but his proposal was rejected.[2] Instead, the States preferred to send occasional messengers or emissaries to Moscow (Massa functioned more or less in that capacity) or, when the need arose, to dispatch a larger, higher-caliber embassy, with all the required diplomatic etiquette, lavish gifts, and so forth. Thus, from 1615 to 1616 an embassy under Reynhout van Brederode, Dirck Bas, and Albrecht Joachimi was sent to mediate between Sweden and Muscovy; an embassy under Johan van Veltdriel and Albert Burgh visited Moscow in 1630–31; those of Jacob Boreel came in 1665; Nicolaas Heinsius in 1669–70, and Koenraad van Klenck in 1675–76.[3] Regrettably, a history of Russian-Dutch diplomatic relations (or, for that matter, of any relations between the two countries, economic, cultural, etc.) has never been written.[4]

When the van Klenck embassy left Moscow in 1676, one of its prominent members, the Chief Steward Johan Willem van Keller (who had also accompanied Heinsius in 1669), stayed behind in the Nemetskaia Sloboda to attend to Dutch interests in Muscovy. Initially without a particular rank, he was recognized and appointed by the States in 1677 as the formal representative of the Netherlands.[5] He became the first permanent agent of the Dutch government at the tsar's court, serving from 1676 until his death in March 1698.[6] Thus with his appointment regular diplomatic connections between the two countries began; from the other side, Andrei Artamonovich Matveev was soon appointed to the States General in The Hague.

Very little is known about this new political and commercial agent from the Netherlands. We know neither the time nor place of his birth, nor anything of his early career except that he had been canon (member of the Chapter) of the Cathedral Church in Utrecht and the secretary of Nicolaas Heinsius, the Dutch envoy in Sweden.[7] In 1680 he was accorded the title of baron (Freiherr) by the Swedish king. According to his successor, Jacob de Bie, "resident" from 1711 to 1718, van Keller was a man of means—that was why he could support the Dutch Reformed Church in the Moscow foreign suburb.[8] He knew Latin (he used numerous Latin proverbs and quotations in his dispatches to the States), French, and German, and apparently also some English and Italian; and he learned Russian. His style is for a diplomat lively and rather civilized.[9]

It seems that he was constantly and immovably in Moscow, a permanent fixture amidst ever-changing political circumstances, ever-alternating diplomats, constantly traveling foreigners, as well as successive monarchs (Fedor, Ivan and Peter with the regent Sophia and, finally, Peter the Great) for over twenty years. "One of the most respected foreigners in Moscow," he was a faithful, conscientious correspondent, penning an endless series of reports to his principals, the "High Mighty Gentlemen" (*Hooch Mogende Heeren*) in the Hague.[10] He passed on to them political and commercial news, some emanating from the Kremlin or elsewhere in Russia or from abroad, some extracted from diplomatic missives. He had his own correspondents and informants both in Moscow and abroad.[11] As Andrew Lossky writes, van Keller was "probably the best-informed foreign diplomat in Russia." "Whenever it is possible to compare van Keller's reports with other sources one is impressed by the accuracy of his information and by the speed with which he obtained it." [12]

The General State Archive in The Hague contains some 270 of his letters,[13] which amounts to an average of one letter per month during his entire stay in Moscow.[14] In the 1840s all the material in the State Archive relating to Russia, at the initiative of Tsar Nicholas I and with the cooperation of his sister, Queen Anna Pavlovna, the wife of King William II of the Netherlands, was copied and sent to the Archive of the Ministry of Foreign Affairs in St. Petersburg, where it was translated (partly into French, partly into Russian).[15] On that occasion, the letters were numbered, but at times a letter was skipped, so that the numbering is inaccurate.

Van Keller's correspondence has never been published, but it has not been totally overlooked and forgotten. Jacob Scheltema quotes extensively from the Baron's letters, notably in volume II of his *Rusland en de Nederlanden*. Moritz Posselt, in his book on Lefort, gives even more quotes and paraphrases of van Keller's dispatches (especially in volume I). Other historians have cited him indirectly, using one of the above sources.[16] The Dorpat librarian and archivist V. A. (Benjamin) Kordt intended to publish these letters at the beginning of this century, but his plan was not fulfilled.[17] A dissertation on "The Dutch resident in Moscow J. Keller and His Letters" was defended in Leningrad in 1947 by M. I. Belov, but it was not published. The same Belov did publish a relatively short paper, "Johan van Keller's Letters in the Collection of Dutch Diplomatic Documents" in 1964.[18] He based the paper on the Russian and French translations in the Petersburg archive (now the Leningrad Division of the Historical Institute of the Soviet Academy of Sciences), dealing mainly with van Keller's reports on the *Strel'tsy* rebellion of 1682, for which he considers them "an important, valuable source."[19]

It would be impossible, in a paper of limited size, to do full justice to van Keller's epistolary legacy as a source of information on Russia and the political situation in Europe in the last quarter of the seventeenth century. He wrote relatively little about the social and economic conditions in Muscovy, the life circumstances and current events in the Foreign Suburb, or his personal life, thoughts and experiences. Primarily, he focused on the international political scene as it was observed and reacted to by the Muscovite rulers and the foreign diplomats in Moscow. From his dispatches one obtains a fairly clear picture of the political situation, the balance of power—or rather the struggle for power—in contemporary Europe. It is regrettable that he kept no diary, as did Gordon and Lefort, for he must have amassed a wealth of impressions and experiences during those two decades. He came to know the Russians well, as he shows on several occasions.

The chief forces striving for political, military, and economic domination in contemporary Europe were the Holy Roman Empire under the Hapsburg Emperor Leopold I; France under Louis XIV, the Sun King; Great Britain with its successive kings, Charles II, James II, and William III; the Republic of the United Netherlands; the Polish *Rzeczpospolita* with its king Jan III Sobieski; Sweden under Charles XI; and finally Turkey under the Sultans Mehmed IV and Suleyman IV, with its allies, the Crimean Tatars. Further from the Kremlin were Spain and Venice; two smaller powers, Brandenburg emerging as the nucleus of what would later become Prussia and the Danish kingdom, were closer at hand. A dividing line could be drawn between the Catholic South and the Protestant North with Orthodox Russia as a rapidly emerging giant in the East; and Muslim Turkey, still a redoubtable force, in the Southeast. Alliances arose between Protestant states (or monarchs) against Catholic ones and vice versa; but often economic, geopolitical and power factors superseded religious affinities. Thus, for example, the ambitious king Louis XIV, desirous of dominating Europe, would thwart his Catholic confrère and rival Emperor Leopold and secretly ally himself with the latter's arch-enemy, the Turkish sultan. Holland, with its decisive stake in the Baltic trade, would alternately side with either Denmark or Sweden, thus inevitably antagonizing the other of these two powers.

It is fascinating to see how these diverse European political and economic configurations and developments are reflected in van Keller's correspondence. He managed to receive European news relatively rapidly, through his own channels and, we may assume, through Dutch newspapers that reached Moscow (usually not by way of Archangel, but with special couriers through Danzig and/or Riga). He became a source of information about international events, both at court and in the Suburb. Van Keller was a convinced Calvinist, with strong prejudices against Rome and notably against the Jesuits, a dedicated representative of the United Netherlands, a perceptive diplomat, and an assiduous, conscientious letter writer. He had the advantage of representing a state which, although not a formal political ally, posed no threat to the Russian government and was viewed as a potential ally, a congenial force in Europe, and one of its main trade partners. He gained the confidence of various high-ranking functionaries: Vasilii V. Golitsyn, the long-term chief minister and generalissimus, was among the close friends with whom he regularly conferred.[20] So were Iurii Dolgorukii, Artemon Matveev, Vladimir and Vasilii P. Sheremetev and other dignitaries at the Kremlin. A faithful emissary of the Dutch Republic, he felt it his task as a "resident" to defend and propagate Dutch political views and commercial interests at the court and among the foreigners in Moscow. He did so by seeking the company of the most influential personalities and trying to obtain a reduction of the very high tariffs on imported Dutch merchandise (in which he seems to have been at least partly successful).

Van Keller and Anglo-Russian Relations

There is little doubt that van Keller warned the Muscovite government about the English and intrigued against them; previous Dutch envoys had done the same, and the English acted likewise vis-à-vis the Dutch. The two seafaring nations had been rivals in Russia from the very beginning of the century, as they were in other parts of Europe and the world. Three wars between them (1652–54, 1665–67, and 1672–74) had exacerbated relations. England was a problem for Muscovite politicians: Tsar Alexis and his entourage had been shocked by the regicide of 1649, and the court was disturbed by the reign of James II (1685–88), a Catholic, who aligned himself with the French king. There was a clear tendency in Russia to trust and favor Protestant regimes over Catholic ones—among the latter Russia's guileful neighbor, Poland—especially because of the fear of the restless proselytizing activity of Rome and its executive force, the Jesuit order.

As a result of Russian suspicions British trade was hindered during the second half of the century. British merchants lost the privileges they had enjoyed, and their numbers decreased drastically during the seventies and eighties. A clear chill in political relations is evidenced by complaints from the Kremlin that the English king had neither sent a delegation to Moscow with condolences on Tsar Fedor's death nor with congratulations on the accession of the two boy-tsars; this was countered by British complaints that the tsars had not congratulated James on his accession.[21] After John Hebdon in 1677, for a long time no English envoy or resident was sent to the Moscow court.

Van Keller's personal relationship with Patrick Gordon, the most prominent man from the United Kingdom in Moscow during the last quarter of the seventeenth century, was somewhat complicated. They were on good terms, and regularly visited each other as members of the European colony, the Sloboda; they were both friends and advisors of Peter, of Golitsyn and other courtiers. At the same time, van Keller was wary of the Scotsman, who was, after all, a subject of a rival country, Great Britain, and, worse, a Catholic. This aroused van Keller's suspicion especially in the mid-eighties,[22] when he noticed more and more attempts by Catholics—Jesuits in the first place—to get a foothold in Muscovy, and when England was ruled by a Catholic king. On February 5, 1686, he reported that Gordon, General-Lieutenant in the tsar's service, had departed for England via Holland under the pretext that he had to be in Scotland briefly for personal reasons; however, van Keller adds, he had been informed that Gordon had received letters from friends, one of high rank at the English court, advising him that "something extraordinary might be expected as far as military activity is concerned," and that was why Gordon had decided to go back.[23] Van Keller adds some information about the Scotsman; originally he had been a Calvinist, but during his stay in Poland he had been converted by Jesuits (this was incorrect: Gordon was born in a Catholic family) and now he was "most zealously and bitterly popish"—he had even converted several Scots and other officers in Muscovy's service to Catholicism. In England and Scotland Gordon would do nothing good for the Protestant churches, he warned. He was said to be one of those who had initiated the recent malicious rumors about Protestants in Moscow and who had brought a Jesuit to the Suburb and obtained at least temporary permission for him to continue celebrating Mass.[24]

Gordon, who had left his wife and children in Russia, was promoted during his absence to the rank of General of the Infantry, the force he was to lead against the Tatars (letter of June 5, 1686). In van Keller's missive of July 3, 1686, he reports (probably informed by the Dutch envoy to Great Britain, Arnout van Citters, with whom he conducted a secret correspondence) that Gordon had had a talk with the British Secretary of State. The latter had indicated that perhaps a special delegation would be sent with him to Moscow to compensate for the political oversight mentioned above. Van Keller adds a warning (repeated on September 10): such a conciliatory embassy might be a first step toward reestablishing old British commercial privileges and, therefore, be prejudicial to Dutch interests.

The September 10 letter announced that Gordon had arrived in Moscow but would probably be called back to London. And on September 25 this was confirmed: a letter of recall had arrived, asserting that Gordon, as a military expert, was needed in England.[25] Gordon visited van Keller on November 17, 1686; however, writes Posselt, the latter "absolutely refused to be somehow involved in Gordon's affairs."[26]

Wishing to improve Anglo-Russian relations, Gordon strongly urged at the Kremlin that a Russian delegation be sent to London. An envoy was dispatched with the announcement that a war with Turkey and the Tatars was imminent and would be very costly. The king was asked for a generous monetary contribution in exchange for grain and other merchandise (letter of September 21, 1686). If the king wanted to send an ambassador to Moscow, it was indicated, he would be very well received. From van Keller's letters of December 3, 1686, and January 21, 1687, it appears that, in response to this hint, King James abandoned his idea of calling Gordon back to England and contemplated appointing him as a British Minister to the tsar's court. "This move appears very suspicious to me," van Keller wrote (December 3), "because, if he were admitted to such a position, the most negative actions could be expected from him, regarding commerce as well as in other respects. We now have the malignant and damaging Jesuits on our necks. I'll do everything I can to see which steps can be taken in this case." However, the idea was flatly rejected when it reached the *Posol'skii Prikaz*—whether partly under van Keller's influence is not known. How could a person in the tsar's active service simultaneously be an official representative of a foreign power? Moscow now decided to send an envoy to London (letter of February 18, 1687).

Despite van Keller's negative assessments of Gordon's role, the personal contact was continued. In June 1688 he was one of the godfathers of Gordon's daughter (at a Catholic christening ceremony!).[27] In the same year Gordon visited van Keller, and there he heard the news of the Dutch Prince William III's landing in England.[28] Thereafter their contact became less intimate. In December 1694 Gordon mentions another visit with van Keller, and on December 16, 1695, he visited him at his sick bed.[29] Was this the beginning of van Keller's lingering disease, thus explaining his lack of activity during the last three years of his life?

The fact that Prince William III, military leader of the United Republic, had crossed the North Sea, ousted his father-in-law James, proclaimed himself King of England, and defeated both the Irish and French, signified a dramatic turn in the situation. Van Keller tells how he rushed with the news of William's victories to the younger of the two tsars, Peter, who "jumped to his feet with joy and jubilated," then "gave orders that on his newly constructed five ships they should merrily fire at full blast" (July 1, 1692). (These five ships, built under Dutch supervision, constituted his whole navy).

To Peter and the Russians this event made perfect sense; finally these two maritime nations, practically neighbors but always bickering and begrudging each other any commercial advantage, were now united under one king, a great king, an inveterate adversary of and valiant victor over France. William was Peter's "foremost hero among Western leaders."[30] He would meet him twice during his first visit to Holland.

The situation in Holland had always puzzled the Russian tsars and politicians. To them, power and authority in a country were embodied in a monarch, an absolute ruler. Thus they would address themselves to the Stadtholder, the Prince of Orange, only to find that he was virtually power-less in political matters and merely a military commander. They had to turn instead to an abstract, polyarchic and rather plebeian body, the States General.

Now that Anglo-Dutch relations had improved so strikingly (a joint Dutch-British fleet battled against the French), van Keller's attitude towards the British also became more positive. However, when the States wrote him about English subjects in Moscow, he answered: "At the court here there is not a single English minister. And the number of English traffickers here is not very considerable either: there are no more than six, four of whom live ordinarily here in town, and two others in Archangel." He asks whether he should "take care of the affairs of these few Englishmen," adding that the British in Archangel are very close to the local Dutchmen anyway (November 1, 1689).

In his letter of July 1, 1692, he writes that, according to Peter, King William would like to report directly to him, van Keller, on important matters, so that he might act as a direct intermediary between the two monarchs. Peter had stressed that he took very much to heart the dealings of his brother-king, William. "Here at the court it is mentioned *hautement* that it would not be inexpedient if His Majesty the King of Great Britain would honor me with some qualification with the sole purpose of maintaining a courteous contact in both directions. I could report on the noteworthy things happening in this country as well as in Poland, Tartary, and on the Turkish borders; and I could spread the word in these parts about the feats and triumphs of His Majesty King William. If this were approved, I would claim no remuneration." The suggestion that he be appointed British as well as Dutch resident, was not taken.[31]

We have thus far focused on van Keller's reactions to international politics connected with Great Britain. It would be equally worthwhile to follow his communications and comments on political and military events regarding the relations of Moscow with other European countries. In almost every letter special attention is paid to the Turco-Tatar problem, the war that was either raging or threatening in the South, the horrific devastations, plunderings, massacres and mass abductions of civilians into slavery in the Ukraine and Poland. He repeatedly denounces the Crimean Tatars as an "evil and perfidious rabble" (boos en trouweloos canaille, April 22, 1687).

In many of his letters he expresses the hope that the European powers, particularly those harassed by the infidels, or those who might become their next victims, would conclude and keep peace among themselves and form a united front against the Turkish and Tatar barbarians. He reports soberly on the two gigantic campaigns against the enemies in the far South under Generalissimus Golitsyn, which failed so miserably, and on Peter's equally unsuccessful Azov campaign (1695), with which he began his career as emperor and military leader. But he was as elated as the Russians themselves at the news of the taking of Azov the next year, thanks to the assistance of Peter's new navy, built with miraculous speed near Voronezh. He reports how thanksgiving services were held in all churches in celebration of this first victory of Russian arms since the times of Tsar Alexis.

Closely connected with the Turkish question were Russo-Polish relations. On the one hand, van Keller was extremely suspicious of the "Heeren Polen," whom he regarded as fanatic Catholics and consequently as adversaries; but, on the other, he favored Poland's peaceful coexistence with Muscovy and their active collaboration against the common enemy in the South. It becomes tedious to read his dutiful reports to the States General concerning Polish envoys or embassies to Moscow: they are sometimes merely mentioned, but often announced as reported coming, then truly on their way, held up, finally arriving in Moscow (in some cases), leaving again, not always with positive results. Although there was no question of a military conflict between the Polish *Respublica* and Muscovy during all those years, a spirit of mutual distrust prevailed. Van Keller was particularly on his guard against the Jesuits who used Poland as a staging ground to infiltrate Russia.

Russo-Swedish Relations

As not all aspects of van Keller's correspondence can be dealt with here, I propose to restrict myself in this final section to contacts with the Scandinavian countries. Sweden had been playing an increasingly important role in Russian foreign policy, as a potential or actual enemy. Kliuchevskii, writing about the three formidable powers with which seventeenth-century Muscovy was confronted—Turkey, Poland, and Sweden—pointed out that "Tsar Alexis's government was already faced with the impossibility of simultaneously waging war on three fronts. Therefore, Muscovite statesmen of the seventeenth century began to select their enemies, looking for rapprochement, or merely for peace, with one or two of them in order successfully to cope with the third."[32] The tense situation on the northwestern front was to culminate in the protracted Great Northern War of 1700–1721. However, during the period from 1661 (the Treaty of Kardis, by which Tsar Alexis had to acquiesce in the Swedish acquisition of large areas on the eastern shore of the Baltic) to 1700, peace prevailed between the two, although at times the situation was explosive.

Connections between Holland and Sweden as well as between Holland and Denmark were ambivalent and sensitive throughout the seventeenth century. Baltic trade rapidly became the principal interest of the mercantile republic, and the States sought free, peaceful, unhampered trade throughout the Baltic area. This policy was bound to collide with the interests of both Sweden and Denmark. In the so-called First Northern War (1643–45) Holland had supported Sweden against Denmark; then, during the Second Northern War (1656–60), the United Republic had turned against Sweden, and the Dutch Admiral de Ruyter had forced the Swedish army to capitulate at Nyborg. Thereafter, Holland controlled the situation in Northern Europe, thanks to the clever policy of Grand Pensionary Johan de Witt.

In 1674, when the "Skåne War" broke out, Holland sided with Denmark. It declared war on Sweden in 1675, but hardly any hostilities took place. Curiously, in the same year the Swedish envoy Ehrensteen succeeded in concluding a trade agreement between the two countries in The Hague. It was followed in 1679 by a treaty of peace and commerce, ratified in 1681 and amplified as a "Guarantee Treaty," aimed at maintaining the status quo in Europe.[33]

Let us now return to van Keller. He seems to have served in the Dutch legation to Stockholm prior to coming to Moscow. In the very first letter preserved in The Hague archives, dated Moscow, June 14, 1676, he first describes Koenraad von Klenck's departure and the respect with which he had been treated by the Tsar and his grandees, to the extent that "the Swedes residing here, to their regret, had to admit they had never seen any ambassador treated in like manner at this court." Then he mentions the state of tension at the Russo-Swedish border, where delegates from both sides were supposed to convene to draw up a proposal for the establishment of a stable border and to resolve other moot points. "The Muscovite commissars destined to reach an agreement on the long-pending question of delimitation with the Swedes have not had a meeting yet," he writes. "It is believed that the Russians, the present conjuncture being as it is, are careful to proceed at the right speed: they want to see what fate will befall the Swedes and be positioned to make their calculations accordingly, while their armies [. . .] stay put at the frontier."

This question of meeting and negotiating between Swedish and Russian delegates at the border to solve specific problems (still unsolved fifteen years after the official peace treaty) becomes almost a fixture in his dispatches for many years. His next letter (June 21, 1676) reports that Tsar Fedor had summoned seven German colonels to reinforce the army facing the Swedish forces. Mutual distrust was so great that negotiations were soon thereafter broken off until further notice; however, they were resumed already the following year. In other letters of the same period, van Keller more clearly manifests a pro-Russian, anti-Swedish attitude (after all, his country was formally still at war with Sweden, which was, moreover, an ally of France, a country he strongly disliked and mistrusted). The fact that the Russians keep a considerable Swedish military force busy on their border, he writes on August 30, 1676, is one of the "beneficial effects of the Swedes' abusing and abandoning the right party [i.e., the anti-French governments] and their fraternizing with France."

Meanwhile, van Keller's attention was constantly drawn to the Danes, who were allies during his first years in Moscow, but after the Dutch-Swedish treaty was concluded (1679) became (potential) enemies. Denmark considered Muscovy an important cornerstone of its anti-Swedish policy and kept a permanent resident in Moscow to observe and, if possible, to influence political developments. The year of van Keller's arrival in Moscow was marked by the departure, after four years of service, of the resident Mogens Gjöe and the arrival of the new resident Frederik Gabel (the son of the prominent statesmen Christoffer Gabel). Gabel soon proved to be an extremely clever, agile, aggressive diplomat. Van Keller describes him as "a nobleman who has traveled extensively and has several languages, one of them reportedly being German, which is very necessary here, and commonly used, even among our Dutch traders." He came to replace Gjöe, who apparently could not get on with the Russian authorities (to which van Keller quotes one of his Latin sayings: "Si fueris Roma, Romano vivito more, / Si fueris alibi vivito sicut ibi": If you live in Rome, behave as the Romans do; if you are elsewhere, live as people live there).[34]

It was Gabel's explicit mission to bring about an offensive treaty against Sweden.[35] He spent about a year in Moscow and worked with great energy to incite the Russians against Sweden and provoke a war. However, he was unsuccessful, as Moscow was too heavily engaged in the difficult war with the Turks and Tatars to risk a second war. In the same year, 1676, London had sent to the Kremlin an envoy, John Hebdon, who with no less vigor agitated against Denmark and for cooperation with England and Sweden. In the struggle between these conflicting tendencies, van Keller was clearly on the side of the Danes. He considers it his obligation, he writes, even though he lacks instructions "to assist Gabel in all possible ways" (March 13, 1677), which he must have done quite energetically. And Gabel himself, as van Keller puts it, "is working with hands and feet to get the desired resolution from His Royal Majesty" (May 15, 1677). However, as already stated, the tsar and his advisors were adamant.

Hebdon had as little luck as his Danish counterpart. To begin with, he fell ill on his way to Moscow and was detained for a long time in a border town. He finally arrived in early January, 1677, as van Keller writes: "with a train of seventeen persons, all dressed in new mourning clothing" (for the deceased Tsar Alexis); however, the mourning period had ended on January 1, and van Keller adds not without some unholy glee: "They'll be obliged now to change it all into colors" (letter of January 7, 1677). Then Hebdon had to wait for four months, to his chagrin, before the tsar finally deigned to receive him. Envoys to the tsar were not allowed to see any foreigners before they had had their first audience; during that period, they were treated practically like prisoners. Neither his proposal for mediation in the Russo-Swedish controversies nor his plea for restoration of English commercial privileges was accepted. Both he and Gabel left at the end of 1677.

Gabel's departure is memorable in that he agreed to include in his large retinue Juraj Križanić, the Croatian priest and writer who had spent eighteen years in Muscovy—fifteen years of the total in Siberian exile. With Gabel's help, Križanić was finally enabled to leave Russia for Poland.[36] Van Keller does not mention the Croat, but he does mention the difficulties Gabel encountered when "he was denied the right to take with him a few servants whom he had hired here and who are not subjects of His Majesty the Tsar" (October 10, 1677), which seems to refer, among others, to Križanić.

Van Keller manifests a critical attitude towards Hebdon and some malicious pleasure at his lack of success. "I am counteracting Hebdon's plans as much as I can," he admits on June 17. But their relations were not strained: when Hebdon held a big party on the occasion of Tsar Fedor's name day, van Keller was also invited. He felt hampered by the fact that he still did not have an official position; but finally the States granted him the status of Resident Minister of the Netherlands. On January 23, 1678, he was received in audience by Tsar Fedor and pronounced his "Oration, recited *memoriter* before his Royal Majesty and His Princes and State Councilors in the

Cremel Castle in Moscow." In this flowery text he expressed his happiness at being granted the privilege of seeing His Majesty's clear eyes in his function of Dutch resident; he also congratulated him on the taking of the fortress of Chigirin in the Ukraine; and he announced Prince William's marriage to Mary of York.[37] On January 1, 1679, he mentions the arrival of the Brandenburg diplomat, Hermann D. Hess, who had previously been in Moscow. Hess was to continue Gabel's efforts to lure Muscovy into a war with Sweden.

However, in the course of the years 1679–81 the entire political constellation in Europe, and with it the state of affairs in Moscow, changed drastically. Louis XIV's France, although at the height of her power, found herself more and more isolated. William III of Orange concluded a treaty with the Brandenburg Elector and then the secret "Augsburg League," in which the German Emperor and Charles XI of Sweden also took part. With this realignment, Sweden gave up its traditional role as France's ally, a role now assumed by Denmark. Automatically, Denmark lost and Sweden gained the confidence of the Muscovite court.

For the Russians, this was a welcome development, because the Turks and Tatars were a serious problem, and they needed peace on their northern borders. Sweden and Denmark also switched places as allies of the States General, and that changed van Keller's position and attitude. The tsar decided to send a legation to Stockholm, consisting of Chancellor Iurii P. Lutochin, a Colonel, and the *d'iak* Vasilii I. Bobinin,[38] "two dyed-in-the-wool chaps," as van Keller described them. (twe gerafineerde quanten), partly to find out the purport of Charles IV's measure by which royal power was increased to the detriment of the Diet's authority and the nobility lost its dominating position. The old distrust was not immediately surmounted: on March 23, 1680, van Keller reported that the Swedish king was extremely disturbed by the concentration of Russian troops on the Livonian border.[39]

In July 1681, he mentions for the first time the name of Hildebrand von Horn, the Danish envoy, and he is obviously amused when he tells how the tsar, after a brawl van Horn had with a German councilor in Moscow, ordered the Dane to leave Muscovy.[40] But von Horn was back in Moscow with a Danish mission in 1682–84.[41] The permanent Danish representative was Henrik Butenant von Rosenbach (1674–98). Again, some Schadenfreude may have played a role when van Keller reports that, as a result of the *Strel'tsy* rebellion of 1682, the Dutch in Moscow were not in danger, whereas Butenant had been dragged out of bed and interrogated (May 23, 1682). In mid-1682, the Swedes were still concerned about possible Russian aggression; they considered it conceivable (according to reports from Rumpf, no doubt) that their port and stronghold, Riga, would be besieged from the sea as well as by 'land. However, our correspondent did not anticipate Russian aggression because of the menace of the infidels in the South.

On August 1 and September 5, 1682, he reports that Brandenburg is sending Hess, and Denmark von Horn, to Moscow; and these gentlemen will throw their money about, he informs the States. Therefore, it is essential that the High Mighty Lords quickly pay his voucher (he repeatedly had to insist on reimbursement of his expenses for representation). Von Horn was detained for some time at the border, but finally arrived; Hess did not come for a long time, which clearly frustrated the Danes (letter of July 30, 1683). Van Keller was very much aware that the Danish and Brandenburg envoys were going to cook up something against Sweden (October 25, 1682), although he assumed that, under the present circumstances, they would be unable to achieve anything substantial (September 5). Another observation, made on November 7, shows van Keller's apprehension of French diplomacy: according to his information, France was working towards estranging Sweden from its allies and on setting Moscow against Sweden.[42]

The parley on the Livonian border between Swedish and Muscovite delegates was resumed early in 1683. A new Swedish envoy came to Moscow: Christoffer Koch or Kochen (later knighted as von Kochen),[43] an "experienced Russian expert"[44] whom van Keller had already mentioned in a letter of January 30, 1678.[45] Together with the General-Major in the Russian army Nicholas von Staden (also a Swede), he had been expelled from Muscovy, accused of conspiracy. They had supposedly passed information to the Swedish government on the feelings and tendencies of the Muscovite court, and on the chances that Muscovy would launch an attack against Sweden. Now Kochen came back, and on March 27, van Keller appeared very pleased that he had arrived and already twice conducted negotiations with representatives of Tsar Fedor. These had positive results: a special high-caliber embassy would be dispatched to Stockholm with the purpose of clearing up all controversial issues between the two countries. (In June, Ivan Pronchishchev departed for Stockholm). A solemn embassy from Stockholm to Moscow followed, and an eternal peace was concluded. "In Moscow, Sweden had, in the Dutch resident van Keller, acquired a skillful diplomatic advocate of its cause," writes Zernack;[46] he has "from now on, during his whole long stay in Moscow, always shown an open ear and an amicable interest in Swedish affairs."[47]

Meanwhile, the Dutchman critically watched von Horn's doings. On January 30, 1683, he reports: "Recently von Horn has thrown a big party, probably to make the Swedish side feel bad"; however, he adds, I cannot see

"the blowing of that Horn will do any good for this hunt." Von Horn be-
haved in a friendly way towards Kochen and van Keller, but the latter knew
he was counteracting the Swedish reconciliatory policy. He found it suspicious that von Horn was throwing about so much money; similar remarks
were regularly made in his letters, indicating that he suspected that the
Danish resident was financed by the Danish and/or French government(s)
to intrigue and bribe in Moscow. There is no doubt that van Keller was not
averse to working with gifts and *douceurs* as well, and that many Muscovite
dignitaries (Vasilii Golitsyn, for instance) were accessible to bribery.

On July 3, 1683, he writes that the Danes were constantly agitating to
prevent all rapprochement between Sweden, Austria, and Poland (which
would strengthen the anti-Turkish league, but not be in Louis XIV's interest), "demonstrating they are better Turcophiles than Christians." Almost
every letter of this period contains some gibes at the Danes. "The Danes go
on merrily: they banquet sumptuously every day with violins and trumpets"
(again a clear hint to the States General to pay him his entertainment
expenses). According to him, after the Turks had been defeated at Vienna
in 1683, the Danes looked somber and quieted down (October 15, 1683).

Meanwhile van Keller had entered into friendly relations with Lodewijk
Fabritius or Fabricius, "a soldier of fortune of Dutch parentage" who was
in the Swedish diplomatic service and had returned from a mission to Persia;[48] he shared with van Keller valuable information about this country and
its relationship to Turkey. Fabritius spent some time in Moscow, partly
because the Russians thwarted his passage to Sweden. However, on July 9,
1683, van Keller reported that "Your High Mighty Lords' intercession on
behalf of His Royal Majesty the King of Sweden has been very positively
received by His Royal Majesty," which also served Fabritius well: the
attitude of the Russian authorities toward him greatly improved. Horn
apparently also maneuvered against Fabritius, reporting to the Russians that
the latter had gone to Persia in order to prepare a Persian-Swedish conquest
of Astrakhan'.[49]

On December 3, 1683, van Keller announced that an "eternal peace" had
been concluded between Sweden and Muscovy. He had rushed with the news
to Golitsyn (which means that he was informed even before the Muscovite
Prime Minister!), who was very pleased and grateful. Immediately an envoy
(Prince Odoevskii) was sent to Warsaw to urge the conclusion of a similar
eternal peace treaty with Poland; now that Sweden would no longer pose a
threat at the northwestern border, all forces could be concentrated on the
Turks and Tatars.

"In the meantime," he writes, "the Danish ministers are quite perplexed by these changes. It seems they would like to move heaven and earth to [. . .] draw His Tsarist Majesty into the French alliance, contending all the time that ambassadors are about to arrive from France with very considerable sums of money and extremely advantageous offers which will benefit His Tsarist Majesty and his lands and parts. However, not much attention is paid any more to the singing of these birds, as they have too often changed their tune and failed. At this moment, quite different political issues are at stake than those of recent times; this has caused the Danish gentlemen to quiet down, Your High Mighty Lords—they are beginning to desist from their usual rejoicings, their revelries and regales. So that Your High Mighty Lords' servant, the Dutch resident here, may say without vanity that, with determination and a gentle approach, he has achieved much more than those people with all their bragging, their running around and banqueting."

After this modest self-praise, he reports that a delegation from the Swedish king will come to Moscow in order to finalize the peace treaty, make mutual commercial arrangements and regulate "the excessive tolls that were recently thrust upon [the Swedes as well as other European merchants]." He mentions he has also submitted several memoranda protesting these tolls, but without success thus far, because the *gosti* counteracted him and managed to assert their will. In preparation for the arrival of the royal embassy, a Swedish officer by the name of Gregory Pröbsting had come to Moscow and paid his respects to Tsar Ivan, "as the younger Tsarist Majesty is indisposed (it is said he has smallpox)."

An important remark is made in his missive of March 11, 1684: notwithstanding all the existing controversies and all the violent disputes, finally an agreement between Muscovy and Poland seemed certain, according to which the Russians and the Poles along with the Cossacks would attack the Tatars in a joint effort, and Sweden was also to join them. Evidently, this was an outcome of the "eternal peace treaty": the Swedes had promised to assist the tsars in their struggle against the Muslim forces. However, two weeks later, on March 25, he had to report that a Russo-Polish truce had been negotiated, but the eternal peace (proposed by Poland in a very acceptable form, he had to admit) had been rejected by the Muscovite government. It apparently did not yet feel strong enough to launch a major attack on the Tatars and their Turkish backers. Its financial situation was deplorable and, after all, there still existed a peace treaty with the Sultan (Bakhchisarai, 1681). But the Poles had their reservations, too. They were unwilling, at this stage, to yield to the Russian demand for unconditional cession of Kiev and Smolensk.

When the Swedish ambassadors arrived, led by State Councilor Conrad

Gyllenstierna,[50] and were received in state at the Kremlin, van Keller expressed his hope that this might contribute to a favorable outcome of all these efforts, countermeasures by the Danes notwithstanding. It looks as if finally "the neighboring Christian rulers in this part of the world [. . .] will be brought to a good and sincere mutual understanding and alliance against the infidels" (April 29, 1684). But he was too optimistic. The Swedish delegation tried to mediate, but to no avail. They then departed again, after having paid van Keller a visit. They left Christoffer Kochen as a commercial councilor in Moscow;[51] soon he would receive the title of resident. Kochen had an audience with the tsars, in which he insisted that a solution be worked out for the remaining controversial points. As a result, a delegation under Prince Fedor Shogavskii and the nobleman Petr Potemkin was to be sent to a small border town between Russian Novgorod and Swedish Narva, where they would meet a delegation of four prominent Swedes, among them Jonas Klingstedt, one of the ambassadors to Moscow the previous year, and the royal councilor Stiernhöeck. The main matter in dispute was commercial: the Swedes were going to agitate vigorously against the high import duties imposed by a recent Russian *ukaz*. Eliminating these duties is also a major Dutch interest, van Keller remarks, and consequently, he has asked Rumpf in Stockholm to be vigilant. He trusts this encounter will lead to positive results, so that the "the golden tree of commerce will one day really flower here." But later that year he had to report that the negotiations were at a standstill. On September 9 he writes that Kochen is on his way to Moscow with a letter to the tsars, reportedly with expressions of dissatisfaction and complaints about new disagreements at the border. The content of a diplomatic dispatch or of an envoy's message was already known before it reached Moscow.

Visiting van Keller in early June 1686, Kochen told him he had received orders from his king to "keep a very confidential relationship" with van Keller, since Holland and Sweden were now united in a close alliance and by mutual friendship. The letter of August 6, 1686, speaks about a failure of the talks at the border town; this probably refers to continuing disputes over details, not to a total failure of the negotiations. An envoy of the tsars to the Swedish king had returned with a missive explaining the Swedish point of view. Yet van Keller keeps believing the remaining issues can be easily solved. In his next dispatch he mentions that the tsars, as was their habit, had returned from a vacation (a sojourn in the country, usually in various monasteries) on or just before September 1, when the Russian New Year was festively inaugurated with ceremonies in the Kremlin, to which he was invited together with the Swedish and Danish residents (apparently Kochen and Butenant von Rosenbach).

In the same letter, he mentions he has spoken to Count Benedictus (Bengt) Oxenstierna, Grand Chancellor of Sweden, and warned him that the recently renewed Swedish-Muscovite friendship was not deeply rooted in Moscow and that another message from the Swedish king would not improve the situation. However, in the present political-military circumstances no act of aggression was to be expected on the Russian side. He repeats this on October 29, 1686: if Moscow had not directed all its energy against the Tatars and Turks, in conjunction with Poland (with which a "Treaty of Eternal Peace" had just been concluded), new conflicts with Sweden would have arisen. The Danes are fomenting these frictions, he adds, while he worked on settling the disagreements. The next letter announced that an epistle from King Charles could be expected which might add fuel to the irritated mood in the Kremlin; for the Swedish resident had complained in Stockholm that he was given to understand he was not welcome at the court "and had experienced some snubs."

Because of continuing small border conflicts, an angry letter from the Swedish king was expected in late 1686 (van Keller reports in November 1686), but the letter turned out to "contain nothing that could be shocking or in any way disagreeable here, about which I am happy" (December 3).

On March 25, 1687, van Keller notes the departure for Stockholm of Lodewijk Fabritius, back from another trip to Persia, and of an envoy of the tsars to the Swedish and Danish courts. Next there is a Dutch-Danish conflict about the closing of all Norwegian ports to Dutch merchants and skippers; van Keller arranged that Dutch timber merchants would be accommodated on North Russian soil (June 17, 1687). And in February 1688 he was involved in averting a potential conflict when a Danzig newspaper printed some libelous, abusive nonsense about the Muscovite court and government, supposedly written in (Swedish) Riga. Van Keller surmised that the Polish Jesuits were behind it, as they wanted to disunite Muscovy and Sweden.

The next development of some import is reflected in the letter of July 5, 1689. Rumpf had communicated to van Keller that, according to Polish sources, the tsars had allied themselves with Denmark; in case of a Danish-Swedish conflict they would take Denmark's side. He had asked van Keller's opinion about this rumor, and the latter had investigated it and concluded that it was unfounded, which he communicated in a letter to Bengt Oxenstierna. He stated that by now the Russian government, because of the negotiations between Denmark and France, was definitely more pro-Swedish than pro-Danish. In the meantime, Denmark and Sweden sought rapprochement and concluded an agreement regarding Holstein, thanks to the powerful intervention of the Dutch States General. He added that the tsars were very pleased with "Your High Mightinesses' counsels and negotiations" and had high expectations of the united Anglo-Dutch navy (August 2, 1689).

During the last years of his residency in Moscow, in the nineties, Scandinavian issues were rarely discussed in his reports; the interest among the Russians, and also van Keller's interest, in the northern neighboring countries had receded, as all attention became focused on the South, where one battle after another was fought against the Sultan's and the Khan's armies. Undoubtedly, van Keller would have been deeply shocked had he lived ten years longer and seen the eruption of the Great Northern War.

A similar overview of his statements and remarks regarding other countries could be compiled: regarding the "evil and sly French" (de loose en boose Franssen), for example, or towards Austria, a Catholic ally of the States General in this period, which explains his accommodating attitude and active support of the emperor's embassy to Moscow in 1689,[52] or regarding Poland, or Turkey and the Crimean Khanate and their relations and wars with Muscovy.

The question may be asked: what was the concrete effect of van Keller's diplomacy on the politics of the Russian government from the mid seventies to the mid nineties? This is very hard to estimate or to establish. When J. Gagarin writes: "One of Peter's first measures was to order their [i.e., the Jesuits'] expulsion . . . , at the suggestion of the Protestants, who had easy access to the young tsar,"[53] one wonders who these Protestants were: probably not Frans Timmerman and Zacharias van der Hulst, who were not politically influential or ambitious, or any other Protestant close to Peter at that time (there were hardly any), but rather the Dutch resident, who was, according to Lefort, "reformé, mais fort," and very much trusted by Peter and his entourage.[54] And we know van Keller's strong feelings towards the Jesuits! He became the spokesman for the Protestant nations at Peter's court, as a counterforce to (but never an open enemy of) Patrick Gordon. In commercial politics, it was certainly thanks to van Keller's tenacious intervention that, after a crisis during the period 1664–85, the complaints of the Dutch merchants were heard and new favorable measures taken, so that foreign trade (through Archangel) was well into the eighteenth century overwhelmingly in Dutch hands.[55] Van Keller thought positively about Peter;

he was the first to call him the Great ("den Groten Heer en Vorst Zaar Pieter Alexeïwits," June 19, 1691), in which he was soon followed by Lefort, Gordon and others. Another aspect of Peter's foreign policy that seems to have been clearly influenced by van Keller was his attitude towards France: more than England, the French Kingdom was Holland's mortal enemy in the period 1667–1715; in accordance with the views and allegiances obtaining in The Hague, van Keller shows a strong anti-French bias in his letters, and no doubt conveyed his feelings to the Russian ruler, who distrusted the French no less deeply.[56]

Yet the political ideas defended by the Dutch resident were not destined, or only partially destined, to be realized in the years after his death. I have referred already to the devastating Northern War that was soon to break out. True, in the years to come France would lose its dominating position on the European political scene, but so would the Dutch Republic; and England was soon to become, both politically and economically, the leading European and world power. Van Keller was a good observer, but he did not delve deeply into the culture, the language, the history, the social habits, or way of life of the Russians. However, as a diplomat he was useful both for the Dutch and the Russian governments. The above survey, though very incomplete, tries to give at least an idea about his opinions and his role in a turbulent period of Russian history.

Notes

1. See Inna Lubimenko, "Les étrangers en Russie avant Pierre le Grand: Diplomates, militaires, intellectuels," *Revue des études slaves* 4 (1924): 90.

2. A[ntonius] van der Linde, *Isaac Massa van Haarlem, een historische studie* (Amsterdam, 1864), 34; also Isaac Massa, *Histoire des guerres de la Moscovie (1601–1610)*, ed. M. Obolensky and A. van der Linde, (Brussels, 1866), I, xlvii; and more recently Isaac Massa, *A Short History of the Beginnings of These Present Wars in Moscow under the Reign of Various Sovereigns Down to the Year 1610*, ed. G. Edward Archard (Toronto, 1982).

3. The account of the Brederode-Bas-Joachimi Embassy is published (in Dutch and Russian) by A. Polovtsov (*Otchet niderlandskikh poslannikov . . . o ikh posol'stve v Shvetsiiu i Rossiiu 1615–1616 gg.*) (SPb., 1878); that of the Veltdriel-Burgh embassy by V. A. Kordt: *A. Burgh, J. Fel'tdril, Otchet . . . o posol'stve ikh v Rossiiu v 1630 i 1631 gg.* (with a survey of the relations between the two states up to 1631) (SPb., 1902). The Klenck embassy has also been described: *Historisch verhael of beschrijving . . . Koenraad van Klenk* [by Balthasar Coyet] (Amsterdam, 1677), likewise reissued in Russia

with a Russian translation: *Posol'stvo Kunrada fan-Klenka k tsariam Alekseiu M. i Feodoru A.*, introduction by A. N. Loviagin (SPb., 1900).

4. It is ironic that the best, or rather the only, survey of these relations, still often quoted, was published in 1817: Jacob Scheltema's *Rusland en de Nederlanden beschouwd in derzelver wederkeerige betrekkingen* (Russia and the Netherlands Considered in Their Mutual Relations), 4 vols. (Amsterdam).

5 "He himself had to shape the form in which he could perform his task," wrote Moritz Posselt in *Der General und Admiral Franz Lefort, sein Leben und seine Zeit* (3 vols., Frankfurt/Main, 1866), III, 189.

6. Cf. J. Scheltema, II, 348–52; Scheltema mistakenly mentions 1697 as the year of van Keller's death. See L. Bittner and L. Gross, eds., *Repertorium der diplomatischen Vertreter aller Länder seit dem Westfälischen Frieden*, I: 1648–1715 (Berlin, 1936) under Dutch-Russian relations, and *Repertorium der Nederlandse vertegenwoordigers, residerende in het buitenland 1584–1810*, O. Schutte, comp. (The Hague, 1976), 286–87. M. Posselt, I, mentions 1696 or 1697 as the year of his death.

7. See J. Scheltema, I, 294, 348. The *Biografisch Woordenboek der Nederlanden*, G. D. J. Schotel, ed. (Haarlem, n.d. [1876]), VII, 30, repeats the date mentioned by Scheltema.

8. Mentioned by M. Posselt, II, 158.

9. He once wrote to the States General that remarks about his supposedly rather jovial style had reached him and asked whether anything in the language of his dispatches was not to their liking; but they responded that his style was well appreciated and that he should continue writing as before (Scheltema, I, 349).

10. Robert K. Massie, *Peter the Great, His Life and World*, (N. Y., 1981), 111.

11. See M. I. Belov, "Pis'ma Ioganna fan Kellera v Sobranii niderlandskikh diplomaticheskikh dokumentov," *Issledovaniia po otechestvennomu istochnikovedeniiu, sbornik statei, posviashchennykh 75-letiiu professora S. N. Valka* (Moscow and Leningrad, 1964) (AN SSSR, Institut istorii, Leningradskoe otdelenie, *Trudy*, vyp. 7), 378.

12. Andrew Lossky, "Dutch Diplomacy and the Franco-Russian Trade Negotiations in 1681," *Studies in Diplomatic History: Essays in Memory of David Bayne Horn*, ed. Regnhild Hatton and M. E. Anderson (London, 1970), 33.

13. Algemeen Rijks Archief, s'-Gravenhage, lias 7364. Six letters are preserved in the "secrete kast Duitsland", 12584. In the following, letters will be simply indicated by their date.

14. M. Posselt's claim (I, xv–xvi) that van Keller wrote nearly every week and often answered the messages by return of post is not substantiated except for the earliest period. A curious remark is made in one of his first letters (December 2, 1676): the "Postmaster of His Majesty the Tsar," van Keller's fellow countryman Andrei A. Vinius, had "confided" to him that other residents, like the Dane Gjöe and the Brandenburger Hess, used to write to their governments only once in two or three weeks; the remark obviously implies that he would like to do the same because of the "sterility of life at the court."

15. Belov, 375. According to him the material arrived in 1843; however, it is noted on all van Keller's letters that they were copied in February 1848.

16. See, e.g., M .M. Bogoslovskii, *Petr I: Materialy dlia biografii*, 5 vols. (Moscow, 1940, rpt. The Hague, 1969), I, 122, 145, 149, etc.

17. Belov, 375.

18. Belov, 374–82. Another study by the same author, mentioned on p. 382, "Rossiia i Gollandiia v poslednei chetverti XVII veka," was not available to me.

19. Belov, 382.

20. On Vasilii V. Golitsyn and his role see, V. O. Kliuchevskii, *Sochineniia*, 8 vols. (Moscow, 1956–59), III, 352ff., and now Lindsey A. J. Hughes, *Russia and the West: The Life of a Seventeenth-Century Westernizer, Prince Vasily V. Golitsyn (1643–1714)* (Newtonville, 1984).

21. See van Keller's letters of July 3 and September 10, 1686.

22. Gordon, when he was in Kiev in March 1685, mentions that he received a letter from van Keller "with compliments and foreign news." *Tagebuch des Generals Patrick Gordon*, trans. and ed. M. C. Posselt (SPb., 1851), 61.

23. This seems to be a more or less accurate translation: the wording is not quite unambiguous (". . . in militaire emplooyen wel haest jets sonderlinx te doen mochte voorvallen").

24. In the same letter, van Keller signalizes a calumnious Catholic campaign that even reached the Kremlin: allegedly, both the Lutherans and Calvinists slandered and disgraced the Holy Virgin, upon which the Lutherans in Moscow had been required to show their confession of faith, which was then translated into Slavonic and was submitted and read at the tsar's court. It was concluded that the accusers were lying.

25. Van Citter's dispatch, communicating the news to van Keller, and a copy of King James's letter are enclosed in the collection of van Keller's correspondence in the Rijksarchief.

26. *Tagebuch des Generals Patrick Gordon*, II, 161. It is not clear which

affairs are meant; the remark seems to indicate, however, that van Keller, though friendly, refused to enter into closer personal relationships with Gordon.

27. Ibid., 220–21.

28. Ibid., 239.

29. Ibid., 500, 639.

30. Massie, 197. Shortly before, in his letter of June 24, 1692, van Keller had reported that "the young hero often expressed the desire to be in His Majesty King William's army and take action against the French or to assist in a sea battle against them."

31. William's letter to the tsar with the announcement of his ascension to the British throne was, after some procedural problems, handed to Peter by van Keller; he also transmitted the reply (see *Tagebuch des Generals Patrick Gordon*, II, 328–31).

32. V. O. Kliuchevskii, *Sochineniia*, IV (*Kurs russkoi istorii*, part 4).

33. See Sven V. Palme, "Sverige och Holland vid Lundakrigets utbrott, 1674–1675," *Karolinska Förbundets Årsbork* (Stockholm, 1938), 134–35. See also the subchapter "Krigsforklaringen och handelsavtalet," 160ff.

34. He took a dim view of the Russians; he is quoted as saying: "Cette nation est changeant et qui veut conclure avec elle doit estre viste à la besogne." (Klaus Zernack, *Studien zu den schwedisch-russischen Beziehungen in der 2. Hälfte des 17. Jahrhunderts.* I: *Die diplomatischen Beziehungen zwischen Schweden und Moskau von 1675 bis 1689.* Giessener Abhandlungen für Agrar- und Wirtschaftsforschung des europäischen Ostens, vol. 7 [Giessen, 1958], 60.) Gjöe called all statements by Russian diplomats "des pures rodomontades" (ibid.), see van Keller's letter of June 28, 1676.

35. *Dansk biografisk leksikon*, VII (Copenhagen, 1935) s.v. Gabel (Gjöe was not deemed worthy of an entry).

36. See Vatroslav Jagić, *Život i rad Jurja Križanića* (Zagreb, 1917) (Djela Jug. Ak. Znan. i Umjet., vol. 28) 186–189.

37. The oration is included in the file with his letters.

38. Van Keller's spelling is: Lutoshin and Bobin. Cf. Kochen's account, quoted by Zernack, 102, footnote.

39. Much information must have come from Christiaan C. Rumpf (or Rumph), who served as Dutch resident in Stockholm even longer than van Keller in Moscow, from 1674 to 1706; he was succeeded by his son, Hendrik W. Rumpf (1702–43).

40. *Dansk biografisk leksikon*, X (1936), s.v. Horn. There is also information on him in Zernack.

41. Zernack, 121.

42. See Andrew Lossky, *Louis XIV, William III, and the Baltic Crisis* (Berkeley-Los Angeles, 1954) (Univ. of Calif. Publications in History, 49) for a detailed discussion of the political events around 1683 in Northern Europe.

43. *Svenskt Biografiskt Lexikon*, ed. E. Grill 21 (Stockholm, 1977), 439.

44. Zernack, 102.

45. In that letter Kochen is called a merchant, although he had come to Moscow as a commercial agent; but these things could very well be combined.

46. Ibid., 116

47. Ibid., 117.

48. Anthony Cross, ed. *Russia Under Western Eyes, 1517–1825* (London, 1971) 120; Fabritius's short biography on p. 383. Van Keller calls him a "Hagenaer" (man from The Hague), although he was born in Brazil. He enlisted in the Russian army in 1660 (fighting Poland), and later entered service in Sweden, where he was knighted in 1696.

49. Zernack, 129.

50. Cf. *Ekonomicheskie sviazi mezhdu Rossiei i Shvetsiei v XVII veke* (Dokumenty iz shvedskikh arkhivov) (Moscow-Stockholm, 1978), 154–59.

51. According to van Keller's letter of June 24, 1684; however, Kochen had already been in Moscow in 1676 and 1683. On March 3, 1685, van Keller reports that Kochen had arrived recently, but he was going to leave again.

52. J. Scheltema, II, 81–82.

53. Quoted by Posselt, *Lefort*, 454.

54. Quoted ibid., 450, footnote.

55. Ibid., 502–4.

56. Andrew Lossky, *Louis XIV* . . ., notes 10 and 39; also his "La Piquetière's Projected Mission to Moscow in 1682 . . ." in A. P. Ferguson and A. Levin, eds., *Essays in Russian History* (dedicated to G. Vernadsky) (Hamden, Conn., 1964), 71–106.

KLIUCHEVSKII'S PUPILS

TERENCE EMMONS

The idea of looking into the relations between the great Russian historian V. O. Kliuchevskii (1841–1911) and his pupils came to me while reading a remark by Hayden White, the man who would make formalists of us all:

> What is usually called the "training" of the historian consists for the most part of study in a few languages, journeyman work in the archives, and the performance of a few set exercises to acquaint him with standard reference works and journals in his field. For the rest, a general experience of human affairs, reading in peripheral fields, self-discipline, and *Sitzfleisch* are all that are necessary. Anyone can master the requirements fairly easily.[1]

This view resonates with Paul Veyne's observation, in his very stimulating book *Comment on écrit l'histoire,* that "history has no method" of its own; it shares a common critical method with any number of other disciplines.[2]

If there is no historical method, what do we teach our students? Narrative techniques? But Jack Hexter was right to say there are no handbooks on how to write history; that is, how to get from our note cards or data bases to the proverbial "write-up."[3] Is history a science or an art?

It seemed to me that some scrutiny of the relations between Kliuchevskii and his pupils ought to be interesting in the context of this perennial question. In Russian historiography Kliuchevskii is, of course, the preeminent challenge for those who would take sides in the debate about history as science or art: a scholar who subscribed throughout his life to the idea of scientific history of the mid-nineteenth-century sociological positivist variety and was at the same time an artist whose lectures were major cultural events, described in the memoirs of many auditors as unforgettable aesthetic experiences, and whose *Course of Russian History* instantly became one of the great monuments of modern Russian literature when it was published at the beginning of this century.[4]

What did Kliuchevskii give to his pupils—science or art, method or inspiration, an agenda or a coherent view of Russian historical development, all

A version of this paper was first presented at the 1987 annual meeting of the American Association for the Advancement of Slavic Studies in a session dedicated to the memory of Petr Andreevich Zaionchkovskii (1904–1983).

of the above or some part of it? It was with these rather obvious questions that I decided to poll Kliuchevskii's pupils.[5]

Two caveats at the outset: the first is that I did not set myself the task of tracing the filiation of concepts or interpretations about specific issues—the four phases of Russian history elaborated by Kliuchevskii; his well-known views on the socioeconomic structure of Kiev Rus', the origins of serfdom, the national assemblies (*zemskie sobory*) of the sixteenth and seventeenth centuries, the enserfment-disenserfment (*zakreposhchenie-raskreposhchenie*) cycle, etc. Kliuchevskii's interpretations, especially his overall periodization scheme, have of course been enormously influential, on his immediate pupils to varying degrees and on much broader circles and succeeding generations of historians: one has only to look at the table of contents of Nicholas V. Riasanovsky's popular textbook to see that influence.[6] But that is a vast subject I deliberately eschew, although some very general comments about it appear here and there. All I have done is look at what Kliuchevskii's pupils themselves have to say about their relations with their teacher—primarily in their memoirs and the introductions to their principal scholarly works; a glance at the works themselves has seemed in order from time to time as well.

The second caveat is that by "pupils" I mean not the tens of thousands of students who sat in on Kliuchevskii's lectures over the long course of his career in several institutions, or even the hundreds, perhaps thousands, of students over more than thirty years who "took" his course while formally enrolled in the historico-philological faculty of Moscow University. I refer, somewhat arbitrarily, to the graduates who were "ostavleny pri kafedre," kept on to write dissertations and prepare for teaching at the university, and who actually defended their dissertations before Kliuchevskii. Of these there were only six:

P. N. Miliukov	(May 17, 1892)
M. K. Liubavskii	(May 22, 1894)
N. A. Rozhkov	(May 19, 1900)
M. M. Bogoslovskii	(November 2, 1902)
A. A. Kizevetter	(December 19, 1903)
Iu. V. Got'e	(December 3, 1906)

(The dates are the dates of their *magistr* [*Magister*] dissertation defenses. Although several of them went on to write doctoral dissertations, only one of these, Liubavskii's, was defended before Kliuchevskii [May 28, 1901]). A number of others who went on to make names for themselves as historians, including M. N. Pokrovskii, A. I. Iakovlev, V. I. Picheta, S. V. Bakhrushin, S. K. Bogoiavlenskii, V. A. Riasanovsky, M. M. Karpovich, and G. V. Ver-

nadsky, quite rightly considered themselves Kliuchevskii's students—there
was a curriculum only at the undergraduate level; but they either did not
take higher history degrees at the university or did so after Kliuchevskii's
retirement (in fact, Bogoslovskii, Kizevetter, and Got'e from the above list
also defended their dissertations after Kliuchevskii's formal retirement from
the *kafedra* in 1901; but he continued to participate in dissertation defenses
for several years, and, indeed, he continued to lecture until shortly before his
death in 1911.)

First, I will consider the testimony of Kliuchevskii's pupils identified
above. Then I will proceed to a few observations that seem warranted, or
are at least suggested, by this evidence. In doing all this, I do not in any way
want to suggest that Kliuchevskii exercised an exclusive or even dominant
influence on these historians, whose professional-intellectual formation, like
that of Kliuchevskii himself, involved exposure to a large and cosmopolitan
body of historical, sociological, and philosophical literature.

The view is widespread that Kliuchevskii inspired but did not teach: he
inspired with the art of his lecturing and the original and penetrating insights about the Russian past that he presented in his lectures, but his *modus
operandi* was not accessible to students; even his seminars were lectures; he
presented his students with an unapproachable *fait accompli*. In all this
Kliuchevskii stood in particular contrast to P. G. Vinogradov (later Sir Paul
Vinogradoff), who drew the students in his seminars on ancient and medieval European history into "hands-on" work with sources, showing them
how to criticize and interrogate them and involving the students in active
discussion of the historian's craft. This view derives in large part, one suspects, from the well-known memoirs of P. N. Miliukov (1859–1943), who
was Kliuchevskii's first "graduate student" and was already pursuing his undergraduate studies at Moscow University when Kliuchevskii succeeded to
the chair of Russian history following the death of S. M. Solov'ev in 1879:

> His insight was amazing, but its source was not accessible to all of us.
> Kliuchevskii read the meaning of Russian history, so to speak, with an
> inner eye . . . This kind of "intuition" was beyond us and we could not
> follow in our teacher's footsteps.

And a little further:

> The professor imposed his elegant, finished structure on our *tabula rasa*.
> We saw by his example that Russian history could also be a subject of
> scholarly study, but the door to this structure remained closed to us.
> As is evident from the above, I worked mostly with P. G. Vinogradov; it
> was impossible to work with V. O. Kliuchevskii.

At this point, of course, Miliukov has to explain why he nevertheless chose Russian history as his field of specialization, and he gives a rational explanation that has nothing to do with Kliuchevskii:

> My main motive in this choice was that working in Russia on the history of foreign states would be "carrying coals to Newcastle," the more so that degree dissertations were written in Russian and did not reach foreigners; and further work after receiving the degree would necessarily be hampered by lack of material and the difficulty of communicating abroad.[7]

Miliukov's memoirs need to be supplemented by his reminiscence about his first encounter with Kliuchevskii, which he gave in a memorial lecture in 1912. It throws a rather different light on the matter of Kliuchevskii's influence on him:

> I have mentioned that I first met Kliuchevskii as a professor in 1879. . . . We didn't know Russian history then and felt no need to know it. But we had already learned the latest words of European scholarship, and we made certain demands of any teacher before submitting to his influence. If Kliuchevskii conquered us immediately, it was of course not only because he told historical anecdotes in a charming and effective way. We sought and found in him primarily a thinker and a researcher whose views and methods corresponded to our requirements [zaprosy].
>
> What were these requirements? The answer even now, after thirty-odd years, is given by the first two lectures of V. O. Kliuchevskii's *Course of Russian History*. Despite certain later accretions of phraseology and thought, the essential content of Kliuchevskii's methodological views on the study of Russian history remains the same there as we knew it then and as it had taken shape under the direct influence of the contemporary needs of our generation in matters of methodology and philosophy of history.

These "needs" or "requirements" (zaprosy), Miliukov goes on, included the eschewing of externally imposed schemes or goals, whether Westernizer or Slavophile, and the study of Russian history

> like any other, from the point of view of the general scientific problem of the internal organic evolution of human society.
>
> We did not yet call this problem a *sociological* problem . . . We only wanted to ascertain manifestations of regularity [zakonomernost']. We sought "laws" in history.
>
> To these demands of ours V. O. Kliuchevskii responded not with discourses and theories, but with the very fact of his relation as a researcher to Russian history as a subject of study. We read his discourses on this matter later in the first lectures of volume I, and found their deductions to becorresponding to our own.[8]

Miliukov summed up the significance of Kliuchevskii for his generation of students in a memoir about A. A. Kizevetter, who was one of Miliukov's first pupils as well as a pupil of Kliuchevskii:

> We were united above all by our common deference to our teacher, V. O. Kliuchevskii, whose talent and erudition seemed to us unattainable heights. His construction of Russian history immediately became our guideline in the labyrinth which that same Russian history had seemed to us in the treatment of Kliuchevskii's predecessors. For us, Kliuchevskii was a genuine Columbus, who had opened the way to unexplored lands. . . .
> In the friendly exchange of our circle, which was held together by our acceptance of the new tasks and methods recommended by our university teachers (in addition to Kliuchevskii, P. G. Vinogradov should also be mentioned here), we elaborated common views of history as a science and identified suitable timely themes for scholarly studies. All this taken together also later gave a common character to the Moscow historical school.[9]

And indeed, in his first major work, his *magistr* dissertation on state finances and administration under Peter the Great, Miliukov acknowledged his intellectual debt to Kliuchevskii, "whose university lectures have determined to a very great degree the substance of my views on the question at hand."[10] He was referring here undoubtedly to Kliuchevskii's critical judgment of Peter's reforms and the emphasis on their reactive character and heavy costs, themes that Kliuchevskii had raised in his lectures on Peter in a much more incisive way than had Solov'ev.[11] In the same introduction, Miliukov seems to acknowledge a debt to Kliuchevskii that goes beyond interpretation of the reign of Peter to the historiographical agenda as a whole:

> [Historical] science, in our understanding of its contemporary tasks, has put on the agenda the study of the material side of the historical process, the study of economic and financial history, of social history and the history of institutions: these are all branches in relation to Russian history that still await their foundation through the mutual efforts of many scholars.[12]

This declaration bears a marked resemblance to the manifesto of the "new history" with which Kliuchevskii began his doctoral dissertation on the Boyar Duma (*Boiarskaia duma*), first published in 1880–81 in the journal *Russkaia mysl'*:

> Thus in the history of our ancient institutions the social classes and interests concealed behind them and through which they operated remain in darkness. Having examined attentively the exterior of the old state edifice and cast a quick glance at its internal structure, we have not studied

adequately either its foundations or its structural material, or the concealed internal relations that held its parts together; and when we will have studied all this, then perhaps the formative process of our state order and the historical significance of the governmental institutions supporting it will appear to us in a rather different light from that in which they appear to us now.[13]

As several commentators on Kliuchevskii's work have pointed out, this was in its day an unprecedented "new history" manifesto. The sociological bent of Kliuchevskii's approach was pointed up in the two-line summary following the title, which did not survive into the book edition:

In the present inquiry the boyar duma is examined in connection with the classes and interests that dominated in old-Russian society[14]

It is noteworthy in this regard that Kliuchevskii's name does not figure in the theoretical-sociologizing introduction to the early editions of Miliukov's great synthesis, *Ocherki po istorii russkoi kul'tury* (*Essays on the History of Russian Culture*), which began to appear in 1896. But this is hardly surprising, considering that Miliukov's theoretical stance was already well developed before Kliuchevskii's appearance at the university; that Kliuchevskii's sociology was derivative from well-known sources; and that, in any case, his theoretical "discourses" were not in print, and Miliukov was no longer a student in the one year of 1884/85 when Kliuchevskii gave an entire course on "methodology."[15] The fact remains that Miliukov's discourse in his theoretical introduction to the *Ocherki* on how the peculiarities of Russian historical development reflected universal sociological laws bears a striking resemblance to Kliuchevskii's remarks about the theoretical value of studying local (that is, national) history in the opening lecture of his *Course,* first published in 1904.[16]

Miliukov does refer to Kliuchevskii in the introduction to the first volume of the "jubilee edition" of the *Ocherki,* published in 1937, where, after an extensive exposition of his updated sociology, he attributes the tendency in his *Ocherki* to emphasize the peculiarities of the Russian historical process more than its similarities to the general-European to the probable influence of Kliuchevskii:

[The author] has built the Russian historical process on a synthesis of both features—similarity and peculiarity [*skhodstvo i svoeobrazie*]. Withal, however, features of peculiarity are emphasized rather more sharply than features of similarity. In this is reflected, most likely, the influence of my university teacher, V. O. Kliuchevskii—the most original [*svoeobraznyi*] of Russian historians.[17]

Miliukov's *chef d'œuvre* as a whole constitutes a complement to Kliuchev-skii's *Course,* supplying the discussion of cultural and intellectual develop-ments (only from the Muscovite period forward, of course) that the latter largely lacks.[18]

The published remarks of M. K. Liubavskii (1860–1936), Kliuchevskii's second "graduate student," about his teacher are much less extensive than Miliukov's and are mostly of a celebratory kind—speeches on the occasion of Kliuchevskii's nomination as an honorary member of Moscow University and following his death (both in 1911). Although the occasions may have been conducive to exaggeration in regard to continuity, there seems little reason to doubt that Liubavskii saw his own work as a direct-line continua-tion of Kliuchevskii's or more precisely as work on an agenda established by Kliuchevskii. He quotes approvingly the preface to the *Festschrift* pre-pared for Kliuchevskii in 1909 (it seems not unlikely that he wrote it himself):

> We went further into specific questions, studying the Time of Troubles, the reforms of Peter, Lithuanian Rus', the history of the Russian monarchy and of state obligations, the fate of the Russian village, the past of the Russian town; from the southern borders of the Muscovite state we proceeded through the Moscow region to the far Maritime North with its peasant communities—whatever we worked on, we have always proceeded from your *Course* and returned to it as the matrix whose individual parts we studied.[19]

Liubavskii's article on Solov'ev and Kliuchevskii, in which he emphasized the continuity between the two great historians, with Kliuchevskii essentially "extending the agenda" of his teacher from the history of legal forms and state institutions to their social and economic content, can probably be read as a paraphrase of his own perceived relation to his teacher, Kliuchevskii.[20]

In his monographic work on the history of the Lithuanian-Russian state (based, as was much of Kliuchevskii's work, on the Moscow archives of the Ministry of Justice, in Liubavskii's case specifically on the Lithuanian *metri-ka*) and historical geography (or the role of geographical factors in Russian historical development), Liubavskii clearly saw himself proceeding from Kliuchevskii's work.

Liubavskii's work on the history of Lithuanian Rus (*Litovskaia Rus'*) has been seen as a partial reversion to the more legalistic and political-institutional approach characteristic of the state school,[21] but overall the work bears a striking resemblance to Kliuchevskii's in *Boiarskaia duma*: there is the same kind of attention to the social content of institutions; or, perhaps more precisely, the same kind of approach to sociopolitical "realities" through the study of institutions. Even the title of his doctoral dissertation bears a close resemblance to Kliuchevskii's doctoral work: *The Lithuanian-Russian Seim. An Inquiry into the History of the Institution in Relation with the Internal Order and Public Life of the State.* The first sentence in the introduction to that work states: "One can say that in [the laws of the 1566 statute relating to the "Great Free Seim"] is expressed the most general summation of the sociopolitical history of that state over the period of its independent existence.[22]

Liubavskii's rationale for his inquiries is rather narrowly academic, but his focus on the history of political decentralization and "estate-representation" in the west-Russian past harks back to Kliuchevskii's remarkably present-minded rationale in the introduction to the first printed version of *Boiarskaia duma*, which included providing an answer to the question:

> Have there been social relations in our past that could still be revived and made to serve the interests of the present; and are there in society of today forces and elements capable of bearing the burden of public initiative, which would not complicate but rather facilitate the government's activity in the interests of the national welfare?[23]

For Kliuchevskii, this question—that is, the question of the future political evolution of the country—had been put on the agenda by the emancipation and the other "great reforms" of the 1860s; it was hardly less pertinent at the turn of the century when Liubavskii was writing, and the "actuality" (*aktual'nost'*) of Liubavskii's inquiries into the causes of political decentralization and institutionalized limitations on the power of the crown in a part of modern Russia's historical patrimony does not seem fortuitous.

When Liubavskii got around to publishing his own general course on Russian history in 1915 (*Lektsii po drevnei russkoi istorii do kontsa xvi veka*), he intended it to complement Kliuchevskii's work:

> By way of explanation for the sketchy and uneven presentation [here], I must say that this presentation was prepared with the intention that V. O. Kliuchevskii's classic *Course of Russian History* be studied obligatorily by the students. My own course was in certain cases an expansion and supplement of that course, and on the other hand it dealt summarily with matters treated particularly fully and thoroughly by Kliuchevskii. It goes without saying that in addition to these differences, the arrangement and content of my course was also determined by differing views on certain aspects of the Russian historical process.[24]

Kliuchevskii's third "graduate student," N. A. Rozhkov (1868–1927), had very little to say explicitly about his relations with his teacher. He made no contribution to the 1909 *Festschrift*, nor to the memorial literature that appeared shortly after Kliuchevskii's death in 1911.

Kliuchevskii's contribution to Rozhkov's passionate search for a science of society, which dominated his historical writing subsequent to his *magistr* dissertation on sixteenth-century agriculture (that is, after about 1900), appears to have been considerable: Kliuchevskii's teaching, along with the writings of Comte, introduced him to the sociological perspective on history.[25] In a way, Rozhkov's "economic materialism," his idiosyncratic but consistent monism based on a combination of Comtian positivism and Marxism, was the playing out, into the second generation, of Kliuchevskii's commitment to the search for "historical laws," which the master's turn of mind and addiction to applied research had prevented him from pursuing.[26]

In contrast to his later work, Rozhkov's dissertation, an inquiry into the state of agriculture and the economic crisis of the late sixteenth century, was the kind of broadly-conceived "economic history" that fitted very well into the Kliuchevskii-inspired corpus: it deals with climatic and soil conditions, demographics, trade, and property relations as well as agriculture *in sensu stricto*. It was based, also typically, on a vast amount of archival research, and in its elucidation of the material conditions underlying the process of enserfment it has been read as a confirmation of Kliuchevskii's theory on the genesis of serfdom.[27]

Rozhkov's subsequent work took leave of the conventional historical framework, but in *Gorod i derevnia v russkoi istorii* (*Town and Country in Russian History*), his *tour de force* 84-page sketch of Russian economic history first published in 1902, despite its novel, consistently materialist, or economic, determinist, viewpoint, the essentially Kliuchevskian four-phase periodization was still preserved: Kievan, appanage, Muscovite, and pre-reform Imperial (Rozhkov only added a fifth period, the post-reform era).[28] The fundamental place of demographic change in Rozhkov's economic-determinist version of Russian history may also owe more than a little to Kliuchevskii.

If Rozhkov was the most theoretically oriented of Kliuchevskii's pupils, his near-coeval and Kliuchevskii's fourth dissertation student, M. M. Bogoslovskii (1867–1929), was probably the least so. In his article for the 1912 Kliuchevskii memorial volume, Bogoslovskii, like Liubavskii, emphasized the continuity between Kliuchevskii and his teacher, Solov'ev. He quotes approvingly from memory Kliuchevskii's remark, "I am Solov'ev's pupil— that is all I have to be proud of as a scholar."[29]

Bogoslovskii rather obviously saw himself standing in the same relation to Kliuchevskii as he saw Kliuchevskii vis-à-vis Solov'ev. In 1911, following

Kizevetter's resignation in the Kasso affair along with many other faculty members, Bogoslovskii was appointed to the chair of Russian history. He wrote about that occasion the following comment in his unpublished memoirs:

> Having stayed, I was quite right to take the chair left empty after Kizevetter's departure, and it was a good thing I did. If I hadn't taken it, Dovnar-Zapol'skii or someone worse would have been put in it and would have propagated his own school. But I preserved for the Moscow chair the traditions of the head of our school, V. O. Kliuchevskii. I preserved them in their purity, and have the right to be proud of that.[30]

Bogoslovskii also insists on Kliuchevskii's aversion to abstract thought ("His mind always needed concrete, real factual material, like fuel for a fire. For him, facts seemed to take the place of logical constructs"), the strictly inductive character of his historical reasoning, and his heroic capacity for sifting documents in the archives ("a truly Solov'evian capacity for work"). He concludes, with an obvious dig at Marxism:

> That is why he was organically incapable of setting himself the task of extrapolating the entire course of Russian history from any kind of abstract principle.[31]

Bogoslovskii nevertheless allows that Kliuchevskii had a predilection for certain groups of facts—political, social, and economic facts, particularly social; within these groups his interest lay especially with the history of "social classes": "If it were necessary to define Kliuchevskii's main, dominant inclination as an historian, I would call him an historian of social classes." Moreover, it was particularly the history of the political elite that held his interest:

> In both *Boiarskaia duma* and his course he studies in detail the evolution of the elite ruling strata: the commercial aristocracy of Dnepr' Rus', the landowning retinue [*druzhina*] and monastery society of Upper-Volga [Rus'], the titled Moscow boyardom [*boiarstvo*] of the fifteenth and sixteenth centuries, and its successor, the variegated small landowning gentry [*melkopomestnoe dvorianstvo*] of the eighteenth and nineteenth centuries, which carried out palace coups through the guards regiments.[32]

In his unpublished memoirs, Bogoslovskii makes the comparison, familiar from Miliukov's memoirs and echoed by several other students, between Kliuchevskii and Vinogradov as teachers. Unlike Vinogradov's, Kliuchevskii's strength was not in the seminars, where he was a "dogmatic," laying out his prepared conclusions and never ending his critical comments with a question mark. Bogoslovskii came to the conclusion as a student that

Kliuchevskii was at home in the lecture hall, where the student would passively listen to his conclusions but not in a laboratory where the student would learn methods through independent work under the guidance of the instructor. It was Kliuchevskii, nevertheless, who suggested the theme of his undergraduate thesis: "The origin, content, and significance of the census books [*pistsovye knigi*] as sources for the history of the Muscovite state in the fifteenth, sixteenth, and seventeenth centuries."[33]

It is interesting to look at Bogoslovskii's own work in the light of these remarks. From his first undergraduate dissertation on the *pistsovye knigi,* through his massive *magistr* and doctoral dissertations, *Peter the Great's Local Reform* [*Oblastnaia reforma Petra Velikago*] (1902), and *Local Self-Government in the Russian North in the Seventeenth Century* [*Zemskoe samo-upravlenie na russkom severe v xvii veke*] (1909–12), to his final unfinished *opus magnum,* the biography of Peter the Great, that work is characterized by a strong penchant for massive, detailed work in previously unused and ill-organized archives.[34] His undergraduate paper, which comprises five thick, bound notebooks in his archive, carried the epigraph:

> *V nauke priatno byt' i prostym chernorabochim.* [In scholarship, it is good to be a simple toiler].[35]

Bogoslovskii's *magistr* thesis seems to continue the line of confronting the theory of the Petrine reforms with their reality that is characteristic of late-nineteenth-century scholarship and can be traced back, through Miliukov, to Kliuchevskii. His doctoral dissertation, like Liubavskii's work on the Lithuanian-Russian state, pursues the line issuing from Kliuchevskii's agenda in the introduction to *Boiarskaia duma*: precedents and alternatives to autocracy or, more precisely, to bureaucratic absolutism, in the pre-Petrine Russian past. In Bogoslovskii's study of the institutions of self-government in the Russian north, where he found them to be surviving intact into the mid-seventeenth century, the task is set in the terms established by the master in his introduction to *Boiarskaia duma* (and pursued in Bogoslovskii's first dissertation, of course): to get from the legislation on the self-government [*zemskie*] institutions of Muscovy to the reality behind it, "how [it] was in fact carried out and to what extent it became reality." The element of present-mindedness in his inquiry is clearly betrayed in his conclusion:

> In developing an absolutist central power and emerging under its aegis from the feudal order, the Muscovite State passes through two successive stages in the development of its form of government, distinguished by the instruments utilized by the autocracy. In the period [from the mid-sixteenth

century to the mid-seventeenth century] the Moscow State may be called
an *autocracy of the land* [*samoderzhavno-zemskoe*]. From the middle of the
seventeenth century it becomes a *bureaucratic autocracy* [*samoderzhavno-
biurokraticheskoe*].

In the first of these periods

> The entire state structure, with the national assembly [*zemskii sobor*] at the
> top and the self-governing counties and townships [*samoupravliaiushchiesia
> uezdy i volosti*] at the bottom, is imbued with the principle of popular self-
> governance [*zemskoe samoupravlenie*]; it is entirely bound up with this prin-
> ciple, and the *zemskii sobor* at the top rests on the district and township
> self-governments as on a necessary foundation. Popular representation at
> the center was the inevitable crowning [*zavershenie*] of local, county, and
> township autonomy.[36]

If a penchant for pathbreaking archival research and a present-minded
interest in Old-Russian political institutions linked Bogoslovskii to his
teacher, so too did his abiding interest in the history of the political elite,
which he carried over into the study of the eighteenth-century nobility.[37]

Among Kliuchevskii's pupils his most pious admirer, and apparently his
favorite student as well, was A. A. Kizevetter (1866–1933).[38] "It would be
inadequate to say," Kizevetter wrote in an obituary article about Kliuchevskii,

> that Kliuchevskii advanced or reformed the science of Russian history. We
> will be much closer to the truth in saying that he founded that science.[39]

For Kizevetter, Kliuchevskii represented the unique combination of scholar
and poet that it takes to make a truly great historian:

> Scholar and poet, a great systemist-schematist and a sensitive portrayer of
> the concrete phenomena of life, a first-class master of broad generalizations
> and an incomparable analyst who valued and loved detailed, microscopic
> observations—such was Kliuchevskii as an historian.[40]

There is little reason to doubt that Kizevetter aspired to be a "most
remarkable scholarly researcher and brilliant teacher of his science"[41] himself. Kizevetter was in fact generally considered to be the best literary stylist
and lecturer among Kliuchevskii's students. Even the sober Miliukov was
willing to allow that he fulfilled this aspiration to a considerable degree:

> We all tried in those days to imitate more or less Kliuchevskii. But
> Kizevetter had special talents for that. . . . The ability to paint vivid word
> pictures, to find the right colors and to make unexpected connections that
> penetrated to the essence of a subject, distinguished Kizevetter as a lecturer
> and a teacher to the end of his days.[42]

It was Kliuchevskii's talent as a teacher, that is primarily as a lecturer, that
Kizevetter chose to write about in his contribution to the 1912 memorial
volume; he describes there in great detail the nature of Kliuchevskii's art as
a lecturer, by which

> imperceptibly but with unusual force the underlying concrete basis of his
> complex and subtle scholarly generalizations was made clear.[43]

There is some reason to believe that Kizevetter's attention to Kliuchevskii's
art as a lecturer went as far as imitating some of his unusual speech patterns.[44]

In any case, this talent, Miliukov goes on, was indeed combined with a
real love for detailed historical analysis and for rooting in the archives, and
he approvingly refers the reader to Kizevetter's memoirs on that score.[45]
Kizevetter's monographic work on the Russian town in the eighteenth century, especially his monumental dissertation, *The Urban Estate in Eighteenth-
Century Russia* [*Posadskaia obshchina v xviii st.*] (1903), certainly qualified
him as a follower of Kliuchevskii on this side of the ledger as well: it was
the plowing of new ground based on archival research (the Moscow archives
of the Ministry of Justice for the most part), and it aimed at illuminating the
socioeconomic and political realities behind the institution (the *posadskaia
obshchina*) that served, again typically, as the focal point of the inquiry.[46]
Kizevetter's study has properly been considered the pioneering study of Russia's "third estate" in the eighteenth century.

Like his colleagues Miliukov and Bogoslovskii, Kizevetter emphasized the
tragic gap that separated the schemes of the eighteenth century absolutist
state from the "Muscovite" reality that lay behind them, and the judgment
was negative:

> The entire government policy of the eighteenth century toward urban self-
> government can be characterized as an attempt to reach a completely
> unreachable goal: realization of the elevated cultural tasks of internal policy
> on the old foundation of servitude [*tiaglo*]. As a result the elevated cultural
> goals were not achieved, and the urban obligations became heavier than
> before; and only one conclusion was forthcoming in the consciousness of
> the urban population: that the paternalistic attentions of the government
> cost very dearly, that life had become harder, not better.[47]

One is instantly reminded of the memorable phrase with which Kliuchevskii
characterized the "modern period" in Russian history:

> *Gosudarstvo pukhlo, a narod khirel* [the state grew fat, but the people wasted
> away].[48]

The conclusion Kizevetter drew from his observation in this dissertation defense speech points up how much his work was also true to type as a present-minded inquiry into the historical roots of self-government in Russia:

> Historical study of past epochs in the development of our self-government leads . . . to the same conclusion as observation of our present situation: one thing above all else is desirable for the satisfaction of the most urgent needs and requirements of our motherland—that all the doors and windows of Russia's state edifice be opened wide to the principles of genuine public initiative.[49]

Iurii Vladimirovich Got'e (1873–1943), the last of Kliuchevskii's pupils to defend his dissertation before his teacher, has left two reminiscences about his relations with Kliuchevskii during his student years between 1891 and 1895.[50] On the whole, Got'e confirms the familiar impression of Kliuchevskii as a rather distant and magisterial teacher, whose seminars were more like lectures and whose general course, which he informs us was read virtually unchanged from year to year, inspired his students, above all "to love the history of their native land."[51]

Like the others, too, Got'e compares Kliuchevskii in this respect to Vinogradov, whose seminars "taught [him] how to work. . . . He was precisely what a professor ought to be in relation to his students: unceremonious and accessible within the limits that separate a genuine major scholar from beginning students." Moreover he attributes the greatest influence on his formation as a historian of Russia to the seminar of P. N. Miliukov, which was conducted, he writes, "fully in the Vinogradov style":

> The same attentiveness, both pedagogical and scholarly, in the selection of topics, the same attentive relations with the students, the same restrained strictness and attention to the analysis of the topics.

And it was in fact for Miliukov that Got'e prepared his undergraduate thesis on the defense of the southern borders of the Muscovite state in the sixteenth century, in the preparation of which he met frequently with Miliukov at the university and at Miliukov's home to discuss details, get bibliographical and source references and the like.

> Work in Miliukov's seminar and, perhaps, even more so the work on the undergraduate thesis under P. N.'s direct supervision deepened and defined my scholarly interests. I decided definitely to become a Russian historian. And for this supervision I will always be grateful to P. N. Miliukov, whom I consider to be my teacher just as much as V. O. Kliuchevskii.

Got'e summed up the influence of his two teachers as follows:

> [Kliuchevskii] lit a special interest for Russian history in me, and in Miliukov's seminar I completed my first scholarly work.[52]

According to Got'e, however, Kliuchevskii's influence on him went considerably deeper than a matter of general inspiration, and he rejects the common view that Kliuchevskii was "a great man, but not a pedagogue." He recounts the story of how he tried to get some detailed advice about the literature on the questions that had been selected for his *magistr* exams and was finally told by his irritated teacher to "get it for himself," to "look it up in Mezhov" that is, the works of Russia's greatest bibliographer, V. I. Mezhov, (1830–94). He understood later, he writes that this was not indifference on Kliuchevskii's part, but part of a deliberate pedagogical strategy to make aspiring professionals aware of their own responsibility in "getting it for themselves" and of the primary importance of sources, rather than secondary literature:

> In his refusal to lift the curtain of scholarship for the uninitiated; in a certain skepticism toward those who had not succeeded in demonstrating their love and devotion to their chosen activity; in his demand that such a person "get it for himself," deepen his own knowledge, and grow accustomed to independent scholarly work; and finally, in his warm involvement with and generous help to those who in his opinion had demonstrated or were demonstrating their sincere love for their chosen subject and were showing some talent for finding their own way and writing independently— in all this one cannot fail to see the conscious devices of an original scholarly pedagogy that had been worked out through long years of practice and the lengthy meditations of a powerful and original mind.[53]

Got'e's major works, his *magistr* and doctoral dissertations, fit squarely into the Kliuchevskian pattern familiar from the work of Kliuchevskii's earlier pupils. *Zamoskovnyi krai v xvii veke. Opyt issledovaniia po istorii ekonomicheskogo byta moskovskoi Rusi* (*The Moscow Region in the Seventeenth Century. An Attempted Investigation into the History of Economic Conditions in Muscovy*), first published in 1906, is based in large part on the study of the *pistsovye knigi,* like Rozhkov's first thesis and Bogoslovskii's second, and is the kind of economic history or "history of economic conditions" that one would expect from the Kliuchevskii school: it includes the study of administrative structures ("regional divisions," as per Liubavskii), population geography and landholding relationships, in addition to the strictly "economic" matter of agricultural production. Rozhkov investigated the socioeconomic background of the Time of Troubles; Got'e studied its socioeconomic aftermath.[54]

Got'e's monumental history of regional administration in Russia from Peter I to Catherine II, of which the first volume was published in 1913 as his doctoral dissertation, in characteristic fashion attempts to go beyond the administrative statutes and structures to the operational and social realities. In a manner analogous to Kizevetter's work on the *Posadskaia obshchina,* Got'e looks at the entire post-Petrine eighteenth-century experience of regional administration from the perspective of the origins of the corresponding Catherinian reforms. (The second volume, completed in 1922 but published only in 1941, is largely devoted to the immediate background and results of the 1775 reform).[55]

As the youngest of this group of Kliuchevskii's pupils, Got'e conceived of his own work as a continuation not only of the master's work but also of that of his older fellows. And indeed, according to his own testimony, he got the idea of his first dissertation from Rozhkov's work on the sixteenth-century economy, and the second was conceived as a continuation of Bogoslovskii's thesis on the regional reforms of Peter.[56]

Another characteristic of Got'e's work, again according to his own testimony, was its central concern with the history of the political elite, the *dvorianstvo.* In the diary he kept during the revolution and civil war, he describes *Zamoskovnyi krai* as "in essence the history of the nobility in the seventeenth century in its main features" and the history of the eighteenth-century regional administration as "nothing other than the *everyday* history of the nobility from Peter to Catherine II, when they essentially conquered everything."[57] In the fall of 1919 he set down a sketch of his life's work, both those parts completed and those left to be done, a "series of monographs in which all my views on the entirety of Russian history would be developed." The result, he wrote, "would be an integrated cycle on the history of gentry Russia [*dvorianskaia Rossiia*], which arose in the fifteenth-sixteenth century and fell in the twentieth."[58]

In this way, the youngest of the first generation of Kliuchevskii's pupils aspired to complete an agenda that had been Kliuchevskii's own.[59] Got'e's fascination with the role of the nobility in modern Russian history seems akin to that of his teacher: the fascination of a plebeian who through education shared the European culture which had been historically, in Kliuchevskii's words, "the caste monopoly of the masters"; it was a role *manqué:* having been exposed to enlightenment and attained the status of a privileged estate by the late eighteenth century, the nobility, content with its privileges, failed to develop into a true first estate, thereby retarding Russia's development into a modern European nation.[60]

This remark raises the interesting question of the social background of

Kliuchevskii's pupils, which may serve as a kind of capstone to this little survey. It would be somehow satisfying to learn that they all, like Kliuchevskii himself, were of plebeian origins. Four of the six in fact were: Liubavskii had been a seminarian like Kliuchevskii (that is, he was born into the clerical estate, the *dukhovenstvo*), and Bogoslovskii's father had been a seminarian; Rozhkov was the son of a "third-element" provincial school teacher, that is, he was from the petty or "democratic" intelligentsia; and Got'e was from a merchant family of booksellers (his great-great-grandfather was a French bourgeois named Gautier who immigrated to Russia during the reign of Catherine). Miliukov, however, was from a modest serving-noble (*chinovnik*) family on his father's side (his mother was from a more elevated gentry family), and Kliuchevskii's favorite pupil, Kizevetter, was the son of a privy councillor (*tainyi sovetnik*); that is, he was from the upper stratum of the serving nobility.

Statistically their collective social background was, at any rate, more plebeian than that of the Moscow university faculty taken as a whole, or of the historico-philological faculty in particular. Especially noticeable is the absence of individuals of landed-gentry background among Kliuchevskii's pupils.[61] Nor did they include anyone in their number who could be considered an apologist for noble interests.

Kliuchevskii's pupils were otherwise a diverse lot politically and ideologically, ranging (in terms of a simple indicator) from the sometime Bolshevik Rozhkov on the left to the very moderate constitutional monarchist Liubavskii on the right. In between were the probably equally moderate constitutional monarchist and sometime Octobrist Bogoslovskii, the slightly more left-oriented and sometime Constitutional-Democrat (Kadet) Got'e (whose political views were very close to those of Petr Struve),[62] the radical democrat and leader of the Kadet party Miliukov, and his close party associate Kizevetter. The *popovichi* (priests' sons) were the most conservative, and the "third elementer" was, not surprisingly, the most radical, followed by the scions of the service nobility. The most European or ecumenical in outlook were probably Miliukov[63] and Rozhkov, in their different ways, followed by Kizevetter, while the others were more nationalist in outlook. None of them, however, could be called slavophile or populist, at least not in the sense of idealizing Russian ways or the peasantry.

* * *

This review of Kliuchevskii's pupils leads to several observations, following more or less directly from the evidence presented. According to a number of influential Soviet historiographers, there was no "Kliuchevskii school" of historians, and this for the simple reason that Kliuchevskii lacked a coherent theory of history. Not only did he have a wrong idea of what a social class is and fail to grasp the ultimate historical motor force, the class struggle—he did not have any monist conception of history at all: despite his inclination toward "economic materialism" (read: primacy of the economic factor without the dialectic), he was in the end an eclectic. No theory = no method = no school. It was stated most colorfully, if not most respectfully, by Pokrovskii, the leading figure in the first generation of Soviet Marxist historians, who apparently never got over having been flunked on his *magistr* examination by Kliuchevskii:

> One is accustomed to speak of the "school" of Kliuchevskii. If there ever was a scholar organically incapable of having a school, it was precisely the author of *Boiarskaia duma,* whose only method consists of what used to be called in the old days "divination." Thanks to his artistic fantasy, Kliuchevskii was able to resurrect an entire picture of everyday life from several lines of an old charter, to reconstruct an entire system of relations from one sample. But he couldn't any more teach someone how to do this than Chaliapin could teach someone to sing as he does. For the one you need the voice of a Chaliapin, and for the other you need the artistic imagination of a Kliuchevskii.[64]

The same essential argument has been used by Kliuchevskii's biographer, and Pokrovskii's student, M. V. Nechkina. It was Kliuchevskii's "tragedy," Nechkina wrote in her 1930 essay on the historian, that he didn't make it to Marxism,[65] and she held to that view in all her later writing about Kliuchevskii.

If, however, we can accept the idea that history is a sublunary enterprise (I borrow the phrase from Paul Veyne) that really has nothing to do with metaphysics or the discovery of "laws,"[66] then at best Pokrovksii, Nechkina, and their seconders in Soviet historiography have come to a defensible conclusion for the wrong reasons. It may, indeed, be wise to shun the term "Kliuchevskii school," or even "Moscow school" (which has the advantage of pushing the heritage back at least as far as Solov'ev, Kliuchevskii's teacher), if only because the influence of both Solov'ev and Kliuchevskii was pervasive throughout Russian historiography of the late nineteenth-earlier twentieth century, as can be seen by examining the work of such outstanding representatives of the "Petersburg school" as S. F. Platonov or A. S. Lappo-Danilevskii.

Nevertheless, certain persistent characteristics of historical scholarship as it was practiced in and around Moscow University in the last two decades of the nineteenth century and the first two or three decades of this century bear the imprint of Kliuchevskii's influence. Some of them are pointed out by Nechkina in her biography of Kliuchevskii: the posing of broad questions, significant chronological scope, distinctive problem-orientation; typically, the study of political forms and relations, but penetrating to the social and economic background; extensive use of archives; and presentation of new "facts." Nechkina also notes the general tendency of Kliuchevskii's pupils to push the chronological boundary forward into the eighteenth century.[67]

These points are well taken, as far as they go. By looking at legal and institutional records as sources for a large variety of social and economic structures and processes, Kliuchevskii's "school" so extended the agenda of historical inquiry, the definition of the "eventworthy" (Veyne's "l'événemential") in a single generation as to transform the face of Russian historiography.[68] Some of this work is astonishingly modern in its wide-ranging treatment of the "eventworthy," presaging by about a generation the similar flowering of the *Annales* school in French historiography. If Kliuchevskii's pupils for the most part adhered to a positivist view of history as the accumulation of documentation, which discouraged the kind of bold cultural-anthropological and sociopsychological interpretations made by the best practitioners of the *Annales,* they nevertheless greatly expanded the agenda, and it was their fundamental respect for the documents that gave their work its enduring value.

The animadversions of Soviet historiography about "the crisis of bourgeois historiography" notwithstanding, the last two decades of the nineteenth century and the first years of the twentieth before the outbreak of the Great War was a period of great progress in the writing of history, for progress in historical writing over time has been for the most part a matter of what Veyne calls "l'allongement du questionnaire": the extension of those areas of human experience that are deemed eventworthy, rather than a matter of attaining deeper levels of explanation or a more perfect metaphysics—a horizontal, not a vertical process.

Judging from the accounts of his pupils, Kliuchevskii's part in all this was central. Pokrovskii & Co. got it all wrong: what Kliuchevskii taught was not "method" with a small "m"—this was a common property of scholarship and could be learned from others—nor was it "Theory" with a capital "T," metaphysics. It was the demonstration, in part through his monographic work but especially through his course, of the breadth of the agenda and the great variety of phenomena—economic, social, political, demographic, geographic—that could be employed in the construction of rational historical explanations; in a word, the very "eclecticism" that Nechkina called his "tragedy."

In the introduction to the first volume of his *Course,* Kliuchevskii justified his "eclecticism" in abstract, sociological terms:

> The endless variety of associations [*soiuzov*] that make up human society arises from the fact that the basic elements of social life in various times and places do not have the same arrangement, they come in various combinations, and the variety of these combinations arises in turn not only from the quantity and arrangement of the component parts, the greater or lesser complexity of the human associations, but from different relations between the same elements—for example, from the dominance of one over the others. In this variety, whose basic cause lies in the endless changes in the interaction of historical forces, the most important thing is that the elements of social life in various combinations and situations display unequal properties and effects, show different sides of their nature to the observer. As a result, one and the same elements behave differently even in the same kind of associations.[69]

"Here," Nechkina interjects in exasperation, "you have a complete rejection of historical monism, in the first place, and in the second a rejection of philosophy of history in general."[70] She was certainly right in the first instance; we can say she was right in the second as well only if we accept her historicist (in Karl Popper's sense), teleological notion of "philosophy of history."

Together with his analytical eclecticism went Kliuchevskii's insistence, also backed by demonstration, on the utilization of the variety of documentation in the archives.[71] It seems to me these were the two elements of his "teaching" that had the greatest impact on his pupils and formed the basic characteristics of the "Kliuchevskii school." Neither the now-apparent inadequacy of some of Kliuchevskii's explanations nor the logical inconsistencies in his periodization scheme should prevent us from appreciating the impact of his approach to the Russian historical past on the following generation of Russian historians.

A secondary characteristic of the "Kliuchevskii school" was its highly critical attitude toward the bureaucratic-absolutist state and its ability, historically, to carry out reforms beneficial to the country as a whole. To a considerable extent, this tendency in the historiography of the last decades of the nineteenth century and the first years of the twentieth reflected the declining reputation of the autocracy that re-emerged very broadly in Russian educated society (*obshchestvo*) during the period of the so-called "counterreforms" under Alexander III and the first decade of the reign of Nicholas II, which is all part of the story leading up to the revolution of 1905. In academic historiography the line of filiation seems to go straight back to Kliuchevskii, and through him, from what we know of his formative years, to the "realism" of the 1860s; like so much else in *fin de siècle* Russia, it all begins in the turmoil of the reform epoch. (The issue of anti-noble bias, which runs like a thread through the "school" as well, is a related phenomenon that can probably be understood in the same terms.)

A closely related characteristic of the work of Kliuchevskii's pupils—one that points up the present-mindedness of these academics—is the very large amount of attention paid to the search for traditions of decentralization and self-government in Russian history. Like the judgments on the autocracy's capacity for reform, this was part of a broader wave of literature on political theory and the history of Russian political institutions that reached flood stage in 1905, and it is possible, in a few cases quite likely, that these academics saw their weighty monographic researches as, in part, a contribution to the social movement. The inspiration can also be traced back to Kliuchevskii, both to his programmatic statements, as in the introduction to *Boiarskaia duma*, and to his Course. Of course, the civic-mindedness of Kliuchevskii's pupils was by no means entirely attributable to their teacher's influence. Some such attitudes were characteristic of a great many Russian academics in these years. But the element of present-mindedness in the research strategies and conclusions of the Moscow historians does appear to have been more pronounced than in the work of their Petersburg counterparts, who tended to hew to the nominalist tradition of K. N. Bestuzhev-Riumin (1829–97).[72]

These comments about the research strategies of Kliuchevskii's pupils raise the interesting question of the extent to which these strategies were the subject of discussion and coordinated effort. In this respect, the testimonies of Miliukov, Kizevetter, and Got'e suggest that the extent may have been considerable and that the circle of students and instructors grouped around Miliukov during his nine-year teaching career as a *Privatdozent* in the late 1880s and early 1890s, when all of the group were at the university, was the main forum. It may be that the Kliuchevskii school owed a good deal of its particular identity to the efforts of Miliukov, whose political and ideological activism was already well developed in those years (and led, of course, to his removal from the university in January 1895). This seems to be an interesting subject in need of further inquiry.[73]

Finally, I would like to raise the question of how, if at all, Kliuchevskii's theoretical views, his sociology, affected his students.

We have to begin by asking how they affected Kliuchevskii's own work as a practicing historian. On this score we find that such ideologically divergent critics of Kliuchevskii as G. P. Fedotov and M. V. Nechkina have denied any connection between the two, at least any connection of a positive sort.

Fedotov, the émigré historian of Russian religious thought, wrote that Kliuchevskii "was not, of course, a sociologist, he was not a theoretician at all," but that as a man of his time (that is, the 1860s and 1870s) he felt obliged to "justify his work before the tribunal of Sociology." That was the only meaning of the theoretical introduction to his *Course:*

> The historian in Kliuchevskii was terrorized by sociology and pretended to accept its social mandate. But only his pupil, Rozhkov, on the basis now of Marxism, made an attempt at a 'sociological' construction of Russian history.

The negative side of Kliuchevskii's commitment to "sociology," according to Fedotov, was that it kept him from any kind of adequate treatment of the individual and, therefore, of spiritual culture in Russian history.[74]

Nechkina describes Kliuchevskii's course on methodology (1884–85) and then concludes:

> Perhaps the most dramatic aspect of Kliuchevskii's eclectic system was the fact that it was for all practical purposes useless to him. . . . His methodological conception was stillborn in his own creative work and was of no use to him in his research work.[75]

These conclusions are, in my opinion, quite misguided. They amount to acceptance of Pokrovskii's view that Kliuchevskii's "method" was nothing but "divination"; that it was, in the final analysis some kind of unanalyzable "art," a matter merely of striking images and unexpected connections—a curious conclusion to be coming, in Nechkina's case, from a scholar who spent a considerable part of her very long career analyzing Kliuchevskii's work and capped it off with a 600-page book. All this amounts to a nearly total failure to come to terms with what was in fact a remarkably coherent, sophisticated, and innovative methodology.

It is true, of course, that Kliuchevskii was not very successful in formulating his theoretical-methodological views in abstract terms, as a reading of his lectures on methodology or even the passage from the theoretical introduction to his general *Course* cited above clearly shows: the terminology is derivative (Kliuchevskii's debt to the great philosopher and historian of law, B. N. Chicherin, is especially remarkable), the language stilted, especially by comparison with his usual narrative style. This was due in part, of course, to the need for brevity in the introduction to his general course. But, as Miliukov notes in his memoirs, Kliuchevskii's theoretical views were best leveloped in the body of his substantive work, in the context of specific historical problems. As S. I. Tkhorzhevskii points out in his 1921 study—to my mind, the best treatment of Kliuchevskii's theoretical views we have—these views comprised a sophisticated and coherent political philosophy, sociology of law and sociology of ideas, all of which were brought to bear on his main enterprise, which was revealed already in the subtitle of *Boiarskaia duma*—not political history, or economic history, or the history of social classes, but "the history of society," of the nation as an historical entity. From this perspective,Tkhorzhevskii argues—correctly, in my opinion—the problem of the primacy of economics or politics, state or people, ideas or material conditions, in regard to which Kliuchevskii has been accused of eclecticism, is irrelevant.[76]

Kliuchevskii's two attempts to develop his theoretical views in abstract formulations were not simply tributes to the tyranny of the "Sociology" regnant among the Russian intelligentsia during his formative years as a historian.[77] In the introduction to his Course published in 1904, when he was over 60 years old, he tells us in so many words that he considers his history of Russian society to be a contribution, of a preparatory kind, to the science of society. His theoretical statements there are a testimony to his abiding commitment to that enterprise, as well as a guide, when compared to his course on methodology, to the honing of his theoretical views through many years of applying them to the historical record. The rather awkward discourse there on "historical forces," "human associations," and "the elements of social life," which was quoted earlier, was not a jejune attempt to impose externally received concepts on his historical analysis, but an effort to sum up in "scientific" language the results of long years of profound reflection on how things work historically.

The obverse of this proposition would seem to be that sociological concepts and the general idea of a possible science of society had somehow helped the decidedly undogmatic Kliuchevskii to expand vastly the agenda of the "eventworthy" left him by his teachers, to focus on the historical process rather than the history of forms and institutions as such, and to deal with complex problems of historical explanation with great nuance and originality.

Kliuchevskii was not a sociologist; he made no contribution to sociological theory. He was an historian whose work—written in jargon-free literary Russian of uncommon grace and economy—was informed with a sociological perspective. It is impossible to say much more about the relationship between "theory" and "practice" in Kliuchevskii's work without a detailed analysis of the structure of his historical writing, a task yet to be undertaken.

By the same token, my provisional response to the question about the influence of Kliuchevskii's theoretical views on his pupils is to beg it: that influence is to be found in the body of their work, just as Kliuchevskii's views were for the most part communicated to his students not in formal discourses or theories but, to quote Miliukov once more, in "the very fact of his relation as a researcher to Russian history as a subject of study."

None of his students makes any note of having been influenced by Kliuchevskii's formal theoretical statements. As a matter of fact, it appears that none of them heard his lectures on methodology, and they were all mature scholars by the time the first volume of the *Course,* with its theoretical introduction, was published. Only two of his students showed an abiding interest in sociological theory: Miliukov and Rozhkov; and, as Fedotov noted, Rozhkov was the only one to go on to work out an explicitly "sociological construction of Russian history," carrying on in a highly idiosyncratic way, one might say, Kliuchevskii's commitment to the idea of a science of society. Miliukov came to Kliuchevskii with his own positivist sociological views already well developed and found Kliuchevskii's views and general orientation compatible with his own. Rozhkov may have owed much to Kliuchevskii in developing his early views on the sociological imperatives involved in the study of history. For the others, their theoretical views, and therefore the answer to the question of Kliuchevskii's influence in purely theoretical matters, must be sought in a detailed analysis of the explanatory structures embodied in their own historical writings.

The story of Kliuchevskii and his pupils is, of course, only part—albeit a very important part—of the story of the great florescence of Russian historical scholarship in the late nineteenth and early twentieth century. It is a story that involves pathbreaking Russian contributions to world scholarship in the study of the history of the ancient world, of medieval Europe and Britain, and of eighteenth century France and the French Revolution, among other subjects. A common characteristic of all this work is the expansion of the agenda to problems of social and economic history. The Russian historians' precocious turn to social and economic history can be traced back to a common intellectual-ideological origin in the 1860s and 1870s;[78] it was undoubtedly sustained by the ongoing, rapid transformation of the society in which they all lived.

Notes

1. Hayden White, *Tropics of Discourse* (Baltimore, 1978), 40.
2. Paul Veyne, *Comment on écrit l'histoire* (Paris, 1978), 9: "Non, l'histoire

n'a pas de méthode: demandez donc un peu qu'on vous montre cette méthode."

3. J. H. Hexter, *Doing History* (Bloomington, Indiana, 1975), 48 and ff.

4. M. V. Nechkina has surveyed the memoir literature and the public response to Kliuchevskii's *Course* in her massive biography of the historian. What it makes up for in biographical detail it unfortunately lacks in critical analysis of Kliuchevskii's narrative work. M. V. Nechkina, *Vasilii Osipovich Kliuchevskii: istoriia zhizni i tvorchestva* (Moscow, 1974).

The four completed volumes of the *Course* were first published between 1904 and 1910 and then underwent numerous subsequent editions. The most recent Soviet edition of the complete course, including the unfinished volume 5, was in the 1956–59 edition of Kliuchevskii's works: *V. O. Kliuchevskii: sochineniia v vos'mi tomakh,* vols. 1–8 (Moscow, 1956–59); a new edition is currently under way. The only full translation into English of the *Course,* by C. J. Hogarth (New York and London, 1911–31), mangles the sense and style of the original almost beyond recognition. Good English translations exist only of the parts of the *Course* devoted to the seventeenth century and the reign of Peter I: V. O. Kliuchevsky, *A Course in Russian History—the Seventeenth Century,* trans. Natalie Duddington, intro. Alfred Rieber (Chicago, 1968); V. O. Kliuchevsky, *Peter the Great,* trans. and intro. Liliana Archibald (New York, 1959).

5. Obvious though they are, these questions have been almost completely ignored in the Soviet historiographical literature. The reasons for this neglect are explained below.

6. Nicholas V. Riasanovsky, *A History of Russia,* 4th ed. (New York, 1984).

7. P. N. Miliukov, *Vospominaniia (1856–1917),* 1 (New York, 1955) 89–93.

8. P. N. Miliukov, "V. O. Kliuchevskii," in *V. O. Kliuchevskii: Kharakteristiki i vospominaniia* (Moscow, 1912), 189. In the English translation by Hogarth, Kliuchevskii's two introductory lectures on theoretical issues were omitted from the first volume and were later added as an appendix to volume 5.

9. P. N. Miliukov, "Dva russkikh istorika (S. F. Platonov i A. A. Kizevetter)," *Sovremennye zapiski* 51 (1933): 323.

10. P. Miliukov, *Gosudarstvennoe khoziaistvo Rossii v pervoi chetverti XVIII stoletiia i reforma Petra Velikogo,* izdanie vtoroe (St. Petersburg, 1905), xiii.

11. On historians' interpretations of Peter's reign, see N. V. Riasanovsky,

The Image of Peter the Great in Russian History and Thought (New York, 1985), especially 166–76.

12. Miliukov, *Gosudarstvennoe khoziaistvo,* xi.

13. V. O. Kliuchevskii, "Boiarskaia duma Drevnei Rusi. Opyt istorii pravitel'stvennogo uchrezhdeniia v sviazi s istoriei obshchestva," *Russkaia mysl',* 1880, no. 1, 48. The book edition of Kliuchevskii's doctoral dissertation omitted this statement.

14. Ibid., 40.

15. This course, "Metodologiia," is the only one of Kliuchevskii's cycle of lecture courses on "historiography" that remains unpublished (mimeographed copies of an auditor's notes are available in several libraries). On Kliuchevskii's special courses, see Nechkina, chapter 6.

16. Cf. P. N. Miliukov, *Ocherki po istorii russkoi kul'tury,* 1, 3rd ed. (St. Petersburg, 1898), 12; and V. O. Kliuchevskii, *Sochineniia,* 1 (Moscow, 1956), 25–26.

Kliuchevskii: "The individual history of a particular nation can be important because of the uniqueness of its phenomena, regardless of their [universal] cultural significance, when they make it possible for the investigator to observe those processes that reveal the mechanism of historical life especially clearly, processes in which historical forces appear in circumstances that are rarely repeated or are unobserved anywhere else, even though these processes have had no significant influence on the general historical movement. In this respect, the scientific value of the history of any given nation is determined by the quantity of unique local combinations and the qualities of whatever social elements they reveal."

Miliukov: "In its pure form, the inherent tendency of the social process is only an abstract possibility. In order to go from possibility to reality, this tendency must be refracted in the prism of real conditions of historical life. Under the influence of given geographical, climatic, soil, and other conditions, the basic direction of historical life can vary infinitely, to the point that it becomes quite impossible to recognize the presence of the same basic underlying tendency. It is the direct responsibility of the historian, not only to discover the presence of this underlying tendency, but to explain the causes of its manifestation in precisely this given concrete form, in each individual variation."

Both historians thus subscribed to a kind of theory of contrasts, according to which the very peculiarities of Russia's history (vis-à-vis Europe) made it a particularly promising candidate for study by the "historian-sociologist" (Kliuchevskii, ibid.). The issue of scholarly legitimacy for the study of

Russian history seems to lie not far beneath the surface of this argument.

17. P. Miliukov, *Ocherki po istorii russkoi kul'tury,* 1, iubileinoe izdanie (Paris, 1937), 29.

18. See Iu. V. Got'e, "Universitet," *Vestnik moskovskogo universiteta. Seriia 8. Istoriia,* 1982, no. 4, p. 23, for a contemporary student's opinion.

19. *Sbornik statei, posviashchennykh Vasiliiu Osipovichu Kliuchevskomu ego uchenikami, druz'iami i pochitateliami ko dniu tridtsatiletiia ego professorskoi deiatel'nosti v Moskovskom Universitete (5 Dekabria 1879–5 dekabria 1909 goda)* (Moscow, 1909), ii–iii.

20. M. K. Liubavskii, "Solov'ev i Kliuchevskii," in *V. O. Kliuchevskii: Kharakteristiki i vospominaniia,* 45–68. This point is made by Dorothy Atkinson in an unpublished seminar paper.

21. Karpovich saw this "legalistic reversion" as a significant tendency among the younger generation of historians. Michael Karpovich, "Klyuchevski and Recent Trends in Russian Historiography," *Slavonic and East European Review* 21 (1943): 37. On the "state school," whóse most prominent representative on the history faculty had been Solov'ev, see, in English, the work by Riasanovsky cited in note 11. The most interesting piece on the place of the "state school" (or "juridical school") in Russian historiography remains Miliukov's essay, which he gave as his introductory lecture upon receiving a Privatdozentship at Moscow University in 1886: "Iuridicheskaia shkola v russkoi istoriografii (Solov'cv, Kavclin, Chicherin, Sergeevich)," in *Russkaia mysl',* 1886, kn. vi (June), 80–92.

22. M. K. Liubavskii, *Litovsko-russkii seim. Opyt po istorii uchrezhdeniia v sviazi s vnutrennim stroem i vneshneiu zhizn'iu gosudarstva* (Moscow, 1900), 1.

23. Kliuchevskii, "Boiarskaia duma," 50.

24. M. K. Liubavskii, *Lektsii po drevnei russkoi istorii do kontsa xvi veka,* 3rd ed. (Moscow, 1918), "Predislovie." Liubavskii took particular exception in his lectures to Kliuchevskii's characterization of Kievan Rus' as a state founded on trade (64–69).

25. N. A. Rozhkov, "Avtobiografiia," *Katorga i ssylka,* 32 (1927): 161–65.

26. This was G. P. Fedotov's point: G. P. Fedotov, "Rossiia Kliuchevskogo," *Sovremennye zapiski* 50 (1932): 353–54.

27. N. Rozhkov, *Sel'skoe khoziaistvo Moskovskoi Rusi v xvi veke* (Moscow, 1899). On the relation to Kliuchevskii's thesis, see V. I. Picheta, *Vvedenie v russkuiu istoriiu (istochniki i istoriografiia)* (Moscow, 1923), 174.

28. N. A. Rozhkov, *Gorod i derevnia v russkoi istorii (Kratkii ocherk ekonomicheskoi istorii Rossii),* 3rd ed. (St. Petersburg, 1913), 6–7.

29. M. M. Bogoslovskii, "V. O. Kliuchevskii kak uchenyi," in *V. O. Kliuchevskii: Kharakteristiki i vospominaniia,* 31.

30. GIM, f. 442, d. 4, 1. 230 ob. (Bogoslovskii's diary, 1917), as quoted by L. V. Cherepnin, *Otechestvennye istoriki xviii–xx vv. Sbornik statei, vystuplenii, vospominanii* (Moscow, 1984), 111.

31. "V. O. Kliuchevskii kak uchenyi," 36.

32. Ibid., 38.

33. Cherepnin, *Otechestvennye istoriki,* 98–99. The text excerpted by Cherepnin, Bogoslovskii's 1927 memoir about Vinogradov, has recently been published: M. M. Bogoslovskii, *Istoriografiia, memuaristika, epistoliariia (nauchnoe nasledie)* (Moscow, 1987), 69–93.

34. M. M. Bogoslovskii, *Oblastnaia reforma Petra Velikogo: Provintsiia 1719–1727 gg.* (Moscow, 1902); *Zemskoe samoupravlenie na russkom severe v xvii v.,* I. *Oblastnoe delenie Pomor'ia. Zemlevladenie i obshchestvennyi stroi. Organy samoupravleniia* (Moscow, 1909); II. *Deiatel'nost' zemskogo mira. Zemstvo i gosudarstvo* (Moscow, 1912); *Petr I. Materialy dlia biografii,* 1–5 ([Moscow], 1940–48).

35. Cherepnin, 99.

36. *Zemskoe samoupravlenie,* 2:260.

37. On the "gentry theme" in Bogoslovskii's work, see Cherepnin, 102–105

38. Several colleagues attest Kizevetter's particular closeness to Kliuchevskii; Kliuchevskii supported Kizevetter's candidacy (over Bogoslovskii's) for the chair in Russian history in 1911. V. O. Kliuchevskii, *Pis'ma, dnevniki, aforizmy i mysli ob istorii* (Moscow, 1968), 216–17.

39. A. A. Kizevetter, "Pamiati V. O. Kliuchevskogo," *Russkaia mysl',* 1911, no. 6, p. 135.

40. Ibid., 139.

41. Ibid., 135.

42. Miliukov, "Dva russkikh istorika," 324.

43. "V. O. Kliuchevskii kak prepodavatel'," 167.

44. Got'e testifies to this from personal experience: Iu. V. Got'e, *Time of Troubles: the Diary of Iurii Vladimirovich Got'e, Moscow, July 8, 1917 –July 23, 1922* (Princeton, 1988), 347.

45. Miliukov, "Dva russkikh istorika," 324–25.

46. A. A. Kizevetter, *Posadskaia obshchina v Rossii XVIII st.* (Moscow, 1903). The focus of the work is, to be sure, on relations with the state; it is not a social history of the Russian town in the eighteenth century.

47. A. A. Kizevetter, *Istoricheskie ocherki* (Moscow, 1912), 271. (From Kizevetter's speech at his dissertation defense.)

48. Kliuchevskii, *Sochineniia,* 3:12.

49. Kizevetter, *Istoricheskie ocherki,* 273.

50. Iu. V. Got'e, "V. O. Kliuchevskii kak rukovoditel' nachinaiushchikh uchenykh," in *V. O. Kliuchevskii: Kharakteristiki i vospominaniia,* 177–82; and "Universitet," cited earlier.

51. "Universitet," 21.

52. Ibid., 23.

53. Got'e, "V. O. Kliuchevskii," 182.

54. Iu. V. Got'e, *Zamoskovnyi krai v XVII veke. Opyt issledovaniia po istorii ekonomicheskogo byta moskovskoi Rusi* (Moscow, 1906; vtoroe, prosmotrennoe izdanie, 1937).

55. Iu. V. Got'e, *Istoriia oblastnogo upravleniia v Rossii ot Petra I do Ekateriny II.* Tom I. *Reforma 1727 goda. Oblastnoe delenie i oblastnye uchrezhdeniia 1727–1775 gg.* (Moscow, 1913); Tom II. *Organy nadzora. Chrezvychainye i vremennye oblastnye uchrezhdeniia. Razvitie mysli o preobrazovanii oblastnogo upravleniia. Uprazdnenie uchrezhdenii 1727 g.* (Moscow, 1941).

56. Got'e *Time of Troubles,* 302.

57. Ibid., 303.

58. Ibid.

59. Bogoslovskii, "V. O. Kliuchevskii kak uchenyi," 38. Nechkina also remarks Kliuchevskii's abiding fascination with the history of the "first estate."

60. Kliuchevskii, *Sochineniia,* 3:10 et passim.

61. In 1906–08, of the twenty-two members of the historico-philological faculty, eight (36%) were of *dvorianstvo* background, eight (36%) were from the *dukhovenstvo,* and three (14%) were of *chinovnik* background. In addition, there was one faculty member from the *kupechestvo,* one of military background, and one foreigner. As it was, that faculty had the lowest proportion of gentry and the highest proportion of clergy of any faculty at the university: the totals for the entire university faculty were 43% and 13% respectively. (Data compiled by Mark von Hagen.)

62. See Richard Pipes, *Struve: Liberal on the Right, 1905–1944* (Cambridge, Mass., 1980).

63. See Thomas Riha, *A Russian European: Paul Miliukov in Russian Politics* (Notre Dame, Ind., 1968).

64. M. N. Pokrovskii, *Marksizm i osobennosti istoricheskogo razvitiia Rossii. Sbornik statei, 1922–1925 gg.* (Leningrad, 1925), 76.

65. M. V. Nechkina, "V. O. Kliuchevskii," in M. N. Pokrovskii, ed., *Russkaia istoricheskaia literatura v klassovom osveshchenii,* II (Moscow, 1930), 345: "Analysis of the class struggle led him toward new generalizations, but he failed to reach them. That is the tragedy of Kliuchevskii . . .".

66. Veyne, *Comment on écrit l'histoire,* 99 et passim. "Comprendre l'his-

toire ne consiste donc pas à savoir discerner de larges courants sous-marins par-dessous l'agitation superficielle: l'histoire n'a pas de profondeurs."

67. Nechkina, *Vasilii Osipovich Kliuchevskii,* 375.

68. In this frame of reference, the "school" should include a number of important Moscow historians who came along after Kliuchevskii's retirement (that is, approximately between the two revolutions of 1905 and 1917) and probably S. F. Platonov of St. Petersburg, who owed much of the inspiration for his great work on the Time of Troubles to Kliuchevskii. See Picheta, *Vvedenie v russkuiu istoriiu,* chs. 17–18; A. N. Tsamutali, *Bor'ba napravlenii v russkoi istoriografii v period imperializma* (Leningrad, 1986), ch. 2 (S. F. Platonov).

69. Kliuchevskii, *Sochineniia,* 1:23–24.

70. Nechkina, "V. O. Kliuchevskii," 311.

71. Several contributors to the recent collection, "Kliuchevskii's Russia: Critical Studies," raise questions about Kliuchevskii's mastery of archival sources; the most ardent of these critics goes so far as to argue that Kliuchevskii stopped intense work in the archives after his magister dissertation, that is, in 1872, *before* beginning work on his doctoral thesis, *Boiarskaia duma.* It seems difficult to reconcile that assertion with the virtual unanimity with which Kliuchevskii's pupils expressed awe for his mastery of the sources for old Russian history. (By the late nineteenth century, of course, a great many of the sources for early Russian history had been published). *Canadian-American Slavic Studies,* vol. 20, nos. 3–4 (Fall-Winter 1986), "Kliuchevskii's Russia: Critical Studies," edited by Marc Raeff.

72. Bestuzhev-Riumin rejected the idea of specifically historical laws and was generally suspicious of broad generalizations; he was a perennial critic of Solov'ev's great history on both accounts. He accordingly steered his students toward archeographic studies. N. L. Rubinshtein, *Russkaia istoriografiia* (Moscow, 1941), 411–14.

73. It may be that the framework for such discussions was laid in Vinogradov's rather formal monthly discussion circles, to which various historians, legal scholars, and economists were invited. Its meetings, which were held regularly throughout the 1890s to 1898, when the university's official Historical Society was established, were customarily devoted to discussions of new works of European history and social science. Miliukov, Liubavskii, Bogoslovskii, and Kizevetter were among the young scholars (Privatdozents) who were considered members of the circle. Bogoslovskii, *Istoriografiia, memuaristika, epistoliariia,* 85–87.

74. Fedotov, "Rossiia Kliuchevskogo," 352–55.

75. Nechkina, *Vasilii Osipovich Kliuchevskii,* 263.

76. S. I. Tkhorzhevskii, "V. O. Kliuchevskii kak sotsiolog i politicheskii myslitel'," *Dela i dni,* 1921, kn. 2:152–79. On Chicherin, whose courses at Moscow University Kliuchevskii took in the early 1860s, see the new book by Andrzej Walicki, *Legal Philosophies of Russian Liberalism* (Oxford, 1987).

77. See P. S. Shkurinov, *Pozitivizm v Rossii XIX veka* (Moscow, 1980).

78. On Russian scholars of world [*vseobshchaia*] history, including such well-known names as Vinogradoff, Rostovtzeff, and Louchitsky, whose work was part and parcel of the general trend, see V. Buzeskul, *Vseobshchaia istoriia i ee predstaviteli v Rossii v XIX i nachale XX veka.* 2 vols. (Leningrad, 1929–31). Among the many books dealing with intellectual currents of the 1860s–70s—"nihilism," "realism," "subjective sociology," and positivism, *inter alia*—one that concentrates on the origin and development of the idea of a "science of society" is Alexander Vucinich, *Social Thought in Tsarist Russia. The Quest for a General Science of Society, 1861–1917* (Chicago, 1976).

PUŠKIN AND THE *FEMME FATALE*

Jealousy in *Cygany*

LEIGHTON BRETT COOKE

BOSWELL: "To be sure there is a great difference between the offense of
infidelity in a man and that of his wife."
JOHNSON: "The difference is boundless. The man imposes no bastards
upon his wife."

Boswell, *Life of Johnson*, October 10, 1779

Ревность

Plan for *Цыганы*

1. Fateful Passions

Puškin's final pronouncement on the tragic events of *Cygany* (*"The Gypsies"*) is uncharacteristically universal in tone:

И всюду страсти роковые
И от судеб защиты нет. (204)[1]

and everywhere there are fateful passions, and from the Fates there is no
defense.

Readers can hardly fail to notice the weighty message of these lines. Most,
no doubt, accept the notion that passions and/or fate affect everyone. Still,
the full implications have not been understood, at least partly because
Puškin could not have been consciously aware of them, and therefore did
not articulate them explicitly. Bypassing Puškin's likely mystical belief in
fate, one wonders why it is so closely associated here with "passions." Given
the semantic link between "rokovoj" and "sud'ba," Puškin implies that the
"passions" are the vehicles of "fate" and that they are ineluctable.

Yet what is this "fate" and why should the "passions" range everywhere?
Puškin devotes a lot of space in the *poèma* to making neat behavioral distinctions between the Gypsies and the *Gadje*—i.e. everyone else, in particular
people from cities and civilization. Aleko is told that he was neither "born"

nor "adapted" to the Gypsies' nomadic life (186, 201, 186). He does become "accustomed," but the narrator doubts this transformation and awaits the reemergence of his fateful passions (188,184).[2] We are not disappointed: in due time Aleko kills Zemfira, his unfaithful Gypsy wife and her Gypsy lover. Her father's condemnation caps the narrative poem by concluding that, indeed, people are different in nature with regard not only to their way of life but also to their emotional attitudes. His pronouncement especially pertains to the unstated but obvious central issue of the whole work, female chastity.

Finally, Puškin contradicts the Starik's summation with lines at the end of the epilogue that insist on the commonality of human emotional response. Reminded of Freud's dictum that "anatomy is destiny," we suggest that Puškin's conclusion, as well as the rest of this narrative on human nature, can best be understood when placed in the context of sociobiology. This new science studies universal features of human behavior by tracing their utility in the evolutionary process of natural selection. In our modern understanding, the passions are "fateful" and ineluctable because they are encoded in our common genetic heritage. They are triggered by relationships such as comprise the major themes of the *poèma*: sexual attraction, exogamy, pair-bonding, kin altruism, reciprocal altruism, infidelity, male sexual jealousy, and aggression. Such sociobiological themes are critical to comprehending the nature of a literary classic. That no one is wholly free of these potential responses enables all readers, including those living in different cultural contexts, to react to the same emotions when reading Puškin's universal tale.

2. Story of a Love Story

Puškin's own interest in the Gypsies certainly involved the "fateful passions." In the epilogue, he makes the remarkable claim that he actually lived with them, something few *Gadje* have done. Puškin speaks of sharing their simple food, listening to their songs, and sleeping by their fires. He recalls how he "tverdil" ("repeated") the "nežnoe imja" ("tender name") of Mariula, known to the reader as Zemfira's wayward mother (203). He also referred to this same sojourn in the 1830 lyric "Cygany" and in Chapter 8, Stanza 5, of *Evgenii Onegin.*

But the narrator, veritably Puškin, does not explain why he describes those "dni" ("days") as "svetlye" ("bright") and "pečal'nye" ("sad") (203). One possibility is that Puškin had some sort of love affair with a *cyganka* while living with the Gypsies. In 1908, Z. K. Ralli-Arbore cited a tale related by her aunt, Ekaterina Zaxarovna Stamo, who heard from her brother,

Arbore's father, Konstantin Zaxarovič Ralli, how he and Puškin visited a group of Gypsies who belonged to the Ralli family estate. There they met a "starik buli-baša" ("elder Buli-Basha") noted for his authority amongst the Gypsies. This elder had a beautiful daughter named Zemfira. She was tall, with large black eyes and long curly hair. She dressed like a man, wore colorful "šarovary" ("pantaloons"), a sheepskin hat, and an embroidered Moldavian "rubaxa" ("shirt"), and she smoked a pipe. Stamo recalled "čto Alek. Sergeevič prosto-naprosto sxodit s uma po cyganke Zemfire."[3] Puškin persuaded Ralli they should stay with the Gypsies. B. A. Trubeckoj says this visit lasted from July 28 to August 20, 1821, during which time Puškin began to live in the elder's tent.[4] Ralli witnessed Puškin and Zemfira wandering off together, holding hands and sitting silently. She knew no Russian and Puškin no Romany, the Gypsy language, so they communicated by means of pantomime. According to Stamo, this relationship might have continued for a while, had Puškin not suspected Zemfira of being inclined toward a certain young Gypsy. One morning Puškin woke up in the elder's tent, quite alone; Zemfira had vanished. He tried to pursue her, but she apparently was warned, and Puškin never saw her again. Sometime later, while Puškin was living in Odessa, Ralli wrote to inform him that Zemfira's beloved Gypsy had stabbed her to death.[5] It was at about this time that Puškin began to write *Cygany*.

Of course, it is difficult to accept this story as genuine. John Bayley calls it "apocryphal."[6] After all, certain details had to have passed from Puškin to Ralli to Stamo to Arbore, and the anecdote was only recorded about eighty-six years after the purported events. The *poèma* must have played a role in bringing the story to light, whether as actual memoir or as fiction. As we shall see, some details ill accord with ethnographic studies of Gypsies. But the account does agree with Lev Puškin's report that the poet "isčez i propadal neskol'ko dnej" (disappeared and was lost for several days), spending them with a Gypsy *tabor* ("camp").[7] Indeed, Ralli's name is mentioned in a variant of the epilogue held by Lev Puškin:

> И нежны имена твердил
> Рали, Земфиры, Мариулы (463)

And I repeated the tender names of Rali, Zemfira and Mariula.

However, Soviet scholars who have studied Puškin's sojourn in Moldavia accept the anecdote as genuine.[8]

If the Arbore story was not composed with a backward glance at the *poèma*, it sheds some interesting light on the tragic events of *Cygany*. Certainly the basic story line and essential characters are there, with the exception of Mariula. A young man from proper Russian society, somehow with legal problems, comes to a Gypsy *tabor*. As a *Gadjo*, he is at a disadvantage in his new milieu and susceptible to jealousy. His decision to live with the Gypsies is principally based on his affection for an exotic beauty named Zemfira. The only daughter of a respected Gypsy elder, she is aggressive, and she expresses her sexual freedom by choosing her own mates. She tires of the jealous *Gadjo* and prefers a young man closer to her way of life. In the end, she is knifed to death. There are important differences between the anecdote and the *poèma*. Puškin did not end up socially bereft; he could and did return to Kishinev. And it was not he but his rival who killed Zemfira.

If Puškin composed the *poèma* on the basis of his actual experiences, then Aleko performs like the poet's alter ego. D. D. Blagoj notes that, among other autobiographical similarities, "Aleko" seems to be a Gypsy variant of Puškin's first name.[9] The *poèma* then is a form of role-playing, akin to Puškin's dressing up like a Gypsy while in Kishinev. Aleko does what Puškin might have done. He establishes a sexual relationship with a *cyganka*.[10] Later he murders her in a jealous rage. We will never know what Puškin would have done had he caught up with his Zemfira. He hardly could have won her back. Puškin's behavior with the populace of Moldavia commonly was described as outrageous, and he fought a number of duels during this time. Although the likelihood of violence over Zemfira was probably faint, one should remember that fifteen years later Puškin died fighting over his wife, that is, in an attempt to demonstrate she was still "his." Nevertheless, it makes little difference to us if the story is false, for similar emotions certainly came into play in the writing of the *poèma*.

Puškin's love story, in any case probably more imagined than real, did not end there or with the completion of *Cygany*. The ensuing stages of the narrative give some idea of the strong passions it conveys. Within a few years of the *poèma*'s appearance in 1827, it provided the basis for four opera libretti; young Mixail Lermontov tried his hand at another, and Raxmaninov composed *Aleko* in 1892.[11] At some point during the next twenty years Puškin's *poèma* came to the attention of Prosper Mérimée. The Frenchman had taken an early interest in Russian literature; he studied Russian under the future Decembrist Vil'gel'm Kjuxel'beker and socialized with a number of Russian writers and some of Puškin's friends, as well as with the poet's brother.[12] Although his main study of Russian was in 1840, Mérimée's letters show him trying to collect Puškin's works shortly after the poet's death.[13] Although only fragments of *Cygany* were published before 1827, the story's impact was already felt in France in 1825, when Jakov Tolstoj placed an article about it in *Revue encyclopédique*. One L. Maidel did an illustration during the 1830s, and the poem received its first French translation in 1846.[14] Precisely when Mérimée first read *Cygany* remains unclear, but it was certainly before 1849, when he described it in a letter to Puškin's friend Sobolevskij as "après tout le chef-d'œuvre" of the Russian's works.[15] Mérimée drew illustrations in the margins of his own translation—*Les Bohémiens* appeared in 1852—and he wrote further appreciative remarks on the work in 1854 and 1868.[16]

Perhaps the greatest gesture of appreciation was conveyed by Mérimée's most famous work, *Carmen*, written in 1845. This novella contains some of the same story elements as Puškin's *poèma*, although it includes many more incidents and characters and is set in Spain. It is not possible to say which came first, Mérimée's interest in *Cygany* or his writing *Carmen*. E. M. Dvojčenko-Markova claims the *poèma* influenced the novella, a view tacitly shared by other commentators who speak of the two works in the same breath.[17] Mérimée did not lack for other sources, such as a legend that Don Pedro I of Castille had a Bohemian mistress, the missionary George Barrow's books on the Gypsies, and Mérimée's own flirtation with a *gitana* ("Gypsy woman") named Carmencita in 1830 near Granada; the narrator of the 1845 novella refers to events which occurred "fifteen years ago." [18] If this is not a case of literary influence, then surely it demonstrates a shared intense interest in the ethnography of the Gypsies, in the female promiscuity embodied by their heroines, and ultimately in the interaction of civilization and unspoiled human nature—the latter supposedly represented by the Gypsies, who were at once misunderstood to be "noble savages" and at the same time available all over Europe.

This mutual fascination with free-loving *cyganki* generated the story's continuing history. In 1875 Georges Bizet composed *Carmen* to a libretto prepared by Henri Meilhac and Ludovic Halévy. There is some evidence that the librettists looked not only at Mérimée's novella but also at his translation of Puškin's *Cygany*. Compare the first line of Carmen's Act I "Chanson et Mélodrame,"

> Coupe-moi, brûle-moi, je ne te dirai rien,

to Mérimée's translation of Zemfira's song,

> Coupe-moi, brûle-moi, je ne dirai rien[19]

In this, the greatest French opera, Carmen was widely recognized as the embodiment of passion and freedom, albeit not so much for her outlaw actions as for her lack of sexual inhibition. She was one of the first of the many *femmes fatales* who became so important in late nineteenth-century art. In a veritable paroxysm of male masochism, artists conjured up images of aloof, powerful, and erotically gorgeous demi-goddesses who offered viewers imaginary destruction via ecstatic contact with their devouring flesh.

Such were certainly the associations Aleksandr Blok made with Carmen when he fell under the influence of the opera in 1914. He saw it many times, read the novella, and cited the libretto frequently in the cycle of ten poems he then wrote under the title *Karmèn* (*Carmen*). Like Mérimée and, as we have speculated, Puškin, Blok had an actual woman in mind; he immortalized the singer Ljubov' Aleksandrovna Del'mas, also his lover, as the aggressive seductress. It is to her destructive will that the persona, as Don José, surrenders himself.

In each work unconstrained female sexuality constitutes a sharp threat to the masochistic male. This ultimately derives from a Moldavian song which Puškin translated and at one time intended as an epigraph to *Cygany*:

> Мы люди смирные, девы наши любят волю — Что тебе делать у нас? (453)

> We are a gentle people, our maidens love freedom, what is there for you to do here with us?

The oft-noted lack of violence amongst Gypsies contrasts with Aleko's/Don José's alien nature and hence propensity for violence. The song's interest in uninhibited women resounds throughout all four texts. Zemfira boldly announces her love for another man. Later she complains to her father,

> Его любовь постыла мне
> Мне скучно, сердце воли просит. (191)

> His love is hateful to me; I am bored, my heart craves freedom

In turn, the Starik advises the disconsolate Aleko that there is no use trying, to constrain her; he compares her to a moon illuminating one cloud after another. This statement of free love later finds a place in Bizet's famous "Habanera":

> L'amour est un oiseau rebelle

—which Blok incorporated into his cycle as

> *О, да, любовь вольна, как птица*

> *O, yes, love is free, like a bird* [20]

This freedom is so essential to Zemfira and Carmen (at least in Mérimée and Bizet) that both defiantly accept murder rather than renounce their sexual independence.

Yet danger lurks for the intruding male amongst these "smirnye" people. Zemfira sings to Aleko of her adultery in the same breath with which she mentions his knife; later, of course, he will carry out this implied threat to stab her. His punishment, exile from society, is the Gypsy equivalent of execution.[21] Notably, all we see in the last lines of Puškin's narrative is the cart left to Aleko; Gypsy funerals often involve the burning or destruction of the deceased's vehicle.[22] In Mérimée's novella the narrator first meets Don José in prison, where the latter is awaiting execution; his murder of Carmen, which he freely confesses, is also tantamount to suicide. In the opera Don José's murder fulfills only the first half of Carmen's fateful prophecy that he will die after her. Through their passion for Gypsy women, Aleko and Don José work their own destruction.

Blok's cycle never gets beyond the second act of the opera; it climaxes with Don Jose's submission to Karmen. But ominous hints abound that sexual contact with the *femme fatale* will bring about the male's future demise. The persona repeatedly notices her teeth. He speaks of the "strašnyj čas" ("dreadful hour") he met her, of the "xiščnaja sila" ("predatory force") of her hands, and of his fear. He refers to himself as a "pogibšij čelovek" ("lost man"). It is not hard to see why; at one point, Blok's Karmen paraphrases another *femme fatale*, Puškin's Kleopatra, with

Ценою жизни
Ты мне заплатишь за любовь![23]

With your life
You will pay me for my love!

3. Puškin the Gypsologist

One problem with Puškin's treatment of free love, endangered males, and violent revenge is that these qualities may have little to do with actual Gypsies. Puškin's portrait, and those of Mérimée, Bizet, and Blok after him, are not necessarily accurate representations of Gypsy mores. Puškin was well acquainted with Gypsies. He encountered them throughout his sojourn in Moldavia and less frequently elsewhere in Russia. He collected some of the songs they sang and translated them into his own verse. But it was on his trips to Bessarabia that he saw large groups of them set apart from *Gadjo* society and had a chance to witness their way of life. Whatever he might have done with Ralli, the poet did visit Gypsy camps with Liprandi in December, 1821. There are a number of drawings of Gypsies to be found in Puškin's papers, including in the drafts of *Cygany,* which he composed well after he left the area. One depicts a bare-breasted woman feeding her baby inside a tent, a spectacle few Gypsy men, let alone *Gadje,* are permitted to witness.[24]

Puškin's impressions must have been strong, for the *poèma* refers to many characteristic features of the Gypsies. Many commentators, Prosper Mérimée among them, have praised *Cygany* for its profusion of ethnographic detail on Gypsy life. As Puškin depicts them, they are nomads who make their living by selling metalwork, performing as musicians, dancers, and animal trainers; the women also tell fortunes. At about the same time as he worked on the *poèma,* Puškin drafted brief "Primečanija k 'Cyganam' " ("Notes for *The Gypsies*"). These mention the unusual status of Gypsies in Moldavia, where they technically had been enslaved since the fourteenth century, but this, Puškin notes, hardly affected their way of life. Interestingly, he claims the Moldavian Gypsies are honest, unlike Gypsies elsewhere, who have a well-earned reputation as petty thieves. This likely is based on his own experience, for he also refers to English scholarship on the Gypsies, when he sketches the now familiar argument that the Gypsies originate from India, citing linguistic, ethnographic, and physiological evidence.[25]

Other vestiges of Gypsy life appear in the text. After the murder there is some hint of a *kris,* a tribal meeting, wherein Aleko's punishment is decided. The central role typically is accorded the *tabor's* patriarch, here Zemfira's father, who announces the verdict.[26] Modern sociologists agree with the Starik on the *relative* lack of violence amongst Gypsies.[27] According to John McLaughlin, "In *Romani* ["Gypsydom"] there is no specified punishment for murder because it is considered such a serious crime that gypsies will not admit that it would be perpetrated by a gypsy. Of course, any gypsy who committed murder would be *mahrime* ["unclean"] and an outcast forever."[28] Notably, Aleko is so punished.

Gypsies are so family and tribe-oriented that they prefer to live together in large tents and rooms.[29] In the opening scene of *Cygany* Puškin repeatedly describes the Gypsies as members of families, who eat and sleep peacefully together:

> Как вольность, весел их ночлег
> И мирный сон под небесами
>
> . . . .
> Горит огонь; семья кургом
> Готовит ужин;...
>
> . . . .
> Заботы мирные семей,.. (179)

Like freedom, their camp site for the night is gay, and their sleep peaceful beneath the heavens. . . . a fire burns; around it a family cooks its supper; . . . the peaceful cares of the families

Gypsies have retained their highly visible and exposed separate identity despite persecution and hostile environments for around eleven hundred years, thanks to their social solidarity, their avoidance of outsiders, and their strict moral code.[30] How much Puškin was able to understand of this is unclear; the picture of Puškin unable to talk to his Gypsy beauty in the Arbore anecdote should remind us that he had no real access to their culture.[31] Fluency in Romany is only a start, for all Gypsologists complain that it is difficult to gain straight answers from a people who have no regard for *Gadje* and see no need to tell the truth.

There are many features in *Cygany* which are in conflict with modern sociological studies. Gypsy funerals are elaborate and normally last three days, unlike the quick burial performed the morning after the murder in Puškin.[32] Mariula's desertion of her daughter belies the specially close relationship noted between Gypsy mothers and their children. The Starik's account of Ovid's sojourn on the Black Sea actually derives from Moldavian, as opposed to Gypsy, sources.[33] It also clashes with observations of a people who have little interest in their past, let alone that of an ancient Roman who lived centuries before the Gypsies left India (probably around 800 A.D.). Puškin is correct in saying that they scorn the "shackles of civilization"; Gypsies are nonliterate, and they resist efforts to educate them (188). There is no oral tradition which could serve as the basis for a history, and as a result Gypsy history has been reconstructed from careful analysis of their language and life style.[34]

Gypsies do not assimilate into or with other peoples. At heart their cultural ideology is hostile to *Gadje*. Their hospitality is a ruse, one often employed with an eye to fraud. Puškin actually may have lived in a Gypsy tent, but the *Rom*, nomadic Gypsies, who consider *Gadje* unclean, do not share utensils with them and usually reserve a separate set and a chair for visitors.[35] Cohabitation may lead to a recognition of marriage, as may be the case with Aleko and Zemfira; however, intermarriage is rare.[36] Mixed marriages are not fully accepted, especially when they involve a Gypsy woman who tries to introduce a *Gadjo* to Gypsy society.[37] Their women in particular are taught to avoid *Gadjo* men, who are considered "polluted"; *Romni* ["Gypsy women"] know that they will be regarded as permanently *mahrime* if they marry a *Gadjo* and many consider the notion "physically repulsive."[38] As Bernice Kohn remarks, Gypsy "women must be faithful to their own men; otherwise the Romany race would soon disappear." Their oft-noted physical difference makes it clear that they have done so.[39] There are exceptions to the rule, possibly including the real Zemfira, but these are rare.

The preservation of the Gypsy way of life also derives from the extremely conservative nature of their society. When Puškin refers to their freedom, "volja," and "dikaja dolja" ("wild way of life"), he seems to equate their lack of written laws—remember, Gypsies are nonliterate—and their effort to evade other legal systems with a total lack of rules. This would be a serious mistake. Rather, as McLaughlin puts it, "the Gypsies are not a group of loosely-knit nomads, but rather a highly regulated society with a specific and definite code of behavior." Their laws are expressed mostly as taboos.[40] *Cygany* is replete with contradictions with regard to ethnographic detail. For example, the Starik says, "My diki, net u nas zakonov" ("We are wild, we have no laws"), as he expels Aleko from the tribe for murder; this punishment, indeed, suggests there is an unwritten law being applied here (210).

The Starik does speak like a true Gypsy elder in two respects: as patriarch, his "final word is considered law," and, as McLaughlin said of actual Gypsies, his "judicial rhetoric is colorful and flamboyant, filled with lengthy and poetic arguments, exaggerated claims and standard formulas."[41] Yet in so doing another inconsistency creeps in. Here the Starik exercises his full authority, while earlier he did virtually nothing to prevent the inevitable catastrophe, although he had been warned. At no point in the narrative does he play the role of a proper Gypsy father; he does not try to control his daughter's sexuality. Normally, her dishonor would damage his social standing. But Zemfira does what she pleases. Her statement,

> Он будет мой —
> Кто ж от меня его отгонит?

He shall be mine: who shall drive him from me?

can be read as defiance (181). In addition, the opening scene suggests his low status. Puškin depicts him awake, alone late at night, sitting by a dying fire, his "ubogij užin" ("miserable supper") getting cold while his daughter is off wandering (180). In virtually all patriarchal societies, women prepare the meals and serve men; besides, amongst Gypsies it is usual for a single parent to attach himself to another family.[42]

Enjoying superior status in the family, the father arranges marriages for his children; this is the prime motive for their nomadism.[43] Since bride-purchase is common, he will demand a higher *daro* ("bride-price") if his daughter is a virgin, preferably between twelve and fourteen.[44] Besides Zemfira being "moloden'kaja" ("young"), little, if any, of this is reflected in the *poèma* (180). Normally the couple will live with the groom's parents, and the bride will assume the lowest place in the female hierarchy. If a groom cannot come up with the bride-price, his "only way to get a wife" may be to move in with her family. However, he will be treated with contempt as a "house *rom*" ("husband").[45] Such may be true for Aleko.

The quality of Puškin's ethnographical insight becomes crucial when he addresses the central issue of the *poèma*, the supposed absence of female chastity amongst Gypsies. This is expressed at various points in the narrative:

> a. Zemfira's nocturnal wandering in the opening scene. The reader might wonder what a "deva" ("girl") is doing in a "pustynnoe pole" ("deserted steppe") late at night. "Guljat' " ("to take a walk"), of course, has sexual connotations. Notably, Zemfira does not return alone (180).

> b. Zemfira's willful choice of Aleko as her mate.

> c. Her baiting song and Aleko's reply that he does not trust her heart. This song, as the drafts inform us, was composed by a "žena nevernaja" ("unfaithful wife") (421).

> d. Aleko's nightmare, which he explains only in part—

> > Мне снилась ты
> > Я видел, будто между нами . . .
> > Я видел страшные мечты! (192)

> I dreamed of you. I dreamed that between us . . . I dreamed terrible dreams.

> —but the context makes the adulterous content of the dream quite clear.

> e. The Starik's flip explanation that "serdce ženskoe—šutja" ("a woman's heart loves jestingly"). He follows this up with a rhetorical question,

> > Кто сердцу юной деве скажет,
> > Люби одно, не изменись (193)

> Who shall say to the heart of a young girl: love one alone, do not alter?

> f. The Starik's narration of how he tacitly accepted the manner in which he was abandoned by his wife, Mariula.

> g. Last, and most significant, Zemfira's illicit trysts—two are depicted—with a young Gypsy.

These passages present an untypical picture of Gypsy mores. Bernice Kohn claims that "chastity is of extreme importance to Gypsies."[46] Many Gypsologists note the practice of virginity rituals, such as the display of the bride's bloody nightgown.[47] Instead of the Gypsy promiscuity promulgated by many *Gadjo* artists, McLaughlin maintains that "sexual intercourse involves strict moral and cleanliness rules and, as such, is engaged in only as custom rules." Moreover, "since the core of Gypsy loyalty is the *fami-*

lia, . . . marriage is of paramount importance in gypsy culture."[48] In the "Appendix" to *Carmen*, Mérimée remarks, "One of the names they give themselves, the *Rome*, or the married folks, seems to me to attest to the respect of the race for the married state."[49] It follows, as Kohn adds, that their "marriages are among the most stable in the world," divorce is rare and, of interest to us, "infidelity amongst married couples is almost unheard of."[50] Okely notes how the fidelity prescribed for women readily translates into other forms of "chaste" behavior: "To maintain her reputation, [a wife] must even avoid being alone with another man or being seen in conversation with him on the camp, lest she risk the accusation of infidelity."[51] Padmashri W. R. Rishi claims there "are no women in the world more modest than Gypsy women."[52]

Aleko's non-Gypsy status may make him vulnerable to parasitism, but this does not excuse the Starik's remarks. In fact, Gypsy punishments for female infidelity can be harsh. Elwood B. Trigg describes the gruesome measures the Gypsies take to stigmatize their unfaithful wives; these include various forms of torture, mutilation, and death carried out by the wronged husband.[53]

Puškin had reason to doubt his claims of Gypsy promiscuity and tolerance of female adultery. One acquaintance, A. F. Vel'tman, said there were no Zemfiras amongst the Gypsy *tabors*.[54] Another possible, albeit fictional, source is Cervantes's "The Little Gipsy"; Jack Weiner and E. F. Meyerson present a number of parallels between that novella and Puškin's *poèma* to support their contention that the Russian read the story, probably in French, before he wrote *Cygany*.[55] However, there is an important contrast between the two works in that, as Cervantes's Elder describes, the Gypsies kill their adulterous wives; they "bury them among the forests and deserts with the same readiness as if they were noxious animals." The Elder says that "under this dread and fear they take care to be chaste, and we . . . live secure."[56] Of course, Puškin, like Mérimée, probably had flirted with a Gypsy girl. Gypsy women will often pose as prostitutes, but this is only a ruse to enable them to steal from the unwitting; Mérimée's narrator flirts with Carmen and soon discovers his watch is missing.[57] Do they do more than flirt? McLaughlin says, "Sexual contact between gypsies and non-gypsies is strictly taboo, particularly between a female gypsy and a *gadjo*. A female gypsy who [actually] engaged in prostitution would be *mahrime* for an extended period of time, if not forever."[58] As many sociologists have pointed out, Gypsy appearances and *Gadjo* impressions of the same sharply conflict with Gypsy reality.[59]

Puškin's critics did not overlook his questionable ethnography. Vel'tman found Moldavian Gypsies to be filthy, "ne stol' mily, kak v poème" ("not so lovable, as in the *poèma*").[60] Writing at the time of the *poèma*'s first full publication, Ivan Kireevskij deduced that the supposed female promiscuity of Puškin's Gypsies would require male tolerance and the absence of marriage. But this ill accords with the Starik's nostalgia for his inconstant wife. Kireevskij concludes "the whole poem contradicts itself" and the Gypsies' way of life "fades away at our first attempt to consign it to our imagination."[61] Following Kireevskij's lead, John Bayley suggested that "the reader would do better to ignore the Gypsy question altogether and to regard the old Gypsy not as any kind of ethnic representation but simply as an abstract figure," one who stands for the "universal lot" of mankind.[62]

As Bayley puts it, Puškin's Gypsies "can hardly be allowed to exist."[63] The point is, they do not. But if Zemfira and her father are not Gypsies, where do these characters come from and what are they doing? We suggest it would be more accurate to view them as externalizations of Puškin's and the reader's common anxieties regarding female promiscuity. In this light the *poèma* has appeal that is not anchored in any one culture, such as Romany or Russian, but is universal in scope.

4. The Biological Context of Aleko's Crime

The critical literature on *Cygany* comprises a curious contradiction of critics who praise the work for its local color, note the role it played in the development of realism, yet at the same time view the narrative as "universal" and "abstract." The "realism" of *Cygany* incorporates a significant portion of fictional, that is, idealized, elements. Indubitably real was the emotional response the *poèma* elicited amongst both Puškin's contemporaries and later readers. Upon its appearance, it was enthusiastically greeted as his best work. Some later quibbled over the details, but no significant critic tried to tear the *poèma* to shreds.

A rational and objective reading of *Cygany* does call many of the narrative's interrelationships into question. Yet despite these inconsistencies and anomalies, *Cygany* thrives; it is read as an emotional whole and accepted as a true masterpiece. This suggests that beneath the irrational surface of the narrative there operates an emotional logic which we can attempt to explicate in a rational, elegant, and universal manner. From these substrata derive our fateful passions. Indeed, these and the central issues of *Cygany* best can be explicated by modern sociobiological insights into the genetic basis of behavior. This heritage does not control human behavior, but it comprises ranges of behavioral propensities that shape the likelihood of certain actions in the context of differing environments. According to this framework, emotions are but enabling mechanisms which influence the frequency and strength of behavioral protocols.

However, it is important to remember that the individual will usually be unaware of such "ultimate causations"; these comprise the various strategies which serve the basic biological drive of trying to replicate one's genetic material either in one's own offspring or via that of relatives. "Proximate" media like culture and psychology will intervene to increase the likelihood that the individual will act "as if he knew" how best to promote the fortunes of his genes.

One gross mistake often encountered in the critical literature on *Cygany* is that Aleko's crime derives from his civilized upbringing. Rather, sociobiological research demonstrates that "male constraint of female sexuality appears to be a cross-cultural universal," one effected by the threat or use of violence.[64] Although societies vary, no society has been demonstrated to be free of such constraints. Male competition for women, the root of this constraint, is probably the leading cause of homicide. As in the case of wife-battering, husbands kill their wives much more for suspected infidelity and feared desertion than for any other reason.[65] It appears that the development of modern Western culture has tended to mitigate male sexual violence. Many Western societies in recent decades have developed institutions for preventing episodes of such violence, caring for its victims when they occur, and punishing its perpetrators—all of these virtually unknown hitherto and elsewhere.

Zemfira's infidelity is not as characteristic as Puškin and many other authors of the nineteenth century might lead us to suspect. In liberal societies men are at least twice as likely to commit adultery; the proportion is much higher in more constrained societies. Indeed, Aleko seems to contrast the Gypsies with the relatively loose morals of city women who "ljubvi stydjatsja" ("are ashamed of love"), "gde net ljubvi" ("where there is no love"), and whose "Izmen volnen'e" ("excitement of betrayals") he was happy to have left behind (185,186).

Male sexual jealousy significantly exceeds its female equivalent in frequency and in force of expression. The literary focus on female, as opposed to male, infidelity reflects not actual behavior patterns, but rather exaggerated male anxieties. Recent research also shows male and female jealousy to be different in character. A jealous woman worries about the loss of her mate's attention and provision of resources. A man fantasizes about the illicit sexual act itself.[66] Note, for example, how Zemfira even exacerbates

Aleko's jealousy by taunting him with explicit sexual allusions. She describes
how she "laskala" ("caressed") her lover "v nočnoj tišine!" ("in the quiet of
the night!") (190). Aleko implicitly refers to this tryst when he recalls their
own lovemaking:

> Как она любила!
> Как нежно преклонясь ко мне
> Она в пустынной тишине
> Часы ночные проводила! — (194)

How she loved! How tenderly she leaned towards me and spent the hours
of night in the quiet of the wilderness!

Puškin apparently shares this anxiety; Zemfira twice is shown in her lover's
arms, while Aleko remains entirely faithful.

Sociobiologists ascribe the gender asymmetry of propensities for sexual
jealousy to the problem of paternal confidence. Human children are slow in
developing to maturity; in most societies the father's assistance in protecting
the family and providing it with resources is crucial to its prosperity, if not
its actual survival. However, owing to internal fertilization, men cannot
identify their own children with certainty. Hence, in return for the provision
of resources, they typically demand that their wives act in a manner that
increases their confidence that they are supporting their own children and
not those of another man. This is the basis of the infamous double standard,
and it has ramifications well beyond the prohibition of female adultery, to
dress, premarital virginity, ultimately to everything that might be associated
with chastity, including the expressions of affection which contribute to the
stability of the conjugal contract and submissive behavior by the wife.
Following Claude Lévi-Strauss's lead that men—fathers, husbands, and
brothers—treat women as property in most societies, sociobiologists postulate that ultimately men want women as breeders. Signs of fertility like
youth and physical attractiveness raise the value of women; these qualities
are reflected in literary characterizations of women. Infertility is common
grounds for divorce; the barren woman is expendable. Notably, Zemfira and
Mariula each have a child; their fertility augments the degree of their
betrayal.

This asymmetry is expressed in legal statutes regarding adultery. Only
rarely and recently have husbands been legally punished, if at all, for
infidelity. A wife, however, especially a young mother, has in many cultures
been tacitly regarded as her husband's property. The cuckolded husband is
the victim, as it were, of a theft, namely, of her fertility.[67] Likewise, in many
cultures laws take only the adulterous woman's marital status into question;

they often call for her and her lover (ignoring his marital status) to be punished harshly, sometimes with death. Although Gypsies have no written laws, they also observe the double standard. While their unfaithful wives are tortured and sometimes executed by their husbands, Trigg says, "there is little evidence that men were ever punished for infidelity."[68]

Some *Gadjo* laws exonerate a husband who witnesses his adulterous wife with her lover *in flagrante delicto* and is driven to kill one or both, as Aleko does. In societies where such murder is criminal, juries often will vote to acquit the husband, reasoning, no doubt like Blackstone, that "there could not be a greater provocation."[69] This notion was not alien to Russia. A defense of this outrageous legal position appeared in the *Dux žurnalov*, 1820, where an anonymous critic virtually summarized the sociobiological description of paternity confidence:

> Везде за прелюбодейство муж имеет право предать смерти виновных: ибо сим охраняется союз семейства, и отец уверен, что не чужих детей любит, воспитывает, хранит и о них печется. Разврат и скорая погибель настоит близко, когда сей закон будет презрен.[70]

> Everywhere for adultery the husband has the right to put the guilty parties to death; by these means the family union is protected, and the father is assured that he is not giving his love, raising, protecting and looking after the children of another man. Corruption and early ruin are imminent when this rule is scorned.

Indeed, Aleko refers to "prava moi" ("my rights") in describing how he would kill his adulterous wife (195).[71]

The use or threat of violence triggered by male sexual jealousy is readily interpreted as an anti-cuckoldry device that has the effect of raising paternity confidence. Comparison of the text with sociological and sociobiological research demonstrates how well Aleko fits the profile of the sexually violent male. Although Aleko already knows of Zemfira's lover, he presumably wishes to constrain her sexuality for his own benefit.[72] He directly rejects the Starik's advice to tolerate her adultery.

Sociobiologists postulate that for each concern the individual possesses a variety of behavioral protocols. These are triggered per different contexts, such as upbringing and environment. Aleko's choice of murder is surely the worst alternative, but it is a likely one. However grotesque and inappropriate this overreaction, it may come into play when other methods of preserving a desired relationship or social status either fail or are unpromising.[73] Aleko suits the profile of the sexual criminal as a "loser." An alien in an exotic context, he feels isolated, especially after the Starik's misbegotten advice.[74] He also seems to occupy the lowest rank. Ryleev and Vjazemskij criticized his degrading station as a bear-trainer. He has no resources, shows no likelihood of improving his material state, and, given his legal difficulties, has nowhere to go. He is probably scorned as a "house *rom*," and he is certainly frustrated in dealing with Zemfira's infidelity. Puškin's poem thus illustrates a theme often expressed in police files concerning murders committed by jealous husbands. Interestingly, convicted wife murderers often claim that their victims contributed to their own demise by boasting of their new lovers, attacking their husband's sexuality, or threatening to leave.[75] Zemfira sings of her lover's youth and laughs at Aleko's age, although he is elsewhere described as young (189, 180, 183, 193). Obviously their marriage is on the rocks. With Aleko's family "happiness" in ruins, the Starik has no justification for condemning him as a "gordyj čelovek" ("proud man") (210). The epithet better suits his victims.[76]

Only one alternative is presented to Aleko, and iʟ hardly looks promising. The Starik narrates how he sublimated his own sexuality and chose not to defend his "marital rights." Victor Erlich points out how "the hidden cost of Gypsy tolerance" is paid out by the Starik's "years of quiet grief, of unrelieved loneliness. (Free-love casualness seems to have been in this instance a one-way street!) To be sure, resignation, hurt borne in silence, is a more humane response than murder, but it too is a far cry from 'happiness.'" As Erlich concludes, "there are no easy solutions."[77]

There is an additional anthropological background to Erlich's remarks. Cuckolds are scorned or mocked in most, if not all, societies. Certainly the duped husband gains no respect for his misfortune. This calls into question how the Starik gained his position of paramount authority. Male honor is ultimately based on the chastity of related women: wives, sisters, and daughters.[78] The reverse does not apply, nor is there a female equivalent for "cuckold." This biologically derived concern is reflected in the important distinction between a husband's suspicion of his wife's infidelity and open social knowledge of the same; in some societies deceived men must take violent action if they are to avoid stigmatization.[79] This drive is certainly present when Aleko tells the Starik how he would have responded to cuckoldry. His response, in the context of literature, is emotionally gratifying. Consider how different our reactions to *Cygany* would be if (a) all the gender roles were reversed, or (b) Aleko took no action, like his father-in-law.

None of the above should be construed as an apologia for any form of sexual violence. Careful study of the biological basis of behavior in all aspects of its expression is essential to better effect a just social order. Because biological propensities originated in prehistoric times, they often

ill-accord with recently developed rational notions of justice. The first more
or less equal adultery law was enacted only in 1852.[80] While reason may pull
us forward, our emotional responses to liberal behavior may hold us back,
creating a tug-of-war evident almost everywhere. This differential pace of
slow biological change and rapid cultural adaptation does make for many
situations where genetic and cultural tendencies collide, and it provides a
rich compendium of emotional concerns for narrative art, as exploited in
Cygany.

Puškin himself was obviously uncomfortable with Aleko's response. He
offers no justification for the murder. Aleko makes no defense for his
actions. Described as "strašen" ("terrible in aspect"), he sits quietly while the
Starik reads him a lesson (201). But he is not so easily disposed of, given his
distinctly autobiographical traits. Prince Mirsky sees this "ruthless and
sincere study of jealousy" as an effort to exorcise this quality, particularly
with regard to Amalia Riznić, a married woman with whom Puškin was
amorously involved in Odessa.[81] Aleko's crime is foreshadowed in "Černaja
šal' " ("Black Shawl"), written in 1820, shortly after Puškin came to
Moldavia. Walter N. Vickery recently showed how the poet wrestled with
his emotions over old love affairs in poems of the 1820s.[82] The mere pro-
longation of this issue suggests the incomplete success of Puškin's struggle.
After all, in 1836 he tried to save his reputation from mockery as a cuckold
by challenging his wife's purported lover to a duel. He never found a good
solution.

Puškin's wrestling with jealousy suggests a new vision of narrative art.
Such fiction, as a part of culture, is itself a biological construct which helps
an individual or a society to practice various behavioral protocols vicarious-
ly. The central issues of *Cygany* were imagined, not observed, the better to
allow Puškin and his readers to confront their own quandary over a just and
at the same time emotionally satisfactory response. Narrative art can pose
compelling problems which are difficult to solve but which also train the
reader by encouraging productive thinking. This pedagogic function constitutes an important aspect of the adaptive quality of literature.

5. The Sociobiology of the *Femme Fatale*

By her nature, the *femme fatale* frustrates simplistic solutions. Like the
genetic composition of any individual, the *femme fatale* constitutes a conflu-
ence of many different factors; however, her literary "genes" are valued in
extremes of good and bad. She is very attractive; if she did not seduce men,
she would be of no interest to us. And she is obviously dangerous. Reading

about her is like playing with fire; she usually tempts men to some serious transgression, ultimately to their doom. This is the kind of fatal allure evoked by fictional Gypsy women. Her contradictory attributes lend her the fascination of a mystery and enmesh the viewer in the moral struggle so typically part of a *femme fatale* narrative. On the one hand, the *femme fatale* is divinely human; she manifests vitality, if not the passion of life. To kill her is a crime. On the other hand, readers find her disruptive and, perhaps as a result, she often ends up dead.

The tenets of sociobiology can help us understand various aspects of the *femme fatale*'s contrary nature. However, the *ultimate causations* that we trace per sociobiology are expressed by means of various *proximate mechanisms*. These, in turn, may be subjected to sociobiological analysis; hence, sociobiology complements other avenues of scholarly and scientific inquiry, including those applied in the arts, like psychology and cultural history, to mention just two. For example, why is the *femme* so *fatale?* Why fear a woman who merely takes the initiative and tries to satisfy her sexual appetite? The answer partly appears to be that men are built that way. If a woman displays even a little self-motivation, she is readily regarded as "masculine," or, from a psychoanalytic viewpoint, "phallic." This common association—horrifyingly sexist—harks back to the infantile image of the ego-devouring mother, who, as Melanie Klein stated, "in the deepest strata of the unconscious is specially dreaded as a castrator."[83] Hence the common link between aggressive sex drives and sharp objects like knives and teeth in a woman "do užasa znakoma" ("horribly familiar"), as Blok says of his Karmen.[84] The voice, important to the singing Zemfira and Carmen, constitutes another phallic image in that it conveys potency and penetrates.[85] Meanwhile, the moon, so often associated with Zemfira's free sexuality in the *poèma*, threatens castration (179, 180, 181, 191, 195, 197, 198, 199). A common symbol of mother-goddesses, the moon is associated with menstruation,[86] treated with particular revulsion by the Gypsies, who observe many strict menstrual taboos. Commonly interpreted as an unconscious reminder of the *vagina dentata* in psychoanalysis, menstruation provokes castration anxiety. From these associations derives the dire character of the sexual challenge made by the *femme fatale*.

Meanwhile, the male is described as weak and vacillating, if not passive, like Aleko. Set beside a dominating *femme fatale,* maternal in scope, he is a child, dominated by events out of his control; indeed, Aleko is compared to a child in the drafts (414). While sleep is associated in the *poèma* with love-making and family harmony, of which sex is the cement, it also conveys the male's child-like vulnerability to the *femme fatale*. Aleko moans as he dreams of Zemfira's infidelity, and when he witnesses her illicit tryst, he wonders if it is a dream; in the drafts he sits as if asleep during the Starik's final declamation (191–92, 198, 431). There is little wonder: much as Mariula betrayed the Starik, Zemfira attacks the marriage, that is, Aleko's sexuality, while he is asleep. Daniel Rancour-Laferrière claims that because "the love for the adult/sexual partner is linked with the feelings once felt toward the parent(s), . . . the wife tends to be a mother-icon for the husband"; this creates the potential for castration anxiety on the part of the man.[87] Rancour-Laferrière suggests castration anxiety has adaptive significance, in part because it is one of the mechanisms that prevent the man from mating with his mother instead of with the mother-icon. The male propensity for castration anxiety also may be a "superadded mechanism to reverse (or keep reversed) the direction of dominance in his relationship with the mother-icon from what it was in his relationship with his mother.[88] Because of these maternal associations, the *femme fatale* is both alluring and threatening. Her prevalence in the unconscious as well as in arts may be one of the factors impelling men to deprive women of power because it induces men to prefer the submissive and to regard assertive women as somehow "fatal."[89] This also serves to emphasize the male masochism at the heart of *Cygany*. Herbert S. Strean notes how often the victim of adultery "has unconsciously aided [his] mate in initiating and sustaining the affair." In the case of an adulterous wife, the "victim husband" will often refuse to believe that his spouse has been unfaithful, even if she flaunts her infidelity, much as Aleko passively listens to Zemfira's song. Strean points out that the immature victim of adultery will seek a parental icon in his mate and react to adultery as if to a faithless mother.[90] This line of argument can also be applied to Puškin. The Arbore account pointed out how his jealousy caused the actual Zemfira's desertion; he brought his misfortune upon himself. Then, whether or not the anecdote is genuine, Puškin indubitably conjured up the attack on the sexuality of his alter ego, Aleko, that *Cygany* constitutes.

Zemfira's likely youthful promiscuity and aggressive traits are signs that she is hardly an ideal wife; *femmes fatales* disrupt long-term pair-bonding, often by destroying their mates. Certainly the reader expects no "happily ever after" at the end of *Cygany*. According to Rancour-Laferrière, castration anxiety also serves to deter sexual misbehavior by the man, especially in illicit relations with a loose or dangerous woman, the kind which are unlikely to provide the long-term mate most favored by evolution. Rancour-Laferrière suggests that "a male suffering from a constant low, subliminal level of castration anxiety would have been less likely to wastefully divert altruism from his mate/offspring to other females whose offspring might not even turn out to be his."[91] If a man is going to limit his sexual activity, he needs to choose his partner with care; Rancour-Laferrière notes that "the woman with a dangerous vagina is the one who is perceived as *too* erotic," in which guise we recognize Zemfira and her *fatale* sisters. Men feel they need to be in control; hence they are susceptible to the *femme fatale*'s sexual challenge. Notably, there is a link between male impotence and his lack of control over his mate.[92] Aleko clearly despairs of controlling Zemfira; until he murders her out of desperation, he does nothing. Her defeat of the man, his destruction, or his inability to assert his dominance are all tantamount to castration; in this way, too, *Cygany* serves as a warning against assertive women.

This psychoanalytically driven misogyny has obvious repercussions on cultural development, wherein the arts serve to promulgate dominant ideologies. Despite the liberal atmosphere of *Cygany*, outer limitations on feminine liberation are to be discerned. For all of Zemfira's promiscuity, one may question whether she really has any freedom. She is always described in relation to someone else, usually a man, whether as daughter, wife, mother, or lover. She is not allowed to be free-standing, like Aleko the outsider, and her age, the prime of her fertility, is a characteristic feature in this regard. This is hardly unusual in the depiction of women, who are always, as it were, under surveillance. Beth Ann Bassein laments how the "almost universal identification of women with sex and the historical tendency to see sexuality as their main or only function" in literary classics serves to limit or otherwise damage women's "sense of self-worth" by presenting "only partial truths about women's lives, leaving the rest unvoiced or relegated to the unimportant."[93] Because the woman with initiative so often dies in major nineteenth-century novels, Bassein worries that such works of literature "more insidiously" than pornography "evade reality, set up constructs that feed our tendency to enjoy suffering, and perpetuate addiction to the kind of personal relationships that build passiveness in women."[94] That Zemfira, like Carmen, dies for her excesses constitutes such a warning; indeed, she both finds Aleko and later meets her Gypsy lover in a graveyard (180, 197ff). With this linkage between love and death, literature works as a mechanism of social defense against innovation. Traditional patriarchies are built around the protection and constraint of women, as a limited reproductive resource. Their marital fates are central to biological reproduction and, thus, constitute the major cement of society, as is particularly evident amongst real Gypsies. This, in part, is what Zemfira threatens.

She is not given like a prize to whatever mate the plot deems best, as in so many narratives. Rather, Zemfira is aggressive; she finds Aleko and boldly states he will be "moj" ("mine").

But cultures are biological constructs that enable much more rapid adaptation to environmental change; like species, cultures are not static, and their success varies. We should note that *Cygany* was written in the midst of about a four–hundred-year process of the gradual emancipation of women.[95] In the 1820s women were taking new roles in society and playing an ever greater part in the selection of their husbands. Puškin's portrait of one of the first *femmes fatales* in modern literature participates in this process, and it is to our benefit. If this view of social dynamics is correct, one might conclude from comparison of liberal and conservative societies that less constrained societies, that is, those with a greater number of liberated women, are more flexible and better developed and enjoy greater security; for all of the taboos she breaks, the *femme fatale* now may be adaptive. *Cygany,* with its extreme statement of a woman's right to love whomever she wants, tested contemporary morals, raised questions about traditional attitudes, and thus gave a push in the right direction.

The confrontation of these contrary perspectives creates another kind of tug-of-war just beyond the limits of social decency. Sociobiology leads us to expect that fictional plots will deal with such minor degrees of transgression. The best literature, like that of the *femme fatale,* works both to warn readers and to stretch us a little; its themes must continue to matter deeply to us and to tantalize. Thus they are assured a continuing role in the nonending process of bio-cultural evolution. From a sociobiological point of view, the best narratives work by throwing one genetically derived "passion" against another, creating the "protivorečija strasti" which Tomaševskij saw as the "uzel tragedii" ("tragic knot"); this we may conceive here as the clash of anachronistic but genetically driven proclivities with recent cultural innovations and rationality.[96] For example, the Starik makes rational sense: let Zemfira go. But such rationality does not satisfy our emotions. Consider how often narratives depict men fighting over a woman, in effect, denying her a choice. Our emotional reactions may be morally objectionable, but they exist owing to biological evolution, and we have to cope with them; narratives often force us to confront ourselves. So it is that Puškin's purported Gypsy lover is long since in her Bessarabian grave, but, because of this literary classic, we still are prompted to seek a middle course between Aleko and the Starik and to find a wholly satisfactory way to deal with the *femme fatale.*

Notes

1. All references to *Cygany* and its drafts derive from A. S. Puškin, *Polnoe sobranie sočinenij v semnadcati tomax*, ed. M. Gor'kij et al. (Moscow, 1937–49) II, and will be noted by page number only. Translations of the *poèma* are adapted from John Fennell, ed. and trans., *Pushkin* (Baltimore, 1964); translations of the drafts and other Russian texts are my own. An earlier version of this paper was read at the Russian School of Norwich University Symposium on Alexander Pushkin, 1987. I wish to thank Simon Karlinsky and Daniel Rancour-Laferrière for their helpful comments.

2. These are described as "strasti rokovye" ("fateful passions")—an anticipation of the conclusion—in the drafts (415).

3. "That Alek. Sergeevič simply is crazy about Zemfira"; cited in B. A. Trubeckoj, *Puškin v Moldavii*, 5th ed., augmented (Kishinev, 1983), 303.

4. Ibid., 304.

5. V. Veresaev, ed., *Puškin v žizni: Sistematičeskij svod podlinnyx svidetel'stv sovremennikov s illjustracijami na otdel'nyx listax,* 2 vols., 6th ed., significantly augmented (rpt., Chicago, 1970), I, 198–199.

6. *Pushkin: A Comparative Commentary* (Cambridge, 1971), 91.

7. "Disappeared and spent several days." Veresaev, I, 198.

8. See Trubeckoj, 303–4 and E. M. Dvojčenko-Markova, *Puškin v Moldavii i Valaxii* (Moscow, 1979), 24.

9. *Tvorčeskij put' Puškina (1813–1826)* (Moscow-Leningrad, 1950), 319.

10. Mario Praz reminds us that "a love of the exotic"—which is so evident in this narrative poem—"is usually an imaginative projection of a sexual desire." *The Romantic Agony*, trans. Angus Davidson, 2nd ed. (London, 1951), 197.

11. Dvojčenko-Markova, 97.

12. Z. I. Kirnoze, ed., *Merime—Puškin* (Moscow, 1987), 6–7.

13. Ibid., 420, 421.

14. Ibid., 11, 177, 11.

15. Cited in Ibid., 422.

16. Ibid., 11, 408–9.

17. Dvojčenko-Markova, 97.

18. Maxwell A. Smith, *Prosper Mérimée* (New York, 1972), 143; Prosper Mérimée, "Carmen," in Antoine Prevost, *Manon Lescaut* and Prosper Mérimée, *Carmen* (New York, 1966), 173. H. Schroeder—"Puškins 'Cygany' und Mérimées 'Carmen'," *Zeitschrift für Slavische Philologie*, 21 (1952),

307–20—does not believe the *poèma* could have influenced the novella; indeed, he notes the many dissimilarities in the characterizations of Zemfira and Carmen.

19. Meilhac, Henri and Ludovic Halévy, libretto for Georges Bizet's *Carmen*, trans. Joseph Allen (London: E.M.I. for Angel recording SCL–3767, 1970), n.p; Kirnoze, 199.

20. Meilhac and Halévy, Act I; A. A. Blok, *Stixotvorenija, poèmy, teatr,* ed. V. Orlov, two vols. (Leningrad, 1972), II, 167.

21. Bernice Kohn, *The Gypsies* (Indianapolis-New York, 1972), 64; Judith Okely, *The Traveller-Gypsies* (Cambridge, 1983), 228.

22. Okely, 195.

23. Blok, II, 164–8.

24. See T. G. Cjavlovskaja, *Risunki Puškina* (Moscow, 1980), 74–75, and S. A. Fomičev, "Rabočaja tetrad' Puškina PD No. 835 (iz tekstologičeskix nabljudenij)," *Puškin. Issledovanija i materialy,* 9 (1983):47. With regard to breast-feeding, see Okely, 208, Elwood B. Trigg, *Gypsy Demons and Divinities* (Secaucus, N.J., 1973), 59 and Jan Yoors, *The Gypsies* (New York, 1983), 230.

25. A. S. Puškin, *Polnoe sobranie sočinenij v semnadcati tomax,* ed. M. Gor'kij, et. al. (Moscow, 1937–1949), XI, 22.

26. John B. McLaughlin, *Gypsy Lifestyles* (Lexington, Mass., 1980), 12, 22–23.

27. Gypsy tribes will engage in fisticuffs at weddings; Okely notes that women are expected to know how to fight; 206.

28. McLaughlin, 86.

29. Ibid, 12.

30. This history of persecution leads us to question the lack of worries Puškin attributes to the Gypsies as well as the hospitality accorded them "vezde" ("everywhere"); 188.

31. For all of the *poèma*'s renowned *couleur locale,* Puškin includes no examples of their language; Jack Weiner and E. F. Meyerson, "Cervantes's 'Gypsy Maid' and Puškin's 'The Gypsies,'" *Indiana Slavic Studies,* 4 (1967), 212–13.

32. McLaughlin, 30–31; Okely, 192ff.

33. G. Bogač, *Puškin i Moldavskij fol'klor,* 2nd ed. (Kishinev, 1967), 76–107.

34. McLaughlin, 31; Yoors, 5.

35. McLaughlin, 21.

36. That their "cohabitation" is soon "consummated" is suggested by the manner in which the Starik awakens them, apparently sleeping together, the

very next morning: "Ostav'te, deti, lože negi! . ." ("My children, leave your couch of bliss"); 182. The drafts are a bit more suggestive; Zemfira invites her new acquaintance to bed, saying "Moej ljubov'ju nasladis' " ("Delight in my love"); 411.

37. Okely, 155; Kohn, 50.

38. Carol Miller, "American Rom and the Ideology of Defilement," in Farnham Rehfisch, ed., *Gypsies, Tinkers and Other Travellers* (London, 1975), 45; Anne Sutherland, *Gypsies: The Hidden Americans* (New York, 1975), 13, 247, 251.

39. Kohn, 64.

40. McLaughlin, 25,19.

41. Ibid., 22, 23.

42. Okely, 152.

43. Yoors, 123.

44. McLaughlin, 27.

45. Ibid., 14–15; Miller, 47–48; Sutherland, 229–30; Yoors, 129.

46. Kohn, 48.

47. Ibid., 48; McLaughlin, 30; Okely, 203; Sutherland, 226–27; Trigg, 89; Padmashri W. R. Rishi, *Roma: The Panjabi Emigrants in Europe, Central and Middle Asia, the USSR, and the Americas* (Patalia, India, 1976), 22. However, Gypsies are not perfect; Daniel Rancour-Laferrière cites the Gypsy practice of killing a bird in order to fake virginity loss; *Signs of the Flesh: An Essay on the Evolution of Hominid Sexuality* (Berlin-New York-Amsterdam, 1985), 180. Also see Yoors, 203–4.

48. McLaughlin, 96, 27.

49. Mérimée, 212; also noted in Werner Cohn, *The Gypsies* (Reading, Mass., 1973), 47–48.

50. Kohn, 50. Also see Cohn, 68, Sutherland, 237, Trigg, 62, and Rishi, 22.

51. Okely, 203.

52. Rishi, 21.

53. Trigg, 62–63. Also see Yoors, 1983, 206 and Rishi, 22.

54. A. F. Vel'tman., "Vospominanija o Bessarabii," in V. È. Vacuro, et. al., eds., *A. S. Puškin v vospominanijax sovremennikov*, 2 vols. (Moscow, 1985), I, 298.

55. Weiner and Meyerson, 210–11.

56. Miguel de Cervantes, "The Little Gipsy," trans. N. Maccoll, in Joseph Ellner, *The Gipsy Pattern* (Freeport, N.Y., 1969), 258.

57. Mérimée, 175.

58. p. 81.

59. See Okely, 201–2. This same contradiction between hostile alien

perception of promiscuity and actual Gypsy chastity was observed amongst Russian Gypsies by Basil Ivan Racoczi. Racoczi bemoans that "comparatively little work on the origins, language and the customs of the Gypsies has been undertaken in the USSR." "An Artist's Visit to the Gypsies of Southern France and to the U.S.S.R.," *Journal of the Gypsy Lore Society*, 3rd Series, 40 (1961):126. This is adducible in part to the Gypsies' resistance to Communist social policies. It also derives from Russian attitudes. In 1911, D. F. de L'Hoste Ranking noted that there were few Russian studies of Gypsies, mostly of their language, and rarely of Gypsy society; "The Gypsies of Central Russia (Part I)," *Journal of the Gypsy Lore Society*, New Series, 4 (1911):195ff. No Gypsologist finds a significant distinction between Gypsies in the USSR and those living elsewhere; Gypsy culture usually is described by scholars and by Gypsies as one whole—although regional and tribal distinctions inevitably exist.

60. Vel'tman, I, 296.

61. "On the Nature of Pushkin's Poetry," in Paul Debreczeny and Jesse Zeldin, ed. and trans., *Literature and National Identity* (Lincoln, Neb., 1970), 10–11. Blagoj finds Zemfira more Moldavian than Gypsy and also doubts the ethnography of the Starik; 329. E. M. Černickij arrives at a similar conclusion by citing the contradictions between Puškin's draft variants; he concludes that artistic choice took precedence over ethnographic accuracy. See "Poèma A. S. Puškina 'Cygany,'" in A. T. Boršč, et. al., eds., *Puškin na juge: Trudy Puškinskix konferencij Kišineva i Odessy* (Kishinev, 1958), 79–80.

62 Bayley, 91, 106.

63. Ibid, 91.

64. Martin Daly, Margo Wilson and Suzanne J. Weghorst, "Male Sexual Jealousy," *Ethology and Sociobiology*, 3 (1982):11; also see Donald Symons, *The Evolution of Human Sexuality* (New York, 1979), 240–46, and Rancour-Laferrière, 91–96.

65. Daly, Wilson and Weghorst, 13–15.

66. Ibid, 18.

67. There is usually no punishment for sex with an unattached woman, but in traditional societies few women have no close male relative.

68. Trigg, 63.

69. Cited in Daly, Wilson and Weghorst, 12–13.

70. Cited in B. V. Tomaševskij, *Puškin*, 2 vols. (Moscow-Leningrad, 1956 and 1961), I, 624.

71. In one draft variant, these "rights" are "svjaščennye" ("sacred"); 452. Mérimée's Carmen herself tells Don José, "As my *rom*, you have the right to kill your *romi* ("wife")." Mérimée, 209.

72. True, he also destroys it. It is important not to idealize all biological mechanisms. Those that exist evolved because they were more effective than alternate tactics, but this does not mean that they are perfect or directly suited to a desired end. As a result, they can be misapplied in untypical situations. One example is the pattern of incest avoidance observed amongst *unrelated* children in Israeli kibbutzim; sociobiologists postulate that children who are raised together between ages 2 and 6 as if they were related will come to regard one another as siblings, irrespective of their heredity. As a result, there has been no intermarriage within any of these groups. Another consideration is that violent constraints must be enacted occasionally if they are to be effective in future situations, such as when a wife-murderer re-marries.

73. Randy Thornhill and Nancy Wilmsen Thornhill, "Human Rape: An Evolutionary Analysis," *Ethology and Sociobiology,* 4 (1983):137–73; William M. Shields and Lea M. Shields, "Forcible Rape: An Evolutionary Perspective," *Ethology and Sociobiology,* 4 (1983):115–36.

74. See Peter D. Chimbois, *Marital Violence: A Study of Interspousal Homicide* (San Francisco, 1978), 58.

75. See Chimbois, 51–52. The police files Chimbois consulted were Canadian.

76. Tomaševskij, I, 630–31, reaches a similar conclusion.

77. Victor Erlich, "Puškin's Moral Realism as a Structural Problem," in Andrej Kodjak and Kiril Taranovsky, eds., *Alexander Puškin: A Symposium on the 175th Anniversary of His Birth* (New York, 1976), 173.

78. Martin Daly and Margo Wilson, *Sex, Evolution and Behavior*, 2nd ed. (North Sciutate, Mass., 1983), 295–97. In the opera, Don José kills Carmen partly to keep her from returning to Escamillo, "infamous creature, to laugh at me in his arms!"; Meilhac and Halévy, Act IV, n.p.

79. Daly, Wilson and Weghorst, 24; Kate Millett, *Sexual Politics* (Garden City, N.Y., 1970), 43. Zemfira's young Gypsy may be trying to stigmatize Aleko when he tries to keep her with him until dawn; public awareness that he cuckolded Aleko will likely win him some admiration. Herbert S. Strean says that adulterers will often act, consciously or unconsciously, to incriminate themselves; *The Extramarital Affair* (New York, 1980), 162.

80. Daly, Wilson and Weghorst, 12.

81. D. S. Mirsky, *Pushkin* (New York, 1963), 72.

82. Walter N. Vickery, "Problems with the Odessa Connection: Some Puškin Love Lyrics Examined" (paper presented to the 1987 Puškin Scholarship in America Today Conference, Madison, Wisconsin).

83. Cited in Rancour-Laferrière, 321.

84. Blok, II, 165.

85. Daniel Laferrière, *Five Russian Poems: Exercises in a Theory of Poetry* (Englewood, N.J., 1977), 72–73.

86. Robert S. McCully, "The Two Phases of the 'Great Mother,'" in Gerald G. Neuman, ed., *Origins of Human Aggression: Dynamics and Etiology* (New York, 1987), 108, 113–15.

87. Rancour-Laferrière, *Signs of the Flesh,* 197–98.

88. Ibid, 328.

89. Ibid., 329.

90. Strean, 164, 162, 165.

91. Rancour-Laferrière, *Signs of the Flesh,* 313–14.

92. Ibid. 324, 325ff.

93. Beth Ann Bassein, *Women and Death: Linkages in Western Thought and Literature* (Contributions in Women's Studies, Number 44; Westport, Conn., 1984), ix, 69.

94. Ibid., 61.

95. Wolfgang Lederer suggests that the invention of "penis-envy" was a male reaction to the emancipation of women in the nineteenth century; *The Fear of Women* (New York, 1968), 217. The same may be true for the *femme fatale.*

96. Tomaševskij, I, 632.

THE HISTORICAL FRAMEWORK OF
NIKOLAJ GOGOL'S "STRAŠNAJA MEST'"

PAUL A. KARPUK

Nikolaj Gogol's "Strašnaja mest'" could be defined as a tale of the super-natural in a historical setting. For the most part scholars have ignored the historical aspect of the tale, owing, perhaps, to the almost universal tendency to regard Gogol as a careless historian who did not care about facts and dates, and from whom, therefore, neither consistency nor verisimilitude in referring to historical circumstances is to be expected. However, a detailed examination of Gogol's allusions to historical events in the story, when considered in light of the factual sources from which he drew his interpretation of these events, reveals a historical framework too consistent to have evolved merely from what V. V. Gippius called Gogol's "intuitive sense of rightness,"[1] and refutes the common supposition that the author was some-how incapable of distinguishing one century from another.

"Strašnaja mest'" is set during roughly the same historical period as "Taras Bul'ba" and Gogol's unfinished historical novel "Get'man," that is, during the period of Cossack rebellions against Poland beginning at the close of the sixteenth century and continuing into the mid-seventeenth century.[2] In all three of these works Gogol treats the conflict between the Poles and the Cossacks as almost exclusively religious; he considers the Cossack uprisings of this period to have been caused chiefly by the establishment of the Uniate Church at the Brest Union of 1596 and the religious persecution which supposedly followed. This interpretation, as scholars have noted with respect to "Taras Bul'ba,"[3] appears to reflect the influence of the *Istorija Rusov, ili Maloj Rossii*, a work originally attributed to the archbishop of Belorussia, Georgij Koniskij, but the authorship of which subsequently became a matter of dispute. Not published until 1846, the *Istorija Rusov* nevertheless circulated widely in manuscript at the time Gogol was writing. And indeed in "Strašnaja mest'" also, some scholars have detected, in the references to Polish and Jewish oppression of the Cossacks, "traces of a fleeting acquaintance" with the *Istorija Rusov*.[4] Gogol's use of this source is plausible if one considers that the story was probably written in mid-to-late 1831, and Gogol may have become acquainted with the *Istorija Rusov* via Puškin at this time.[5] It is probably not coincidental that the *Istorija Rusov* has also been cited as an influence on one of the "Get'man" fragments, "Neskol'ko glav iz neokončennoj povesti," which was written at about the same time as "Strašnaja mest'."[6]

It is generally know that the *Istorija Rusov*, which attracted the attention of Gogol and his contemporaries because of its great artistic power, has almost no reliability as a factual historical source. In particular, scholars have long since dismissed as fables its tales concerning how Jews, during the period of the *Unija,* supposedly became landlords of Orthodox churches and took advantage of this to desecrate church property and charge taxes for the performance of Orthodox rituals.[7] If Gogol believed these fables and indeed made them the cornerstone of his interpretation of this period in Ukrainian history, it is less a reflection on Gogol's qualities as a historian than of the fact that his Russian contemporaries also believed them.

One of these contemporaries was, in fact, the preeminent historian of Ukraine during the period Gogol was writing, Dmitrij N. Bantyš-Kamenskij, whose *Istorija Maloj Rossii* is considered the first scholarly history of Ukraine. This work was first published in 1822 but substantially rewritten and expanded for a second edition, which appeared in 1830. Gogol mentions it more than once in his correspondence from early 1834, when he was working on his own history of Ukraine "in six small or four large volumes" (10:297); from his letter of March 6, 1834, to I. Sreznevskij we know that he consulted it at this time as a bibliographical source (10:300; see also 10:303). However, there can be little doubt that he must have begun using it much earlier. The publication of, in particular, the second edition of Bantyš-Kamenskij's history was an "epoch-making event" which could hardly have escaped the attention of anyone interested in Ukrainian affairs.[8] Furthermore, Bantyš-Kamenskij included in his history a chapter on Ukrainian customs, dress, and popular beliefs (for the most part pirated, however, from other sources); and as we know from his "Kniga vsjakoj vsjačiny" and several letters to his mother,[9] Gogol at the time of the publication of the second edition was actively searching for ethnographic information on Ukraine, evidently for use in the stories which later became part of the *Dikan'ka* cycle.

Unfortunately, the problem of determining precisely which historical source may have influenced Gogol at any particular point is complicated by the nature of the sources he was using. On the surface it would seem rather easy to identify Gogol's sources, since he often used material from them almost verbatim, particularly in "Taras Bul'ba."[10] However, it was customary for historians of the time to cite, or paraphrase closely, primary source documents or other historians to an extent that in our day would certainly be considered plagiarism, although these historians were usually careful at least to cite their source. The result was that the same material could be duplicated almost word for word in a multiplicity of sources, any of which Gogol might have used. As a case in point, the material on the *Unija* which Gogol incorporated into "Taras Bul'ba," "Get'man," and "Strašnaja mest'," which is invariably attributed to the *Istorija Rusov*, could equally well have been taken from the second edition of Bantyš-Kamenskij's history, where it is cited almost verbatim.[11] In the present work we will have many occasions to refer to material as having been borrowed from the *Istorija Rusov*, but if we do not in each instance mention Bantyš-Kamenskij's history as a potential source for the same material, it is simply to avoid repeating a point, which, once made, the reader should bear firmly in mind as our argument proceeds.

Thus textual evidence alone is not enough to determine whether Gogol used a particular source; biographical circumstances, i.e., the likelihood that Gogol encountered, or evidence that he knew of, a particular source must be taken into consideration. And in fact biographical circumstances, together with textual evidence to be presented below, suggest that Gogol was well acquainted with both the *Istorija Rusov* and the *Istorija Maloj Rossii* at the time he was writing "Strašnaja mest'."

In "Strašnaja mest'" there are several passing references to the various types of persecution which, according to the *Istorija Rusov*, were visited upon the Ukrainian populace in connection with the establishment of the Uniate Church in 1596; these references recall the descriptions of such abuses in the *Istorija Rusov*, of which Gogol made much more extensive use in "Get'man" and "Taras Bul'ba."[12] At the beginning of chapter II of "Strašnaja mest'" the narrator explains the mood of despondency among the Cossacks by noting, among other things, that ". . . Catholic priests are already swarming over Ukraine and rebaptizing the Cossack people into Catholics," and besides ". . . the Horde had fought for two days at Solyonoe Ozero" (1:246). The reference to the forced conversion of the Ukrainian people to Catholicism appears to draw on two passages from the *Istorija Rusov*, indicating that "the Roman clergy, spreading out in triumph over Little Russia to supervise and coerce adherence to the Uniate faith, was conveyed from church to church"[13] and that many Ukrainian nobles, for fear of losing their privileges, yielded little by little to the *Unija* and subsequently were completely converted to Catholicism.[14] The reference to a battle with the Crimean Tatars at "Solyonoe Ozero," i.e. "Salt Lake," appears to be an invention on Gogol's part, but is representative of the frequent Tatar raids on Ukrainian territory during this period, which are referred to repeatedly in the *Istorija Rusov*.[15] The seriousness of this situation is underscored by the fact that Solyonoe Ozero is located in the vicinity of Novhorod-Sivers'kyj, and the presence of a Tatar army there would have represented a very deep penetration into Ukrainian territory. The location may have been suggested to Gogol by a completely unrelated incident described in the *Istorija Rusov*, the siege of Novhorod-Sivers'kyj by the Poles during the wars with Russia at the beginning of the seventeenth century, for which Ukraine became a "theater of operations." During this engagement the Polish army set up camp, according to the *Istorija Rusov,* at Solyonoe Ozero.[16]

Another passing reference to the ills created by the establishment of the Uniate Church occurs during the quarrel between Danilo and Katerina's father related in Chapter III. Danilo suggests that Katerina's father is not only a traitor to the fatherland, but is worse than a convert to the Uniate faith:

> «Слава Богу, ни в одном еще бесчестном деле не был; всегда стоял за веру православную и отчизну; не так, как иные бродяги, таскаются, Бог знает где, когда православные бьются на-смерть, а после нагрянут убирать не ими засеянное жито. На униятов даже не похожи: не заглянут в Божию церковь».

(1:251)

The reference to the Orthodox being engaged in a fight to the death places the action in the middle of the religious wars which, according to the *Istorija Rusov*, resulted from the establishment of the Uniate Church (the term "Unijat," we might note, is used specifically in the *Istorija Rusov*, in reference to the fact that adherents to the Uniate faith, in order to obtain an Easter cake free of charge were required to wear on their chests a rag with the inscription "Unijat").[17] A similar reference is found at the beginning of Chapter VI, where the narrator cites, as the reason the sorcerer has been imprisoned, his participation in the conspiracy to betray Ukraine to the Catholics: "Sidit on za tajnoe predatel'stvo, za sgovory s vragami pravoslavnoj russkoj zemli prodat' katolikam ukrainskij narod i vyžeč' xristianskie cerkvi" (1:261).

The author of the *Istorija Rusov* cites numerous examples of depredations committed by the Polish forces of occupation in connection with the enforcement of the Brest Union:

> «Рыцарство Руское названо Хлопами; а народ, отвергавший Унию, Схизматиками... города заняты Польскими гарнизонами, а другие селения их же войсками. Им дана власть все тое делать народу Рускому, что сами схотят и придумают, и они исполняли наказ сей с лихвою, а что только смыслить может своевольное, надменное и

пьяное человечество, делали то над несчастным народом Руским без угрызения совести. Грабительства, насилие женщин и самых детей, побои, мучительства и убийства превзошли меру самых непросвещенных варваров. Они, почитая и называя народ невольниками или ясыром Польским, все его имение признавали своим... На прислуги... Духовенству выбираемы были Поляками самые краснейшие из девиц Руских.[18]

The behavior of this "capricious, haughty, drunken" crowd, the treatment of and reference to the Ukrainian people as "slaves" ("xlopami"), the coercion and appropriation of women, and the reprehensible behavior of the Roman Catholic priests sent to enforce the *Unija* appear to be recalled in Chapter VIII, in which a crowd of Polish soldiers gather in a tavern and plot an attack on Danilo's estate.

На пограничной дороге, в кормче, собрались ляхи и пируют уже два дни. Что-то не мало всей сволочи. Сошлись, верно, на какой-нибудь наезд: у иных и мушкеты есть; чокают шпоры; брякают сабли. Паны веселятся и хвастают, говорят про небывалые дела свои, насмехаются над православьем, зовут народ украинский своими холопьями и важно крутят усы, и важно, задравши головы, разваливаются на лавках. С ними и ксенз вместе. Только и ксенз у них на их же стать: и с виду даже не похож на христианского попа. Пьет и гуляет с ними и говорит нечестивым языком своим страмные речи. Ни в чем не уступает им и челядь: позакидали назад рукава оборванных жупанов своих, и ходят козырем, как будто бы что путное. Играют в карты, бьют картами один другого по носам. Набрали с собою чужих жен. Крик, драка!... Паны беснуются и отпускают штуки: хватают за бороду жида, малюют ему на нечестивом лбу крест, стреляют в баб холостыми зарядами и танцуют краковяк с нечестивым попом своим. Не бывало такого соблазна на русской земле и от татар... Слышно между общим содомом, что говорят про заднепровский хутор пана Данила, про красавицу жену его...

(1:264–65)

A very similar scene, we might observe, is enacted in one of the "Get'man" fragments, "Glava iz istoričeskogo romana," in the depiction of the debauched behavior of the Polish noble, a "great sinner," who also recalls the sorcerer in "Strašnaja mest'."[19]

The *Istorija Rusov* recounts numerous instances of murderous acts committed by the Poles against children: ". . . mladency, posle ubityx materej, polzavšie po ulicam, podnimaemy byli na kop'jax, a inye sxvačeny za nogi i ubity golovami ob steny" (from the description of the battle at Novhorod-Sivers'kyj); ". . . ostavšixsja že po materjam detej, brodivšix i polzavšix okolo ix trupov, perežgli vsex v vidu ix otcov na železnyx rešetkax, pod koi

podkidyvali ugol'ja i razduvali šapkami i metelkami" (from the description
of the execution of Hetman Ostrjanycja and his officers); ". . . vojska Pol-
skie . . . neskol'ko raz povtorjali proizvedennye v Varšave ljutosti nad
nesčastnymi Malorosijanami, neskol'ko raz varili v kotlax i sožigali na
ugol'jax detej ix v vidu roditelej" (during the period of renewed persecution
following the suppression of the Ostrjanycja uprising).[20] These appear to be
recalled in a despairing speech pronounced by Katerina in Chapter III:
"Tvoi kosti stanut tancovat' v grobe s vesel'ja, kogda uslyšat, kak nečestivye
zveri ljaxi kinut v plamja tvoego syna, kogda syn tvoj budet kričat pod
nožami i okropom" (1:252). Gogol made extensive use of this same material
in the second edition of "Taras Bul'ba," though in most cases these atroci-
ties are attributed therein to the Cossacks rather than the Poles (see 2:83,
168, 169).

According to the *Istorija Rusov*, the introduction of the Uniate Church in
Ukraine and the attendant persecutions of the Orthodox were initiated
following the suppression of the Nalyvajko uprising in 1597–98. However,
during the Hetmancy of Konaševyč-Sahajdačnyj, from 1598 until his death
in 1622, the *Unija* was largely allowed to lapse, because the Poles needed
Sahajdačnyj's help in wars against Russia and the Turks. Following his
death, the religious persecution of the Orthodox was resumed; this precipi-
tated the uprising under Hetman Taras Trjasylo in 1624 (1628–29 according
to most other sources). Though this uprising was successful, Taras failed to
solidify his gains, and after his death the *Unija* was gradually reintroduced.
The failed uprising under Hetman Ostrjanycja in 1638 was followed by another period of renewed repression, which continued until the Xmel'nyc'kyj
rebellion in 1647–48.[21] One of these periods of renewed repression seems to
be recalled when Danilo suggests to Katerina that the Poles are about to
"reappear": "Odnako ž znaeš' li ty, čto za goroju ne tak spokojno. Čut' li
ne ljaxi stali vygljadyvat' snova" (1:253).

Noting that "the hero, Danilo, reminisces with melancholy about the
glorious days of the Hetmancy of Petro Konaševyč-Sahajdačnyj and complains that the Cossacks are immobilized by internecine strife and lack of
leadership," Leon Stilman asserts specifically that the action "takes place
between the death of Sahajdačnyj in 1622 and the resumption of the struggle
in 1629 under the new Hetman, Taras Trjasylo."[22] The following speech by
Danilo, to which Stilman refers, does indicate that the action in the story
must take place sometime following the death of Sahajdačnyj:

«Что-то грустно становится на свете. Времена лихие приходят. Ох,
помню, помню я годы; им, верно, не воротиться! Он был еще жив,
честь и слава нашего войска, старый Конашевич! как будто перед

очами моими проходят теперь козацкие полки! — Это было золотое время, Катерина! — Старый гетман сидел на вороном коне. Блестела в руке булава; вокруг сердюки; по сторонам шевелилось красное море запорожцев. Стал говорить гетман — и всё стало, как вкопанное. Заплакал старичина, как зачал вспоминать нам прежние дела и сечи. Эх, если б ты знала, Катерина, как резались мы тогда с турками! На голове моей виден и доныне рубец. Четыре пули пролетело в четырех местах сквозь меня. И ни одна из ран не зажила совсем. Сколько мы тогда набрали золота! Дорогие каменья шапками черпали козаки. Каких коней, Катерина, если б ты знала, каких коней мы тогда угнали!»

(1:265–66)

These sentiments are repeated in the songs of the blind bandura-player described in Chapter XVI: "Sperva povel on pro prežnjuju get'manščinu za Sagajdačnogo i Xmel'nickogo. Togda inoe bylo vremja: kozačestvo bylo v slave; toptalo konjami neprijatelej, i nikto ne smel posmejat'sja nad nim" (1:279). This idealized portrait of the Hetmancy of Sahajdačnyj, and the campaigns against the Turks undertaken by him, is fully in keeping with that provided in the *Istorija Rusov*, in which it is said that "the Poles, respecting the bravery and the services rendered by Sahajdačnyj, did not dare carry out their effronteries in the open during his reign, and moreover even their most beloved Unija somewhat abated and grew cold."[23] The author of the *Istorija Rusov* does, in fact, describe numerous successful campaigns against the Turks and Tatars undertaken by Sahajdačnyj, as a consequence of which the Cossacks collected immense booty, including livestock ("Getman . . . vozvratilsja s plennymi i velikoju dobyčeju v svoi granicy"; "Ves' tabur Tatarskij so vsem tem, čto oni ni imeli, dostalsja pobediteljam v dobyču, a plenniki Malorosijskie, do neskol'ko tysjač oboego pola duš, ne tol'ko čto osvoboždeny iz nevoli, no i nagraždeny lošad'mi i veščami Tatarskimi dostatočno, i vozvratilis' v svoi žilišča, ravno i Getman s svoim vojskom pribyl v rezidenciju svoju blagopolučno i so slavoju mnogoju").[24] Gogol also seems to be following the *Istorija Rusov* in his use of the terms "bulava" (mace) and "serdjuki" (according to Dal', who cites Koniskij, this is a term used to refer to regular infantry among the Ukrainians).[25] According to the *Istorija Rusov*, the "bulava" or mace was a symbol of office first bestowed upon the Ukrainian Hetmans by King Stefan Báthory.[26] The term "serdjuki" is mentioned in the *Istorija Rusov* by way of explaining the origin of the word "kozak": "Takim obrazom i Ruskie voiny nazvalis' konnye Kozakami, a pešie strel'cami i serdjukami, i sii nazvanija sut' sobstvennye Ruskie, ot ix jazyka vzjatye, na primer strel'cy po strel'be, serdjuki po serdcu ili zapal'čivosti, a Kozaki i Kozare, po legkosti ix konej, upodobljajuščixsja koz'emu skoku."[27]

The use of infantry during Sahajdačnyj's campaigns, in particular, is referred to repeatedly in the *Istorija Rusov*.[28]

Danilo's speech continues with a characterization of the present state of affairs in Ukraine, to which past glories are contrasted:

> «Ох, не воевать уже мне так! Кажется, и не стар, и телом бодр; а меч козацкий вываливается из рук, живу без дела, и сам не знаю, для чего живу. Порядку нет в Украйне: полковники и есаулы грызутся, как собаки, между собою. Нет старшей головы над всеми. Шляхетство наше всё переменило на польский обычай, переняло лукавство... продало душу, принявши унию. Жидовство угнетает бедный народ».
>
> (1:266)

The reference to the entire nobility having converted to Polish ways, including "slyness" and having accepted the Uniate faith, recalls two passages in the *Istorija Rusov* describing the aftermaths respectively of the failure of the Nalyvajko uprising and of the death of Hetman Sahajdačnyj:

> Чиновное Шляхетство Малоросийское, бывшее в воинских и земских должностях, не стерпя гонений от Поляков и не могши перенесть лишения мест своих, а паче потеряния ранговых и нажитых имений, отложилось от народа своего и разными происками, посулами и дарами, закупило знатнейших урядников Польских и Духовных Римских, сладило и задружило с ними и, мало по малу, согласилось, первее на Унию, потом обратилось совсем в Католичество Римское. В последствии сие Шляхетство, соединяясь с Польским Шляхетством свойством, родством и другими обязанностями, отреклось и от самой породы своей Руской, а всемерно старалось, изуродовав природные названия, приискивать и придумывать к ним Польское произношение и называть себя природными Поляками.... Следствием переворота сего было то, что имения сему Шля<хет>ству и должности их возвращены, а ранговые утверждены им в вечность и во всем сравнены с Польским Шляхетством. В благодарность за то приняли и они, в рассуждении народа Руского, всю систему политики Польской, и подражая им, гнали преизлиха сей несчастный народ.[29]

> А что знатнейшее Малоросийское Шляхетство все почти обратилось к ним в Католичество и осталось в Руской религии из народа одно среднее и низшее сословие, то дали они новый титул Униятству, назвав его: «Хлопска вяра».[30]

It is important to observe that Gogol was far from consistent or conscientious in transposing even those pseudohistorical "facts" into the fictional setting of "Strašnaja mest'." In a passage cited previously, the narrator refers to the "Cossack people" being rebaptized into Catholicism by Roman Catholic priests (1:246), whereas the author of the *Istorija Rusov* mentions the acceptance of Catholicism only by the nobility, and the forced conversion of the people as a whole, not to Catholicism proper, but only to the Uniate faith. Danilo's reference to the acceptance of the *Unija* by the entire nobility is consistent with the *Istorija Rusov* only to the extent that this was an initial stage in what ultimately was a complete conversion to Catholicism, and that the entire nobility was involved. However, Danilo makes no reference to the further conversion of the nobility to Catholicism as such, and the indication that they "accepted" the *Unija* therefore seems inconsistent with the reference, in the *Istorija Rusov*, to the fact that the nobility came to hold the Uniate faith in contempt, unless "prinjali" here simply refers to the acceptance of a religious policy rather than the faith itself. Danilo's reference to the oppression of the people by Jews, we might add, draws upon those passages in the *Istorija Rusov* which depict Jews as the primary agents of the Poles in the religious persecution of the Orthodox, to which repeated references are made in "Taras Bul'ba" and "Get'man."[31]

Danilo's reference to internecine feuding among the Cossack officers is interesting, inasmuch as the *Istorija Rusov* mentions few cases of fratricidal warfare among the Cossacks, unless one includes references to the conflicts between the mass of true "patriots" and the few "traitors," such as Hetman Perevjazka or Hetman Barabaš, who sold themselves to the Poles.[32] This suggests that Gogol may in fact have been drawing on another source. The connection drawn by Danilo between feuding among the Cossacks and the absence of a senior leader is particularly revealing in this respect, as this characterizes above all the period *following* the death or disappearance of Hetman Taras as it is described in Bantyš-Kamenskij's *Istorija Maloj Rossii*. Bantyš-Kamenskij, in contrast to the author of the *Istorija Rusov*, who maintains that Taras "died peacefully" in 1632,[33] notes that it is not known what fate befell him, and even suggests that the Cossacks betrayed him into the hands of the Poles: "Neizvestno, kakaja učast' postigla Tarasa. Dolžno polagat', čto on byl smenen bespokojnymi Zaporožcami, ne ljubivšimi dolgo povinovat'sja odnomu Načal'niku, ili, možet byt', vydan imi Poljakam."[34] Bantyš-Kamenskij then relates a curious tale concerning overtures made by the king of Sweden, Gustavus Adolphus, to Ivan Petražyc'kyj [Petrižickij], who replaced Taras as Hetman in 1631:

При нем [Петрижицком — Р.К.] Шведский король Густав Адольф старался, посредством Рижского Губернатора, Руселя, привлечь Козаков на свою сторону, обещая им нанарушимое сохранение вольностей и религии их, как благородным Рыцарям, храбрым воинам, Обладетелям Днепра и Черного моря, защитникам веры Греческой. Может быть Петрижицкий и поднял бы оружие против Польши, еслиб в след за сим Густав не лишился жизни, сражаясь с Имперцами при Луцене и не явился на правой стороне Днепра другой Гетман, Гаврилович, который произвел междоусобную брань, поглотившую обоих виновников оной.[35]

The reference to fratricidal warfare between the two Hetmans of Left and Right Bank Ukraine, Petražyc'kyj and Havrylovyč, seems clearly recalled in Danilo's allusion to the absence of a senior leader and infighting among the Cossack officers. According to Bantyš-Kamenskij, Petražyc'kyj and/or Havrylovyč was then succeeded as Hetman by Semen Perevjazka, who, however, was quickly deposed by the Zaporožan Cossacks for adhering to the Polish side and even conspiring to infiltrate Ukraine with Polish troops (which recalls Danilo's suggestion that the Poles had begun appearing again).[36] This account of the brief Hetmancy of Perevjazka is substantially the same as that in the *Istorija Rusov*, but in the latter no mention whatever is made of Petražyc'kyj, Havrylovyč, or the feud between them; Perevjazka, it is stated, was the immediate successor of Hetman Taras.[37] After the deposing of Perevjazka, the Zaporožan Cossacks, according to Bantyš-Kamenskij, "continued to elect and replace Hetmans." In 1632 they were led by Arlam, in 1633 by Sulyma.[38] Neither of these is mentioned by the author of the *Istorija Rusov*, who skips directly from Perevjazka to Hetman Pavljuk.[39]

A vital clue to interpreting the historical time-frame of "Strašnaja mest' " is found at the beginning of Chapter II, in which Danilo refers to rumors that the Poles intend to build a fort to cut off communications between Ukraine and the Zaporožan *seč'*: "Ja slyšal, čto xotjat ljaxi stroit' kakuju-to krepost', čtoby pererezat' nam dorogu k zaporožcam" (1:247). This is a reference to an actual historical event, the building of the fortress of Kajdak (sometimes spelled Kodak, Kadak, or Kudak), which was intended for precisely this purpose. The building of this fortress is referred to both by Bantyš-Kamenskij and in the *Istorija Rusov*, as well as in a few other sources Gogol might have been familiar with at the time, most notably the memoirs of the French engineer Beauplan, who indeed was its designing architect. Bantyš-Kamenskij gives the following account of the historical circumstances surrounding the building of the fortress at Kajdak, which demonstrates its close proximity in time to the period of fratricidal warfare referred to above:

Запорожцы продолжали, между тем, избирать и сменять Гетманов. В 1632 предводительствовал ими Арлам, с 1633 Сулима, воевавшие против Турков на Черном море. Возвращаясь однажды из своего хищнического похода, Сулима изумился, увидя на первом Днепровском пороге крепость, построенную Поляками, овладел оною, изрубил находившийся там Польский гарнизон, состоящий только из двух сот человек под начальством Полковника Мариона, но в скором времени, окруженный Конецпольским, принужден был сдаться и отослан в Варшаву, где его четвертовали.[40]

In a footnote Bantyš-Kamenskij observes that this fortress, "named Kudak," was built by the engineer Beauplan in July, 1635, and taken by Sulyma in August of the same year.[41] The historian goes on to relate that in 1639, following the suppression of the uprisings under Ostrjanycja (1638) and Hetman Poltora-Kožux (1639), Crown Hetman Koniecpolski (referred to in the passage cited above) undertook to reconstruct the fortress:

...Коронный Гетман Конецпольский с 4000 человек отправился в Кудак, возобновил при себе крепость сию, разоренную Козаками, снабдил оную сильным гарнизоном и поручил своему Инженеру Боплану осмотреть и исследовать все пороги, вероятно, чтобы воспрепятствовать Запорожцам собираться впред в тех местах.[42]

A somewhat more detailed account of the construction of the Kajdak fortress is given in another source which Gogol could possibly have used at this time, Aleksandr Rigel'man's *Letopisnoe povestvovanie o Maloj Rossii*.[43] The references in Rigel'man's account to the planning stages of the fortress and to its strategic purpose are strongly reminiscent of the corresponding passage in Gogol's text:

А чтоб приглашать Запорожских Низовых Козаков и иных людей к себе и сами бы к ним переходить они не могли, подал совет Коронный Хетман, Конецпольский, построить бы при Днепре, между жилищами Украинскими и Низовых Запорожских Козаков на урочище, Кайдаке, крепость, и тем бы пресечь им к сообщению их всю удобность сухим и водяным путем.... Сами ж тотчас послали на Кайдак (место при самом Днепровском первом или верхнем пороге Кайдацком, на правой стороне) строителей, работных людей и военную команду для прикрытия оных строить крепость со всяким поспешением.[44]

...узнавши о городовом уже на Кайдаке строении и что, наконец, им от того воспоследовать может, тотчас собрались [Козаки] к препятствию оного и, сообщась с Запорожцами, разбили там французского полковника, Мариона, который в Кайдаках уже с 200-ми военными людьми приставлен был для прикрытия работников, так что ни единый жизнию не спасся. А как, сверх чаяния, услышали, что Конецпольский поспешно поспешает к ним с великим числом войска, то в великое сумнительство пришли о Хетмане своем, Савалтовиче. Они, обвиняя его в том изменою, и признав заподлинно, тотчас его в куски изрубили...[45]

[В 1639 году Поляки] усильно постарались достроить помянутую крепость Кайдак, а паче чрез старание Коронного Хорунжего (знаменоносца) Конецпольского, и чтоб населить оную народом Польским и Немецким вооруженным, и тем бы их [Козаков — Р.К.] на обои стороны обуздать и усмирить.[46]

Rigel'man, we might note, appears to be confusing Savaltovyč with Sulyma. According to Bantyš-Kamenskij, Savaltovyč was not elected Hetman until 1638, whereas, according to the account of Beauplan, whom Bantyš-Kamenskij follows, the initial stage in the construction of the fortress and its destruction by the Cossacks took place in mid-1635.[47] However, like Rigel'man, Bantyš-Kamenskij also indicates that Savaltovyč was suspected of treachery and therefore "cut to pieces" by the Cossacks.[48]

The construction of the fortress at Kajdak is also mentioned in the *Istorija Rusov*, although the account it gives is, as we shall have reason to see, hopelessly garbled; among other things, the author of the *Istorija Rusov* confuses Crown Hetman Koniecpolski with the *podstarosta* of Čyhyryn, Daniil Czaplicki (Czaplinski), and fuses the two stages in the construction of the fort into one, relating the entire episode to the year 1638:

...Польское правительство, под распоряжением Чаплинского, наместника Гетманского, или иначе дозорцы Чигиринского, по планам и разводам инженеров французских, в 1638 году воздвигнуло нарочито сильпую крепость, Кадаком названную, над рекою Днепром, между пределов Малоросийских и Запорожских устроенную с политическим умыслом, чтобы воспящать сообщению между сих единокровных народов, а паче их войск, одно другому вспомогающих...[49]

Danilo's allusion to infighting among the Cossack officers makes it clear that Gogol must have been influenced by some source in addition to the *Istorija Rusov*, in which the Cossacks are portrayed rather consistently as presenting a united front to the Poles and turn against one of their own kind only when he is suspected of collusion with the Poles. Gogol most likely was influenced in this particular instance by Bantyš-Kamenskij, who not only refers specifically to a period of fratricidal warfare under the "two Hetmans," but also suggests instances in which Cossacks betrayed their own leaders (Taras, Savaltovyč). The electing of and deposing of a rapid succession of Hetmans by the unruly *zaporožcy* in the early 1630s, and the general confusion during this period (which is even reflected in the disagreements between Rigel'man and Bantyš-Kamenskij as to which Hetman succeeded which and in what order), certainly seems to be recalled in the portrait drawn by Danilo of the current state of affairs in Ukraine.

The above-cited material from Gogol's historical sources, which included at the very least the *Istorija Rusov* and Bantyš-Kamenskij's history, and possibly also Rigel'man's chronicle (cf. the reference to the planning stages in the construction of the fortress at Kajdak, to which Danilo seems to allude), allows us to pinpoint rather definitely the time at which the action in "Strašnaja mest' " takes place. The references to Polish intentions to build a fortress to cut off communications with the Zaporožan Cossacks, to the reappearance of the Poles and the abuses connected with the introduction of the Uniate faith, to feuding among the Cossacks, and to the period following the death of Sahajdačnyj, suggest that the action takes place in the early 1630s, i.e., not between the death of Sahajdačnyj and the uprising under Taras, as Stilman speculates, but directly following the death or disappearance of Hetman Taras. It was at this time, according to the *Istorija Rusov*, that the Poles little by little reinstituted the religious persecution that had been rolled back during the Hetmancy of Taras and garrisoned Ukraine with additional troops in order to enforce it;[50] that Ukraine, according to Bantyš-Kamenskij, was engulfed in fratricidal warfare between the Hetmans of Left- and Right-Bank Ukraine, Petražyc'kyj and Havrylovyč; and that plans for the building of the Kajdak fortress, referred to in all three sources cited above, were getting under way.

One additional reference in the story to historical circumstances serves to confirm this general impression. At the beginning of Chapter V, Danilo mentions in passing that only last year he had been preparing to go to war together with the Poles, with whom he still at that time maintained an allegiance, against the Crimean Tatars (1:260). Gogol need not be referring here to a specific campaign, for campaigns against the Turks and Tatars were an almost constant fact of life during this period. However, the indication that the Poles and Cossacks had still been allied only a year earlier could refer, giving Gogol some allowance for the contradictory dates in his sources, to the period immediately preceding the brief Hetmancy of Taras, when the Cossacks were still nominally allied with the Poles (during which, according to Bantyš-Kamenskij, there were several Cossack raids against the Turks and Tatars, though he does not mention Polish participation in them and in fact indicates that the Poles attempted to curb such raids).[51] According to Rigel'man and Bantyš-Kamenskij, the uprising under Hetman Taras took place in late 1628 and early 1629,[52] but the author of the *Istorija Rusov* assigns the date 1624.[53] According to Bantyš-Kamenskij, Taras in 1631 (i.e., one or two years later) had already been replaced as Hetman by Petražyc'kyj,[54] but Rigel'man claims that Taras was succeeded in 1633 by Sulyma.[55] There is a possibility that Gogol, if in fact he was referring to a specific historical event, could have had in mind the joint Polish-Cossack campaign against the Turks which ended with a Turkish victory at Tsetsora, which in the *Istorija Rusov* is loosely related to the interregnum between the death of Sahajdačnyj and the uprising under Taras (which would tend to support the time period we have assigned here to the story);[56] Bantyš-Kamenskij, however, gives the date 1620,[57] i.e., before Sahajdačnyj's death (which would tend to support Stilman's hypothesis). Gogol mentions, however, war not against the Turks but the Tatars. Another campaign which is related by Bantyš-Kamenskij to the period following Taras's victory over the Poles at Perejaslav, but in which he makes no mention of Taras participating, suggests somewhat more strongly the historical circumstances referred to by Danilo, and fits neatly into the historical time-frame we have suggested:

> Вскоре Козаки пустились на многих ладиях в море Черное и, упоенные поражением Поляков, дерзнули ночью войти в самый канал Констан-тинопольский, овладели двумя неприятельскими галерами, причинили значительный вред Турецкому флоту, возвратились с богатою добы-чею. Обладетель Музульманов не удовольствовался обещаниями По-сланника Польского, отправил тайное повеление к Хану ворваться в Польшу с сильным войском. Полководцы Сигизмундовы умели отра-зить хищных Татар.[58]

This episode reflects the complex state of political affairs in southeastern Europe of the time: the Cossacks undertook an independent raid against the Turks, perhaps in spite of the objections of the Poles, and in retaliation the Turkish leader ordered the Tatars to attack the Poles, who were considered responsible for the actions of the Cossacks because the latter were still nominally subjects of the Polish crown. Though there is no specific mention of an alliance between the Poles and Cossacks, there is a reference to war between the Poles and Tatars in which the Cossacks were involved. In any case, the complex political picture, the frequency of warfare between the Poles and Cossacks on the one side and the Turks and Tatars on the other, and the contradictory facts given in Gogol's sources, suggest that we need not hold the author too closely in this instance to the fine points of historical fact.

It is interesting that while the main action in "Strašnaja mest' " can thus be related rather specifically to a definite historical period, the semilegendary "pre-history" of the tale describing the quarrel between Ivan and Petro, which is related by the blind bandura-player in Chapter XVI, is also set firmly in historical time (since the bandura-player precedes this narrative with songs about Sahajdačnyj and Xmel'nyc'kyj, this entire scene may have been suggested to Gogol by Bantyš-Kamenskij's observation that "up to the present day blind bandura-players sing of the exploits of Xmel'nyc'kyj, Palej, and other renowned military leaders of the fatherland").[59] This quarrel is said to have been the consequence of a search by the King of Poland, Stefan Báthory, for a hero who could aid him in the war against the Turks:

> За пана Степана, князя Седмиградского, был князь Седмиградский королем и у ляхов, жило два козака: Иван да Петро.... Воевал король Степан с турчином. Уже три недели воюет он с турчином, а всё не может его выгнать. А у турчина был паша такой, что сам с десятью янычарами мог порубить целый полк. Вот объявил король Степан, что если сыщется смельчак и приведет к нему того пашу живого или мертвого, даст ему одному столько жалованья, сколько дает на всё войско. «Пойдем, брат, ловить пашу!» сказал брат Иван Петру. И поехали козаки, один в одну сторону, другой в другую.

(1:279)

The portrait of Báthory as a wise, benevolent ruler is consonant with that provided in the *Istorija Rusov* and by Bantyš-Kamenskij, who indeed cites the *Istorija Rusov* to that effect.[60] Bantyš-Kamenskij observes that "the Ukrainian chroniclers speak with exemplary praise of this sovereign, calling him a friend and a father of humanity, and comparing him with Emperor Titus," and it is undoubtedly for this reason that Gogol also treated him as something of a hero. Báthory is mentioned again both in "Get'man" and in the first edition of "Taras Bul'ba." In the former, the narrator describes a picture hanging on the wall of Ostranica's *svetlica*, in which Ostranica's grandfather is shown fighting side by side with Báthory (3:293–94); in the latter, Taras is said to have been one of the original colonels of the Cossack regiments established by Stefan Báthory (2:284; this reference is absent in the second edition). The designation of Stefan Báthory as "Knjaz' Sedmigrad-skij" must have been taken by Gogol from Bantyš-Kamenskij's history (" . . . Stefan Bátorij, Knjaz' Sedmigradskij, xrabryj, krasnorečivyj, veliče-stvennyj naružnostiju, provozglašen Korolem . . .");[61] this title is not used in the *Istorija Rusov*. "Sedmigrad" is a calque of the German "Siebenbür-gen," i.e., Transylvania; thus "Knjaz' Sedmigradskij" refers to Báthory's title of Prince of Transylvania before he became King of Poland. The implication in Gogol's text that Báthory participated personally in a campaign against the Turks may be rooted in Bantyš-Kamenskij's statements, not only to the effect that Báthory was courageous and experienced in military affairs, but also that after his arrival in Kraków, the new king gave his solemn oath always to take personal charge of military campaigns.[62] In fact, however, Bantyš-Kamenskij mentions only Báthory's personal participation in wars against Russia. The dates provided by Bantyš-Kamenskij for the reign of

Stefan Báthory, 1576 to 1586,[63] allow us to establish approximately the historical time frame of the "pre-history" of Gogol's tale.

Although we have cited numerous instances of what appear to be borrowings from the *Istorija Rusov* in "Strašnaja mest'," it is important to reiterate that virtually all this material, with the exception only of Gogol's fleeting reference to Solyonoe Ozero, would have been available to Gogol from Bantyš-Kamenskij's history, where the passages in question from the *Istorija Rusov* are quoted verbatim or paraphrased closely.

It should be clear enough from the preceding discussion that at the time "Strašnaja mest'" was composed, Gogol was much more familiar with and made far greater use of source material on Ukrainian history than is implied by the customary references to Gogol's lack of historical knowledge,[64] or by Ajzenštok's reference to the presence in "Strašnaja mest'" of "traces of a fleeting acquaintance" with the *Istorija Rusov*. The mere absence of *numerical* dates in "Strašnaja mest'" should not blind us to the fact that Gogol shows considerable awareness of historical time, notwithstanding repeated assertions in the critical literature to the contrary. If only for this reason, it seems legitimate to take a closer look at Gogol's references to historical time in "Get'man" and "Taras Bul'ba" also.

Notes

1. V. V. Gippius, *Gogol*, ed. and trans. Robert A. Maguire (Ann Arbor, 1981), p. 65. All quotations from Gogol's writings in this article are taken from the Academy edition of his complete collected works, i.e., N. V. Gogol', *Polnoe sobranie sočinenij*, 14 vols. (Moscow and Leningrad, 1937–52). Quotations from Gogol's own writings in this edition are cited in the text in parentheses, with volume number followed by page number. Citations from the commentaries in this edition (or the commentaries and Gogol's writings in combination) are given in endnotes using the abbreviation *PSS*.

2. Although it is commonly asserted that in "Taras Bul'ba" Gogol confuses his chronology by entire centuries and ascribes the action sometimes to the fifteenth, sometimes the sixteenth, and other times the seventeenth century (see, for instance, Gippius, pp. 63, 65), a closer look at the text reveals this assertion to be fallacious. In the second (i.e., canonical) edition of "Taras Bul'ba," there are, in fact, no references whatever to the sixteenth century. The one reference to the fifteenth century concerns the date of the origin of Cossackhood (2:46), not the time of the action in the story. See M. B. Xrapčenko, *Nikolaj Gogol'. Literaturnyj put'. Veličie pisatelja* (Moscow, 1984), p. 168. The approximate time of the action is indicated by

Gogol in his characterization of Bul'ba's *svetlica:* "Svetlica byla ubrana . . vo vkuse togo brannogo, trudnogo vremeni, kogda načalis' razygryvat'sja sxvatki i bitvy na Ukrajne za uniju"(2:43–44). Bearing in mind that Gogol, following the *Istorija Rusov,* attributes the Cossack wars against the Poles to the founding of the Uniate Church, i.e., to the act known as the *Unija,* the time "when the skirmishes and battles in Ukraine over the *Unija* began to be played out" is clearly to be identified as the end of the sixteenth and the first half of the seventeenth century.

Vasilij Gippius takes the "Get'man" fragments as another example of Gogol's supposed proclivity for confusing chronology by entire centuries, noting that the dates ascribed to (or suggested by) the action in the fragments do not match up. But Gippius asserts far too confidently that these fragments all belong to one novel; in fact (as Vsevolod Setchkarev, among others, observes) the relationship between them is not clear, and there is no need for the dates to match up if different novels are involved. See Gippius, p. 63; Vsevolod Setchkarev, *Gogol: His Life and Works,* trans. Robert Kramer (London, 1965), p. 139.

3. See particularly Romana Bahrij-Pikulyk, "Superheroes, Gentlemen or Pariahs? The Cossacks in Nikolai Gogol's *Taras Bul'ba* and Panteleimon Kulish's *Black Council,*" *Journal of Ukrainian Graduate Studies,* 5, no. 2 (1980), p. 34; Romana Bahrij-Pikulyk, "The Use of Historical Sources in *Taras Bul'ba* and *The Black Council,*" *Studia Ucrainica* 2, University of Ottawa Ukrainian Studies, no. 5 (1984), p. 58; Romana Bahrij-Pikulyk, *"Taras Bul'ba* and *The Black Council*: Adherence to and Divergence from Sir Walter Scott's Historical Novel Pattern," Diss., University of Toronto, 1978, p. 141. Gogol's use of the *Istorija Rusov* in the writing of "Taras Bul'ba" has been commented on extensively in the critical literature. See, for instance, I. Ja. Ajzenštok's commentary to "Taras Bul'ba," *PSS* 2:718–20, 722; E. I. Proxorov, "Istoričeskie i fol'klornye istočniki 'Tarasa Bul'by,' in *Taras Bul'-ba,* Literaturnye pamjatniki (Moscow, 1963), pp. 201–3, 209–10; S. Mašinskij, *Istoričeskaja povest' Gogolja* (Moscow, 1940), pp. 97–100, 104–5.

4. *PSS,* 1:544.

5. *PSS,* 1:544, 3:715.

6. *PSS,* 3:714–15; George Gregory Grabowicz, "The History and Myth of the Cossack Ukraine in Polish and Russian Romantic Literature," Diss., Harvard University, 1975, p. 473.

7. I. Kamanin, "Naučnye i literaturnye proizvedenija N. V. Gogolja po istorii Malorossii," in *Pamjati Gogolja: Naučno-literaturnyj sbornik,* ed. N. P. Daškevič (Kiev, 1902), pp. 105–7; *PSS* 2:719.

8. Dmytro Doroshenko, "A Survey of Ukrainian Historiography," *The*

Annals of the Ukrainian Academy of Arts and Sciences in the U. S., 5–6, no. 4(18)–1, 2(19–20) (1957), p. 109.

9. *PSS* 9:495–533, 656–57; 10:141, 144, 150, 162, 167–68, 171, 178–79, 208–9, 214–15. See also *PSS* 1:501–2, 523–24, 529–30, 540; N. L. Stepanov, *N. V. Gogol': Tvorčeskij put'*, 2nd ed. (Moscow, 1959), pp. 21–22; George S. N. Luckyj, *Between Gogol' and Ševčenko*, Harvard Series in Ukrainian Studies, 8 (Munich, 1971), pp. 102–3.

10. Mašinskij, pp. 100–101.

11. Dmitrij Bantyš-Kamenskij, *Istorija Maloj Rossii* , [2nd ed.] (Moscow, 1830), 1:178, 198–99, 203, 217.

12. See the sources cited in notes 3 and 6.

13. Georgij Koniskij [pseud.], *Istorija Rusov ili Maloj Rossii* (Moscow, 1846), p. 40.

14. *Istorija Rusov*, p. 41.

15. *Istorija Rusov*, pp. 14, 20, 24, 31, 44.

16. *Istorija Rusov*, p. 43. In the notes to "Strašnaja mest' " in the 1983 seven-volume edition of Gogol's collected works, it is asserted that "Solenoe ozero" refers here to the Sivaš (the gulf at the west end of the Sea of Azov), evidently because the Sivaš is very salty, ergo a "salt lake." Therefore, it is assumed, Gogol must be referring to a battle which was fought on the shores of the Sivaš during a campaign which the Zaporožan Cossacks, led by Sahajdačnyj, undertook against the Crimean Tatars in 1620. See N. V. Gogol, *Sobranie sočinenij v semi tomax*, ed. S. I. Mašinskij and M. B. Xrapčenko (Moscow, 1983), 1:474. This does not seem possible, inasmuch as Sahajdačnyj is dead at the time the story begins. The Sivaš is sometimes referred to as "Gniloe more" ("Putrid Sea") or even the "Beloe more" ("White Sea"), but not to my knowledge as "Solenoe ozero." In "Neskol'ko glav iz neokončennoj povesti" the Cossack Pud'ko refers to the Sivaš simply as the Sivaš: ". . . Kuzubija guljaet s rybami na dne Sivaša i tjanet gniluju vodu vmesto gorelki' " (3:282); however, the statement that Kuzubija is now drinking "putrid water" instead of vodka is evidently a reference to the alternate name "Gniloe more." A battle fought at such a distant location would not have caused the concern which is expressed in "Strašnaja mest'."

17. *Istorija Rusov*, p. 48.

18. *Istorija Rusov*, p. 40.

19. *PSS* 1:545.

20. *Istorija Rusov*, pp. 44, 56.

21. *Istorija Rusov*, pp. 40–41, 48–49, 52, 56–57.

22. Leon Stilman, "Nikolaj Gogol and Ostap Hohol," in *Orbis Scriptus. Dmitrij Tschižewskij zum 70. Geburtstag*, ed. Dietrich Gerhardt et al.

(Munich, 1966), p. 821. In Gogol's texts and in the sources he used, Russian spelling is used for Ukrainian personal and place names. When quoting such texts in the original Russian, I have adhered to the spelling in the text. Elsewhere, I have preserved the Ukrainian spelling for Ukrainian personal and place names, transliterated according to the transliteration table on p. xii of Dmytro Čyževs'kyj, *A History of Ukrainian Literature*, trans. Dolly Ferguson et al., ed. George S. N. Luckyj (Littleton, Colo., 1975).

23. *Istorija Rusov*, p. 48.

24. *Istorija Rusov*, pp.45, 47.

25. Vladimir Dal', *Tolkovyj slovar' živogo velikorusskogo jazyka*, 4 (St. Petersburg-Moscow, 1882; rpt. Moscow, 1980): 175.

26. *Istorija Rusov*, p. 26.

27. *Istorija Rusov*, p. 19. Gogol could also have known about "serdjuki" from Puškin's "Poltava," in which they are mentioned during the scene of Kočubej's execution (second canto). However, Puškin's text ("Skačut serdjuki") indicates that they are mounted, in disagreement with Dal's definition of "serdjuki" as infantry. In a footnote Puškin defines "serdjuki" as "vojsko, sostojavšee na sobstvennom iždivenii getmanov." See A. S. Puškin, *Sobranie sočinenij v desjati tomax*, 3 (Moscow, 1975), 197, 212. Bantyš-Kamenskij also mentions "serdjuki," but indicates that they are first mentioned by Ukrainian chroniclers only in the year 1674, and were probably established by Dorošenko; in this case, Gogol's reference to "serdjuki" in connection with the Hetmancy of Sahajdačnyj would be clearly anachronistic. According to the *Istorija Rusov*, which Bantyš-Kamenskij cites in the second edition of his history, they were later used by Mazepa as a kind of personal bodyguard, which echoes the definition given by Puškin. See *Istorija Rusov*, p. 186, and Dmitrij Bantyš-Kamenskij, *Istorija Maloj Rossii* [2nd ed.] (Moscow 1830), 3:233. Danilo's indication that Sahajdačnyj was surrounded by "serdjuki" ("vokrug serdjuki") seems to indicate that Gogol was also visualizing them as a kind of bodyguard.

28. *Istorija Rusov*, pp. 44, 45, 46.

29. *Istorija Rusov*, p. 41.

30. *Istorija Rusov*, p. 48.

31. See sources cited in notes 3 and 6.

32. *Istorija Rusov*, pp. 52, 59.

33. *Istorija Rusov*, p. 52.

34. Bantyš-Kamenskij, 1:204.

35. Bantyš-Kamenskij, 1:205–6.

36. Bantyš-Kamenskij, 1:206.

37. *Istorija Rusov*, p. 52.

38. Bantyš-Kamenskij, 1:210.

39. *Istorija Rusov*, p. 52.

40. Bantyš-Kamenskij, 1:210.

41. Bantyš-Kamenskij, 1: notes, 36.

42. Bantyš-Kamenskij, 1:218.

43. Gogol refers to Rigel'man's chronicle in his March 6, 1834, letter to Sreznevskij (10:299).

44. Aleksandr Rigel'man, *Letopisnoe povestvovanie o Maloj Rossii i ee narode i kozakax voobšče* (Moscow, 1847), 1:42.

45. Rigel'man, 1:43–44.

46. Rigel'man, 1:47.

47. [Guillaume le Vasseur le] Sieur de Beauplan, "A Description of Ukraine . . .," in *A Collection of Voyages and Travels . . . In Eight Volumes,* 1 (London, 1752): 452.

48. Bantyš-Kamenskij, 1:217.

49. *Istorija Rusov*, p. 50.

50. *Istorija Rusov*, p. 52.

51. Bantyš-Kamenskij, 1:199–200, 202.

52. Bantyš-Kamenskij, 1:202–4; Rigel'man, 1:40.

53. *Istorija Rusov*, p. 51.

54. Bantyš-Kamenskij, 1:205.

55. Rigel'man, 1:41.

56. *Istorija Rusov*, p. 49.

57. Bantyš-Kamenskij, 1:186–87.

58. Bantyš-Kamenskij, 1:204.

59. Bantyš-Kamenskij, 3:214.

60. *Istorija Rusov*, p. 28; Bantyš-Kamenskij, 1:137, 149, 154.

61. Bantyš-Kamenskij, 1:137.

62. Bantyš-Kamenskij, 1:137.

63. Bantyš-Kamenskij, 1:137, 154.

64. See, for instance, *PSS* 3:714–15.

TRANSCENDING POLITICS: VYACHESLAV IVANOV'S VISIONS OF *SOBORNOST'*

BERNICE GLATZER ROSENTHAL

Vyacheslav Ivanov (1866–1949), one of the most important poets and theorists of Russian symbolism, was oriented toward metaphysics, not politics; but the severity of the socio-political situation in Russia induced him to reflect on how to resolve it. He regarded the revolutions of 1905 and 1917 as surface manifestations of a profound spiritual and cultural crisis, which was in turn part of an eschatological transition to a new era. He believed that the conflict-ridden present would be transcended by a new spiritual ideal—*sobornost'*, originally an ecclesiastical concept, which connoted the unity of all believers in the mystic body of Jesus Christ. *Sobornaya Tserkov* is the Slavonic translation of the words Catholic Church in the Creed. Its application to secular matters is specifically Russian and Slavophile and derives from a verbal coincidence: the Russian word *Sobor* also means council. Thus the suggestion of temporal political or social ramifications is inherent in the word.[1] It was the Slavophiles, especially Aleksei Khomiakov (1804–1860), who first applied the term *sobornost'* to secular matters. Khomiakov considered *sobornost'* the essence of the Russian Orthodox understanding of the Church. As he used the word, *sobornost'* meant unity in multiplicity, an organic union of believers in love and freedom, and pertained to the Church as an idea, not as an institution. But he also used *sobornost'*—the idea, rather than the word itself—"to explain world history, to assail everything he disliked in life, and to promote all the institutions and all the doctrines he championed."[2] The peasant commune (*mir*) exemplified *sobornost'*; *sobornost'* was the Russian answer to class conflict, the antipode of the rationalism, legalism, compulsion of the West, and so on. Other Slavophiles contributed their particular emphasis to the idea, which exerted, in various permutations, a broad influence on nineteenth-century Russian thought. Vladimir Soloviev's (1853–1900) socio-political ideal, Free Theocracy, is a variant of *sobornost'*, as is his concept of All-Unity. Symbolist poets and writers of the early twentieth century, including Ivanov, used both the word and the general idea to express their own quest for a new kind of society characterized by freedom, beauty, and love.

As a youth Ivanov had been a revolutionary and an atheist, but the assassination of Tsar Alexander II (1881) had led him to recoil from terrorism and to lose faith in populism. He studied Greek and Roman history and philology, turned inward, and wrote lyric poetry. Intent on establishing a clear sense of personal identity and on situating himself in a larger entity, a universal community (*obshchina*), he was particularly impressed by Friedrich Nietzsche's depiction (in *The Birth of Tragedy*) of the loss of self in the ritual ecstasy of the cult of Dionysus and of the culture-forming power of myth.[3] Ivanov's vision of *sobornost'* was influenced more by Nietzsche and Soloviev than by any other thinkers, except perhaps for Dostoevsky.[4] Particularly important was Soloviev's idea of Free Theocracy and his view of art as a theurgy, a path to a higher reality or truth.

For Ivanov *sobornost'* was at once a metaphysical and a socio-political ideal, for he regarded it as the earthly reflection of a higher reality. *Sobornost'* symbolized his hope of transcending politics and resolving social conflict; it was his alternative to Autocracy on the one hand and to materialistic Western liberalism and socialism on the other. The centrality of *sobornost'* in Ivanov's thought is somewhat concealed by the vatic language he used, and by the vague terms he coined, e.g., "supraindividualism," "mystical anarchism," "mutual attraction," "the Russian Idea," "monantropism," to describe his ideal—a spiritual community, a free union of individuals bonded together by powerful unconscious ties of passion and myth. Evoking and developing these ties was the task he set himself. This paper will describe Ivanov's most important attempts to forge the bonds of inner unity: 1. a cultic theater (1904–08); 2. "the Russian Idea" (1908–19); and 3. "monantropism" (1919–21). We will see that as the impossibility of realizing an otherwordly ideal on this earth became obvious, Ivanov moved from relative optimism to the brink of despair and from a dream of a loosely knit "new organic society" to an integral vision of unity that all but obliterated the individual. Ivanov ceased writing about *sobornost'* after 1921, perhaps because the consolidation of Bolshevik power made the issue moot. Neither the word nor the idea is important in his doctoral dissertation, "Dionysus and Predionysianism" (1923).[5] He left Russia voluntarily in 1924, settled in Italy, and converted to Roman Catholicism.[6] In emigration he wrote far more poetry than prose and expressed himself in Dantean universals devoid of any direct reference to contemporary concerns.

In terms of the Slavophile-Westernizer discussions of the mid-nineteenth century, Ivanov was clearly a Slavophile, for he perpetuated the Slavophiles' communal emphasis, their rejection of politics, legalism and rationalism, and their basic tenet: unity in freedom and love. But Slavophilism was the product of a stable era in Russia (compared with turbulent western Europe); its passionless *agape* and gentle Orthodoxy did not meet the emotional needs of people experiencing social collapse and cultural crisis. The reintegration for which he yearned required stronger measures—enlisting the power of the passions, directing unconscious drives, engendering new group dynamics. Moreover, the backward-looking orientation of classic Slavophilism, its hope to restore pre-Petrine Russia, did not mesh with the eschatological expectations and utopian ardor of a revolutionary epoch. Going beyond Slavophile exaltation of the Russian past, Ivanov dreamed of an entirely new kind of society, one which would include elements of other cultures, especially ancient Greek, and would be based on freedom and love, but not as the Slavophiles understood those terms. Thus in Ivanov's writings Slavophile anti-legalism became antinomianism; Slavophile apoliticism became anarchism; Christian love (*agape*) was supplemented, perhaps even supplanted, by sexual love (*eros*) to a degree which would have shocked the Slavophiles; freedom meant the absence of all external constraints; and Ivanov's Dionysian Christianity, tinged with occult elements, replaced conventional Russian Orthodoxy as the spiritual center of society.

A Cultic Theater

Ivanov first began to write about *sobornost'* in 1904 as the way to transcend the escalating social and political conflicts of that year. Asserting the need for a spiritual/cultural solution to Russia's problems, he took as a model the Dionysian theater of ancient Greece as described by Nietzsche. The German, however, had treated Dionysianism as a primarily aesthetic phenomenon. Ivanov stressed its religious and psychological aspects, the actual worship of Dionysus and the orgiastic, ecstatic elements of the Dionysian rituals. He believed that the rituals created in the participants a feeling of oneness with each other and with all that exists and called this feeling the "religious-psychological phenomenon of Dionysianism."[7] Implying a close connection between the life-giving force of Eros and the world soul, he linked sexual passion to the religious experience of catharsis and claimed that passion causes the participants to lose consciousness of the distance between themselves and others, to feel themselves one with the cosmos, with all existence.

Ivanov viewed the cultic community as an example of *sobornost'* because it was united by love and faith. He hoped that in a resurrected cultic theater the chorus would articulate a new all-Russian myth. Ivanov regarded myth as the artistic perception of an event in mystical reality and as the expression of a timeless suprapersonal higher truth lying beyond the Dionysian flux.

Believing that myth constituted a people's internal self-definition and situated the individual in society and in the cosmos, he maintained that specific forms of the myth change, but that their essence is eternal. He considered Dionysus a precursor of Jesus Christ and believed that a new formulation of the Christ/Dionysus archetype could reintegrate Russian society. He wanted the theater to return to its religious origins and become a "common festival and service," a liturgy, so that it could fulfill its historical mission of uniting the intelligentsia and the people.[8]

Toward this end, Ivanov urged his fellow symbolist poets to end their isolation from the people and become myth creators, to forge new myths (actually reformulate the old) around which the intelligentsia and the people could unite. He considered the chorus the "living symbol of *sobornost'*" and used the terms chorus and people (*narod*) interchangeably. (Refusing to consider material factors, he made no mention of economic or class categories at all.) Ivanov's mystique of the chorus derived primarily from Nietzsche's description of the Dionysian rites, from Richard Wagner's idea of the theater-temple, and from his own research on the Dionysian cults, and secondarily from the prominence of the choir in Russian music and in Slavophile thought. He admired Richard Wagner's operas for their rejuvenation of German myth, but objected to the passivity which Wagner induced in his audiences. Ivanov's theatrical ideal, which he called "choral activity," emphasized the chorus as an active participant in the ritual, an actual creator of the myth.[9] The actors in the Dionysian rites, he constantly emphasized, were not performers, but participants in a religious rite in which they truly believed, members of a religious commune, for which Ivanov co-opted the Russian term *obshchina*. Ivanov never clarified who, if anyone, would conduct the chorus, but his general orientation suggests a new hierarchy with the artist as priest. Neither did he consider exactly how the new myths would emerge or how they would permeate society. He simply assumed that in the cultic theater, choral action would lead to myth-creation, to the new unifying all-national myth.

Ivanov viewed history as a series of cycles, each characterized by its own mythic vision, and believed contemporary events had their precursors in antiquity. In his eyes the Russo-Japanese War was the successor to the Punic Wars between Carthage and Rome and a warning of the danger of "pan-Mongolism," as expounded in Vladimir Soloviev's famous poem (1894) about the conquest of Europe by a resurgent Asia:

> Our first Punic War with Yellow Asia began. War is a touchstone of the popular consciousness and a trial of the spirit; not so much a test of eternal power and eternal culture as of the internal energy of the self-affirming

potential of the collective [*sobornyi*] personality. Yellow Asia moved to fulfill her ordained task—the task of trying the spirit of Europe: is her Christ living and active in her?

Yellow Asia asked us first, what [is] the nature of our self-affirmation? But we were filled only with disharmony. And in our sick writhings an internal process began, whose true meaning consisted in efforts at self-definition. We yearned for freedom, for self-definition.[10]

Carthage, of course, was in Africa, but this was not the issue. Ivanov believed that humanity was separating into two camps, for and against Christ, and that Russia must define herself in Christian terms. To him, the Christian people (*narod*) represented the "new barbarians," the carriers of the elemental creative forces destined to revitalize Russia, just as the barbarians had destroyed cultured Rome and initiated the Christian era.[11]

Ivanov's belief that the society of the future would be characterized by *sobornost'*, a free union of individuals, led him to support, with inner reservations (he liked "the idea of anarchy," but not necessarily its literal implementation), Georgii Chulkov's doctrine of Mystical Anarchism and to provide an introductory essay, "On the Non-Acceptance of the World,"[12] for Chulkov's pamphlet *On Mystical Anarchism*. Mystical Anarchism has been described elsewhere.[13] Briefly, its main tenets were the abolition of all external constraints on the individual (including morality, ethics, government, and law) and the achievement of *sobornost'* by means of some sort of "new religious synthesis," based on Eros, ecstasy, and mutual "inner experience." Ivanov and Chulkov based their theory on the "mystical person," who expressed himself through love and sacrifice as distinct from the egotistical power-seeking "empirical person." They never explained, however, who or what would be sacrificed and for what purpose, for their emphasis was on the attractive aspects of their doctrine—emotional gratification, belongingness, personal authenticity, harmony with one's self and others— rather than on self-denial. They objected to liberal individualism's emphasis on legal rights, which, in their view, separated people from one another and severed their link to the cosmos. Ivanov expected a new kind of individualism, which he called "supraindividualism," to emerge, linking the latter to *sobornost'* and describing it, not at all clearly, as the "affirmation of the inner unconscious mystical ties formed by their common link to a suprapersonal suprarational entity, the World Soul."[14] He objected to Kant's morality of duty, because he believed that human action should be motivated by love, and refused to bind the "flowing energies of the infinitely self-liberating soul by external norms or forms of any kind." Mystical Anarchism, he said, was "beyond 'yes' and 'no' "; its morality was the "morality of the passionate aspirations of the spirit," the affirmation of Eros and ecstasy.[15] He recognized that the "terrible freedom" he was proposing could be dangerous, but believed that Russia's self-definition required such freedom, for the "spirit breathes where it wishes" (an allusion to John 3:8).[16]

Struggling with God (*Bogoborchestvo*) is the most prominent theme of "On the Non-Acceptance of the World"; the entire essay is Promethean and rebellious in tone. Carrying the anti-legalism and anti-rationalism of the Slavophiles to an extreme conclusion, Ivanov rejected all external constraints on the individual and virtually ignored the Christian concept of original sin, for he believed that a new type of human being was in the process of being born. He attacked traditional Christianity and Buddhism for their passivity, their denial of this world, and rejected the "negativism" of the Ten Commandments ("Thou shalt not"). He described Mystical Anarchism as positive, life-affirming, as saying a "dazzling 'Yes'" to the world.[17]

The frequent recurrence of the words "differentiation" and "fragmentation" in his writings of this period underscores Ivanov's desire for reintegration, for "a new organic society," characterized by *sobornost'*. He insisted that self-affirmation must be expressed within the community and not apart from or against it, but also emphasized that the bonds which hold the community together must be internal (spiritual, emotional, psychological) and voluntary.

Ivanov's concept of *sobornost'* excluded parliaments, constitutions, legal guarantees, which he disdained as mere "formal freedoms" or "external freedoms." In his view, the "civic *obshchina*" (a legal and economic entity) was inferior to the "prophetic *obshchina*" (a holy or religious body). He considered political parties divisive and warned that the newly constituted Parliament (*Duma*) was superficial. "Only when the choral voice of the *obshchina* becomes the genuine referendum of the people's true will, will real political freedom exist."[18] "Liberal forms" such as a Parliament did not "answer [his] expectations"; he found liberalism devoid of a life-creating spirit, of a higher ideal.[19] Seeking in *sobornost'* an extrapolitical alternative to Western liberalism, Ivanov exalted myth over law and chorus over parliament. Myths, he said, constitute the link between the "inner experience" of the individual and the timeless suprapersonal I of the World Soul and have theurgical significance. Again and again he lauded the chorus, describing it as the "breeding ground of folk creativity and prophecy," an "instrument of myth-creation," an "organ of social self-definition," and maintaining that in a new cultic theater the embryo of a "new religious synthesis of life" could be formed. "Enough of spectators," he proclaimed, "we don't need circuses.

We want to gather together to create—'to act'—communally and not just to contemplate . . . Enough of pseudo-action; we want action."[20] Theater, rather than Parliament, would be the focus of a "new organic society," its unity cemented by the new all-national myth, created collectively by the people. Thus would the spiritual/emotional bonds of the "new organic society" be created.[21] The cultic theater, the seed of *sobornost'*, would replace the church and state as the basic institutions of the postrevolutionary era. He even tried to persuade Peter Struve to abandon his political theorizing to do cultural work.[22]

The questions Ivanov posed in his diary belie the Prometheanism and lawlessness of his public pronouncements. They testify to his deep misgivings about the course of events in 1905 and to his Christian loyalties. He asked himself whether the new New Year (1906) would bring more funerals, punishment, or a miracle and whether "the insatiable hunger of the despairing and feverishly rebelling people for the truth of God, the truth of the earth, and the law of Christ in people—deep, unconscious, and spiritual, this hunger which first of all and in spite of all torments the people in its deepest bowels—[will] be satisfied, when, by external appearances [it] rejects every truth and abolishes every law?" He grieved that "Russia rushes about without consciousness," that the spiritually unifying force necessary to achieve *sobornost'* is still lacking.[23]

The disappointing results of the Revolution of 1905 confirmed Ivanov's belief that politics is superficial. The October Manifesto turned out not to be the "white light of the sun of freedom . . . that would illuminate the quiet depths of azure *sobornost'*,"[24] but the prelude to even more bloodshed and violence. A flood of pornography followed the relaxation of the censorship laws. Contemporaries, appalled by the nihilism and immoralism of the youth, blamed them on Nietzsche. The subtleties of his own views (e.g., on anarchism as a metaphysical rather than a literal concept), Ivanov realized, escaped most people. Even Chulkov, he complained, did not understand him.[25] The death of his beloved wife, Lydia, in October, 1907, also had a chastening effect on him. For all these reasons Ivanov concluded that "Dionysus in Russia is dangerous."[26] Its result was not creativity, not a revaluation of values on a high theoretical plane, but nihilism, destructiveness, and vandalism. He blamed the absence of positive content in Russian nihilism for Russians' passivity, for their readiness to submit to authority. From then on, references to the ecstatic elements of the Dionysian rites, to Eros and ecstasy, virtually disappeared from his writings. He continued to regard the chorus as the "new democratic center" (by democratic, he really meant popular or *narodnyi*) and still referred to the "choral principle" and to Dionysus, but without the orgiasm. When he wrote of self-affirmation, it was as "Luciferian" or "demonic" self-affirmation, a condemnation of the "Luciferian wish to be as gods." Recognizing that the Dionysus myth, choral activity, and a cultic theater were too diffuse to foster *sobornost'* and too remote from most Russians' "inner experience" as well, he began searching for a more focused image or idea that would guide Russians through what he now believed would be a long and slow eschatological transition to the new era.

"The Russian Idea"

More than ever, Ivanov viewed the eschatological transition as a primarily internal process and concentrated especially on self-definition, for to him, the crucial distinction between *sobornost'* and impersonal collectivism was that in *sobornost'* the elements retained their own distinctive identity. He believed that the chaotic forces that led to the revolution had spent themselves and that the revolutionary ideals must be expressed in new and positive forms.[27] In Nietzschean terms, this implied the Apollonian principle (form, individuality, structure),[28] rather than Dionysian dissolution. From around 1908 on, Ivanov emphasized concrete and particular symbols, images, and ideas that would inspire and guide Russians as they progressed from "the real to the more real" (ultimate reality).[29] His vocabulary and imagery changed. The symbol became the Word with its explicit Christian connotations. Christianity and not just a vague "new religious synthesis" became the new all-unifying myth. (He treated Christianity, in rather unconventional terms, as a mythic vision.) The "face" of Jesus replaced the abstract archetype of Christ/Dionysus because it symbolized Jesus's personhood and because it distinguished Christianity from diffuse mysticism, from the faceless All of Buddhism, and from "impersonal" (soulless) secular ideologies. The cultic community became a transcendental church or nation (depending on the context), and the passions became the Russian soul. He placed ever-greater emphasis on articulating "the Russian idea," for he regarded nations (which he defined in cultural rather than political terms) as the persons of collective humanity. Specifically rejecting the notion of Russia as any "arithmetic computation of parties and groups," he insisted that Russia is a spiritual whole.[30] Each person, he admonished, is linked to his ancestors and his descendants in a chain that must not be broken.[31] Neither individuals nor groups may assert themselves apart from or against the whole. Soloviev's ideal of Free Theocracy became ever more important in his thought. In a 1910 speech, "The Religious Deed of Vladimir Solo-viev," he alluded to Russia's religious mission: to lose her personal soul in order to serve the principle of the universal Church—the totality of the mystic body of Christ—was presumably to be reborn in it.[32] Emphasizing the cosmic aspects of *sobornost'*, Ivanov frequently used the words *sobornost'* and "church" interchangeably. He defined the church as a mystical essence, an invisible union of souls which form the divine-human body, and explicitly excluded internal organizations or denominational collectives (e.g., of the sectarians) from his definition of a church.[33] Ivanov's idea of the church was complex and even contradictory but accentuated its transcendental character.

Most prominent in his writings of this period was emphasis on "the Rus-sian idea" as the needed integrating force. Every nation, he wrote, in a 1909 essay on the subject, had its own "idea," the essential quality that distin-guished it from other nations. It was a basic fact of history, "a product of the psychological substratum of the unconscious spheres of the collective [folk] soul" and should not be misunderstood as national egoism or confused with the concept of the State.[34] Asserting that Russians' collective inner experience was different from that of other nations, even other Christian nations, Ivanov repeated the long-standing platitude (which misrepresents Western beliefs) that the Russian emphasis on Easter rather than on Christ-mas testifies to the Russian belief that Golgotha, self-sacrifice, will be followed by Resurrection in "Divine All-Unity."

He insisted that the "Russian idea" was a Christian idea and contrasted the "primitive" or "organic" Christian culture to the "critical culture" of the modern era marked by differentiation, egoism, and self-will—the culture of the "scions of Cain."[35] "Primitive culture" however, was characterized by *sobornost'*; a basic conception of the divine and the human permeates every aspect of its life and is embodied in common principles, laws, and social norms that are recognized by all.[36] (Note his implicit acknowledgement of the need for law.)[37] He considered Christianity a form of "primitive culture" which arose in response to the "critical culture" of Rome and ultimately prevailed over it because the new Christian faith was couched in the form of mystery. All new religious truths, Ivanov believed, must be "hidden in mystery, in the form of myth." The religious innovations of Pisistratus, for example, founder of the Orphic mystery religion, were so in tune with the subliminal yearnings of the people that their novelty was forgotten. Pisistra-tus is remembered as a tyrant, but not as a renegade from the popular faith. By contrast, Socrates, the founder of critical rationalism, was perceived as a heretic and a danger to the state; he did not understand the people, and

they did not understand him.[38] The secular Russian intelligentsia has repeated the error of Socrates. Religious innovations (he did not specify what
these would be) must be expressed in mythic form and incorporated into
Christian mystery, because the Russian soul is Christian. It "expresses the
central Christian idea, the categorical imperative of the descent and burial
of the light and the categorical postulate of the Resurrection."[39] In "going
to the people," the intelligentsia followed the imperative of descent, but the
people wished to ascend, to be resurrected. Intelligentsia and people could
meet and be reunited on the basis of an all-Russian idea.

Evoking religious/mythopoetic imagery, Ivanov explained that the "imperative of descent, this call to the dark earth," is an act of love and
sacrifice, the bringing down of the divine Light into the darkness of the
lower spheres that seek illuminations. As such it represents a reformulation
of the Russian image of the kenotic Christ and a reaffirmation of the Christian ideal of sacrifice and resurrection. "In Christianity, the law of self-
preservation is turned into the law of the preservation of the light—not of
the empirical person but its suprapersonal divine content." The intelligentsia
"always knew" that they had to go to the people, merge with them, but they
did not realize that the Christian narod declined to merge with the atheistic
intelligentsia. Their merger, Ivanov maintained, could occur only in a third
world, in the still invisible "light of Christ." The phrase has a double
meaning: the first is conventionally Christian, but the second alludes to
Anthroposophy, the occult doctrine of Rudolf Steiner, which held that
Christ's spirit resides in the cosmic ether and will be visible to man after the
Second Coming. For this to occur, however, "the law of the descent of the
light must be realized in harmony with the law of the preservation of the
light, not of the empirical person, but of its suprapersonal divine content."[40]
The intelligentsia must strengthen the light in itself, purify itself, be initiated
in the word of Christ, and only then should it act—descend to the people in
the name of God.[41] This too is an allusion to Anthroposophy; purification,
initiation, and action allude to the stages of becoming an adept of a secret
society, a kind of "inner church." The descent of the divine Light into the
darkness of the lower spheres is a tenet of Anthroposophy also, as well as
of Gnosticism, the Kabbala, and Elena Blavatskaia's Theosophy.[42]

Ivanov maintained that the Russian idea revealed "the deepest meaning
of our striving for all-nationality, our energy of sovlechenie—in our yearning for descent and service."[43] Exactly what Ivanov meant by sovlechenie,
however, is not clear, for he provided several definitions and used the term
in different contexts, among them: casting off material possessions and

defenses, laying oneself bare in order to merge spiritually with others, and unmasking hypocrisy and lies. All Ivanov's definitions of *sovlechenie*, however, denote his rejection of egoism, his emphasis on voluntary union, and his conception of *sovlechenie* as passion, energy, will, and as the entelechy of the Russian idea, the moving force of Russian life. In "On the Russian Idea" (1909), Ivanov attributed the intelligentsia's descent to the people to the "passion of *sovlechenie*," and alluded to *sovlechenie* as the basic trait of the Russian character, the "creative energy in our souls." He "defined" it, not at all clearly, as the "yearning to incorporate oneself into every chasuble, every vestment, and to envelop every mask and decoration with the naked truth of things."[44] He also maintained that the Russian "love for descent" was apparent in all forms of *sovlechenie*, positively and negatively. According to Ivanov, the bold, incorruptible, and relentlessly logical nature of Russian thought stemmed from *sovlechenie*, but so did the Russian intelligentsia's striving to deflate values, to create idols; its nihilism; its hatred of any culture that isolates, elevates, and attains; its tendency to reduce everything to the same level.[45] In a 1908 essay, however, Ivanov counterposed *sovlechenie* to the law of Moses, stating that the latter was based on natural law—the law of self-preservation of the "empirical person," a biological entity—while *sovlechenie* pertained to the "mystical person."[46] In this context he "defined" *sovlechenie* as the morality of "self-destruction" practiced by mystics and Christians which enables them to transcend the limitations of the natural order, including a sense of property. Elsewhere in the 1908 essay, however, Ivanov "defined" *sovlechenie* as "self-dissipation," associating it, ambiguously, with the destruction of the ego which precedes the discovery of one's authentic inner self prior to its merging with the cosmos. He also related *sovlechenie* to the Christian conception of perfect love which overcomes fear (including, according to Ivanov, fear of self-annihilation) and to Zarathustra's concept of "overflowing," a giving of oneself from plenitude, from love, rather than from the negative motivations of guilt or self-denying altruism, and to Nietzsche's concept of "love for the distant." That Ivanov was unable to provide a clear and consistent definition of what he considered the most basic aspect of the Russian identity did not bode well for the realization of his vision of *sobornost'*.

As Ivanov's concept of *sobornost'* became ever more otherworldly, the borders between individual and community faded, and the person was virtually submerged in mystical "all-unity." More oriented to the distant past and to the distant future than to the present, he had no interest at all in practical issues. Even the occasional references to the events and circumstances of the real world that appear in his writings, e.g., the need for a new kind of church, show that he perceived them through the filters of a mystical prism. Although new political events—World War I and the Revolutions of 1917— entered into his consideration of *sobornost'*, its otherworldly character not only persisted, but became even more emphatic.

World War I stimulated Ivanov's Slavophile sentiments, reawakened his sense of eschatological imminence, and motivated him to reinterpret Slavophilism along "democratic" lines. Like many of his compatriots, he believed that the war had opened a new, constructive era. Proclaiming that "the time is Slavophilizing" and that a suprapersonal, supranational force was moving Russians toward voluntary self-definition,[47] he endorsed the Slavophile tenet that Russia is a mystical entity, quoted Tiutchev's verse "one must simply believe in Russia," and asserted that Soloviev had been a Slavophile at heart. He lauded Slavophilism as a metaphysic of national self-definition, an intrinsically religious metaphysic, because of the Slavophile emphasis on Holy Russia. But he considered Slavophilism dangerous when utilized to provide theoretical justification for the existing system and/or as a progressive cloak for reactionary views, e.g., Danilevsky's concept of biologically determined "cultural types." To Ivanov the "sin" of Slavophilism was its inclusion of factors extraneous to purely spiritual experience, such as a state church, in its metaphysic.

The Slavophiles had criticized Western political thought for viewing state power as an alien force, as the result of military conquest and the consequent subordination of the populace. Following this reasoning, Ivanov claimed that Western liberalism contained a fatal contradiction: an increase in popular freedom entailed the disintegration of state power. (The liberal Provisional Government did disintegrate in 1917, but Western governments have become more powerful than ever.) By contrast, Ivanov argued, Slavophilism contains the seeds of a different resolution, full of popular freedom and a transcendental state, because it is based, not on the feudal contractual concept of governmental power (nor on the liberal concept of the social contract that followed it), but on the Roman concept of "deposition." Typically, Ivanov neglected to define "full popular freedom" and "transcendental state," nor did he discuss practical issues, such as who would govern or how an invisible entity with no formal structure would be governed. He simply stated that the popular will is "deposited" in the hands of the person or persons called to power (e.g., the Varangians) and that in this act of "deposition," popular sovereignty is thereby affirmed, not diminished, for it has simply redefined itself as monarchical rule. The monarch, moreover, is responsible to God. This implicit popular sovereignty, Ivanov continued, accounts for the Tsar's distrust of the Slavophiles, because the concept of "deposition" can be turned around and used to justify a new democratic order based on religion:

> It is clear that the national and religious conception of the desired growth in our political freedom is formulated in the living legacy of the Slavophile ideal—the readiness of the people, in degree corresponding to the development of its historical growth, to accept ever more [responsibility] on itself and ultimately, full religious responsibility for the fate of the fatherland.[48]

The immanent sanction Slavophilism accorded the monarch thus became a transcendental sanction, as the state itself achieved *sobornost'* by turning into a free theocracy based on internal and voluntary bonds. Presumably the monarch dissolved the state, but this is by no means clear. Ivanov's attempt to democratize Slavophilism was too vague and impractical to serve as a realistic alternative to either democracy or secular liberalism or socialism.

The otherworldly nature of Ivanov's concept of *sobornost'* is evident in a 1916 essay, "Legion and *sobornost'*." The title is an allusion to the Roman Legions, which Ivanov connected, for reasons he did not fully explain, with the "mystery of evil" because of their impersonality, their "facelessness." In his eyes, the Germans were a variant of the Roman legions, a "human ant-hill," a "new form of evolution of homo sapiens," a Leviathan, a "higher form of the prehuman natural organism," a soulless, mechanical entity.[49] He opposed efforts to organize Russia for the war because he considered organization "a German principle." The Russian principle, he said, is *sobornost'*, a union of persons in which each person has his own singular, unrepeatable, and unique essence, his creative freedom, "his own word," but all are united as "one Word," i.e., are united in God. He reaffirmed his view of *sobornost'* as a target or a goal rather than a given entity. It has never existed in its entirety on earth, and he once again compared it to the Spirit, "which breathes where it wishes."[50] Avoiding any explanation of how Russia would conduct a war without organization, Ivanov simply assumed that if Russians were united by the same Christian ideal, all would be well. Philosophers would clarify its meaning and artists would develop the "creative life forms" necessary for its realization. Elsewhere he described *sobornost'* as the "Slavic recognition of the supreme degree of human common life";[51] his use of the term Slavic rather than Russian indicates his belief in the "inner unity of the Slavic world." Respectful of the Polish "national idea,"[52] Ivanov believed in an ecumenical *sobornost'* of nationalities, as did Soloviev. Nationalism, he said, was not *sobornost'*, but a confusion of the "old national idea" with *raison d'état*.

The February Revolution of 1917 reinforced his eschatological expectations and deepened his conviction that only religious regeneration could save Russia. He continued to insist that Christian *sobornost'* was invisible and internal and reaffirmed his argument that Russian life must be based on a new principle which recognizes holiness as the highest virtue. "Russia stands at the threshold of another existence—and sees God as she thirsts for Him." But the guard at the door, seeing her in savage distortion, says, "This is not Russia," in effect, throwing her into the abyss. To emerge from it, Russia must define her authentic self, change internally, become religious.[53] He described the revolution as not a movement, but a state, a state of chaos, formlessness, and the Russian soul as crossing through a gloomy desert of nihilism, "where only beasts live and where man himself is becoming a beast."[54] Alluding to "terror above and terror below," he complained that no new values had been created because the revolution had ignored religion, the source of values, and there was no sense of unity. Each looked out for himself, affirmed himself against the whole and committed treason against it.[55] As an example of the harmful effects of the non-religious character of the revolution, Ivanov cited a dialogue between Kerensky and a mutinous soldier. Kerensky had extolled the army's duty to freedom and social democracy, but the soldier replied that freedom is useless to the dead. Taken aback, Kerensky did not know what to say. Ivanov believed that Kerensky should have explained the Christian faith in the immortal soul, the Christian precept of self-sacrifice, and the Christian doctrine which holds freedom to be the basis of human relations.[56]

Ivanov attributed the wavering of the Provisional Government to the absence of a unifying religious idea and insisted that religion is not a private matter. Again and again he asserted the need for the principle of a new life, the religious awakening of the people, the realization of Christian truth on earth, and he specifically warned against attempts to return to the past. He bitterly criticized the intelligentsia for its attempt to inscribe "on naked empty tablets . . . the new statutes of the rootless man-God."[57] This statement alludes, simultaneously, to John Locke's concept of the *tabula rasa* (the epistemological basis for liberalism and rationalism), Nietzsche's injunction to break the old tablets of values, and Dostoevsky's warning of the advent of the man-God. Ivanov held the intelligentsia responsible for the present turmoil, because it taught hatred of religion and contempt for the past; he called for national repentance as the first step toward a new national self-definition, as evidence that Russia was not really a mass of mutinous slaves.

A truly creative revolution, a real democracy, he insisted, required the religious awakening of the Russian people. The revolution will either leave Russia a "heap of dried bones or it will inspire real regeneration."[58]

"Monantropism"

Ivanov's final vision of *sobornost'* reflects his interpretation of the Bolshevik Revolution and Civil War as a test or trial, part of the eschatological transition to a new order. He described his generation as lost in a labyrinth in which all exits are enveloped in flames; but, determined not to succumb to despair, he still believed that somehow man would survive this ordeal by fire and find his way back to the whole, become part of a living universal personality. He insisted on seeing the seeds of a new birth. In his 1919 essay, "On the Crisis of Humanism," Ivanov described an emotional shift (*sdvig*), a watershed in human history.[59] In contrast to Alexander Blok, whose essay "The Collapse of Humanism" (also 1919) foretold the end of history, Ivanov insisted on the importance of retaining ties with the past. The new concept of *sobornost'* ("Monantropism," see below) which he advanced in this essay implicitly related contemporary trends to ancient Greece and was, perhaps, his way of keeping faith with his ideal. Obliquely he was responding to the truly inhuman conditions of the Civil War years and to the loss of personal freedom under "war communism," aestheticizing them as parts of a new cosmic process.

"On the Crisis of Humanism," subtitled "Toward a Morphology of Contemporary Culture and on Contemporary Psychology," can be considered the sequel to his 1905 essay "The Crisis of Individualism." In 1905 he had proclaimed the death of individualism, but still championed a kind of humanism ("the sovereign affirmation of the human in ourselves") and the Greek ideal of a harmonious person. In his 1919 essay he announced the death of classical humanism as well. He redefined humanism as "the ethical-aesthetic norms that demarcate the relation of man to all that marks or serves the internal indications of [his] natural belongingness to humankind," noted that it favored the harmonious development of the person, and claimed that it was founded on the "autarky" of the harmonious person.[60] Autarky, a Greek word, was adopted by the Germans in World War I to describe a self-sufficient war economy; Ivanov's application of this term to humanism signals his changed orientation, his rejection of the humanism that began in Greece and had dominated European thought since the Renaissance. Incidentally, he did not consider Plato and Aristotle to be humanists, charging that their political emphasis destroyed the harmonious human personality and created invidious distinctions between people such as "slave" and "free." He found Aristotle's definition of man as a political animal particularly objectionable.

He believed that humanity was now in the process of moving beyond humanism, of returning to the "other side of humanism," to the Hellas of the pre-Socratic thinkers and of Dionysus, i.e., to a different kind of humanism, which he called "monantropism." Etymologically, the term means movement toward one-man-ness or a feeling of one-man-ness. "Monantropism," Ivanov explained, entailed the development of new feelings, new values, the fostering of a mythological rather than a rational consciousness. But it was too soon to predict what the new forms would be, except to state that they would enable man to overcome his old limits (his ego) and to achieve *sobornost'*. He considered the music of Skriabin and the writings of Dostoevsky, Soloviev, and Fyodorov to be portents of "monantropism" and noted that Indian mystics had always realized that man is one. But the new humanism, he asserted, inspired by Christ, would have a face, personhood, be "one Adam."[61] This is a reference to Adam Kadmon, the primordial man of the *Kabbala,* reborn (according to Christians) in Jesus Christ. Ivanov regarded Jesus's "face" as the visible symbol of the new Russia that he still hoped was being born. Contrasting Christian mysticism with the "faceless" mysticism of the Buddhist Nirvana, Ivanov constantly emphasized that Jesus was resurrected, but Buddha was not.

In 1919, Ivanov was employed by TEO, (*Teatral'nyi otdel Narkomprosa*), the theatrical section of the Commissariat of Enlightenment. His anti-individualism, his belief in folk creativity and in the chorus as a democratic entity, were, in some respects, compatible with the Bolshevik desire to create a new culture. The Bolsheviks, then preoccupied with economic collapse and civil war, had not yet defined their own cultural policy and were willing to work with non-Party intellectuals. Ivanov, for his part, may have thought he could shape post-revolutionary culture, or he may simply have needed employment. He wrote articles for *Theater Herald* (*Vestnik teatra*), the organ of TEO, and contributed an introduction to the 1919 Russian translation of Romain Rolland's *Théatre du peuple* [*Narodnyi teatr*].[62] These writings contain allusions to *sobornost'*, "spiritual collective" and "folk collective," but the word "proletariat" is conspicuously absent. Ivanov's concept of *sobornost'* directly contradicted the Bolsheviks' political emphasis, for his goal was reconciliation, harmony, and religious awakening, while the Bolsheviks wished to foster revolutionary militance, a specifically proletarian consciousness, and atheism. Nevertheless, Ivanov's ideas of a cultic theater were a major source of the mass festivals and civic rituals of the early Soviet period and also influenced early Soviet political theater.[63] Ivanov protested against the socialist tendentiousness of the mass festivals and against using festivals for political purposes, but to no avail.[64] Indeed, he was visited and interrogated (but not arrested) by the Cheka sometime in 1919.[65] Unable to secure permission to leave Russia,[66] Ivanov did manage to gain admission to the sanatorium where, in June 1920, he and Mikhail Gershenzon wrote their famous "Correspondence."

The general thrust of Ivanov's "letters" is well known; they reassert the need for cultural continuity, allude to the "original sin of individuation," and regard cults as a manifestation of the eternal longing for unity.[67] They exude the same will to integration that in 1919 he had called "monantropism." But I wish here to call attention to Ivanov's reference to Jean Jacques Rousseau, the progenitor, in a sense, of political romanticism and its successor ideologies of the "right" and "left." Ivanov rejected Rousseau's dream that if society could "unlearn" to read and write, the seductions of culture would be banished. The dream, he said, had originated in Rousseau's lack of religious faith. "The new society without the muses and the letters that you [Gershenzon] envision . . . is a delusion of decadence, like all Rousseauism, unless it is a community of prayer and not a new crop of human beings as corrupt as we are." And, continuing in the same spirit: a *tabula rasa* is impossible; "the very fountainhead of our spiritual psychic life is poisoned. . . . the Orphic and Biblical assertion of some 'original sin' is, alas, no lie."[68] Ivanov was alluding here to Rousseau's *Discourse on the Origins of Inequality* (1755), which was interpreted by many Russians, most notably Tolstoi (who had been a disciple of Rousseau since the age of fifteen), as an injunction to eschew culture and live the simple, natural life of the peasant. A lover of culture, Ivanov opposed "simplification" (*oproshchenie*), but was as vehemently anti-individualist as the Rousseau who wrote *The Social Contract* (1762).

There are other significant elements of affinity between the two thinkers which link Rousseau's civil religion to Ivanov's "all-national myth" and both of them to the civic rituals and mass festivals of the early Soviet period. Ivanov's complaint in "The Crisis of Individualism" that individualism stifles individuality is similar in spirit to Rousseau's statement (in the *Confessions*), "I am like no one in the whole world. I may be no better, but at least I am different" and recalls Rousseau's critique of French society's emphasis on externals as well.[69] Ivanov's political views echo in important respects Rousseau's rejection of English liberalism, in particular John Locke's concept of the Social Contract based on mutual self-interest. Rousseau's critique of what was later called bourgeois society became part of the mainstream of radical thought and, in Russia, shaped both Westernizer and Slavophile perceptions of the West.

The viability of Rousseau's and Ivanov's respective social ideals depends on members of society subordinating themselves to the whole and identifying with it. To accomplish this goal, Rousseau relied primarily, but not exclusively, on law. His advocacy of a civil religion in *The Social Contract*, however, demonstrates that he was just as aware as Ivanov of the need to enlist supernatural forces. There are differences in these concepts, to be sure, but in terms of their social function (restricting self-will) Rousseau's civil religion is the equivalent of Ivanov's "all-national myth" or "Russian idea." Neither considered Parliament the voice of the people. Popular participation is an essential element in their respective visions of the good society. Rousseau advocated direct democracy and realized the need to go beyond the laws. Without an active citizenry, Rousseau warned, the "General Will" would fall dumb. Ivanov insisted that the spectators must be active, must participate in creating the "all-national myth." Both thinkers sought to integrate the individual in a new supraindividual entity: the community as collective personality for Rousseau, "monantropism" for Ivanov. Rousseau's model was Geneva, a small community where everyone knew everyone: in a word, not an impersonal society, but a kind of *obshchina*.

Even Ivanov's theatrical views are similar to Rousseau's. In his *Letter to d'Alembert on the Theater* (1758),[70] Rousseau expressed his desire for a new theater, one that would not merely entertain but uplift. He admired the theater of ancient Greece as a school of civic virtue, condemned the "cellar theater" (small private theaters) of his day, and desired a truly national theater with performances in the open air, as in ancient Greece. He even advocated festivals that would unite the people with "sweet bonds of pleasure and joy." "Let the spectators become an entertainment to themselves, make them actors themselves," Rousseau wrote, "Do it so that each sees and loves himself in the others, so that all will be better united." He believed that a revived Greek theater and national festivals would provide the moral inspiration and civil instruction his social ideal required. The national festivals of the French Revolution derive from Rousseau's ideas on a new theater. Friedrich von Schiller and Romain Rolland incorporated Rousseau's vision into their own aesthetics, which Ivanov knew, and he was almost certainly familiar with Rousseau's political thought as well.

My point is that an unexpected congruity of ideals and values led to similar results. Ivanov's and Rousseau's theatrical ideas were part of a larger social ideal which was too diffuse, too elusive, to be implemented without serious distortion. Rousseau's vision of civic virtue inspired Robespierre's

"Republic of Virtue," and his ideal of an integral community led to the "totalitarian democracy" of the Jacobins.[71] Similarly, Ivanov's theories on creating a collective consciousness, his anti-individualism, and his mystique of sacrifice were easily adapted by the Bolsheviks for their own purposes.

The above is not to deny, of course, the differences which flow from Rousseau's political emphasis and from Ivanov's apolitical stance, nor the fact that Ivanov specifically rejected aspects of Rousseau's and Rolland's theatrical aesthetics, claiming that they ignored the aesthetic demands of the theater and separated art and life instead of combining them.[72] Moreover, Rousseau, writing at the peak of the Enlightenment, was confident of the ability of human reason to shape the ideal society, while Ivanov opposed such presumption and warned against

> establishing outward apparent bonds, where the very roots of conscious-
> ness, the blood vessels, as it were, of our spiritual selves, are not interwoven
> into a single web. In the ultimate depths, where we cannot reach, we all
> form a single universal-circulating system, feeding the single heart of
> humanity.[73]

He predicted that culture would become a cult of God and of the earth and advocated genuine creative freedom (which he never defined) rather than misguided attempts to return to nature.

Conclusion

That Ivanov's vision of *sobornost'* was never realized is not surprising. He himself wavered on whether or not it was a spiritual ideal which would ever be totally realized on this earth. But his progression from cultic theater to the Russian idea to "monantropism," which steadily circumscribed the realm of freedom, serves an object lesson on the danger of an idealism untempered by practicality. Ivanov's diagnosis of the ills of his time was correct, but incomplete. His belief that the political and social conflicts of his time were rooted in a profound spiritual crisis indeed reflected reality. The Orthodox consensus that had cemented traditional Russian society together and given each person his/her place in society and in the cosmos had lost its compelling power. To restore the lost unity, it would have had to be reformulated on a new basis. But Ivanov was treating only one dimension of the problem. Focusing exclusively on internal issues (spiritual, psychological), he ignored the external dimensions of human existence (politics, economics) and never tried to work out the connections between the spiritual and the temporal realms. Intent on avoiding the use of force and detesting materialism, he refused even to consider what belongs to Caesar (the government) and what belongs to God. As the impossibility of combining unlimited self-affirmation and communitarianism became obvious, Ivanov steadily abandoned his optimistic vision of a loosely knit "new organic society," redefined self-affirmation to mean self-definition, and ended up regarding individuation itself as a sin. Sacrifice rather than self-fulfillment became ever more important in his thought. His final vision of *sobornost'*, "monantropism," aestheticized rather than challenged the Bolshevik suppression of the individual and was, in its own way, as much of an integral vision as the integral nationalisms of late nineteenth and early twentieth century Europe. There was however, a major difference. Integral nationalism makes politics into a religion; it subordinates all aspects of life to the state. Ivanov wished to transcend politics altogether and eliminate the state. He was an advocate of the idea of anarchy.

Ivanov's writings are replete with references to what he considered transcendental concepts or metaphysical principles—the idea of anarchy, the idea of a state, the idea of a church, the idea of a nation—but he did not necessarily intend for them to be taken literally. Neither did he offer any guidance on how to embody, even partly, a transcendental idea on earth. An extremely subtle, even evasive, thinker, he regarded words as symbols of a mysterious higher reality and was not particularly careful about definitions. He never clarified the difference between individuality and individualism, nor did he ever explain exactly what he meant by the person or his/her "face." Most importantly, in terms of *sobornost'*, he never defined freedom, except to state that it excluded force. It is clear, however, particularly after his "cultic theater" period, that to Ivanov freedom was an internal concept, similar, in some respects, to the German concept of "inner freedom" described by Leonard Krieger in *The German Idea of Freedom*.[74] For all practical purposes, Ivanov's version of "inner freedom" amounted to a mystic withdrawal from the conflict-ridden world of politics. Thus he never really grappled with the problem of how to prevent the organic society he valued from deteriorating into the "facelessness" he detested, symbolized to him by the Roman legions, by worldly empire. To use the terminology of the Greek tragedy he loved, this was his "fatal flaw."

Notes

1. I am indebted to Fr. John Meyendorf of Fordham University and St. Vladimir's Orthodox Seminary for this information.
2. Nicholas Riasanovsky, "Khomiakov and *Sobornost'*," in Ernest J.

Simmons, ed., *Continuity and Change in Russian and Soviet Thought* (Cambridge, Mass., 1955), 189.

3. O. Deshat, "Vvedenie," Vyacheslav Ivanov, *Sobranie sochinenii,* 4 vols. to date, 1 (Brussels, 1970), 9–16. Henceforth cited as *Sob.* Ivanov left Russia to study in Germany, returning to stay in 1904, and settled in St. Petersburg. In 1912 he left Russia again and upon his return in 1913, settled in Moscow. See also V. Ivanov, "Avtobiograficheskoe pis'mo," 2, 13.

4. For the influence of Nietzsche, see *Sob.* 2:19–20; for Soloviev, "Religioznoe delo Vladimira Solovieva," *Sob.* 3:295–306.

5. *Dionis i pradionisiistvo* (Baku, 1923). In contrast to his earlier study, "The Religions of the Suffering God," serialized in *New Path* (*Novyi Put'*) and *Problems of Life* (*Voprosy zhizni*) in 1904–5, which focused on the mystical and sacrificial elements of the Dionysian rites, the dissertation treated the sources of the religion itself.

6. Isolated from *émigré* circles, for many years Ivanov did not publish in their journals, refrained from direct criticism of the Soviet regime, and was actually quite ambivalent about it.

7. "Éstetika i ispovedanie," *Vesy*, no. 11, (1908), p. 48.

8. *Po zvezdam*, (St. Petersburg, 1909), 54–55; henceforth cited as *Pz*.

9. See, for example, his essays "Poet i chern'," "Novye maski," "Nitsshe i Dionis," "Vagner i dionisovo deistvo," reprinted in *Pz*.

10. *Pz.*, 311–12. This passage was written in the spring of 1905 and incorporated into his 1909 essay "The Russian Idea."

11. *Pz.*, 245.

12. *Pz.*, 103–22. "Ideia nepriiatiia mira" is not included in the reprint edition of *O misticheskom anarkhizme* (Letchworth, 1971); original edition St. Petersburg, 1906.

13. For details, see Bernice Glatzer Rosenthal, "The Transmutation of the Symbolist Ethos: Mystical Anarchism and the Revolution of 1905," *Slavic Review* (December 1977), 608–27.

14. *Pz.*, 118, 121.

15. *Pz.*, 119, 120, 122. See also his remarks on "limitless inner freedom" and his view of *sobornost'* as the "supreme affirmation of ultimate freedom," *Ibid.*

16. *Pz.*, 90.

17. *Pz.*, 108.

18. *Pz.*, 218; see also 213–14, 285.

19. *Sob.* 2:215.

20. In "Novaia organicheskaia epokha i teatr budushchego," *Pz.* 205–6.

21. *Pz.*, 189–219.

22. *Sob.* 2:746 (diary entry June 5, 1906).

23. *Sob.* 3:354–55. (This was written in 1906 and incorporated into a 1917 essay).

24. *Sob.* 1:90.

25. *Sob.* 2:787. (diary entry August 11, 1908).

26. *Pz.*, 360.

27. *Sob.* 2:215.

28. Ivanov was one of the principals in the founding of the new symbolist journal *Apollon* in 1909. Until then, he had virtually ignored Nietzsche's Apollonian principle.

29. For Ivanov's distinction between "realistic" and "idealistic" symbolism, see "Dve stikhii v sovremennom simvolizme," *Sob.* 2:536–61.

30. *Sob.* 3:360.

31. *Sob.* 3:129. The phraseology here is reminiscent of Edmund Burke's *Reflections on the French Revolution*, except that the conservative Burke was arguing for an empirical politics while Ivanov looked forward to a radically new apolitical era.

32. "Religioznoe delo Vladimira Solovieva," *Sob.* 3:306. In the same essay (p. 301) Ivanov stated that the church must assume a new form that would correspond with the differentiated aspects of contemporary culture (i.e., not a state Church), that it cannot be a body, because it is a mystery, and that the Church is an invisible union of souls that form the divine-human body. He now regarded history as humanity's progress to divine-humanity—Soloviev's idea.

33. *Sob.* 3:298.

34. "O Russkoi idee," *Pz.* 309–337; see esp. 316. This is an allusion to Petr Struve's article, "The Intelligentsia and the National Face," (Petr Struve, "Intelligentsia i national'noe litso," *Slovo*, March 10, 1909). Ivanov considered the search for the "national face" the one positive outcome of the Revolution of 1905, but disagreed with Struve's emphasis on political power and economic development.

35. *Pz.*, 325.

36. *Pz.*, 321.

37. In a 1908 article, "On Laws and Ties" ("O zakone i sviazi") he had referred to Zarathustra as a law-giver, not just a law-breaker, but still wanted to replace the Ten Commandments with a positive morality. *Sob.* 3:126–31.

38. *Pz.*, 323. Note the similarity to Nietzsche's critique of Socratic rationalism.

39. *Pz.*, 334–35.

40. *Pz.*, 332–35.

41. *Pz.*, 336.

42. Theosophy and Anthroposophy had many adherents among the intelligentsia at the time. Ivanov was introduced to Anthroposophy by Anna Mintslova, Rudolf Steiner's emissary to Russia. For details, see Maria Carlson, "Ivanov—Belyj—Minclova: the Mystic Triangle," in *Cultura e Memoria (Atti del terzo Simposio Internationale dedicato a Vjačeslav Ivanov)*, ed. Fausto Malcovati (Florence, 1988) 1, 63–80.

43. *Pz.*, 331.

44. *Pz.*, 327–28; see also p. 330.

45. *Pz.*, 327–30.

46. *Sob.* 3:126–27; 131.

47. "Zhivoe predanie," *Sob.* 3:340. The phrase "the time is Slavophilizing" is from a speech by Vladimir Ern.

48. *Sob.* 3:346.

49. "Legion i sobornost'," *Sob.* 3:255.

50. *Sob.* 3:260.

51. *Sob.* 3:261.

52. *Sob.* 4:655–72.

53. "Revoliutsiia i narodnoe samoopredelenie," *Sob.* 3:358.

54. *Sob.* 3:362.

55. *Sob.* 3:359.

56. *Sob.* 3:361.

57. *Sob.* 3:357.

58. *Sob.* 3:364. See p. 360 for Ivanov's belief that religion is not just a private matter.

59. "Krizis individualizma," *Pz.*, 86–101; "O krizise gumanizma i k morfologii sovremennoi kul'tury i o psikhologii sovremennosti," *Sob.* 3:368–82. One of the reasons for Ivanov's attack on the orthographic reform in *Iz glubiny* was his conviction that it broke the "sacred links" to the past.

60. *Sob.* 3:373, 377.

61. *Sob.* 3:378–80.

62. Articles published in *Vestnik teatra* are: "Zerkalo iskusstva," 1919, no. 4, pp. 1–2; "K voprosu ob organizatsii tvorcheskikh sil narodnogo kollektiva v oblasti khudozhestvennogo deistva," 1919, no. 26. p. 4; "O Vagnere," 1919, no. 31–32; and "Mnozhestvo i lichnost', v deistve," 1920, no. 62. The latter is reprinted in *Sob.* 2:219. I am grateful to Lars Kleberg for providing me with a copy of Ivanov's introduction to *Narodnyi teatr* (Petrograd-Moscow, 1919).

63. Konstantin Rudnitsky, *Russian and Soviet Theater*, trans. Roxane Permar (New York, 1988), 7–14.

64. See A. I. Mazaev, *Prazdnik kak sotsial'no-khudozhestvennoe iavlenie* (Moscow, 1978), p. 151. Mazaev finds a hint of annoyance in Ivanov's remark that "since the theater has been seized by the street, the street can be turned into a theater." Mazaev also observes that the liturgical quality of Ivanov's choral principle tended to neutralize revolutionary passion.

65. Lidia Ivanova, "Vospominaniia o Viacheslave Ivanove," *Novyi zhurnal*, no. 149 (December 1982): 122.

66. Lunacharsky had given Ivanov (and Konstantin Bal'mont, the symbolist poet) permission to leave Russia with his family on condition that they refrain from speaking openly against the Soviet regime, but Bal'mont violated the agreement as soon as he reached Reval; as a result, Ivanov's permit was cancelled. For his ailing third wife, Vera, this was tantamount to a death sentence; she died soon after.

67. "A Corner to Corner Correspondence," trans. Gertrude Vakar, in Marc Raeff, ed., *Russian Intellectual History, An Anthology* (New York, 1966), 396.

68. Ibid., 380.

69. *Confessions*, trans. J. M. Cohen (Middlesex, 1967), 17.

70. Trans. Allan Bloom (Glencoe, Ill., 1960), 125–26; for Rousseau's love of the Greek theater see 78–79.

71. This is the argument of Jacob Talmon, *The Origins of Totalitarian Democracy* (New York, 1970).

72. "Predislovie," *Narodnyi teatr*, xiii.

73. "A Corner to Corner Correspondence," 396.

74. Leonard Krieger, *The German Idea of Freedom* (Boston, 1957). According to Krieger, the German concept of inner freedom, which incorporated individual freedom in the state, fostered political quietism, subordinated the individual to the state, and ultimately led to Naziism. See especially pp. 86–138 on Kant and Hegel.

"ПОРУЧИК КИЖЕ" ["LIEUTENANT KIZHE"]

A Discussion[1]

JERRY T. HEIL

The increasing interest in recent years in Iurii Tynianov (b. 1894 in Vitebsk, d. 1943 in Moscow), in the West as well as in the Soviet Union, makes it essential that all of Tynianov's written work undergo systematic scrutiny. This written work includes novels, stories, journalistic writings and theoretical essays on both literary and film topics, and filmscripts.

The most famous of Tynianov's filmscripts was for the FEKS version of SHINEL' [THE OVERCOAT], made in 1926, directed by Kozintsev and Trauberg.[2] It is appropriate to say a few things here about SHINEL' (which is well known in the United States) as a sort of "preface" to the discussion of PORUCHIK KIZHE (which has not been shown in the United States since 1934). SHINEL' was a much-disputed film, to say the least, but it was so well known that it has never been ignored, even if it was only "just mentioned" in the USSR during periods of anti-formalism. The most objectionable thing about this film was that it dared to make radical changes in Gogol's story of the same title (published in 1842). It amused only a few critics by creating, for the first half of the film, a **young** Akakii Akakievich Bashmachkin (this *Vorgeschichte* is loosely adapted from the character of the artist, Piskarev, in another story, *Nevskii Prospekt* [1833–34]); its "distortion" of the canons of the realist cinema through reliance on **grotesque hyperbole** of photographic images further assured the wrath of the critics. As Tynianov wrote in a belated, mocking rejoinder (in 1929), he was called "an illiterate boor" (*bezgramotnyi naglets*), and he and the directors were chastised for "distorting a classic," part of the "people's inheritance" (*narodnoe dostoianie*).[3] Nor did the film show the proper amount of sympathy for the oppressed and victimized civil servant under tsarism (the film's acknowledgement of the accumulated "civic" criticism of Gogol is distanced and ironic, though it is to be found).

The wrath of most critics probably would not have abated even if they had read Tynianov's own explanatory statements on SHINEL', a publicity brochure from Leningradkino for the film upon its release. This short article/brochure remains the best explication to date of the film. In it, Tynianov states that "the ciné-tale SHINEL' is not a ciné-illustration to the famous Gogol story . . . we have before us not a tale based on Gogol, but a ciné-tale **in the manner** of Gogol."[4] The FEKS/Tynianov film is, in fact, **a dense, interpretive discourse on the creative manner of Gogol;** it is bold, innovative, and eccentric. The acting, sets, costumes, and cinematography are all consistently expressionistic (whether German Expressionism was an influence or not[5]). This sustained stylization (the Russian term would be *uslovnost'*) functions most often to depict Akakii Akakievich's myopic, subjective outlook on the world. It renders his **line of vision** as well as his **psychological apprehension** of things, people, and events. Audience expectations conditioned by photographic realism are constantly thwarted by extreme, "subjective camera" angles, by camera techniques that distort whatever might be in the pro-filmic space, by costume and set design, and by stylized acting. The creators of SHINEL' were very adept at finding marvelously cinematic equivalents to Gogol's narrative strategies and to his frequently absurd humor, which "stretch the imagination" by paying little heed to the proprieties of verisimilitude and the logic of the ordinary. This Petersburg is "grotesque," "spectral," "irreal," "Gogolian." SHINEL' was informed by contemporary Formalist literary interpretation and theory,[6] and it is the central text in a concerted and conscious praxis of Formalist film theory as it was being formulated.[7]

Thus SHINEL' was well publicized, well known, very unusually creative, and non-standard. It was also one of the very few films to have been at least partially **theorized** from the outset, and it is plain evidence of Tynianov's serious professional and scholarly involvement in both literature and the cinema and in their respective theories. The evidence of SHINEL' has to be considered in discussions of the two other film projects dating to 1926–27, SOIUZ VELIKOGO DELA (THE UNION OF THE GREAT CAUSE [1927], usually known by its acronym SVD), cowritten by Julian Oksman, a FEKS film directed by Kozintsev and Trauberg, and PORUCHIK KIZHE. But SHINEL' does not form a stylistic "triptych" with *SVD* and KIZHE; the films are quite dissimilar in style (though they share a sort of commonality of theme and historical period). KIZHE is the least photographically "expressionistic" of the three—the film went into production six to seven years after the initial planning, and its director was not a member of FEKS, though the acting might occasionally remind the viewer of the eccentrism of NOSFERATU (1922) or DAS KABINET DES DR CALIGARI (1919), films whose thematics are not even close to KIZHE's. The Tynianov films belong, however, to a single body of work; they are three examples of the Formalist approach to literature and to the cinema. And because Tynianov's mark on all of them is so evident, they qualify him as a film *auteur*.

The "Kizhe texts" must be differentiated. They include two versions of a filmscript ("PORUCHIK KIZHE," written in 1927 and revised in 1933–34), a still extant film (PORUCHIK KIZHE, released in 1934), a musical score for the film written by Prokofiev (in 1933), an orchestral suite elaborated from the filmscore ("Lieutenant Kijé" [1934]), and a *povest'* (*Podporuchik Kizhe*, published in January 1928). Tynianov wrote the script for a **silent** film, but the project was shelved, then revived in 1933 for a **sound** film which was directed by Alexander Feinzimmer. Thus there are two variants of the script.[8]

PORUCHIK KIZHE was apparently a popular film when it was released. Reviews appeared in *The New York Times* and in *Variety* in 1934; there were Soviet reviews as well, of course.[9] But it was largely forgotten until quite recently, until a few "new" scholars had viewed it. One of these, Kristin Thompson, has noted the (intentional) destruction of "naturalistic sync-sound relations" in the opening sequence, as well as the film's overall comic stylization.[10] Ian Christie calls this film "a remarkable working model of Formalist literary theory, couched in the form of a fable on the generative power of language".[11] Mikhail Iampol'skii discusses KIZHE in some detail as a "theoretical film," as well as noting its possible antecedent in, and conscious parody of, certain aspects of E. T. A. Hoffmann's fairytale/novella, *Klein Zaches, genannt Zinnober* (*Little Zaches, called Zinnober* [1819]), as well as of Gogol's *Nos* ("The Nose" [1836]).[12] The annotated script of 1933/34 for the sound film was published in 1984 and again in 1987.[13] But there is only one known print of the film in the West (in Brussels); Moscow's *Gosfil'mofond* preserves the film intact.

Three initial facts should be noted about Tynianov's texts. First, the filmscript provided the basic themes for the story, though the two works were written at about the same time, in mid-to-late 1927.[14] But this pattern of genesis, **filmscript-to-story,** and not the more usual reverse sequence, is also evident in the relationship between "SVD" (written in 1926) and the novella *Chernigovskii polk zhdet* (published in 1932), though these two works have little else in common, with different characters and plots.[15] "KOLOKOL I OBEZ'IANA" ("THE MONKEY AND THE BELL"), a filmscript dated 1932, was likewise the initial "seed" for a story that was left unfinished.[16]

Second, these scripts and stories, as do all of Tynianov's fictional writings, reflect their author's absorption in the history of Russian literature, especially from pre-Romanticism through the so-called age of Pushkin and Gogol (though his scholarly activity also covered the literature of the 1920s and 1930s). Each of the fictional works reflects Tynianov's complex irreverent regard of autocratic rule and its ideological helpmeets; and Tynianov makes plain his concern for **original** art and literature under the *ancien régime* (reverberant "Aesopian" subtexts lend further complexities to Tynianov's scripts, stories and novels). And there are two significant characteristics of Tynianov's working, creative, intellectual **methodologies**: (1) They are **dialectical**, i.e., they are examples of both structural and thematic constructs built upon apparent inconsistencies or paradoxes (thus they are not un-Marxist, but they completely lack any clear references to "Party-line" political concerns of the late 1920s-early 1930s and are thus non-Stalinist); (2) they are practical applications of Tynianov's theories (in his case, the sometimes abusive term "Formalist" seems restrictive, but he was a member of OPOIAZ), although he did not construct his fictions as point-for-point demonstrations of his theories (thus Tynianov manages to elude simple categorization, and he does it in the fictions with no small amount of deliberate vagueness and irony).[17]

Third, Tynianov based his "Kizhe" on two **anecdotes** that apparently date to the reign of Paul I (1796–1801). These two anecdotes tell of a certain Кижъ who is "born" of a scribal error and who rises to the rank of general, and of a nameless officer of dragoons who is mistakenly excluded from the service because of his supposed death.[18] This was surely a conscious homage to Gogol', particularly to *Shinel'*, a story which was elaborated out of an anecdote about a poor civil servant. (Tynianov altered the name **Кижъ** to **Киже**, and provided the nameless officer with a surname, Siniukhaev).

Though there are radical differences between the basic plot elements of the script and the story, there are broad thematic similarities. *Podporuchik Kizhe* has three main characters: the tsar (Paul I/Pavel Petrovich), Kizhe, and Siniukhaev (who does **not** figure in the filmscript or the film). There are several other characters who function more as "signifiers" or "indicators" than as fully-fledged personae. The three main characters are linked thematically, but there are no circumstances where they would actually "meet," and their stories are essentially separate. One ideational strategy in evidence here is that the reign of Pavel Petrovich is to be characterized by a lack of real communication between people; it is a deadening official life, where ritual is all-important and where the state apparatus functions for its own convenience, not for the common good. A real person (Siniukhaev) loses his right to count himself among the living because an official document says he is dead. A use for the scribal error, Kizhe, is found when a scapegoat is needed to be blamed for disturbing the tsar by calling out "*Karaul!*" ["Help!"] outside his window; Kizhe is flogged, exiled, pardoned, returned to the capital, given promotions that enable him to rise in the ranks to General; he marries, begets children, and, when his "existence" no longer serves the purposes of those who have kept him "alive," Kizhe dies and is given a state funeral.

Obviously absent at all stages of his life and career, Kizhe nonetheless acquires prestige and respect; he is the **nothing** that becomes a **something**, a sort of perverse *nihil obstat*. One function of the story is to debunk the Russian autocratic state by ridiculing its inherently ludicrous apparatus. Ironically, and very much to the point, *Podporuchik Kizhe* is a literary work that mocks the significance attached to the written word (of course, the documents that give rise to Kizhe and eliminate Siniukhaev are erroneous); the film serves the same purpose, though more obviously. Tynianov's two treatments of the Kizhe theme are based on real, historical personages and events (even Kizhe has at least one antecedent), but this is a **fiction**, whose strategies are both ideological and artistic; it is not a factually accurate historical treatise. The story version also has an obvious, though superficial, "cinematic structure," being divided into twenty-three sections (I–XXIII) of varying lengths, which function in a manner similar to a series of "alternat-ing" sequences of simultaneous or consecutive events; this is a basic narra-tive film structure (and the basic structure of the standard TV melodrama/soap opera). But the story as written is not very "filmable," because of the selectivity of narrative information, multiple vaguely-limned characters, frac-tionalized scenes, its lack of concreteness, and so on. (It is beyond the scope of this paper to speculate about the theoretical and practical possibilities of making the camera function in a manner equivalent to the literary narrator.) The typographically sectionalized story also gives visible distinctiveness to the three partially independent main story lines. *Podporuchik Kizhe* includes numerous minor plot elements and settings (locations), so much so that the story seems elusive (it is a modernist text which forces the reader to be attentive, to "work" at reading). PORUCHIK KIZHE is less complicated in these respects, but the film scholar will recognize that a **film** sets up a complex of criteria not usually applied in critical discourse on literary works. The mood of the film is less melancholic than the story's, which leaves its readers with an impression of the socio-political malaise of the autocracy. But the principle aim of both texts is to **amuse**.

The bulk of my remaining comments will be given over to the specifics of Tynianov's filmscript and its narrative strategies. "PORUCHIK KIZHE" has a limited number of main characters, each of whom is carefully distinguished from the others, each with strong, identifying personal traits. Tsar Pavel Petrovich is primary among these (excluding Kizhe, for the moment), and it is his residence, the Mikhailovskii Castle [*zamok*] in Petersburg, which functions as the main setting. The other dramatis personae are courtiers and underlings, who range from the historically identifiable to the quasi-historical to the purely fictional: Count Pahlen, Kutáisov (the tsar's barber), Gagarina (presumably the tsar's mistress), her *Freilina* (a lady-in-waiting, who becomes Kizhe's "wife" and then his "widow"), and the Adjutant (named Kablukov, the tsar's adjutant and Pahlen's nephew).[19] (These last two are identified by their titles, capitalized as if they were names.) There is also an ostensibly minor character, the "drunken captain," who functions as a continuity device and whose significance to the intrigue becomes apparent only at the end of the script.

The ideological prejudice of "PORUCHIK KIZHE" is clear, but it is also immersed in irony, comedy, and stylistics. Pavel Petrovich is the butt of a particularly trenchant combination of comedy and the grotesque. He is depicted as petulant and naive, incompetent and cruel, almost boundlessly credulous, and, when his paranoia becomes especially acute (he suspects, correctly, that there is a conspiracy against him) he relies on an imaginary person to save him: *"Kizhe menia spaset!"*. He is ridiculed in a comparison with the ancestor he idolizes, Peter the Great; he is laughed at by the common folk, who nickname him "Daddy Snubnose" (*"Bat'ka kurnosyi"*);[20] his courtiers take advantage of his naiveté, yet they fear his wrath, and Count Pahlen, the main beneficiary of imperial largesse, leads the plot against his life. Pavel Petrovich is even ridiculed in his murder scene by being strangled at the same time the grand state funeral for "General Kizhe" is taking place.[21]

"PORUCHIK KIZHE" is notable for having a title character who is not a physical entity. As Count Pahlen explains to those assembled on the military parade-ground to witness Kizhe's flogging and send-off into exile,

"Arestant sekretnyi, i figury ne imeet."

The solution to this obvious handicap in a film is part of this film's comedic strategies: Kizhe's "space" (frequently described as *"mesto" Kizhe*) acquires increasing significance as Kizhe's existence is verified and his status becomes more and more augmented. But he had been "born" of an error made by a scribe who had been under pressure from the Adjutant to finish a document (a list of promotions) for the tsar to sign. This error, in "the birth of Kizhe" sequence,[22] is essentially as follows: Instead of writing

. . . Poruchiki zhe Platonov, Liubavskii . . . naznachaiutsia . . .

the scribe, trembling under pressure, mistakenly jots down a trio of *k*'s, obliterates the middle *k* by dropping an ink spot on it [*k* ■ *k*] and sees he has written

... *Poruchik Kizhe, Platonov* ...

Allowed no time to correct the error, he adds the requisite "jer" (the "hard sign," Ъ) in the place of the ink spot (which is logical, if one remembers that this is the eighteenth century, long before this letter was eliminated in the orthographic revisions of 1918) to give rise to an officially inscribed fact,

ПОРУЧИКЪ КИЖЕ.

(In the film, the name is emphasized in a close-up shot, the letters are non-cursive, all capitals, and the "jer" is later added by Pavel Petrovich, as it is in section IV of the story; one might remember here that Tynianov observed that a particular letter or sound might carry a parodistic meaning.[23]) Pahlen learns of this error, but realizes how it can be put to good use: Lieutenant Kizhe will be charged as the culprit who had shouted "*Karaul!*" under the tsar's window, thereby disturbing his slumber. Kizhe is to be flogged and sent into exile.

The significance of Kizhe's "space" is first recognized when he is being flogged. Nobody appears, of course, when Pahlen calls Kizhe out from the ranks, but the *palachi* (as they are called), though dumbfounded, lash their whips against the "wooden horse" (*kobyla*, actually a wooden plank, slightly tilted) onto which have been "impressed the traces of human bodies (knees and elbows)." His grenadier escort, less attentive, also do their duty, only somewhat sleepily and sloppily regulating the requisite distance between themselves and the "empty space" (*pustoe mesto*). Kizhe is soon returned from exile, however, because Gagarina has thought up a use for him. Apparently motivated by a need to remover her Freilina as a rival for the tsar's attentions, Gagarina convinces him that he does not have a servant as loyal as Lieutenant Kizhe. The notion of "a loyal servant" (*vernyi sluga*) becomes paramount in Pavel Petrovich's mind as his paranoia is aggravated by the realization that he is, indeed, in danger:

"*Gosudarstvo v opasnosti. Gosudarstvo—èto ia!*"

Most of the latter scenes and sequences in the script where the tsar is the central figure are punctuated by his most frequent utterance,

"*Vse neverno!*"

and/or by his belief in an imaginary savior (who has already been promoted):

"*Polkovnik Kizhe vernyi sluga . . . Polkovnika Kizhe v generaly!*

"*Vse neverno! Kizhe menia spaset!*"

Kizhe is a general by the time he is to marry the Freilina, and while his official status is assured, he causes consternation by being absent at his own wedding (a long sequence in the script and film; cf. section XVII of the story version, where the wedding is but a detail). But Pahlen angrily explains that "the groom is late" and forces the ceremony to proceed between the Freilina and the "empty space." Immediately after the ceremony there is a festive gathering of guests in Kizhe's chambers. In this sequence, and increasingly thereafter, Kizhe's "empty space" becomes **a space to be occupied, a space to be filled**. Kizhe becomes "substantiated"—"he" is replaced by substitutes,[24] first by an armchair, and then by "his" wife's desperate lover, the Adjutant, in an efficient and very funny "conjugal embrace" sequence.[25] (In these and other scenes the upper classes are shown to be aware of the deceptions, but they are willing to play their roles in support of them.) The conjugal embrace sequence ends in a "long fade-out" (*dlinnoe zatemnenie*), which, at the moment of rising viewers' expectations in a love scene, is conventionally a sign of the viewers' (and the camera's) desire to keep on looking—the darkening screen is a teasing device that gradually removes the *voyeur* from the object of his scopophilia.

Pavel Petrovich's belief in Kizhe's existence is never actually tested, as he is never physically placed at a site where Kizhe is supposed to be present. But once Kizhe is married, the tsar demands to see his "protector." The need to present Kizhe to the emperor becomes **a disruption of the norm** (much as Kizhe's "birth" had been, until uses were contrived for him). Pahlen announces that Kizhe has fallen dangerously ill and has been sent to the hospital. There, in a sequence that functions to mock the Germanized/ Prussianized Russian upper classes and professionals, Kizhe continues to inspire awe in his absence. The German doctor (*lekar'-nemets*) waves his arms in astonishment and exclaims,

   "General fon-Kizhe - strannyi bol'noi!"

thereby unwittingly adding to Kizhe's aggrandizement by attributing to him an aristocratic (German) *von*. Count Pahlen (*graf fon der Palen* in the 1926 script [*kadr* 253], for whom the historical model was Count or Baron von Pahlen), soon announces Kizhe's demise, but attributes it to God:

   "General Kizhe, bozh'ei volei, skonchalsia."

and he orders Kizhe's funeral with full military honors but attributes the order to the emperor. The successful maneuvers to deflect responsibility or blame for decisions or manipulations are characteristic of Count Pahlen.

The script's concluding Part 8 contains two simultaneous events (alternating sequences) with two denouements—the funeral of Kizhe and the "regicide sequence. "The funeral procession consists of fifteen carriages with liveries, each drawn by a team of six horses draped in black. **All** of the carriages are empty, as is the open coffin on the hearse at the head.[26] The emperor laments the loss of this "loyal servant" from a distance, safely within his castle, with its moats and drawbridges. But no sooner has he donned his nightcap and crawled into bed than the group of conspirators (*zagovorshchiki*), with Pahlen leading them, breaks down the door and enters his chambers. The script consistently subverts the potential dramatic tragedy of events. Here, Pahlen mechanically offers a glass of champagne,

  "Ne xotite vy stakan lafitu?"

as he has done in the most inappropriate circumstances throughout the script. This "Laffitte" serves to ridicule Pahlen's superficiality (though the historically identified conspirators had also been imbibing), but it also continues a major subtheme of the script, that of drinking and drunkenness, as does the repeated appearance of a seemingly minor character, the "drunken captain" (*"p'ianyi kapitan"*). Significantly, it is this nameless, drunken captain, and not either Count Pahlen or one of the conspiring generals, who is identified as the regicide. He removes his scarf, forms it into a noose, and is clearly meant to proceed to strangle the tsar, who will die a coward's death—the shots of the actual murder are elided from the script, replaced by a shot (#600) of Kizhe's funeral procession. In a final mockery, the drunken captain leaves the room singing his characteristic ditty:

  "Umu Umovichu, Pavlu Petrovichu, ego kapitan b'et v baraban."

Meanwhile, in the funeral procession, Kizhe's "space" is finally occupied by his substitute, the Adjutant, who jumps into the hearse to take his place alongside the "widowed" Freilina, who now agrees to marry him, since he is now a "general" and has completely usurped Kizhe's position. The Adjutant announces the tsar's demise to the crowds,

  "Bat'ka kurnosyi prestavilsia!"

as does Pahlen to the soldiers,

  "Imperator Pavel I pochil v boze."

The soldiers greet the new emperor with a cheer. Accompanied by Pahlen and a general, the white-clad Grand Duke Alexander is seen coming out onto a palace balcony. Thus Tynianov's script echoes an apparently real fear of Pavel Petrovich that he would be ousted, as had been his supposed father, Peter III (by his mother, Catherine the Great, who is called *"poxititel'nitsa prestola"* in the story, section VI, and who had indeed delayed her son's ascent to the throne for thirty-four years, until her own death in 1796). It also acknowledges the possible (or probable) role of Alexander in his father's assassination.[27]

"PORUCHIK KIZHE" is an intensely **signifying** text, resonating on several levels in several directions, extending its meanings beyond the strict parameters of the plot. It communicates the author's playful interpretations of both political and literary history and of the role language plays in an historical epoch, as in the utilization of documents and of spoken dialogue in an approximation of the syntax and lexicon of the late eighteenth century (the use of archaisms is especially notable). As such, it provides more evidence of Tynianov's "semiotic perspective."[28]

It should be stressed that the pseudo-world (the diegetic representations) of PORUCHIK KIZHE is one of extreme artificiality and was scripted as such. It is a stylized, fictional film-work that consistently subverts the norms of the realist cinema (photographic realism, historical verisimilitude), i.e., the picture doesn't "look like" a documentary photo). Its cinematographic style may lack the expressionistic long shadows and chiaroscuro effects of SHINEL' and *SVD*, but the film shows the influence of the FEKS, especially in the "quirky" acting. The esthetic resolutions surely reflect the advisory input of Tynianov and the conscious intention of Feinzimmer to follow the film's original plans. Its **literariness** is almost flaunted (which would be very apparent to any literary scholar who might read the script, though probably less apparent to the usual viewer of the **film;** the latter, however, would surely notice its stylization).

Three aspects of this literariness are of particular interest. (It is already obvious that the script is a written text—films are also inscribed texts— whose plot depends on the effects of a scribal error and on the ideational/ideological importance attached to the official word.) First, the script has several "**literary inserts**" in the form of brief, poetical texts which have place and function within the diegesis. These short poems and "ditties" (folk poems set to music) are not formal, complete written texts, as they are intended as details (signifying, codified details), logically motivated, to be rendered **orally**. Notably **lacking** in the film is the most famous of the "Kizhe songs," found in the "Romance" section of Prokofiev's suite. This is a poem, "Stonet sizyi golubochek," written in 1792 by Ivan Ivanovich Dmitriev (1760–1837). This poem is very far removed from the mood and the thematics of Tynianov's script (and Prokofiev uses only its first three quatrains, eliminating the bathetic last four quatrains). Prokofiev also used a charming "troika song" (in section IV, "Troika"). This appears in the script in a variant of only the first quatrain, sung in rakish fashion by two drunken soldiers.

But the other five of the six literary inserts in the script seem to have been written by Tynianov. Their ironic *épigonstvo* (imitation) is certainly in character; their formal properties, and their functions in the script, constitute an effective demonstration of the "lowering of the 'high style'" (*snizhenie "vysokogo stilia"*) that occurred during the transition from Classicism to Sentimentalism/Romanticism in the late eighteenth/early nineteenth centuries. Their "genres" range from the *bon ton* Sentimental novel to the "elegant" salon song to the vulgar folk ditty. They might be described as a canonical and cliché'd mini-paradigm of the literary and musical genres prevailing at that time. They are also a sure mockery of the trite side of Sentimentalism and of public tastes, and are part of a web of allusions that clearly reflect Tynianov's negative evaluation of some minor personalities in Russian pre-Romanticism.[29] For the most part, the literary figures who are mocked belong to the periphery of literary achievement, but the accumulated evidence in "PORUCHIK KIZHE" also reflects Tynianov's concern with the **marginalia** of literary history that bore such positive results in his writings and editing endeavors. Tynianov's advice to pay more attention to the "lowly genres," which in the 1920s also included the cinema (in the tastes of the traditional purveyors of culture), was no doubt earnestly given:

"Tovarishchi, pobol'she vnimaniia nizkim zhanram." [30]

It would be difficult to argue this point relying only on this quotation and on the evidence in "PORUCHIK KIZHE" of soundly lampooned literary "citations." Happily, Tynianov himself provides irrefutable evidence of his critical, evaluative approach to this period.[31]

The second and third literary characteristics of "PORUCHIK KIZHE" are at once structural and semantic. The overall architectonics of the script seems to be another homage to Gogol, duplicating a Gogolian narrative structure. As was noted by Tynianov's contemporary Aleksandr Slonimskii, in Gogol there is a "fusion of the serious and the comic" and "a general movement from 'merriment' to 'sadness' within the structure as a whole," while one perceives "two opposing directions: one rising into intense *pafos* [emotion] (cf. the strangling of Pavel Petrovich), the other breaking off abruptly into comic anticlimax" (cf. the carryings-on in Kizhe's funeral procession).[32] This abstracted format, which is not necessarily static, is a detectable substructure of Tynianov's screenplay, whether it was utilized consciously or not (though it is extremely diffused in *Podporuchik Kizhe*).

The beginning and ending of "PORUCHIK KIZHE" constitute another very good, more definitive example of Tynianov's sensitivity to structure. The "introductory sequence" consists of a series of fifty shots, passing from the snow-covered city outskirts, gradually moving onto a military parade-ground in the capital and then into the emperor's residence, where the sentries are passing along a message:

"Imperator spit"

(KIZHE was called THE CZAR WANTS TO SLEEP at its New York screenings in 1934). This sequence is extremely stylized, rhythmical, calm, and quiet. There is a series of shot descriptions,

Spit Gagarina. Spit Freilina. Spit sobachka. Zadom k dveri u okna, okru-zhennyi stekliannymi shirmami,[33] spit Pavel.

An intertitle announces that "Someone isn't sleeping" (*Kto ne spit*), where-upon the action/intrigue begins with sequences with Count Pahlen and of the unexpected shout, *"Karaul!"* (the answer to that "mystery": the Adjutant is having a tryst with the Freilina, and, in playful response to a coquettish pinch, has called out for help).[34] In the "**closing** sequence" there is a series of shots, going from the castle courtyard onto a street and over a snowy field on the outskirts of St. Petersburg, wherein the city is shown retiring for the night. The flag is lowered, the streetlamps are extinguished, a snowstorm abates, and a call is heard being passed from the castle to the fringes of the city:

"Imperator spit!"

This sequence recalls the introductory sequence, both of which conclude in quiet and darkness. The disruptions of the norm have been eliminated, the situation has returned to the usual.[35] This reversed repetition, a recapitu-lation of diegetic elements (locations, sounds, characters, rhythms,), even if in a briefer version, **effects a closure**. Considering the sustained, regular, non-realist pace of all elements in the script (including the indicated use of music), it can be called a **poetic** closure, a neat, balanced, rhythmical ending to a text which is, in this respect, contained within itself both as a structure and as a concept, with its apparent ideological message **subordinated to stylistics.**

Notes

1. This paper was first presented in February 1988 at the Slavic Depart-ment, University of Texas, Austin. **Film** titles cited here are in small caps, whereas film**script** titles are in small caps and inclosed in quotation marks. Transliterations follow the Library of Congress system without diacritics (but *è* and, in the notes only, *ë*, are marked for clarity); variant translit-erations are as published elsewhere. I prefer to use Russian titles rather than their English translations, and "englished" personal names instead of some less familiar transliterations (Gogol instead of Gogol'; Prokofiev instead of

Prokof'ev; Meierkhold instead of Meierkhol'd), except in citations from the Russian.

2. FEKS *(Fabrika ėkstsentricheskogo aktëra)*, a group formed in 1921 by the theater enthusiasts and future film directors Leonid Trauberg (b. 1902) and Grigorii Kozintsev (1905–1973). FEKS became an actors' workshop in 1924 and shortly thereafter a film production company. *Shinel'* was their fourth film. FEKS was disbanded in 1929, though its members continued to make films. The FEKS manifestoes, published collectively as *Ekstsentrizm* (1922), deserve their rightful place in the consideration of Futurism and Formalism in post-revolutionary Russia. See the translation, "Eccentrism," in *The Drama Review* 19/4 (December 1975), 95–109. Also see Vladimir Nedobrovó, *FEKS* (Leningrad, 1929), and *Cinema e Avanguardia in Unione Sovietica. La Feks: Kozincev e Trauberg*, ed. Giusi Rapisarda (Rome, 1975). For the film credits and a list of contemporary reviews, see the entry for *Shinel'* in *Sovetskie khudozhestvennye fil'my: Annotirovannyi katalog,* Vol. 1 (1961), item #416, 175–76 (henceforth cited as *SKhF* 1 or 2).

3. Iurii Tynianov, "O fėksakh," *Sovetskii ėkran.* 1929 no. 14, 10, reprinted in *Poėtika. Istoriia literatury. Kino* (Moscow, 1977), 346–48 (henceforth cited as *PILK* (1977).

4. . . . *ne povest' po Gogoliu, a kinopovest' v m a n e r e Gogolia* . . . [Tynianov's italics, JTH]: Iu. Tynianov, *"Shinel'*—libretto" (Leningrad, 1926), reprinted in *Iz istorii Lenfil'ma,* III (1973), 78–80; included as Appendix III of my doctoral dissertation, "The Russian Literary Avant-Garde and the Cinema (1920s and 1930s): The Film-Work of Isaak Babel' and Jurij Tynjanov" (University of California, Berkeley, 1984), 336–37 (henceforth: J. Heil).

5. Kozintsev himself denied that the German Expressionist films "cast a gloom" over *Shinel'*. Grigorii Kozintsev, *Sobranie sochinenii,* I (1982), 109–10 (this first of five volumes was originally published as *Glubokii ėkran* [1966]). Nedobrovó reiterated, approvingly (in 1928), what most observers were saying, that the FEKS had "adopted Expressionism as their style" (*op. cit.,* 58). Most Soviet critics still either deny or play down the Expressionist influence, aligning themselves with contemporary critics in railing against the "Hoffmannism" and "Expressionism of *Shinel'*. See also J. Heil, 196–98 and 312–13, note 81.

6. The concept of the grotesque in Gogol (and hence a broadening of critics' vision of this writer) really began with OPOIAZ and its kindred spirits, as with Boris Eikhenbaum, "Kak sdelana 'Shinel' Gogolia" (1919), and Aleksandr Slonimskii, *Tekhnika komicheskogo u Gogolia* (1923). Tynianov's own studies are of paramount importance here, of course. See his "Dostoevskii i Gogol' (k teorii parodii)" (1921). The production of *Shinel'*

served as a "practicum" for Tynianov's ideas on Gogol as well (he was present at the filming and had an amicable working relationship with the FEKS
on the production), and Gogol is Tynianov's most favored writer to cite.

7. The most important book-length contribution of the Formalists to film
theory was the miscellany edited by Eikhenbaum, *Poètika kino* (1927), which
included Tynianov's important article, "Ob osnovax kino," where Gogol is
the subject of section 12. Tzvetan Todorov cites this **film** article to help
elucidate the somewhat confusing use by the Formalists in their literary
theory of the terms *fabula* and *siuzhet*: "Some Approaches to Russian Formalism," in *20th Century Studies* 7/8 (December 1972), ed. Stephen Bann
and John Bowlt, 16–17 (reprinted in book format as *Russian Formalism, A
Selection of Articles and Texts in Translation* [New York, 1973]).

Poètika kino is available in a reprint (Berkeley Slavic Specialties, 1984)
and in two English translations: (1) *The Poetics of Cinema*, ed Richard
Taylor, no. 9 in the series "Russian Poetics in Translation" (Oxford, 1982);
(2) *Russian Formalist Film Theory*, ed. and with an introduction by Herbert
Eagle, "Michigan Slavic Materials, No. 19" (Ann Arbor, 1981) [This publication deletes Shklovskii's article, but includes Jakobson's "Is the Cinema
in Decline?" (1933)].

For a complete list of Tynianov's film writings (filmscripts and articles),
see J. Heil, 280–86 and *Russian Literature* XXI–IV (Amsterdam, May 1987),
553–39 (henceforth *RL* XXI–IV).

8. Sergei Iutkevich was originally appointed director of the silent film.
"Kijé" is the internationally accepted spelling used for the musical suite.
Podporuchik Kizhe first appeared in *Krasnaia Nov'*, no. 1 (1928), with a
section I that has been deleted from all subsequent republications (it is
included as Appendix IV in J. Heil, 339). A copy of Tynianov's original
script (1927) is located at TsGALI. The variant used for Feinzimmer's (Fain-
tsimmer) film was considered "lost" until I located it in the USSR and
included it in my doctoral dissertation. See notes 4 and 16 here. See also
E. A. Toddes, "Posleslovie" in *Podporuchik Kizhe* (Moscow, 1981), 164–200.
My reference text here is that published in *Russian Short Stories, A Bilingual
Collection,* Vol. 2. ed., trans., and introduced by Maurice Friedberg and
Robert Maguire (Random House, New York, 1965), 507–93. *N.B.* The stress
mark on the first syllable (*Kízhe*) in this edition is invariably incorrect
(though it is logical, considering the origin of the name); the spoken lan-
guage insists on a second-syllable stress (*Kizhé*) (as does Prokofiev's title).
There is a difference in the historical "time spans" indicated in the script and
in the story. "PORUCHIK KIZHE" covers the period from about 1798–99,

from the rise of the historical Baron von Pahlen, to 1801, the death of Paul; its chronology is sequential and, in important instances, simultaneous. The temporal schema of *Podporuchik Kizhe* is vaguer and more enigmatic, but the narration "extends" over the entire reign of Paul I: In section I, Paul, in slumber, remembers the day his mother's death was announced, while in the final section, XXIII, the narrator speaks historically distanced from the final events (Kizhe's obituary in the *St. Petersburg Necrologue;* Siniukhaev's total disappearance; Paul's death "in March of the same year as General Kizhe—according to official reports, from apoplexy").

9. *The New York Times,* 10 December 1934 (16:3), and *Variety,* 18 December 1934. Running time for the film was 69 minutes, and the print had English captions. For a list of contemporary Soviet reviews, see the entry for PORUCHIK KIZHE in *SKhF* 2, item #1261, 50–51. One of these reviews was written by Lev Nikulin (1891–1967), entitled "Zhizn' pod baraban. PORUCHIK KIZHE na ėkrane," *Literaturnaia Gazeta,* 4 February 1934. In the context of the anti-formalist campaigns since 1929, and considering Nikulin's record of affiliation with and loyalty to CPSU ideology in art, his positive evaluation of *Kizhe* deserves mention. He was of the opinion that the "flogging of Kizhe" was very effective (from an ideological point of view) because the viewer was made to **imagine for himself** what a real whip would do to a real man (thus he diverges from the Party's insistence on "realism" in the cinema). At the end of his review, Nikulin states that "the style of the Soviet film, the combination of ideologically significant thematics with a new, nonbanal form, with a new word (*novoe slovo*) in the realm of the cinema, has found its expression in the film PORUCHIK KIZHE," and that the film "ought to be shown to writers."

10. Kristin Thompson, "Early Sound Counterpoint," *Yale French Studies* no. 60 (1980), 130–31. PORUCHIK KIZHE was, it should be noted, one of the first all-sound Soviet feature films (sound-film technology became universal in the USSR much later than it did in the USA); thus the quality of the sound track is "primitive" in comparison with later films.

11. Ian Christie, "Soviet Cinema—Making Sense of Sound," *Screen* 23/2 (July–August 1982), 46–47.

12. M. B. Iampol'skii, "PORUCHIK KIZHE kak teoreticheskii fil'm," in *Tynianovskii sbornik* [II]. *Vtorye tynianovskie chteniia* (a conference held in June 1984), ed. M. O. Chudakova *et al.* (Riga, 1986), 28–43. This critic also recognizes (33, note 15) that the liberal use Tynianov seems to have made of Hoffmann and Gogol might be better called "citation" (*tsitirovanie*). Iampol'skii himself cites Tynianov's silent film script at TsGALI, but he did

not have access to the script for the sound film (see note 13 below). He also discusses the issue of "the mirror" (*zerkal'nost'*) [reflection/refraction/distortion/doubling/multiplying] in KIZHE and in Tynianov's other works (38–43). There is an English version of *Klein Naches: Little Naches, Surnamed* [sic] *Zinnober,*" in *Three Märchen of E. T. A. Hoffmann*, trans. Charles E. Passage (Columbia, South Carolina, 1971), 1–109. For an article on SHINEL' that indirectly relates to PORUCHIK KIZHE, see Iu. G. Tsiv'ian, "Paleogrammy v fil'me SHINEL'," *Tynianovskii sbornik* [II] (1986), 14–27.

    13. J. Heil. (1984), and in "Jurij Tynjanov's Film-Work. Two Filmscripts: 'LIEUTENANT KIŽE' and 'THE MONKEY AND THE BELL' (1932)," *RL* XXI–IV (15 May 1987), 346–558 (entire issue). The annotated "shooting script" (*rezhissërskii stsenarii*) for KIZHE published there is the same as in my doctoral dissertation. See also the scholars cited in note 14 here.

    14. In her notes to *PILK*, 550, Marina Chudakova concludes that Tynianov wrote the script in spring 1927 and the story in summer 1927. Two other Tynianov scholars are in accord. Zorkaia describes it as "rozhdënnyi dlia kinematografa siuzhet." See Neia Markovna Zorkaia, "Tynianov i kino," *Voprosy kinoiskusstva*, 10 (1967), 292. And Sëpman states, "Kharakterno, chto Tynianov istoriiu poruchika Kizhe srazu prednaznachil dlia ëkrana, uvidel ee kak spetsificheskii kinomaterial." See I. Sëpman, "Tynianov-stsenarist," *Iz istorii Lenfil'ma*, III (1973), 75. KIZHE is thus not properly described as an "adaptation" (*ëkranizatsiia*), but rather as a film from an "original script," one not based on a narrative work previously written (in contrast, SHINEL' was a literary adaptation, from Gogol).

    These two articles are important, but neither deals successfully with KIZHE. Zorkaia (291–93) makes the mistake of relying on Belinkov's monograph (see note 18 below), and takes Iutkevich's word that the scripts had been lost. Sëpman (74–76) evidently read Tynianov's silent script (at TsGALI) and Iutkevich's treatment of it (located in the archives at *Gosfil'-mofond*) but criticizes the **film** as "a farce," inferior to the author's original philosophical/psychological tragicomedy. My comparison of the silent and the sound scripts led me to conclude that the radical differences are not philosophical; the two variants differ mostly in the exclusion of certain details and some sequences from the later variant, and in the ordering of some sequences (also the released film was given a different ending). Even much of the dialogue in the sound film has been written as dialogue for the intertitles of the silent film.

    15. *SVD* is a melodrama that is stylistically notable for its strongly contrasting side lighting; the fifty-five–page story is subtitled *dlia detei starshego*

vozrasta. But both works have themes that derive from Tynianov's research on the Decembrist Uprising of 1825; both are highly fictionalized accounts of the revolt as it occurred in the Ukraine. Apparently all prints and the negative of *SVD* lack parts 2 and 6 (one-half hour, or one third of the footage, including the ending, is missing from the original eighty-minute six-part film). See J. Heil, 198–201, and Appendices V(A) and V(B), 340–52 (the Russian intertitles for the whole film and their translation). See also Iu. M. Lotman and Iu. G. Tsiv'ian, "S.V.D.: zhanr melodramy i istoriia," *Tynianovskii sbornik* [I]. *Pervye tynianovskie chteniia*, ed. M. O. Chudakova *et al.* (1984), 46–78.

16. Kozintsev lamented (in 1966) that this script was lost, as were Tynianov's other filmscripts. See Grigorii Kozintsev, *op. cit.*, 101–2, 104. Sèpman also lamented the loss. See Sèpman, 76. Zorkaia wrote that there was no trace of it (by 1967) and that it remained "only a legend" See Zorkaia, 293. "KOLOKOL I OBEZ'IANA" is discussed in J. Heil, 201–7 and 315–16, notes 93–102. I located it in the USSR. It was discussed and first published, with annotations, in *RL* XXI–IV (1987), 378–82 and 497–532. See also notes 4, 13, and 18 here.

17. It is possible (and productive) to isolate examples of Tynianov's theoretical and critical views on literature in his own fictions, but the main point still is that the fictions are not "illustrated theories." It is also true that the historical fictions are not scholarly, objective histories, though there are impressive amounts of known historical facts lodged in them (KIZHE is a case in point).

There are few critical reviews in English of Tynianov's fictional prose, but see Gust Olson II, "Tynianov—Fictionist" (unpublished Ph.D. diss., University of Toronto, 1982), and Evelyn Jasiulko Harden, "Truth and Design: On the Historical Novels of Jurij Tynianov" (unpublished Ph.D. diss., Harvard University, 1966) and her "Truth and Design: Technique in Tynjanov's *Smert' Vazir-Muxtara*," *Mnemozina*, ed. Joachim Baer and Norman Ingham (Munich, 1974), 171–84. See also the bibliographies and works cited by J. Heil, 280–97, and in *RL* XXI–IV (1987), 533–53. A later addition to the list is by Dmitri N. and Zinaida A. Breschinsky, "On Tynjanov the Writer and His Use of Cinematic Technique in *The Death of the Wazir* [sic] *Mukhtar*," *SEEJ* vol. 29, no. 1 (Spring 1985), 1–18. While this article gives valuable information on the novel, it is ultimately quite disappointing—the thesis, a valid one, that Tynianov used cinematic technique in his prose, remains a peripheral motif. Evidence of the author's cinematic literacy is not furnished by the mere incorporation into their text of such terms as "cut to" or "freeze frame" or of pat definitions such as "juxtaposition . . . is montage" (12, which their footnote 33 does not elucidate).

A recent article is useful indeed, but I wish its author had avoided the "film metaphor" of its title: Monika Frenkel Greenleaf, "Tynianov, Pushkin and the Fragment: Through the Lens of Montage," in *California Slavic Studies* XV, *Cultural Mythologies of Russian Modernism. From the Golden Age to the Silver Age,* eds. Boris Gasparov, Robert Hughes and Irina Paperno (Berkeley and Los Angeles: Univ. of California Press, 1992): 264-292. There are two problems here. There is no such thing as a "lens of montage," unless the improbable suggestion here is of a **filming** technique, during which continuities (or intentional **dis**continuities) are established only with in-camera "takes" and without recourse to later "cutting" and "splicing" on an editing table. Then: Greenleaf is going against common and "received" opinion in her discussion of montage and "recombination," **but** she links it to Tynianov's work, and that is the major point of her article, which provides more evidence that Tynianov belongs in the "pantheon" of modern film theorists. The broad perception, which is not confined to "illusionist" narrative cinema, is: "montage" = "editing," the "suturing together" of film pieces or shots in order to establish their relationships (continuities, usually) which would seem to eliminate identifiable "fragments," i.e. the terms are hardly synonymous, unless one can establish their application by linking them in theory and practice to, say, Constructivist films of the 1920s (Eisenstein, Vertov) or modernist film-texts with radically disrupted spatio-temporal relations between syntagmas, however brief or disjointed. And "fragments"/fragmented is not, in narrative film analysis, the same as segments/segmentation. [Greenleaf's article was published after my article here was written, J.H.]

18. Arkadii Belinkov, *Iurii Tynianov* (Moscow, 1960, 2nd ed. 1965), 399–400 (cited from 2nd ed.). Belinkov's source was the collection *Pavel I. Sobranie anekdotov, otzyvov, xarakteristik, ukazov, i pr.,* compiled by Aleksander Geno and Tomich [sic] (1901), 174–75. But Belinkov did not note the genesis of *Podporuchik Kizhe* from a filmscript, and he completely dismisses "PORUCHIK KIZHE" (on 398–400). Sèpman says that Tynianov borrowed the anecdote from Vladimir Dal' "[Dahl]. See Sèpman, 74.

The unfinished "KOLOKOL I OBEZ'IANA" (see note 16 above) also grew from two anecdotes, these about the odd goings-on under the first Romanovs in the seventeenth century. See N. Stepanov (untitled memoir on Tynianov), *Iurii Tynianov, pisatel' i uchenyi,* No. 11 in the series "Zhizn' zamechatel'nykh liudei," (Moscow, 1966), 135–37. For a discussion of the differences between Stepanov's account of the script and the one published in 1987, see *RL* XXI–IV, 378–82 and 393–94, notes 66–74.

19. Count Peter-Ludwig (Alekseevich) Pahlen (1745–1826) was a Baltic German who is supposed to have been Paul's most trusted and powerful confidant (see note 27 below). Ivan Pavlovich Kutaisov (1759?–1834) was a captive "Turk" who served as Paul's valet and achieved the title of *graf* in 1799. Kutaisov introduced the sixteen-year-old Anna Lopukhina to the then forty-four-year-old tsar, who then made her his mistress (in place of his older paramour, Catherine Nelidova, who figures in section XVII of the story but is not mentioned in the script). For propriety's sake, Lopukhina was married off to Prince Gagarin; thus she became Princess Gagarina, whose chambers at the Mikhailovskii Castle were joined by a secret staircase to Paul's. The name "Kablukov" appears only once in the 1933–34 version of the script (in *plan* 422), perhaps a typographical error and/or an oversight during the revision of the silent filmscript. There was an historically factual Sablukov, an officer in the Horse Guards, who was loyal to the tsar. See the discussion of these historical antecedents to the script's characters in *RL* XXI–IV, 452–55 (since which publication, I can confirm the existence of Gagarina and Sablukov), in Leonid Strakhovsky, "The Mad Emperor," chapter I in *Alexander I of Russia: The Man Who Defeated Napoleon* (New York, 1946), 13–24, and in Henri Troyat, "The Reign of Paul," *Alexander of Russia, Napoleon's Conqueror* (New York, 1982), 34–57.

The Adjutant is also called *malen'kii* (*plan* 241) and *karlik* (*plany* 301 and 576). These are some details which Iampol'skii gives as evidence from the 1927 script that link "PORUCHIK KIZHE" to Hoffmann's *Klein Zaches*. See Iampol'skii (in note 12 above), 33–36. It is somewhat clearer in the earlier script, but it seems that Tynianov's strategy here was to set up a contrast (to isolate) and to draw a parallel between the diminutive Adjutant and Pavel Petrovich. The Adjutant is a "reflection," a sort of "double" to the emperor, who is not "up to par," a fact that is emphasized by the contrasts made between him and Peter the Great. See *RL* XXI–IV, *plany* 240–43 and 337–38 of the script, and annotations on 469–70 and 475–76 (the sequences with the statue of Peter I at the Mikhailovskii Castle).

In *Podporuchik Kizhe*, the adjutant's name is Sablukov, and he is more of a manipulator than the Adjutant of "PORUCHIK KIZHE"; it is he, not Pahlen (who barely figures in the story, section XX), who first sees the advantage of Kizhe's existence (in section IV).

20. In the film, the role of Pavel Petrovich is played by an actor, M. Ian-shin, who is rather the opposite of "snub-nosed." He bears no facial resem-

blance to the portraits of Paul I nor to the illustrations to the story by
E. Kibrik as they appeared in the story's first book-format publication in
1930 (see also note 33).

21. The murder, or "regicide sequence," was deleted from the final version
of the film, probably because it was known that Stalin was "sensitive" to
such notions (though Kirov had yet to be assassinated, in December 1934,
after the film's release in March 1934). The film's ending, as given in the
entry in *SKhF* 2 (not entirely reliable in its "plot summaries"), follows the
script's *fabula* to the point where Pahlen is forced to declare Kizhe dead.
Pavel Petrovich then

> remembers the money he had granted Kizhe on his wedding day. The
> emperor orders his adjutant to return the money, not suspecting that it had
> been stolen by that very adjutant. Instead of the money, the adjutant
> delivers an empty trunk and a message, in which "General Kizhe" reports
> that he has squandered the money [*den'gi on proel*]. The infuriated tsar
> orders the late general to be reduced to the ranks [*razzhalovat' v soldaty*].

In his review of the film in *Literaturnaia gazeta* (4 February 1934), Nikulin
remarks that the "story of the theft of 10,000 rubles is strained, foisted [onto
the film] tendentiously, necessary for a traditional finale," but that the
"attention of the viewer is dulled, and after the death of the non-existent
Kizhe, he [the viewer] waits for an ending that is still distant." Sergei
Prokofiev remarked that "the ending of the film was changed several times,
which made it muddled and heavy." See S. S. Prokofiev, *Materialy. Dokumenty. Vospominaniia* (Moscow, 1956), 72. It is evident that the ending was
changed during production.

22. Cf. the "birth" of Kizhe in *Podporuchik Kizhe*, section II, which is one
of the few passages in the story which fairly well "describes" a sequence in
the film.

23. Iurii Tynianov, "O parodii" (1929), first published in *PILK* (1977),
284–310. It is. of course, the tsar himself who makes Kizhe a **legal and
political fact** by inscribing the "jer" and by signing the writ for promotions.
In section IX of the story, the narrator explains:

*Pridirchivyi glaz Pavla Petrovicha [opisku] izvlëk i tvërdym znakom dal ei
somnitel'nuiu zhizn'—opiska stala podporuchikom, bez litsa, no s familiei.*

One might search Tynianov's writings for a theoretical clue to this *nulevaia
persona*. He noted the structural and semantic significance of the *propuski
strof* (the lacunae, the wordless lines of dots—the "nothing" that indeed is
"something") in Pushkin, in "O kompozitsii *Evgeniia Onegina*" [written
1921–22], *PILK* (1977), 59–60; the separability of *fabula* and *siuzhet* is considered in "Illiustratsiia" (1923), *PILK,* 310–18, and in "O siuzhete i fabule

v kino" (1926), *PILK*, 324–25; in the latter sections of "Ob osnovakh kino" (1926), *PILK*, 340–45, Tynianov tackles the problem of the interrelationship of *fabula*, *siuzhet*, and **style**. As Todorov ascertains (*loc. cit.*), Tynianov's concept of *siuzhet* will comprise the complications of style/stylistics/stylization. The explanation remains somewhat inconclusive, as Tynianov relies only on **literary** citations to make his points in "Ob osnovakh kino." It does seem clear, however, that Tynianov uses the **focal point** of "Kizhe's 'space'" (its privileged position in the film both as a *locus* and as a perception) as his own "debunking" of the role of illustrations to literature (which rely on *fabula*), while simultaneously demonstrating the "non-objectiveness" or the lack of "concreteness" (*konkretnost'*) of *siuzhet* (*"Siuzhet veshchi opredelitsia kak dinamiki ee"*). His examples are usually from Gogol, but Tynianov was (in 1926–27) convinced of the "abstract" nature of the cinema and inclined toward denying the legitimacy of **verisimilitude** as a criterion of the cinematic. See "Kino—slovo—muzyka" (1924), *PILK*, 320–22, and "Ob osnovakh kino." My more elaborate discussion of Tynianov's film articles is in J. Heil, 177–84 and 302–7 notes 20–48.

Simply put: Tynianov must have enjoyed the process of creating a dynamic "being" (Kizhe in the various texts) out of a thread of a story (anecdotes) about "nothing," whose breadth and profundities are not yet exhaustively explored by scholars.

24. In the film, the "empty space" at the wedding is filled by a puppet (*kukla*). The notion of "substitute" is inherent in Tynianov's script and story as well. In Part 8 of the script (*plany* 558–63, immediately prior to the funeral procession sequence), there is a conversation between a young and an old soldier (this dialogue is integrated into the story's section IX). The young soldier asks whether there is an emperor, and who it is, to which the old man replies: *"On i est', tolk'ko podmennyi"*(the story uses *podmennënyi*). Besides serving as a reminder that Pavel Petrovich and his father had been displaced by Catherine, this is also a reminder of the rumored illegitimacy of Pavel Petrovich and of the recurrent theme of the "false tsar" in Russian history, most notably the claim by the rebel leader, Emelian Pugachev (1726–75) that he was Peter III, and the claims of the two "false Dmitriis" during the *Smutnoe vremia* (1598–1613).

25. See "PORUCHIK KIZHE," Part 7, *plany* 467–501, and annotations.

26. The shot descriptions (*plany* 566–78) emphasize that the carriages and the coffin are empty. In *Podporuchik Kizhe*, section XXII, the procession consists of "thirty court coaches, some empty, others full. The Emperor had willed it so." Iampol'skii (*op. cit.*, 36) says that the empty coffin also figures in Hoffmann. In actual fact, it is a question of **perception through a glass**

prism (see note 12 above) during the funeral of Zaches/Zinnober: In the "Last Chapter" of *Klein Zaches*, one character looks through a lorgnette

> at the magnificent casket in which Zinnober lay, and it suddenly seemed to him as if there had never been a Minister Zinnober, but rather only a little, uncouth, unruly pygmy whom people had erroneously taken for a sensible, wise minister.

But in addition, this "Last Chapter" includes a "happy ending wedding" (between Balthazar and Candida), as does the ending of "PORUCHIK KIZHE." Despite the variables in basic story line and stylistics, and despite the very heavy sarcasm of *Klein Zaches*, it seems clear that Tynianov linked it to KIZHE as a referential text with a similar political/ideological purpose (and as a concealed, humorous retort to the anti-formalist/anti-Hoffmannists).

27. See note 21 above. In any case, Count Pahlen (among other things, military commander of Petersburg under Paul I) was widely thought guilty of the assassination plot, with the consent of the future Alexander I, who nevertheless exiled von Pahlen to his estate "because of ill health" on 10 June 1801, three months after Paul had been strangled in his chambers at the Mikhailovskii Castle. See also the accounts given by Strakhovsky, 13–24, and by Troyat, 34–57.

28. Herbert Eagle's expression, in his discussion of *Poètika kino* and Tynianov's contribution. See Eagle, 5–9.

29. These literary inserts are discussed in detail in "Music and Poetry in 'PORUČIK KIŽE,'" in J. Heil, 267–79, and in *RL* XXI–IV, 371–77.

30. According to one of his former students, N. N. Afimov, Tynianov would say this in his lectures at Leningrad's State Institute of Art History (*GIII*): *Iz istorii Lenfil'ma*, I (1968), 240. In his memoirs, Grigorii Kozintsev (325) describes the 1920s milieu: *Nizkii zhanr—vot chto togda byl "avangard." "Levoe iskusstvo," "nizkie zhanry"—antiakademizm.*

31. This evidence is less in his scholarly works than in his rather subjective fiction. See the satirical treatment of Iurii Aleksandrovich Neledinskii-Meletskii (1751–1828) in section XI of *Podporuchik Kizhe*, and of Faddei Bulgarin (1789–1859) in section 30 of *Maloletnyi Vitushishnikov* ["The Minor, Vitushishnikov" (1932, published 1933)] (the hard ending on the adjective—instead of the modern *-nii*—was Tynianov's choice, a "sign" of the language as it was in Pushkin's time (see the four-volume *Slovar' iazyka Pushkina*); the spelling with *-nii* is a curious misprint in Iampol'skii's article (42), considering it comes from a Tartu-associated group). See details in *RL* XXI–IV, 453–54.

32. Aleksander Slonimskii, *Tekhnika komicheskogo u Gogolia* (1923, rpt.

Providence, 1963), 24–25; translated as "The Technique of the Comic in Gogol," in *Gogol from the Twentieth Century. Eleven Essays.* ed. and trans. Robert Maguire (Princeton, 1974), 325–73 [the citation is on 338].

33. Pavel Petrovich is not only introduced behind these "glass screens," but he will also die behind them. In *plan* 599, the assassins find him hiding: *V lunnom svete iz-za shirmy vidny nogi Pavla.* The feet, extending stick-like, are characteristic also of Hoffmann's Zaches. Iampol'skii (39) cites *kadr* 327 of Tynianov's 1927 script, where the glass is utilized **both** as a pale reflection of Pavel's *visage* (to himself) and as a diffused, distorted image of Pavel (to the film's viewers): *Pavel vkhodit v komnatu. Zakhodit za shirmu—smotrit v steklo shirmy. Blednoe otrazhenie. Khriplo: "Vsë neverno."* In section I of the story, Pavel Petrovich is introduced "barricaded behind and on the sides by a glass screen," and Kibrik's illustrations to the 1930 edition portray the stylized, puppet-like/toy-soldier-like emperor as such. These kinds of details in Tynianov's work are usually tied to some historical fact, such as (here) the fireplace screen behind which the historical Paul I is said to have been hiding when his assassins entered his room (Strakhovsky, 23–24; with his "bare feet sticking out under a Spanish screen," Troyat, 55). But the glass screens are "cinematized" by Tynianov (as noted above) and function as a sign both of Paul's irreality and of his cowardice—they are not merely a trivial historical detail.

34. The attention Tynianov paid to the importance of a single word prompts the scholar to refer to a dictionary to verify instincts. There are at least two instances here of polysemy:

(1) A word of Turkic origins, *karaul* (as defined in the four volume *Slovar' russkogo iazyka* ([1983])) means: (a) an armed guard, (b) guard duty, c) the location of a guardhouse (arch.), and (d) a call for help (interjection). The word thus functions in the "Kizhe" texts ironically, considering the proximity of the emperor to the source of the ominous cry. In section IV of the story, once he has "legitimized" him, Pavel Petrovich petulantly demotes Kizhe to guard duty (*v karaul*).

(2) Siniukhaev (in the story only) bears a characteronym that functions in a manner parallel to the surname in Dostoevskii's *Brat'ia Karamazovy* (*kara* [Turkic] = black; *mazat'* = to smear): *siniúkha* = (a) cyanosis, a bluish discoloration of the skin due to inadequate oxygenation of the blood, and (b) "Jacob's ladder" (*Polemonium*), a grassy plant with blue flowers that has medicinal properties. Thus one can say that the fates of both Kizhe and Siniuhaev are **symptomatic** of their society, and their "diagnosis" might alleviate or help to eradicate the malaise. Also lodged in this surname (but having no etymological connection to it) is the root of the verbs *niukhat'* =

"to smell," and *obniukhat'* = "to sniff (at)." There are several instances in Tynianov's fiction of various "sniffings" (in addition to various slaps, pinches and "tweaks of the nose" inflicted on underlings) which comprise a creative homage to the Gogolian "nose motif." For examples in "PORUCHIK KIZHE," see *plany* 19–21, 190, 285, 297, 401 and note (*RL* XXI–IV, 480), 535, and 625–27.

35. As Vladimir Propp noted in *Morfologiia skazki* (1928), the "disruption of the norm" or the "complication" (*zaviazka*), as well as the "liquidation of the lack" (to mix up his categories) and the "return to the status quo," typify the folk tale, which is in some ways structurally akin to certain established film genres (based on determined formulae with variations, i.e., the horror film, the western, the gangster film and *films noirs*), especially of the so-called "classic" period circa 1930 to 1950.

In Russian history, the elimination of Paul I did not signal a return to the norm in all respects. The reign of Alexander I (1801–25) is generally considered a positive era (though growing disenchantment after the Napoleonic Wars culminated in the Decembrist Revolt of 1825), especially if compared with the previous one and with that of Nicholas I (1825–55).

MYTHOPOETIC THINKING IN
ALESHKOVSKY'S *SMERT' V MOSKVE*

JOHN M. KOPPER

The theme of death possesses its own inherent literary qualities. While death itself may signify little more than an act of generosity, as it does in the self-sacrifice at the end of *A Tale of Two Cities,* or a monumental throwing back of consciousness upon itself, as in *Hamlet,* the problem of writing death into the literary work retains at all times a formal aspect: the question of closure. The central issue for dying persons and those about them—what will survive this death?—is inevitably re-posed for the literary work and its readers in textual terms: is there anything more to read or to witness? The pleasures of readers or audience are naturally arrayed against the moment when the text expires. Theirs is the indulgence of unbelievers, who have faith in nothing beyond the textual last curtain: at moments when narrative has been embodied in truly popular forms, available to a multitude of listeners or readers, it has taken on the properties of serial extension: the nineteenth-century novel, the oral tales of Greece and medieval Europe, the detective shows of television today. We grow attached to their immortal aspirations. It is hard to shut off the television, the Roland cycle, or Dickens.

Narrative in the modern period—since the French Revolution—has been a special beneficiary of the conjunction of two terms: death as emplotted action and death as textual exhaustion. If one of the central modes of modern literature is irony—or the dual perspective—then the issue of immortality, the problem of consciousness surviving death, becomes not simply a question of life *after* the text, but of life *within* the text, that is, of the voices which lie outside the dying consciousness. There is no greater irony than death, and no more fortuitous an occasion for the writer who wishes to exploit disparity in point of view. Death can partition textual rooms that contain different forms of consciousness.

This happy potential in the death theme would seem to have been largely "mined out" before—or by—the advent of so-called post-modernism. In *To the Lighthouse* death can be a chapter interlude, dividing characters from their own deaths, and beyond death, from their reorganization in the memories of those that survive them. In the section of *Sodom and Gomorrah* entitled "The Heart's Intermissions," Proust describes the impression left by the deceased grandmother on the consciousness of the hero. *The Sound and the Fury* brackets the meditations of a suicide on his last day of life with other chapters that serve to contain and qualify the role of a consciousness facing extinction.

It is only later texts that reformulate the relation between literature and the survival of consciousness. In *Finnegans Wake* the consciousness of the defunct—or dying—hero is not blunted or sharpened by death. Instead it expands to swallow the entire work. In Beckett's *Imagination Dead Imagine* the aggressive minimalism of the fictional universe reflects a failure of literary imagination, leading to the death of art and the disappearance of the text. In these works the ironic balance between what lies inside and what lies outside the dying consciousness is no longer sustained.

If one is to place Aleshkovsky's *Smert' v Moskve* according to its exploitation of the death theme, it must go with the literature of the earlier period. The novel is undoubtedly the scion of two of Russia's great death narratives, most obviously *Smert' Ivana Il'iča* and less obviously *Oblomov*. In all three works the protagonist's mind is ironically constituted in the confrontation of a cluttered consciousness with a cluttered world. The narrator interpolates into this already ironic story the ironic voice of one who has survived.[1]

Smert' v Moskve chronicles the last hours in the life of party leader Lev Zakharych Mekhlis, after Kaganovich the most prominent Jew in Stalin's inner circle. Mekhlis died in February 1953, a month before Stalin. The novel takes place in Mekhlis's Moscow apartment, and the telling is divided between Mekhlis's own thoughts and a narrator who comments freely and extensively. Mekhlis's historically-grounded reflections range from the Revolution and the legacy of Lenin to Stalin and the ongoing Doctor's Conspiracy, the Politburo, the imminent problem of succession, and his own place in Soviet history, which Mekhlis envisions as an entry in the encyclopedia. The main non-historical material in the novel has to do with Mekhlis's sexual liaison with two women, both named Verochka, who are married to instructors of history and geography, respectively. The two Verochkas know all the Kremlin's rumors and frequently pass on Party gossip to Mekhlis. Mekhlis's thoughts are inspired by what he sees and hears in his apartment, which is filled with objects. When a surprise article in *Pravda* announces that he has already died, Mekhlis decides that Stalin is playing one of his jokes, but when he turns on the radio, funeral music is being played. At the end of the novel Mekhlis is carried dying out of his apartment by the teachers of history and geography.

Both *Oblomov* and *Smert' v Moskve* take place largely in apartments crowded to the brim with objects, and both works chronicle heroes who confine themselves to narrow places and spend a great deal of time in bed, the place where minimum physical mobility is joined to maximum mental freedom. *Smert' Ivana Il'iča* begins in larger worlds, but shrinks to the hero's bedroom in Ivan Ilyich's "new" house, a parodic allegory of the divine mansion described by Christ, and furbished by Ivan Ilyich with decorations which become the instruments of his death. Any crude Proppian sequence developed for the nineteenth-century death narrative, a subgenre to which *Smert' v Moskve* belongs, must include the moments of reaching out to familiar objects as a guide, coming to know oneself through what are quite literally one's "effects," and watching the external world turn recalcitrant and remote in the face of death. Formerly a mirror of the mind's order, the realm of domestic objects becomes a chaotic and unresponsive environment, a figure for the resistance the mind encounters when trying to organize itself through memory. This use of the man-made world as a limiting device replaces Romanticism's similar appropriation of nature, and the convention is borrowed by Aleshkovsky in *Smert' v Moskve*. The world lying outside the hero comes to constitute an increasingly large domain, a space of "ongoing life" which stands against the diminution inflicted by death.

Aleshkovsky would then seem to have been a careful student of Tolstoy and Goncharov. He develops the "irony of death" motif by advancing and sustaining a spatial metaphor characteristic of the figural structures of "Smert' Ivana Il'iča" and *Oblomov*. Yet in Aleshkovsky's hands the conceit diverges radically from its nineteenth-century sources. If there is something innovative in Aleshkovsky's use of what one might call the "furniture" topos, it is the boldness with which he asserts figural meaning, a gesture we associate with the philosophical tales of Poe and romances of Hawthorne, but which represents a minor line in Russian literature. Mekhlis's apartment is furnished with the booty of the Third Reich, itself the most notorious pillager of our century. He has a harpsichord that belonged to Goebbels, a rug given to Goering by Mussolini, and a bust sporting what seems to be a wig, but is actually the scalp of a Rabbi from Cologne, placed there by Himmler (pp. 13–14). The scene is blatantly unrealistic, not an "is" but an "as if it were" staging. The figural messages are delivered efficiently: 1) Soviet officials are no different from the Nazis, and 2) the Stalinist inner circle has taken over the talismans of a killer culture, forgetful that this culture was itself conquered and destroyed. As he reflects on his life, then, Mekhlis sees only the relics of death, and if the import of the imagery were not already clear, he is continually bumping into, tripping over, and rearranging the bric-a-brac. For example, the apartment contains a Scottish harp, an emblem of the Aeolian harp, perhaps the most concrete image of transcendence which modern European literature has produced. But the harp is set in vibration only when knocked down, run into, and thrown against the TV set, and it produces merely a cacophony. With symbols like the scalp and the harp, Aleshkovsky violates normal Realist criteria for distinguishing probable from improbable behavior and adjusts his art to the standards of non-Realist genres. Hawthorne's Preface to *The House of the Seven Gables* long ago attempted to legitimize this kind of gesture by distinguishing a non-Realist genre, the romance: "The [Novel] is presumed to aim at a very minute fidelity, not merely to the possible, but to the probable and ordinary course of man's experience. The [Romance] . . . while it sins unpardonably so far as it may swerve aside from the truth of the human heart—has fairly a right to present that truth under circumstances, to a great extent, of the writer's own choosing or creation."[2]

A second intrusion upon the Realist plan of the novel is its use of the fantastic. The climax of *Smert' v Moskve* occurs toward the end, when Mekhlis, asleep in his apartment, dreams an allegory of the "Veršina Vlasti." This dream inverts Goncharov's "Son Oblomova." The Veršina Vlasti is a reviewing platform, precariously balanced on Lenin's Mausoleum, and deriving warmth for its floorboards from the ducts that heat the Mausoleum. When a bevy of naked Pioneer girls parades by, reminiscent of Bulgakov's Black Sabbath imagery, Mekhlis glances down at himself to see if his body has responded sexually. Instantly nudity is transformed from eroticism into bestiality—Mekhlis sees that the leaders on the Veršina Vlasti are naked from the waist down, and their lower bodies are animal-like.

> Ноги-то у всех вождей — вовсе и не ноги, а дикие копыта, покрытые грязновато-жидковатой сивой, гнедой, буланой, пегой и прочими щетинами. Только у Сталина... поставившего, понимаете, себя над партией и народом...нагуталиненные копытища донизу прикрыты густыми, как у породистых битюгов, чубами щетинищи... но, что особенно удивительно, бабки-то у всех вождей разные... У брюхатого Кагановича — кривовато-тонюсенькие, словно у рахитичной антилопы. У Берия — тоже, но с какими-то грязными наростами. А вот у кащеистого Суслова — опухшие, слоновьи тумбы. Аккуратные, в общем-то, мослы лишь у жопоморды Маленкова и у лаптя кромешного Никиты...
>
> (pp. 201–2)

Trying to maintain his balance, Mekhlis grabs Suslov's leg, but falls anyway. As he plummets downward, Mekhlis discovers that the Veršina Vlasti is the summit of a mountain; he gazes at people trying to climb upward, driving their walking sticks into the skulls of the corpses that litter their way. At the foot of the mountain are clock hands ("strelki") pointing upward like a forest of arrows. An instant short of being impaled on these prongs of Time, Mekhlis wakes up. The clock hands figure Mekhlis's own death and make clear that Bolshevik power has abandoned history in order to build its edifice.[3]

We move now to yet another feature of the novel which cannot be considered Realist. *Smert' v Moskve* is about an historical figure, very powerful during the Stalinist years. The nineteenth-century novel tends to use historical figures sparingly and peripherally, since its effort is to find and follow the generic man—the ordinary public official Ivan Ilyich, the lazy noble Oblomov who at the end is literally transformed from proper name to common noun. *Smert' v Moskve* at first glance would seem *not* to be interested in the representative.

The systematic deployment of symbolic structures, the reliance on fantasy, and emphasis on the extraordinary man call to mind not only certain strains of nineteenth-century Romantic literature, but the features of myth. *Smert' v Moskve* is filled with side glances at classical mythology: Krupskaja, Stasova, and Zemljačka are characterized as three furies (and at the end of the novel act like three Fates [p. 256]). The heating ducts of Lenin's tomb evoke the underground stream passages at Delphi, an image that allows the reader to understand that Lenin is the modern oracle (p. 201). These are a few of the novel's direct references to classical mythology, but Aleshkovsky's relation to myth goes beyond mere citation.

If loosely taken, myth is a set of beliefs encoded in story form. It usually contains statements about origins, and because myths are by definition retellable, they provide *current* information on why things are as they are. Agnosticism would seem to preclude the use of myth in any non-ironic context, and indeed a large part of Aleshkovsky's enterprise is dedicated to dismantling at least two powerful Soviet myths, Marxist utopianism and the personality cult of Stalin. Communist man is replaced by the greedy intriguer; Stalin, referred to in capital letters as "Xozjain," is a divinity of fear, loathed by the pantheon of Party leaders over whom he presides. Allusions to a theocracy are introduced as parody. This aspect of *Smert' v Moskve* provides no surprises and is of one cloth with the Realist undertaking. Yet the three features of *Smert' v Moskve* which escape the conventions of the Realist genre—fantasy, allegory, and the use of a well-known historical figure as a representative of common experience—would seem to suggest that the novel's relationship with mythology is not necessarily "anti-."

The logic of myth itself is rather complicated. First, one must distinguish between myths and stories that use myth. According to this distinction, myths would be kernel narratives, by definition 1) significant in every detail and therefore laconic, 2) giving animate form to natural objects, or concepts, or cosmic processes. In Greek mythology, for example, Heaven and Earth give birth to Time, Ocean, and Memory. Time in turn gives birth to the father of the gods. This myth animates nature (heaven and earth) and concepts (time) and imposes a chronology for creation through the analogy of human procreation. The myth is very simple: chronology is a metaphor for causality, and people are metaphors for concepts. In literary terms, this means writing the common nouns with capital letters and having the entities behave like living creatures. The Greeks took common nouns like chronos and mnemosyne and produced divinities like Chronos and Mnemosyne.

Yet myths nearly always contain material which is superfluous to the description of a concept or a natural process. It is easy to see how this expansion takes place. An implicit understanding of the world motivates the story-line of an allegory, however abstracted it is from experience, and at some point, in response to this understanding, the story develops independent life and produces plot sequences of its own. If Zeus and Hera, as principles representing the wandering warrior and the domestic woman, are destined to live in conflict, then they must fight over something. The theme of Zeus's mortal girl friends is produced to fulfill a narrative expectation. In mythologies as ramified as the Greek, this spinning out of stories sometimes produces neat intersections: the Europa tale exemplifies Zeus's infidelity and also explains how Europe got its name. At times, rather than serve as description of *two* events in the mythic system, the myth seems to lose even its original function. Apollo and Helios are both gods of the sun; Hades is both the underworld and god of the underworld, but death is Thanatos. Many of the gods thus cease to be properties and merely possess, or hold title to, the properties, while they spend their time caught up in the domestic politics of the Olympian court. Their stories become elaborate fantasies and, in a skeptical age, can acquire the rococo filigree of the tales in Ovid's *Metamorphoses*.

The Stalinist period was conducive to myth-making because the upheavals and dislocations of the time were so rarely rooted in a visible cause. Myths attribute actions and assign reasons for behavior. This explains the interest Mekhlis possesses as a universally known Soviet functionary, a minor deity in the Stalinist Valhalla. Mekhlis's mythic attraction is his high station. As a Stalinist policy-maker, he is simply a mythologically up-to-date version of a rain-maker or earth-shaker. But myths also produce their own independent stories. I think it possible to see now that the aspects of Aleshkovsky's novel which "exceed" the Realist convention are precisely the qualities of myth which lead to the complicated plot. Mekhlis drifts off again and again into imaginary and remembered conversations with Stalin, formulates policy statements, reviles his opponents, and endlessly justifies to himself virtually indistinguishable shades of official anti-Semitism and anti-Zionism. The novel, with Ovidian invention, spins its entertaining subplots around this ostinato. For example Mekhlis hears a noise in his apartment, which then provokes a discourse from the narrator on sound in childhood, and a metaphysical discussion ensues.

> Не в том ли милый, неуловимо-лукавый, нежно-заигрывающий смысл любого собрания звуков, то есть гармонии, равно, как и звука одинокого, в первые наши дни нелегкого обвыкания с даром Жизни, что любые звуки кружатся, падают, трепещут, взвиваются, посиживают, перепархивают, носятся, словно птицы-ласточки, чайки, попугаи, воробушки, соколы, совы, журавли, синички, — одним словом, шастают любые звуки, пропадая и, к счастью, возникая вновь, как раз промеж устрашившим нас до ужаса, бытием и вполне беззаботной вечностью, разрушаемой зачастую намеренно легкомысленно не пчелами, не черепахами, не ягуарами и китами, но лишь людьми, в безлюбовных праздных организмах, и простите за выражение, безответственных зачатиях?...
> ...И через какое-то время все звуки мира, лишаясь божественной свободы, попадают в плен либо к вещам, либо к явлениям и к живым тварям, не говоря уж о чудесном пленении звука словом, становятся, звуки на взгляд поверхностный, всего лишь рабскими свойствами всего их пленившего.
>
> (p. 246)

Mekhlis imagines his death is being announced on state TV and radio, and throws things at the TV. Here we are in the realm of improvisation. The kernel myth is forgotten, and Mekhlis emerges, like the contentious and touchy gods of Greece, as a personality in his own right. In Rousseau's terms, the "dangerous supplement" to narrative is Mekhlis himself.

Just as Mekhlis's eminence shows its origin in myth, so does allegory. An example descriptive of the genesis of allegory would be the end of the novel. The premature announcement of Mekhlis's death signifies the loss of an orderly chronology in a culture that has abandoned history. But if this were not made sufficiently clear to the reader, in the last scene the two drunken instructors in history and geography, while performing their moonlighting jobs at the city morgue, stumble into Mekhlis's apartment, rob him of a copy of Thucydides, and carry him, still alive, into death. The allegorical reading is transparent enough: geography and history—space and time—survive Mekhlis, but appear in drunken, or Soviet, versions. This allows for a philosophical discussion of Russian history:

> ...Ввещий [sic] Олег сам знает, когда ему сби... кстати, ты заметил,
> Вась-Вась, что, если бы он не сбирался отмстить неразумным хазарам,
> а разумно использовал их способности, энергию и географическую
> неприкаянность, то нынешние рыла «из грязи — в князи» сегодня бы
> не в Африку лезли, а собирали пустую посуду в проклятых «рюмоч-
> ных» и «бутербродных»?
>
> (p. 255)

The seme of drunkenness permits even more comment, equally diverting but at some level sensical, such as the confusion of Mme. de Stael with Ostrovsky's novel: "Мадам де Сталь. Вась-Вась, как она закалялась! Как она закалялась!" (p. 251). Narrative declines from—or better, issues from—the allegory, the mythic elements lose their overdetermination, and the stories and subplots multiply.

The third non-Realistic feature of *Smert' v Moskve,* the fantastic, derives from its allegorical structure. To insist that any implausible action occurring on the allegorical plane must be simultaneously read within the constructs of realism is to produce the fantastic, as Todorov defines it.[4] Moreover, as Sinyavsky has pointed out, this confusion is characteristic of the myth-making apparatus of socialist realism, where the continuity of realistic sequences is constantly disrupted by the pressure to codify action in exemplary forms and elevate it into a theological system.[5] One problem with such literature is that it becomes hard to distinguish the unrealistic portrayal from the unfaithful, or in other words, the potential allegory from the lie. Aleshkovsky's texts parody this ambiguity in socialist realism. In *Smert' v Moskve,* as in Aleshkovsky's *Kenguru,* impossible things happen and characters claim to have done impossible things, just as they do in a canonical Soviet text like *Cement.*

If *Smert' v Moskve,* as it demythologizes Soviet history, simultaneously uses many of the conventions of mythology, where does it finally come down? An answer can be provided by looking at the novel's language. On the surface, its impious discourse would seem to be consistently demystifying and militantly secular. Aleshkovsky's colloquialism is as rich as anything in Russian since Babel' or Zoshchenko, and the invective as exuberantly coarse as Pushkin's privately circulated poems. The play of learned discourse with improvisatory word games reminds one, in its obsessive brilliance, of Rabelais. Like Panurge's disquisitions, the novel is best read aloud.[6]

Nevertheless, any examination of the characteristic features of Aleshkovsky's complex style shows its proximity to religious discourse and religious ritual. First, the language is incantatory. Words break down and become syllables to be chanted: "Зверье, загнан. тупик класс. бор... клетки желнаркомом... в глаз. мольба о прощ... не прост. сердц. отстук. морзе... высш. мер... высш. мер. высш. мер... выр... род... чел..." (pp. 88–89) Sounds occasionally produce lengthy alliterated sentences: "Он знает, за что поддеть, на что подсадить, да подсечь побольнее и помотать, понимаете, помотать..." (p. 144). Syllables also separate and produce word families—the "us" in "bezuslovno," Mekhlis's favorite word, becomes Stalin's "us" or "moustache," and generates a swarm of stinging words:

> Чувство облегчения тут же зловредно улетучилось, а Л. З. вмиг облепила, кусаючи, жаля, подкалывая, стая мухообразных словечек.... УСтал... УСтав... УСтряловщина... УСыпальница... УСкакать... УСнуть... УСпеть... УСтраниться... УСыпленный... УСоп... УСушка...
>
> (p. 223)

Behind this associative play lie two theories of language, both of which apply to Aleshkovsky's novel. One is the mimetic, advanced in Plato's *Cratylus* and carried through the distinguished work of Vico on mythopoetic thinking to its farcical resting place in the Stalinist theories of language promoted by Marr. Stalin, by Aleshkovsky's lights, is the central, determining fact of Soviet existence; the letters "yc," embodying his distinguishing feature, are bound to appear with fearsome regularity in a multitude of Russian words, where the stable semantic value of yc will inevitably and repeatedly invoke the original authorizing figure. But the "us" passage suggests Dostoevsky as well. In "Bobok," also a tale of disintegrating consciousness, language is gradually stripped of its social functions until what remains is an obscenely trivial word. Dostoevsky's morbid characters do not produce the combinatorial linguistic splendors that proliferate in Mekhlis's consciousness, but common to the two texts is the notion that the residue of speech in its moment of decomposition may be the symbolic word.

Second, phrases from a frozen discourse, Soviet political jargon, intrude at unexpected moments, puncturing the tone of the narrative: "жертвы исторически необходимых заблуждений" (p. 88). While having sex, Mekhlis finds that:

> В самом половом акте, в голове его беспорядочно мелькали вдруг приметы и образы служебной действительности, он холодел от их враждебного явления и сам себя раздражительно вопрошал: «какой съезд... какая, понимаете, пятилетка?... да вы что?... где очередные задачи?... орден Ленина?... ложа Большого?... Депутат?... ну знаете...»
>
> (p. 108)

As Priscilla Meyer has noted, the sandwiching of political discourse into
patently non-political speech is characteristic of Aleshkovsky's style.[7] In the
story "Smert' ovčarki," for example, the defendant Mirošničenko concludes
an account of his actions with the words:

> Напоследок мы со свояком налопались от пуза телятины и распили,
> конечно, литровочку за мою предстоящую тюремную жизнь. Думаю,
> что и вы так же поступили бы на моем месте. А в остальном я
> полностью поддерживаю нашу партию в ее продовольственной про-
> грамме и в борьбе за разоружение американского империализма.[8]

In *Smert' v Moskve,* Yuri Levitan's voice over the radio breaks in to
announce the achievements of the women's garment works (p. 150); *Pravda's*
obituary of Mekhlis is quoted at length (pp. 142–43). The identity of
Aleshkovsky's heroes is based on the civic religion of Marxism-Leninism,
and it is constituted in the lapse from proper political activity. As in *Portrait
of the Artist as a Young Man*, religious discourse crowds out individual consciousness by its fixed formulas, and all boundaries between religious man
and private man are threatened with dissolution.

   Third, the text incorporates a Jewish lexicon—"зай гезунд," or the words
of Mekhlis's mother, "Партийная работа — далеко не цимес."

   The pastiche of "Jewish" and "Soviet" speech, as well as the disintegration
and recombination of sounds, creates a verbal and thematic collage, reflecting attitudes toward past, present, and future. In the novel the Jewish theme
signifies history and the past in general, but Judaism for Aleshkovsky has
become a matter of Jews torturing Jews, and it survives in *Smert' v Moskve*
as mere vocabulary. The language of everyday Soviet life stands for the
present, but the Bolshevik dream endures only in Levitan's Communist cant.
Future life is represented by the alliteration and alphabet games, foretokens
of the time when Mekhlis will be entombed in the *Bol'šaja Sovetskaja
Ènciklopedija* as an alphabetically filed entry, "...Рядышком с 'Мехико,'
'меховой промышленностью,' и 'турецким султанеусом Мехмедом II'"
(p. 238). Mekhlis' place in the Encyclopedia thus becomes a coffin between
two entries, and the Encyclopedia itself can be interpreted as a vast Soviet
cultural cemetery. Aleshkovsky's novel appears to suggest that language no
longer bears the weight of meaning, that the mythological systems of Judaism and Bolshevism are dysfunctional, and that only words survive, organized not by cultural codes but by the senseless order of the alphabet. The
various lexical strata of *Smert' v Moskve* are used by Aleshkovsky to destroy
the possibility of a mythological language.

   To leave the argument here, however, is to ignore the most important speech layer in the novel, *mat*. Scurrility consistently reduces speech to the language of the body and body processes. In the words of Rosenbloom, tortured by Mekhlis during the investigation into the Doctor's Conspiracy, "А о кале вы способны сказать что-нибудь большее, чем то, что кал — это говно?" (p. 116). With one motion discourse falls toward the body and language declines to the scabrous. By dint of repetition, *mat* claims its place as an *underlying* level of discourse to which the various other kinds of speech in the novel return, and it replaces the rituals which have failed. Leo Spitzer has written that in Judaism the rights of the body coexist with the claims of the Creator on the immortal soul, and I suspect that Aleshkovsky's *mat* exploits this Jewish idea, enveloping discourse on the body with a religious aura.[9] But Aleshkovsky by no means holds up Judaism as a saving doctrine once he has so convincingly abandoned it. Rather *mat* becomes a ritualistic conjuration of normality, an emphatic voice for sanity.

To understand the relation of Aleshkovsky's *mat* to myth, we need only return to the original model of the kernel myth and to the stories that build upon it. As we saw, Aleshkovsky's novel pretends to be filling out a myth with stories, and it betrays all the earmarks of extended myth. But this raises the question of the kernel myth. The obvious candidate would be the encyclopedia entry describing Mekhlis' life. Here *Smert' v Moskve* shows insight into the mythic process. Myth involves statements about origins in a form which continues to remain valid for a culture. But myths become ritualized by repetition and not only explain but *consecrate* present practice. An alternative kernel myth in *Smert' v Moskve*, the layer to which the text's many plots and voices must inevitably respond, is scurrility. The novel counteracts the impression left by the encyclopedic entry that the origin of the Soviet *polis*, which is "the current state of things," can be described as a succession of *podvigi* performed by a succession of Mekhlises, and suggests that the origin of the current state of things can be described only by profane words. *Smert' v Moskve* uses the conventions of myth not simply to demythologize, but to substitute for a myth that deceives—the encyclopedic entry—a myth that truly provides an explanation for the surrounding world and that neither effaces nor masks.

In summary, *Smert' v Moskve* combines inherited conventions of nineteenth-century Realism with certain features not usually associated with that movement: the story of the prominent historical figure, allegory, and fantasy. These same features are characteristic of myth. *Smert' v Moskve* uses these conventions in part to undo myth, but also to write a more accurate account of Stalinist power than the encyclopedia provides.[10]

It is in its portrayal of Mekhlis and the Kremlin leadership that Aleshkovsky's text seems most contemporary. There have been traditionally three approaches to historical figures in Russian fiction: the piously circumspect, the caustically circumspect, and the larger-than-life biographical. The depiction of Catherine the Great and Pugachev in *Kapitanskaja dočka* and of Beethoven in Odoevskij's "Poslednij kvartet Betxovena" exemplify the first. The portrayal of Napoleon in *Vojna i mir* or of Stalin in *V kruge pervom* are examples of the caustically circumspect. A. N. Tolstoy's Peter the Great is the paradigmatic protagonist placed in a "heroic age." But in Soviet literature of the last twenty years a fourth pattern has emerged, in which high officials, most frequently Stalin himself, are ritually and systematically degraded. One thinks of the portraits of Party officials in Voinovich's "V krugu druzej," Iskander's "Sandro" stories, and Aleshkovsky's own *Kenguru*.

Most of these Stalin satires have been anti-hagiographical. By inverting the tradition of the "positive" hero, they reject the idea that socialist fiction must be edifying, a "mirror of virtue" rather than a "mirror of reality." But *Smert' v Moskve* clearly transcends this current genre; it may use the weapons of Realism to disarm myth, but its non-Realist discourse suggests that myths have value, if their explanatory function is itself not allowed to become sacred and therefore predictive.

Cassirer has remarked of the typical Old Testament prophet that in his struggle with idolatry he ". . . must inject into the mythical consciousness an alien tension, an opposition it does not know as such, in order to disintegrate and destroy it from within."[11] In his effort to deconstruct the ideal image of the Soviet state, Aleshkovsky proposes a rhetoric of defamation and abuse. But this *mat* already contains Aleshkovsky's alternative: an anti-idealistic, earth-bound, ironic discourse. *Smert' v Moskve* is to be read as a visionary book by a prophet of invective.

Because Aleshkovsky's characters are so negatively drawn, they lack the redemptive potential inherent in eschatological prophecy, or even in the visions of Oblomov or the dying Ivan Ilyich. There is a narrative difference between facing limbo and facing Giudecca. Aleshkovsky's protagonists, as one of them himself says, are in "hand-to-hand" combat with those who would follow Biblical virtues, and as active forces for evil, they cannot sustain a myth of expiation and salvation.[12] But the language can. It is *mat*, after all, which demolishes Mekhlis's myth of himself, and more crucially, *mat* which can bring the novel to its end. Once Mekhlis has been reduced to a death-in-life, the story is over, vitriol has done its work, and in the space surrounding Mekhlis's life is left the myth of *mat*, ever susceptible to invocation. Though the protagonist exhausts the narrative with his recitation of lies, profanity is left. To this the reader must bear witness.

Notes

1. Citations are taken from Yuz Aleshkovsky, *Smert' v Moskve* (Benson, Vt., 1985).

2. Nathaniel Hawthorne, *The House of the Seven Gables*, Centenary Edition of the Works of Nathaniel Hawthorne, 2 (Columbus, 1965):1.

3. Incidentally, the scene borrows from the opening chapter of *Alice in Wonderland*, which seems to have become a canonical image book for Aesopian writing in the Soviet Union. The fall itself, the clock images, the white gloves of the leaders, and the objects—papers, glasses, blades of grass, and corpses—which fall with Mekhlis all evoke Alice's tumble into fantasy at the beginning of *Alice in Wonderland*.

4. When he defines the fantastic as "a hesitation" between the natural and the supernatural reading, Todorov specifically excludes allegory (see Tzvetan Todorov, *The Fantastic*, trans. Richard Howard [Ithaca, 1980], 32). Todorov has in mind allegory which can only be read—that is, "explained"—as allegory. But if the supernatural events of a text are to be believed, as they are in *Smert' v Moskve*, then it becomes a moot question whether or not allegory has motivated insertion of the supernatural event.

5. "[Contemporary Soviet writers] try to combine the uncombinable: the positive hero (who logically tends toward the pattern, the allegory) and the psychological analysis of character . . . a high ideal with truthful representation of life." But Sinyavsky goes on, ". . . A really faithful representation of life cannot be achieved in a language based on teleological concepts." See Andrei Sinyavsky, "On Socialist Realism," trans. George Dennis, in *The Trial Begins and On Socialist Realism* (Berkeley, 1982), 214–15.

6. Scholarly hours could be fruitfully spent arguing whether the rapid pitch and plunge of language makes for what Eikhenbaum found to be the essence of Gogolian grotesque, or instead creates a Soviet-style Pantagruelisme as optimistic as its Renaissance forebear.

7. Priscilla Meyer, "*Skaz* in the Work of Juz Aleškovskij," *Slavic and East European Journal*, 28:4 (1984), 455–61.

8. Yuz Aleshkovsky, "Smert' ovčarki," in *Kniga poslednix slov, 35 prestuplenij* (Benson, Vt., 1984), 64.

9. Leo Spitzer, "Three Poems on Ecstasy: John Donne, St. John of the Cross, Richard Wagner," in *Essays in European and American Literature*, ed. Anna Hatcher (Princeton, 1962), 150. Priscilla Meyer uses Boris Uspenskij's discussion of *mat* as the functional "equivalent of prayer" and argues that Aleshkovsky's scurrility serves a "holy purpose" (Meyer, 460).

10. Peter Allan Dale comments on the reversal of values in Thomas Carlyle's *Sartor Resartus*: "The comic inversion of a dominant literary-spiritual ideal does not represent a failure of faith in that ideal. What is involved, rather, is a mature recognition of the realities that tend to undermine or block the ideal, and the hope of somehow redeeming that ideal by indirection." The difficulty one faces in applying this passage to Aleshkovsky's humor shows how far removed his satire is from conventional Romantic irony. (See Peter Allan Dale, "*Sartor Resartus* and the Inverse Sublime: The Art of Humorous Deconstruction," in *Allegory, Myth, and Symbol*, ed. Morton W. Bloomfield [Cambridge, Mass., 1981], 303.)

11. Ernst Cassirer, *Mythical Thought*, trans. Ralph Manheim (New Haven, 1970), 241.

12. "Мы в рукопашные схватки с людьми, променявшими моральный кодекс строителя коммунизма на пресловутые заповеди: не убивай, не лги, не отбивай жену у дружка, не воруй и так далее." ("Ikra dlja Billi," in *Kniga poslednix slov*, 135–36).

PAN TWARDOWSKI: THE POLISH VARIANT
OF THE FAUST LEGEND
IN SLAVIC LITERATURES

A Study in Motif-History

WALTER SCHAMSCHULA

Ever since the Faust legend came into being in the sixteenth century, it has fascinated writers and readers by its dramatic rendering of the elementary conflict between the human mind in search of knowledge and officially-established concepts upheld by the authority of a monopolizing church. Another reason for its success is that it offers a wide variety of potential plot resolutions, ranging from the condemnation of the sinful scholar to his redemption. The Faust legend became a challenge to philosophically minded writers, who sought to shape it into a drama of man in search of truth in an unexplorable universe.

The idea of Dr. Faustus could have originated only under certain circumstances. First of all, an ethical dualism is required in which the powers of good and evil balanced each other, as they do in the Judeo-Christian world view. Here, the good side is with God, the Creator of the universe and holder of the ultimate power, whereas the evil side is with God's opponent, the devil. Moreover, the genesis of the myth of Dr. Faustus is conceivable only at a junction in human intellectual history when two concepts of the world coexisted: one that of a closed society dominated by the medieval church, exerting strict authority over everyone's mind; the other that of humanist emancipation and self-reliance. With the Renaissance and the rise of Humanism, a new human character emerged: the self-assured scholar, poet, artist, the *uomo universale,* who no longer needed the patronage of a church to carry on his creative activity. In such a period of transition from a closed society to the first, rudimentary stage of an open one, conflicts were bound to arise. An independent mind, a scholar perhaps, a doctor whose skill and knowledge were demonstrated in public, was seen by the simple mind as a wizard, a magician whose knowledge and skill were rooted in evil.

A society in transition from church-dominated mind control to free development of the intellect was, in its initial stage, an environment in which an independent and scientifically minded person had to face great hardships. The experiments of alchemists or of physicians who brewed their medications awed common people and gave rise to the idea that such power must be evil and that the devil must even have become the magician's servant by contract, since, as A. I. Beleckij in his study on Faust put it, "witchcraft is illegal wonder, and wonder is legal witchcraft" in the doctrine of the Christian churches.[1] The evidence of alleged supernatural occurrences in sixteenth-century Central Europe—including Bohemia and Poland—is very rich, and there are numerous references to persons called Dr. Faustus or to other active magicians suspected of having supernatural connections. Very instructive documentation of this subject may, among other sources, be found in V. M. Žirmunskij's book *Legenda o doktore Fauste*.[2] Yet this work deals with the Faust legend proper, not with the general idea of a contract with the devil, of which Dr. Faustus is only the best-known and most widespread example.

Another enlightening study, Leopold Kretzenbacher's *Teufelsbündner und Faustgestalten im Abendlande* [3] enlarges the picture and includes other characters related to Faust. We are informed that the motif of a contract with the devil signed with the person's own blood is rather widespread within the extended area of Central Europe. There is a Dutch version where the holder of the contract is a woman and a Hungarian version with a wandering scholar called Garaboncziás-diák as the protagonist. This same character also appears in Eastern Croatia as Grabancijaš, while in the coastal area his name is either grecized as "Negromante, Legromant," or simply given as "Vještac," the wizard. The Slovenes have their version of a "student of the black school" (Černe šole dijak) or the "Student from the Trenta" (Trentarski študent) who occurs in folklore and from there entered literature in Joža Lovrenčič's story "Sholar iz Trente" (1939), which has become something like a Slovene "Faust" epic.

Still more widespread and productive is the Polish version of the Faust motif, which is also quoted in Kretzenbacher's book. The name of the hero is Doktor Jan Twardowski, yet in most cases he is referred to as Pan Twardowski (because he is a member of the Polish "szlachta"), or as "Mistrz Twardowski." Like Faust, Pan Twardowski is said to have a historical prototype, reported to have lived in the sixteenth century in Cracow, where the historical Dr. Faustus is also supposed to have been seen. In Cracow, one of the oldest universities north of the Alps (founded in 1364), around the year 1500 the arts of chiromancy, catoptromancy, crystallomancy, and necromancy (foretelling the future by palmistry, by looking into a mirror, by using a crystal, or by communicating with the dead) were practiced, and there are reports that in the year 1505 two baccalaurei studied witchcraft. Cracow and the Łysa Góra became the setting of the Twardowski saga. Evidence about the historical Twardowski is ambiguous and probably distorted by later accretions. According to one account, Twardowski was a student of the German Reformer Philipp Melanchthon at Wittenberg, yet his name does not appear in the enrollment roster, the "Immatrikulationsbuch." In later years, according to several unattested references, he was a protégé of Franciszek Krasiński, who was to become bishop of Cracow, and also represented him at the court of Sigismund August II, so that—allegedly— Twardowski became a marshal at the court. As with the Faust legend, we are here again confronted with numerous local traditions and orally trans- mitted stories connecting the hero Twardowski with such places as Byd- goszcz, Cracow, Kazimierz nad Wisłą, etc. There are nine taverns by the name of "Rzym" (Rome) which claim to be the place where Twardowski was taken by the devil on his way to hell. They are scattered over the areas of Cracow, Sandomierz, Great Poland, Mazowia and even Belorussia.

The most recent study on Twardowski, and the most instructive, is Roman Bugaj's *Nauki tajemne w dawnej Polsce—Mistrz Twardowski,*[4] in which, while no mention is made of Kretzenbacher's study, the folkloric or semi-folkloric genesis of the Twardowski theme does seem to be properly addressed. In addition, there is much important information to be found in this study. As evidence for Twardowski's existence, a certain manuscript is occasionally referred to as an actual holograph of the magician. This so-called Twardow- ski book is kept at the University Library of Cracow and has been studied repeatedly. In 1932–33 Josef Reiss published his essay "Das Twardowski- Buch. Opus magicum des polnischen Faust."[5] He mentions several strange occurrences connected with the Twardowski book, for example, the fact that it is said to have disappeared under mysterious circumstances between 1620 and 1630 and that on one of its pages there is a black spot, reputed to have been caused by the devil when he tried to grab the book. Recent critical studies by Przybylski, Bandtke, and Dobrovský have demonstrated that its author was Paulus (Paulirinus) de Praga, surnamed Žídek (the Jew), born in 1413. (The book itself deals with botany and the art of medicine. The black spot is just an ink spot.)

The plot of the Twardowski legend, as it appears in literature in the nineteenth century, shows signs of growth from a single story about a con- tract with the devil to a conglomerate of tale-types. I shall try to tell the story as it occurs in such versions as K. W. Wójcicki's "Klechdy narodu pol- skiego,"[6] Ignacy Kraszewski's novel *Mistrz Twardowski* (1839), and Julian Krzyżanowski's scholarly analysis.[7] Twardowski is doomed in a twofold sense. Once he was promised to the devil by his father when the latter was in danger of being submerged in a swamp (in one version) or (in others) of being killed by robbers. He calls the devil for help and promises him the first unfamiliar object he will see in his house after his return. After being saved, he learns that during his absence a son had been born to him; the son now becomes the devil's prey. In some of the versions Twardowski, who has grown up, succeeds in retrieving the devil's contract by entering hell and saying prayers. This introductory story, incidentally, is a tale-type of its own, listed in Aarne-Thompson under the number 756B S222: "Man promises (sells) child in order to save himself from danger or death"—with the appendix: F81.2: "Journey to hell to recover the devil's contract."[8] This is an independent story which also entered literature independently, e.g. in Leonid Andreev's "Legenda o razbojnike Madeje" (1927). In some of the versions Twardowski succeeds in recovering the contract before entering into a new one in exchange for forbidden knowledge and mastery of witchcraft. This second pact, however, contains a great variety of conditions. The most important is that the devil has the right to abduct Twardowski's soul into hell only in Rome, where Twardowski promises to go voluntarily within the next seven years. The seven years go by, but Twardowski stays away from Rome. Now the devil must resort to trickery. Within a day he constructs a restaurant by the name of "Rome." At night Twardowski as a physician receives a call from a patient in "Rome." As soon as the doctor arrives there, the devil confronts him. Twardowski makes the sign of the cross and resists. Now the devil appeals to Twardowski's pride: "verbum nobile debet esse stabile" (A nobleman must keep his word). Twardowski obeys, and the devil takes his prey into the sky over the Carpathian mountains. At this moment an old woman prays to the Holy Virgin (or Twardowski himself prays), and the devil loses his power. He abandons Twardowski's body, which now will remain fixed in the air until the day of the Last Judgment. Twardowski's servant—a kind of "famulus" like Faust's Wagner—in the meantime has been transformed into a spider by Twardowski himself. He clings to his master's coat and from a lofty place high above the mountains spins a web down to earth. This allows him to climb up and down and to stay in contact with the earth. Down on earth he finds out what is going on, then climbs up to his master and tells him all the news.

As we see, there are substantial differences from the Faust legend. The original Faust story ends with the devil's triumph. Faust's soul is abducted into hell, whereas in later, literary versions, especially since the Enlightenment (Lessing, Goethe), Faust is saved from eternal condemnation. Twardowski's fate is a compromise: he is neither saved nor condemned. The

Blessed Virgin, the patroness of Poland, is strong enough to save Twardow-ski from hell, yet his sins are so grievous that they balance the power of the Virgin's intercession. Unlike Faust, Twardowski is not driven by his intellectual curiosity alone, but also by a strong desire to influence his world, to exert political power, to enjoy life, to be successful with the other sex (an element of the Don-Juan motif); in sum, he is all a Polish magnate could desire. Witchcraft is merely a tool. In the oldest reference to the motif Twardowski is synonymous with the magician, and the contract with the devil remains unmentioned. He succeeds in reviving the late Queen Barbara Radziwiłł for several minutes in front of her mourning husband, King Sigismund August. As a magician he also practices medicine. He experiments with human bodies, dissecting them while he keeps their souls in glass vessels so they cannot escape into the other world. After having recomposed their bodies properly, he reunites them with their souls. Another aspect of the Twardowski theme is the quest for eternal youth. Twardowski makes use of his power to try to live forever. After having rejuvenated the mayor of Bydgoszcz he wants to perform the same operation on himself. He lies down in a coffin and asks his servant to watch over the coffin for three years, seven months, seven days, and seven hours. After this period of time a child wakes up from the coffin and grows quickly to manhood. The experiment having been successful, Twardowski transforms his servant into a spider in order to prevent him from performing the operation on others.

In some versions a magic mirror plays an important role. According to some local traditions, this mirror is kept at the Węgrów monastery in Podlesie. Twardowski used it at his lectures at the university in order to revive characters of the past in front of his audience. Whoever looks into this mirror sees only an ugly grimace. A mirror really exists in a Węgrów church (albeit without the ugly grimace) bearing the inscription: "Luserat hoc speculo magicus Tvardovius artes, lusus at iste Dei in absequium est."[9] (With this mirror, the magician Twardowski deceived the arts, and was himself deceived in God's clemency.) An analysis of the frame shows that it originated in the early eighteenth century when, perhaps, the church wanted to demonstrate to its flock the fatal consequences of witchcraft. Yet this does not mean that the mirror itself must be from the same period, since it may be assumed that the inscription together with the frame were in any case added to the mirror after Twardowski's death. Another detail that occurs in some of the versions is Twardowski's desire to travel through the air with the devil's help and to look down on cities from above. Twardowski's devil acts in a rather unsophisticated manner compared to Goethe's Mephisto; at times he is downright stupid and thus open to being deceived.

Unlike the Faust theme, which served as a subject to some of the giants of world literature, such as Marlowe, Lessing, Goethe, Lord Byron, Valéry, Thomas Mann, and of course Puškin, Turgenev, and Bulgakov (the most prominent Russian Faust authors), the Twardowski legend has been accepted in literature only with difficulty, at first in Polish, then also in other Slavic literatures. Let us first examine the Polish literary tradition. The first mention of the magician Twardowski occurs in Lukasz Górnicki's *Dworzanin polski* (1566), which is a Polish version of Baldassare de Castiglione's *Il libro del Cortegiano*. This testifies to the ancient origins of the Twardowski story—no later than the mid sixteenth century, about the same period as the Faust legend. *Dworzanin polski,* like *Il Cortegiano* is a handbook of behavior for the nobleman, an important document of cultural history. It consists of so-called "exempla" or "fabliaux," short instructive stories with didactic messages, but nonetheless entertaining. The story in question says that a person at the court seeking more influence upon King Sigismund August asks someone to supply him with an instructor in black magic. The other nobleman offers his help, pretending that he himself is a disciple of Twardowski. To prove his point he demonstrates his art. He says that upon a magic formula a woman who is selling her pottery in the neighborhood of the castle will destroy all that pottery with a stick. The experiment is a success and is reported to the king. The king asks the nobleman to repeat it. Yet the latter is unable to do so: "I would have once again to make arrangements with that woman," he says. The fabliau with the smashed pottery is not unique to *Dworzanin polski*. It also occurs in a German chronicle, the *Zimmerische Chronik* of the same year, 1566, and in *Till Eulenspiegel*.[10] In some versions of Twardowski the woman who sells the pottery is Twardowski's wife, and Twardowski smashes it by magic in order to upset her. (See Wójcicki's reconstruction, where Twardowski runs over his wife's pottery with his carriage.) Górnicki seems to refer to that aspect, but he demystifies the story and gives it a natural twist.

The first great poet to treat the subject is, of course, Adam Mickiewicz, who, in his ballad "Pani Twardowska" of 1820, focuses especially on Twardowski's marital life. It is a travesty rather than a serious poem, centering around the final scene, when the devil comes to claim Twardowski's soul. Twardowski makes fulfillment of the devil's request dependent on three conditions. The first is relatively easy to meet: the demon must create a few items, such as a live horse from a painted one, shape a whip out of sand, let Twardowski mount the horse and ride into the wood, where a house is to be built out of nut-kernels, etc. The second is more difficult: the devil has to take a bath in holy water. Despite convulsions, sniffing, coughing, and moaning, the devil obeys. The third condition, however, is impossible to fulfill: the devil has to live an entire year with Pani Twardowska. The devil gives up and escapes through the keyhole.

Here for the first time in literature the city of Rome is mentioned as the place where the final transaction must take place. The ambiguous prophecy that tells a person that he or she will not die or be killed except at one particular place, which produces a false feeling of security, is another common motif in folktales, known as "Death in Jerusalem," since in most cases the fatal place is Jerusalem. One of its other appearances is in the twelfth century in Walter Mapes's *Kurienschwänke* (Fabliaux from the Papal Court). Here a woman has foretold that Pope Sylvester will not die before having celebrated a mass in Jerusalem. He feels secure until he learns that he has celebrated a mass in Santa Croce in Gerusalemme.[11] The idea of that episode is that a person is misled by ambiguous prophecies. Destiny deceives the mortal by creating a location of the same name. As far as Rome is concerned, one could ask, "why Rome, exactly?". Rome is, like Jerusalem, a holy place in which the devil is not expected to have any particular power. My assumption is that we may be confronted with a reflection of sectarian ideas. In the Christian heretical movements which merged, first into Hussitism, then into the Reformation, the Pope is seen as the Antichrist, and Rome is possessed by the devil. In consequence the devil is expected to be at home at this place and especially powerful. If we take into account that Twardowski as well as Dr. Faustus are products of the era of the Reformation, and that there seems to be good reason to ascribe their ties with the devil to the superstition or malevolence of the enemies of this movement, the meaning of the plot becomes clear: a scholar who has joined the Reformation and accepted the notion that the devil is at home in Rome naturally promises the devil to meet him at the devil's principal residence. At the same time his refusal to go to Rome may be seen from the Catholic viewpoint as the refusal of a heretic or a person possessed by the devil to come to the holy place. Mickiewicz was the first to introduce this detail into literature, but he must have taken it from the oral or written tradition. Walter Anderson discovered the first evidence of the mention of Rome in the context of the Twardowski legend in the memoirs of the castellan Marcin Matuszewicz from the year 1758.[12] Yet, if my interpretation of the function of Rome in the religious context of the origins of the Twardowski legend is correct, this would mean that Rome as the place of Twardowski's surrender to the devil was part of the plot from its very beginning.

The ballad "Pani Twardowska" was quite successful and influential. It was translated into many foreign languages, once into German by Franz Freiherr von Gaudy (1839), into Ukrainian by Petro Petrovič Hulak-Artemovs'kyj (1827), the latter being a rather free adaptation. When this poem, titled "Tvardoŭs'kyj (Malorosyjs'ka balada)," appeared in *Vestnik Evropy,* there was an introductory statement saying that the character of Twardowski was also known in Ukrainian folklore: "Heroj balady ta joho spilka s bisom vidomi ne menše u Polšči ta za Dniprom, niž u Malorosii j Ukraini." This may have been the reason why Hulak-Artemovs'kyj underscored the folkloric element with particular Ukrainian features. If we may believe Hulak-Artemovs'kyj's contemporary O. Roslavs'kyj-Petrovs'kyj, who wrote the poet's obituary, Mickiewicz read this translation and judged it superior to his own ballad.[13] The translation is so independent that Hulak-Artemovs'kyj extended the original thirty-two verses to fifty-two, adding special Ukrainian details, such as more specifically Ukrainian music playing at the beginning and the end. Twardowski is in the midst of a celebration that sounds very much like a Cossack orgy. Also, Hulak-Artemovs'kyj seems to have enjoyed giving the devil German nationality. Devils in folkloric tradition very often appear in the dress of an unloved neighbor. The Russian devil appears in the Polish national costume,[14] the Polish devil is dressed like a German,[15] and the German devil like a Frenchman. In the Ukrainian version of Pan Twardowski, the poet is not satisfied with Mickiewicz's description: "Diablik to byl w wódce na dnie, istny Niemiec, sztuczka kusa . . ." He adds that the devil's trick of luring Twardowski into a restaurant named Rome is a "German trick": "Se üže nimec'ka štuka . . ."

Another translation into a Slavic language is Karel Havlíček-Borovský's Czech version from the year 1852. Havlíček, the revolutionary Romantic who had to suffer exile for his involvement in the Czech national movement of 1848,[16] translated numerous works from other Slavic literatures, in particular Russian, into Czech, usually trying to add some peculiar twist to his translation. His rendering of "Pani Twardowska," however, is more faithful to the original than is the Ukrainian version. Nevertheless, he too seems to have enjoyed the devil's German nationality (completely suppressed in Gaudy's German translation): "Čertík to byl v vodce na dně,/ pravý Němčík jak koňázra . . ." (It was a little devil at the bottom of the vodka-barrel, a real German [dim.] like a titmouse—i.e. the image of a German).[17]

"Pani Twardowska" is not the only occurrence of Twardowski in Mickiewicz's work. The fragment of the first part of *Dziady* (Forefather's Eve), which was published posthumously, contains another ballad where Twardowski appears as a magician, but the story lacks most of the details of the Twardowski saga. The only appurtenance which plays an important role is the mirror. This is the ballad "Młodzieniec zaklęty," where Twardowski, by his supernatural power, enters a castle. In one of the vaults he finds a young man in chains standing in front of a mirror. The young man is in the process of being slowly transformed into stone. This process has petrified his lower extremities up to the chest. Twardowski enters into a conversation with him and wants to know who he is. It appears that the young man was a contemporary of the fourteenth-century Lithuanian ruler Olgierd, Jagiełło's father. The name Twardowski is unknown to the prisoner, by which the poet wants to indicate that the magician does not stem from one of the ancient families. When Twardowski tries to free the young man, saying: "I know witchcraft, I know the power of that mirror, I shall shatter it now into pieces, to make the mask fall from you," the prisoner stops him: he wants to hold the mirror in his hands before it is destroyed. He kisses the mirror and turns to stone immediately. Twardowski appears here with only a few of his attributes and without the essence of the story, his contract with the devil.

In addition to popular ballads about Twardowski, there now appear full-length books, among which Ignacy Kraszewski's *Mistrz Twardowski* (1839) has become one of the most influential. This is the work that inspired not only literature in and outside Poland, but also other arts. A ballet by the composer Adolf Sonnenfeld under the title "Pan Twardowski" was first performed at Warsaw in 1871 and has been performed many times well into the twentieth century.[18] Poland remains the natural setting for the development of the story, which reached its widest expansion with Kraszewski. Among the many Polish authors of later generations who have treated the subject, I mention only Leopold Staff, whose epic in six cantos "Mistrz Twardowski" was published in 1902. There is also an unfinished Croatian opera by the composer I. Zajic based on a libretto by J. E. Tomić, written in 1911.[19] The subject has also been treated in historical paintings as well as in films.

It was my intention to trace the development of the motif within Polish literature only to the point where it has matured to such a degree that it could affect foreign literatures. Therefore we may now leave the Polish scene and try to find out how the subject crossed the frontiers of Polish culture into other Slavic territories.

As we know, the border between Orthodox Christendom and Catholicism within Slavic territories is not a completely impenetrable one. Ideas and cultural values have migrated from one side to the other. In some instances, however, achievements of one culture find it nonetheless difficult to pass. It is indicative that literary subjects born in Poland are rarely treated in Russia. Polish history appears in Russian literature as the history of the traditional antagonist: cf. *Boris Godunov, Jurij Miloslavskij, Taras Bul'ba,* etc. The difference in religion is certainly one reason for hostile perception. In the case of Polish-Russian relations, however, there is also the antagonism of two immediate neighbors who throughout history have also been in political competition. Pan Twardowski is one of the few exceptions of a Polish theme which penetrated Russian culture.

In one case this reception is characterized by elements of that hostile attitude. In no instance did the spirit of Slavic solidarity play a major role in the acceptance of the story in Russia. The author of this first Pan Twardowski in Russian literature is the historical novelist Mixail Nikolaevič Zagoskin (1789–1852), best known for his novel *Jurij Miloslavskij,* one of the first Russian historical novels in the vein of Sir Walter Scott.[20] *Jurij Miloslavskij* was highly acclaimed by Puškin and his contemporaries, but Zagoskin's subsequent historical novels, written in the 1830s and 1840s, proved ever less successful, and shortly before his death he was almost forgotten.[21] Zagoskin had been a participant in the Napoleonic wars. He joined the army in August, 1812, was wounded at Polock, and rejoined the fighting army in pursuing the Napoleonic forces all the way to Gdańsk. It may be assumed that he became familiar with the Twardowski legend during his stay in Poland. The first result of this encounter was the drama "Pan Tvardovskij" (1828), which has the subtitle "Romaničeskaja opera." The term "romaničeskaja" has to be understood as "romantičeskaja." In fact, the text was used as a libretto by the composer A. N. Verstovskij, and the first performance in 1828 was of the opera. According to Bugaj's data, Zagoskin's friend S. T. Aksakov was coauthor of the text.[22] The way it is written shows the characteristics of a libretto. The prose dialogue is interrupted by poems named "arias" and "choruses." The piece certainly is not a masterwork and exhibits some of the stereotypes of the neoclassical drama, together with elements of the Gothic novel. Zagoskin was fairly well-accepted as a dramatist before he turned to writing historical novels.

"Pan Tvardovskij," a drama placed in the sixteenth century in Galicia, introduces the wizard in the role of a villain who wants to marry Julija, the daughter of the Polish magnate Boleslavskij (Bolesławski), while Julija loves a young man called Krasickij (Krasicki). Twardowski uses his magic art to win Boleslavskij's attention and is about to succeed in marrying Julija when the devil appears in the role of *"deus" ex machina.* A hermit has sent Twardowski a message to repent and abandon his sinful life. When Twardowski refuses, his castle goes up in flames, and he is dragged off to hell. This drama is a rather clumsy attempt to combine the Twardowski theme with a drama based on the traditional love triangle.

A much better and more skillful treatment of the subject forms part of

Zagoskin's collection of prose stories under the title *Večer na Xopre* from the year 1836. This is an unduly neglected piece of prose, consisting of six stories on supernatural events connected by a frame. One of Zagoskin's biographers, N. Vasin, wrote: "vyšedšie v 1836 godu ego 'Povesti' v kotoryx byli pomeščeny ego fantastičeskie očerki: 'Pan Tvardovskij,' 'Beloe prividenie,' 'Neždannye gosti,' 'Koncert besov,' 'Dve nevestki' i 'Nočnoj poezd,' prošli u publiki nezametnymi."[23] All six stories are told in one evening in the house of the landowner Ivan Alekseevič Asanov on the banks of the Xoper in Saratov Province. (The Xoper is a tributary of the Don in the south of Russia.) Part of the fascination of these stories, it is true, stems from the subject matter. All of them are based on certain supernatural events, and Zagoskin is one of the first (next to Žukovskij and Puškin) in Russian literature to introduce this non-religious, Hoffmanesque type of the supernatural into prose. The frame he creates, a circle of narrators all under the spell of magic or some expectation of horrible events, adds to the atmosphere of suspense. Zagoskin's enjoyment of horror stories is evidenced in almost all of his novels. In one of the editions of his prose he confesses his predilection for the supernatural, whereby he blends elements of Russian folk superstition with elements of the English Gothic novel and features of the tales of Hoffmann: "I have always been a fervent admirer of horrible stories. I cannot tell you what pleasure it causes me every time I listen to a story which causes my hair to stand on end, my heart to stop and my spine to be seized by a shiver. Let these learned gentlemen who even doubt that wood-sprites surround passers-by and that you may disarm a person with one word, smile at my credulity[!]. I do not want to bargain their dry, materialistic conclusions against my naive but vivid and warm fantasies."[24]

"Večer na Xopre" tells about a young man, the narrator, who spends a summer in Serdobsk in Penza Province. In Serdobsk the narrator meets a friend who invites him to the estate of his grandfather on the Xoper. The grandfather has the reputation of being an eccentric, even suspected of having ties with the devil. Out of curiosity the narrator accepts the invitation. At the estate he meets a group of war veterans, who start telling one story after the other, all of them with the common denominator of a supernatural event or an event that may be interpreted as supernatural, or rather, parapsychological. Some of these phenomena are no longer considered wholly unreal by modern science, such as telepathy, apparitions, extrasensory perception, etc. The author feels constantly obliged to defend these phenomena as real and thus to argue against the philosophy of the Enlightenment. This may be one of the reasons why "Večer na Xopre" was rejected by critics and the public. The author expresses clearly and without restraint his conservative worldview and takes an almost militant position against the philosophy of the Enlightenment.

The first story of the cycle is called "Pan Tvardovskij" and leads us into the area of Cracow in the year 1772. The Russian army is stationed there under the command of General Suvorov in connection with the Russian-Turkish war and the first partition of Poland. The narrator is a staff officer and has been ordered to provide accommodation for the wife of the commander of the regiment, who insists on accompanying her husband during the campaign. During his search he enters a castle called Biały Folwark. The owner of the estate, a Polish magnate by the name of Dubickij (Dębicki) receives the captain in a unfriendly and condescending manner. When he learns that the captain has been sent to requisition the place as army headquarters and that a whole detachment of soldiers together with the colonel's wife are expected to come, he becomes more responsive and says that the whole estate has only three rooms in which anyone could stay. The rooms on the first floor cannot be occupied, because this is the place where Twardowski was carried away by the devil, and every Friday they are visited by ghosts and devils. A bailiff who once experienced the devil's orgy got so sick that he died three days later. The captain considers this a fabrication and decides to stay overnight in the large hall, claiming that an Orthodox Russian officer does not have to be afraid of any Polish devil. On the walls of the hall there is a gallery of portraits, all of them exceedingly ugly. The most repulsive of all shows the inscription "Twardowski." The captain first falls asleep, then is awakened by a noise. He sees that the neighboring room is lighted. A dining table is set for thirteen persons. In the middle there is a big plate covered by a cloth. Twelve guests appear and invite him to join them as the thirteenth. All of them sit silently around the table. With the twelfth stroke of the clock suddenly the company comes to life:

> Ten minutes passed. All was still; the devils were silent. The wizard was staring; and I gazed on the whole precious company, waiting to see how the matter would end. Now the clock in my chamber began to wheeze, the wheels turned, the bell sounded, one, two, three! Chu! it is midnight.
>
> The twelfth stroke had not ceased sounding when the wizard moved his mustaches and nodded his head. One of the party rose and, bending forward, stretched forth a long bony hand, bent his hooked finger, and snatched away the white cloth covering the dish. Uh, fathers! [batjuški] even now I cannot think of it without terror. I look. On the plate is a human head; and what a head! O thou Lord, my God! Swollen cheeks, a nose as big as my two fists, a mouth reaching both ears, eyes as large as tablespoons. How my heart jumped! What a dish they had ready!
>
> "Eat!" roared the wizard, with his hoarse voice. "Eat!" repeated in chorus the whole unclean power. Oi, oi, oi! this is an evil affair! I wish to

rise, my legs bend under me; I wish to say a prayer, my tongue does not move. The devils and wizard are just burning me with their hellish eyes.

At last I said somehow, "Avaunt, avaunt! Let God arise!" (Čur menja, čur! Da voskresnet Bog!). And what do you think? the head moved, began to mock me with his tongue and gnash its teeth. O heavenly powers! and prayer has no effect—bad! I do not remember how it came into my head, whether from fear or not; but I raised my hand holding the pistol, placed the muzzle almost against the devil's head, cocked the pistol, fired!

Nothing! All the devils roared with laughter; the head opened its enormous gullet, and in a deep bass voice thundered forth, as if out of a barrel, the Polish mazurka.[25]

After this pandemonium, the officer falls to the floor, losing consciousness. When he wakes up, the apparition is gone. He leaves the estate as quickly as possible. Later he learns that at Bjały Folwark a whole company of Polish confederates has been captured together with the landlord Dubickij, and that subsequently the Cossacks burned and destroyed Bjały Folwark. So there is at least the possibility of a natural explanation of the apparition, which, of course, would not account for the head on the table singing the Mazurka (a particularly popular song among Polish nationalists) after being shot by the captain.

In this story, the Twardowski motif is utilized to express the deep conflict between the Polish, Catholic side and the Russian, Orthodox one. Polish culture is alien to Zagoskin and his hero, and this feeling of uneasiness with an alien culture results in demonizing the other nation. The wizard Twardowski is the personification of that feeling of helplessness in the face of an alien culture. At the same time we recognize that Zagoskin makes use of that part of the Twardowski legend which was transmitted orally. Twardowski is the quintessentially Polish wizard; he is endowed with supernatural power and the evil spirit. Zagoskin seems not to have used one of the more complete versions of the story, although the gallery of ugly pictures in the hall reminds us of the Węgrów mirror in which one sees the most ugly grimaces.

Gogol', whose obsession with devils and devilish scenes is well known, may provide us with more evidence that the Twardowski motif was adopted in the Ukraine and from there spread to Great Russia. Although the wizard himself does not appear in his work, some of his devils, especially in his Dikan'ka stories, seem to indicate that they are modeled after the Twardowskian devils: the devil serving-man, the devil in German costume, etc., as Stender-Petersen has pointed out.[26]

In more recent Russian literature, there is another Russian treatment of the same subject matter, based on Polish folk ballads. Its author is the symbolist Konstantin Bal'mont, who was a very active translator from other languages into Russian. In 1908, in the first issue of *Zolotoe runo,* he published a sequence of three popular ballads under the title "Tvardovskij." What attracted a Symbolist like Bal'mont to this seemingly distant subject of semi-folkloric origin? The answer is easy: "Tvardovskij" carries the subtitle "Tajna večnoj junosti." The rhymed balladic parts are introduced and commented on by Bal'mont. These comments are the essence of the entire undertaking. The idea of eternal youth, however, is only part of the philosophy expressed in these accompanying texts. Youth, he says, is inseparably connected to childhood, and childhood has an immediate connection with the transcendental:

> Домыслом тайной мечты, которая сама себя не видит, детство, быть может, ближе к великим запредельным родникам, откуда в нашу жизнь беспрерывно вливается свет нездешний; как слиянье алабастра, который просвечивает; а юность досягает посвященности в таинство страсти, в сладкий ужас и восторг наслаждения. Но страсть уже дышит и в ребенке; когда он тонким молоточком стучится под материнским сердцем, и домысл тайной мечты не покидывает юношу, когда он внезапным поцелуем вызывает на девическом лике страстный румянец или смертельную бледность. Величайшее счастье — быть ребенком всегда и всегда быть юношей, это не только счастье, но единственное достоинство.[27]

The fascination with the trascendental ties of man attracted Bal'mont to the Twardowski saga, yet he overlooks the fact that while Twardowski tried to gain eternal youth, he was carried away by the devil instead. The moral question of a contract with the powers of evil does not interest him at all. It is the perspective of greatness, life's victory over death, that captivates him. This Nietzschean view is all too obvious in the following passage:

> Человек, звездой отмеченный и к высокой звездности предназначенный, не мирится с человеческим — слишком человеческим [Menschliches — Allzumenschliches — W. S.], он хочет большого, предельного, достоверного, и, силою своей воли, переносит в ограниченную жизнь безграничность, изменяет условия времени и пространства; перепутывает возрасты, не перепутывает, а играет ими всеми, как играет искусный игрок на всех струнах, останавливаясь на той, которая ему желаннее, столько, сколько ему захочется. Такой звездоокий может вступить в союз с светлоглазыми Стихийными гениями, может заключить союз и с темноглазыми Стихийными, но раз он вносит в такой союз душу свою целиком, высшее Око это увидит, и он не погибнет ни в медлительной полноводной реке, текущей между мирных берегов, ни в кипящих вспененных волнах горного потока, любящего острые выступы, изломы и паденья с утесов.[28]

Twardowski, then, is the Nietzschean superman, beyond Good and Evil, free to choose between the clear-eyed elemental genii and the dark-eyed ones, and he will not perish because the "highest eye" sees and obviously accepts it. This idea is consistent with the Nietzschean personality, who dreams of the future greatness of the human race and tries to overcome the inherited enslaving moral dualism of the church. Twardowski, viewed from this angle, might be a superman; yet Bal'mont, in order to accommodate him, had to redirect his destiny: in the original version, Twardowski realizes his limitations when the time comes to give account of his life. Bal'mont, however, had to soften the impact of that tragedy and to loosen the power of the moral law. He did so by restructuring the story. There are three segments in his versified text. The first is called "Zerkalo Tvardovskogo." Here the ominous mirror functions like one of those key items which serve as gateways from one world to the other. Incidentally, in the tradition of the Twardowski story, the famous mirror is kept in the monastery of Węgrów in Podlesie, as mentioned above. Węgrów is a city east of Warsaw. In Bal'mont's version this reads: В Венгрии, в старом костеле приходском. . . . This mistake is not necessarily a mistranslation by Bal'mont. Kretzenbacher mentions several Twardowski versions where the place name Węgrów was misunderstood as Hungary.[29]

The second segment contains the scene with Twardowski's intended abduction from the restaurant called "Rome" to hell. The introduction to this piece, called "Tvardovskij," contains a reference to the Faust legend and its most ancient version, Kiprijan of Antiochia, who is the first known person alleged to have concluded a contract with the devil. Finally, the third segment, "Večnaja junost' Tvardovskogo," brings Bal'mont's personal interpretation of the semi-happy ending. In the introduction, he considers it typical that the devil takes Twardowski not down to hell, but into the air, where the powers of good may become active. Interestingly, the power which causes Twardowski to stay in suspense is not a superhuman "beyond good and evil," but human compassion, the good old traditional values of religion, the prayer of his childhood days:

Дьявол получил власть умчать Твардовского, но он влечет его не вниз, а вверх. И чем выше Дьявол его уносит, тем ближе Твардовский к благословенному крещению слезами, к этой поразительно-трогательной возможности — запеть в высоте детскую песню любви, молитву младенческой веры. Чей был этот мощный голос, воскликнувший: «Повисни так, до дня Суда здесь будешь». Быть может, голос оттуда, где Око? Но тогда Твардовский, уже осужденный висеть в воздухе, осужден, уже присужден к каре, и в день Великого Суда, конечно, будет оправдан, ибо правосудие Божеское не есть суд человеческий, или Дьявольский, и дважды оно не наказует за одну и ту же вину.[30]

The ultimate judge is the "Eye," something that is not human, and finally redeems Twardowski through legal sophistry, on the premise that no one may be sentenced twice for the same crime. Hence Twardowski's state of suspense is only a transitory stage before his final redemption.

There is no indication in the text printed in *Zolotoe runo,* or in the Bal'mont edition in *Biblioteka poèta, bol'šaja serija,*[31] what Polish text Bal'mont used. From the way the three segments are organized, however, I conclude that Bal'mont manipulated it in order to adapt it to his philosophy. "Večnaja junost' Tvardovskogo" does not belong to the end but to the middle of the story. It is also worth mentioning that the Soviet edition omits all the prose parts and makes the story appear as just one of the many translations produced by the poet. There is no allusion to Bal'mont's philosophical message, except for the sequence of texts which—in my view—indicates his manipulation of the original.

One of the Slavic literatures in which the Twardowski motif has produced some interesting reflections is Czech. The Czechs became aware of the existence of a Slavic version of the Faust drama rather early. Beside Dobrovský, mentioned above, his contemporary Šebastián Hněvkovský mentions in his epic "Doktor Faust" (1844) the existence of a Slavic Faust theme; and for the first time the idea is suggested that this story may be competing with the basically Germanic Faust story. It is true that Prague is one of the places with Faust reminiscences, and this seems to be the reason why Hněvkovský selects this subject. He emphasizes the Prague scenery without trying to compete seriously with Goethe's *Faust.* His work is a rather dry, belated neoclassical epic, whereas Goethe's *Faust,* whose second part was completed only twelve years earlier, in 1832, is a dramatic poem. Hněvkovský, though he may seem inspired by Goethe's work, did not feel challenged to compete with it from a national point of view, using the Polish Faust story.

There was a different situation when Jaroslav Vrchlický (Emil Frída, 1853-1912) approached the subject. Vrchlický is the Czech poet of the nineteenth century who used his native tongue most perfectly in poetry and seemingly without any effort. He was an unusually prolific writer; his collected poetry alone fills twenty sizeable volumes in the most recent edition. Today his virtuosity leaves us mostly unaffected, yet in his lifetime he was considered, if not the greatest Czech poet, at least the second greatest after Mácha; and he was the first Czech considered for the Nobel Prize, which to his chagrin he never received.[32]

Vrchlický had translated Goethe's *Faust* into Czech before he turned to the Twardowski subject. In an interview, when he was asked about his Twardowski, he said that his work with Goethe had inspired him to create his own version of *Faust*. Why then did he not write Faust, but Twardowski? The beginning of Vrchlický's career is characterized by a cosmopolitan orientation, towards the world of beauty, particularly in the Romance cultures, but also in such distant realms as Arabic, Persian, and Indian literatures. In Bohemia he was criticized for lack of national interest; since the common prescription for a proper Czech writer at that time was to be a fighter for Czech independence, all his intellectual energy was supposed to be devoted to national propaganda. Thus it was imperative for a Czech writer that he turn to Czech or Slavic subjects, or to foreign subjects only if they could be seen as symbolizing a Czech problem. Eliška Krásnohorská was his harshest critic,[33] and it seems that Vrchlický was susceptible to her kind of criticism. International themes, it is true, continued to constitute the major part of his work, yet Czech and Slavic subjects received more attention in later years. Another reason Vrchlický chose Twardowski as his *Faust* may simply be that it was difficult to compete with a monumental work like Goethe's *Faust,* which he knew so well. Thus, while he could not escape the temptation to imitate certain features of that work, he tried to make his own seem more independent. Besides, it should be mentioned that the true Faust theme is not totally absent in Vrchlický's work. In 1886 he published a ballad under the title "Faust v Praze," which contains some satirical thrusts against his nationalistic critics, and some Twardowski reminiscences as well. When Faust on his way from Wittenberg to Italy stays in Prague, his Czech admirers ask him to demonstrate his art in their presence and to revive some famous personages of the past. He does so, and on a canvas on the wall (like a cinema screen) there appear Alexander the Great, Helen of Troy, Albertus Magnus, Abélard, etc. The crowd is not satisfied: "We want domestic subjects," they shout. Here they are: Libuše, Břetislav, Otakar, Charles IV. Even this does not satisfy them: they want to see Jan Hus. So Hus appears on the screen, but soon a red flame catches the canvas and burns the image of the reformer. Faust exstinguishes the flame with a sign of his hand. "A genius always walks through the world in flames," he explains. "No matter whether they are lit by the anger of the idiots or whether they whip them out of his bosom, the important fact being that he lights the darkness around him."[34] It is not difficult to understand the message of that poem. The poet is like Faust, producing images of the past for the public. Those who want to dictate the kind of images to be produced may well end up finding themselves dwarfed by historical reality.

The Twardowski theme appears in Vrchlický's work for the first time in the ballad "Slza Twardowského," which was published in *Lumír* in 1877. This is, in fact, the more appealing work, since it does not pretend to offer an entire philosophical construct, as does the other, which we shall mention as our last example. Nevertheless this ballad is a first approach to the subject, a kind of preliminary sketch for the later full-scale epic "Twardowski," which appeared in 1885 and of which the ballad became a part. As in many of Vrchlický's works, the reader has to have some factual knowledge of the subject in order to enjoy the piece. Here, in the ballad, we are told that the devil takes Twardowski, who had been dissatisfied with his services, on one of his flights over the country. A cloud serves as an aircraft, and Twardowski looks at the world from above, realizing all its injustices: rich people living in luxury and debauchery, poor children starving to death. Suddenly the aircraft seems to come to a stop and threatens to tumble down to earth. Only in the last moment the devil gets it moving again. The devil explains the near-accident: "You cried, your tear/ was caught by the seam of the coat./ And these tears—have weight . . ./ It pulled us down all the the way,/ I blew it off—as a star flies . . ."[35]

Here the question of good and evil is addressed, perhaps in a playful way, as one might expect from a Parnassian, but not without effect. The sense of compassion at the sight of the endless sufferings of poor people is presented delicately, a sudden glimmer that adds a dimension of depth to the story. Certainly, Vrchlický is at his best where he has to deal with a single issue. He is the master of the small form, be it lyrical or epic. When he tries the large-scale epic, he barely masters its complexities.

Hence, the epic "Twardowski" was less than a success from the time of its publication, although not without interest in terms of motif history. This plot of the epic follows the pattern of Kraszewski's novel (as previously outlined) and of a German version called *Twardowski, der polnische Faust. Ein Volksbuch,* published in Vienna in 1861 by J. N. Vogl in the spirit of the "popular reading" in which the Faust saga was first presented, the so-called Volksbuch-version. So we have here the entire story, from the scene where the father unknowingly promises his son's soul to the devil to the very end, when Twardowski is held stationary above the Carpathian mountains. Most striking in this Twardowski version, however, is that Vrchlický irresistibly gravitates towards Goethe's Faust, as may be demonstrated by numerous quotations, among which may be cited:

> " . . . Zřít chci lidským zrakem,
> Co je skryto za oblakem"[36]

> (I want to see with my human eye,
> What is hidden behind the clouds).

and Goethe:

> Daß ich erkenne, was die Welt
> im Innersten zusammenhält.

And the disenchantment:

> Já sklonil sluch svůj k tepnám přírody,
> v řek zrcadlo a v jezer jasnou tůň
> jsem hroužil svoje oko pátrající,
> v báň prahor vryl se jako slepý krt,
> vše nadarmo; je hluchá příroda
> a odpovídat nechce člověku.[37]

> (I inclined my ear to the veins of nature,
> into the mirror of rivers and into the clear
>   depths of lakes
> I directed my watchful eye,
> into the dome of the primeval mountains I
>   dug myself like a blind mole,
> all in vain; nature is mute
> and does not want to answer man.)

Goethe:

> Wie nur dem Kopf nicht alle Hoffnung schwindet,
> Der immer fest an schalem Zeuge klebt,
> Mit gier'ger Hand nach Schätzen gräbt
> Und froh ist, wenn er Regenwürmer findet.

Goethe's *Faust* and Vrchlický's Twardowski also share an extensive reliance on plots and the characters from the classical past. Again, Vrchlický is generous in displaying his extensive erudition. One of the scenes he locates in historical Venice, another time the devil revives Semiramis for Twardowski's enjoyment, just as Mephistopheles revived Helen, the epitome of classical beauty, for the sake of Faust. Unlike *Faust,* Vrchlický's "Twardowski" is only partially dramatized, and part of this dialogue is in prose. On the other hand, the twelve parts of Vrchlický's work show a greater variety of compositional devices. Part of the action is presented in the form of a ballad: for example, "Slza Twardowského," which becomes part VII, and part V, the ballad of the spider, containing the story of how Matěj, Twardowski's famulus, is transformed into that creature. This transformation is not connected with Twardowski's quest for eternal youth, but becomes a rather comical episode in the context of the entire story, a feature which is also underscored by its popular style. When Twardowski is being summoned to the king's palace to save the princess, who is suffering from a deadly disease, Matěj pretends to be the magician. He cuts the Princess into pieces but forgets to keep her soul in a safe place to prevent it from escaping. When he puts the parts together, the princess will not come to life again. At this moment, Matěj is carried through the window by the devil and caught by the guards. He is being accused of being an impostor and sentenced to death by burning. At this moment, Twardowski learns of Matěj's trouble and saves him by taking him from the stake by his hair. Then, in order to punish him, he transforms him into a spider. It is not difficult to recognize in this ballad elements of Goethe's "Sorcerer's Apprentice."

These all-too-obvious references to Goethe predetermined most of "Twardowski's" reception by the critics. It is worth mentioning that Thomas Garrigue Masaryk, who later became the first president of the Czechoslovak Republic, was a very influential critic and rejected the work as unoriginal. In: "Několik myšlenek o literárním eklekticismu. Twardowski p. Jar. Vrchlického,"[38] he described it as too dependent on Vogl's German Volksbuch version. This negative attitude, here and there relieved by more positive commentary, persisted into the 1930s, when Arne Novák wrote "Vrchlický a Goethe."[39] He stated that Vrchlický took the idea of Faust without shaping his work consistently along the lines of that model. He at times introduces the Don Juan motif, switches from burlesque to serious scenes, where the hero is presented as the philosophically-minded scholar who wants to know the essence of things. His criticism climaxes in the statement that Vrchlický seemingly did not understand the message of Goethe's *Faust* and responded only to details accessible to him. Recent critics like Vítězslav Tichý, in his commentary to the 1956 edition,[40] claim that it is inadmissible to criticize "Twardowski" on the basis of a comparison with Goethe. Vrchlický had in mind an independent creation, and those who measure the work by the yardstick of the work of another author do it an injustice. He points out that "Twardowski" is not only a Faust figure but also bears the marks of Don Juan and of a typical Polish magnate. After all, Twardowski is not Faust: he is designed to be his Slavic counterpart, and Vrchlický tries to emphasize the Slavic aspect, among other ways by introducing elements of Polish Catholicism and of the special brand of Messianism as it occurs in Mickiewicz's "Forefathers' Eve." Nevertheless it was detrimental to "Twardowski" that its *Faust* allusions are too numerous and too obvious to remain unrecognized by the public for which the book was written. And still the epic shows a writer who rises far above the average and whose work presents not only weaknesses but also strengths.

This concludes my survey of treatments of the subject in Slavic literatures. Pan Twardowski may be considered a typical example of a tale that originated in the anonymous field of folklore and oral tradition, perhaps based on real historical characters and events, and crossed the borderline into written, "serious," and professional literature. In folklore it continued to grow and acquire new marginal narrative patterns. In literature, however, it developed from unpretentious anecdotes under the auspices of "prodesse et delectare" (Górnicki) into pretentious conceptualizing statements (Bal'mont, Vrchlický) which depart from the idea of literature as entertainment. The subject is charged with a burden of thought which, at times, it finds difficult to bear. We may ask ouselves why the works treating the Twardowski motif have not become works of such exceptional rank as the Faust dramas of world literature, since Faust and Twardowski originated under similar circumstances, in the twilight of folklore, from whence they entered the literary arena. Is it due to the fact that the subject was mostly unknown outside of Poland and inaccessible to writers in the rest of the world? This may not be the only reason. The Twardowski motif is perhaps too universal and unfocused to offer a character capable of carrying a fundamental philosophical message. It has either to be manipulated, as it was by Bal'mont, atomized as in Mickiewicz's successful ballad and Vrchlický's "Slza Twardowského," deprived of its philosophical dimension, as in Zagoskin, or else it risks being unable to carry a heavy load of ideas.

Notes

1. A. I. Beleckij, "Legenda o Fauste," *Zapiski Neofilologičeskogo obščestva pri S.-Peterburgskom universitete,* issue 5 (1911), p. 66.

2. Moscow-Leningrad, 1958. Another recent study on the subject is Günther Mahal, *Faust: Die Spuren eines geheimnisvollen Lebens* (Bern-Munich, 1980), written in a more popular style.

3. Klagenfurt, 1968 (= Buchreihe des Landesmuseums für Kärnten, vol. 23). Cf. also Elisabeth Frenzel, *Stoffe der Weltliteratur* (Stuttgart, 1962), pp. 172–79, and Charles Dédéyan, *Le thème de Faust dans la littérature européenne,* 3 vols. (Paris, 1954–56).

4. Wrocław etc. 1986.

5. *Germanoslavica* 2 (1932–33), 90 ff.

6. *Klechdy, starożytne podania i powieści ludu polskiego i Rusi,* vol. 1, part 2 (Warsaw, 1837).

7. *Paralele. Studia porównawcze z pogranicza literatury i folkloru* (Warsaw, 1977), pp. 135–47. Cf. also *Słownik folkloru polskiego,* ed. J. Krzyżanowski (Warsaw, 1965), pp. 405–7.

8. Antti Aarne, Stith Thompson, *The Types of Folktale, A Classification and Bibliography* (Helsinki, 1973), p. 260

9. Cf. Bugaj, pp. 261–75 (see note 4).

10. It does not occur in "Cortegiano." Cf. Łukasz Górnicki, *Dworzanin polski,* ed. Roman Pollak (Wrocław, 1954), p. 277. According to J. Krzyżanowski, Górnicki introduced this story from *Till Eulenspiegel.* See J. Krzyżanowski, *Romans pseudohistoryczny* (Cracow, 1926), p. 21.

11. Cf. Kretzenbacher, pp. 99–101 (see note 3).

12. "Zu Pan Twardowski in Rom," *Zeitschrift für slavische Philologie,* 25 (1956), pp. 309–11. Andersen rejects D. Čyževs'kyj's opinion *(Zeitschrift für slavische Philologie* 24, pp. 76–78) that Mickiewicz took the motif from Plutarch. He writes: "Das Rom-Motiv ist nämlich keineswegs von Mickiewicz willkürlich auf Pan Twardowski übertragen worden, sondern bildet einen integrierenden Teil der 'polnischen Faustsage'." It might be worth mentioning that in Mixail Bulgakov's Faust novel *Master i Margarita* the devil comes to claim the "master" at a restaurant called "Yalta." Is this a reflection of the Twardowski motif in Bulgakov's work? (I owe this detail to Joan Grossman).

13. Cf. *Istorija ukrains'koi literatury u vos'mi tomax,* 2 (Kiev, 1967), 231.

14. Cf. A. Stender-Petersen, "Der Ursprung des Gogolschen Teufels," *Göteborgs Högskolas Årsskrift,* 26 (Göteborg, 1920), 72–87.

15. Cf. inter alia, V. G. Korolenko's *Istorija moego sovremennika* (1906–08), chapter 5.

16. On his life and work cf. the most recent and well-informed study by Jiří Morava: *C. K. disident Karel Havlíček* (Toronto, 1986).

17. K. Havlíček-Borovský, *Básně* (Prague, 1960) p. 177.

18. Cf. Bugaj, p. 302.

19. Ibid.

20. Cf. Walter Schamschula, *Der russische historische Roman vom Klassizismus bis zur Romantik* (Meisenheim/Glan, 1962) (= Frankfurter Abhandlungen zur Slavistik, vol. 3), pp. 87–98.

21. Cf. the reminiscences of Zagoskin in Turgenev's biography. David Magarshack, *Turgenev. A Life* (New York, 1954), pp. 28–29.

22. Bugaj, p. 302.

23. N. Vasin, "Mixail Nikolaevič Zagoskin. Biografičeskij očerk," *Sobranie sočinenij M. N. Zagoskina v dvux tomax,* 1 (Moscow, 1902), p. x.

24. Cited in Schamschula, p. 92.

25. Michael Zagoskin, *Tales of Three Centuries,* trans. Jeremiah Curtin (Boston, 1891), pp. 49–51.

26. Cf. note 14. I am thankful to Hugh McLean for providing this information.

27. *Zolotoe runo,* 1 (1908), 54.

28. Ibid.

29. Kretzenbacher, p. 99.

30. Bal'mont, p. 58.

31. K.D. Bal'mont, *Stixotvorenija* (Leningrad, 1969), pp. 553–57.

32. Cf. Milada Součková, *The Parnassian Jaroslav Vrchlický* (The Hague, 1964).

33. Cf. Zdeněk Pešat in *Dějiny české literatury* 3, ed. Jan Mukařovský (Prague, 1961), p. 298.

34. J. Vrchlický, *Básnické dílo,* 7 (Prague, 1950), 108-13.

35. *Básnické dílo,* 12 (Prague, 1949), p. 178.

36. *Básnické dílo,* 8 (Prague, 1956), p. 300.

37. Ibid., p. 309.

38. *Naše doba,* 2 (1895).

39. *Goethův sborník. Památce 100. výročí básníkovy smrti vydali čeští germanisté,* (Prague, 1932), pp. 66–97.

40. Pp. 554ff.

SOUTH SLAVIC MUSLIM EPIC SONGS

Problems of Collecting, Editing, and Publishing

ZLATAN ČOLAKOVIĆ

My intention is to try to explain why the products of the South Slavic Muslim art of singing traditional epic songs were collected in the way they were throughout history; where, from whom, and how the songs were taken down; how they were edited and published; and for what reason. It is my hope that a close look at the four main published collections of this epic poetry may provide a clear answer to the question posed and may lead to a solution of an important contemporary issue: how it should be done today.[1] My subject is thus how the traditional art of Muslim epic singing has been represented by its collectors.

Franciscan Collectors

Ivan Franjo Jukić "Banjalučanin" (1818–57), a revolutionary and a stubborn Franciscan monk, courageously fought against Turks, Austrians, and even his own superiors in the Roman Catholic Church for the rights and social welfare of the oppressed "raja" (Bosnian members of the Catholic and the Orthodox Churches in the Turkish Empire). Considered an extremely dangerous person by both Turkish and Austrian high officials, he was imprisoned in Sarajevo in 1852 on the basis of a false accusation by the Turkish government. In jail he was subjected to mistreatment. He tried to commit suicide, and his health failed. Seriously ill, he was forced to travel on horseback to another prison in Istanbul. From there he was sent into exile from the Turkish Empire to Rome. He died in Austria.[2]

Jukić was a passionate follower of the Croatian *Ilirski pokret* (Illyrian movement). In 1842 Ljudevit Gaj, the leader of this national literary and political revival, and Stanko Vraz, the famous Slovene poet, urged Jukić to organize on a large scale the collection and publication of "Illyrian" epic and lyric songs in Bosnia. Jukić started collecting even before 1840, but, influenced by Gaj and Vraz, he asked his Franciscan friends and others to join in the collecting venture.

Jukić was well acquainted with Karadžić's and Milutinović's published collections (see note 9). He asserted that many of the songs from their collections belonged to the Bosnian tradition, and that some of Karadžić's best singers, like Filip Višnjić, came from Bosnia (see Jukić's correspondence with Gaj and Vraz). Therefore he spoke with authority when he expressed his conviction that collecting in Bosnia, the area where the songs originated and still flourished, might result in a more truthful image of the tradition and might produce a greater collection than Karadžić's already world-famous one. He was not able to mobilize as many collectors as Karadžić, but he produced an excellent collection himself of *ženske* and *junačke pjesme* (women's and heroic songs), as well as of stories, proverbs and riddles.

In 1844 Jukić prepared the first volume of "Illyrian" lyric and epic songs for publication. The manuscript contained forty lyric and ten epic songs. The political situation at that time in Croatia had changed dramatically. The Austrians prohibited public use of even the word "Illyrian." The Croatian "Illyrians" in Zagreb were unable to publish the manuscript. Before his death Jukić published part of his collection, together with the songs collected by Grgo Martić, Marijan Šunjić and Đorđe Margetić, in the magazine *Bosanski prijatelj*, which Jukić founded and Gaj printed at his own expense.[3]

We do not know much about the way Jukić collected songs, but it is obvious that he hesitated to collect epic songs from Muslim singers. One only has to recall Jukić's own trenchant words: "The Turks have taken away from the Bosnians everything but their songs." There were some Christian singers in that period who learned to sing Muslim songs and sang them to rich beys for recompense. Jukić as well as Martić collected from one of them only those Muslim songs which were "neutral," i.e., did not have Muslim victories over Christians as their subject. However, he readily collected songs describing Christian victories. Many of those songs clearly originated in the rich Muslim oral epic tradition. Transformed into a pseudo-Christian tradition, they lack mythic meaning and background. Jukić was especially eager to collect "historical" songs describing brutal fratricidal conflicts among the Muslims themselves.

Jukić published his own poems in decasyllables (*deseterci*). He was able to imitate perfectly the style of oral epic literature although he was a rather poor poet. It seems that he made many changes in the texts he collected, but how far he went, we can only guess, since he did not preserve the originals. Finally, Jukić did not provide any information about the singers from whom he collected.

Grgo Martić alias Ljubomir Hercegovac (1822–1905), the closest of Jukić's collaborators, was acquainted from early childhood with traditional singing.

He was a fine poet, and he wrote historical and heroic long epic poems in the traditional decasyllabic line.[4] Praised in his own times, today these epic poems have almost been forgotten.

Martić firmly believed in the Illyrian origin of the South Slavic peoples. For this reason he assumed that the Homeric poems and South Slavic epic poetry were connected. Martić devoted many years to translating Homeric epics into decasyllable lines. He was obsessed with Homer. All his life he proudly used the playful pseudonym Ljubomir Hercegovac ("A Hercegovinian Who-Loves-Homer").

In 1858 Martić published part of Jukić's as well as his own collection of heroic songs.[5] This book contained fifty epics. Some of them are Christian haiduk songs (especially the cycle of seven epics about the haiduk Mihovil Tomić), and some belong to the Kosovo cycle and to the Marko Kraljević cycle. The core of the book, however, consists of the Wedding and Duel songs describing Christians victorious in their struggle against the Muslims. The book also contains eight Muslim epic songs.[6]

In the preface, titled *Razlog* (Argument), Martić claims that Serbo-Croatian and Ancient Greek are "closely related" languages. He believes that in "prehistoric times . . . our original forebears" were related to the Greeks. Martić asks: Where else can we look for an explanation for the incredible similarity between the South Slavic and the Homeric heroic epic? Although a Franciscan, Martić expresses a hubristic wish: he longs to find some South Slavic song preserved from the epoch before the South Slavs "embraced Jesus's word." In that song "would we not recognize the same product as Homer's?"[7]

Like so many contemporary Homerologists, Martić believed that Homer was the supreme poet, who had created a monumental epos using traditional oral epic style and content with incredible individual artistry. He finds a useful parallel to Homer in the work of the famous Croatian poet Andrija Kačić-Miošić (1702–60), who collected traditional oral epic poetry and later incorporated it into his own poetry. He utters yet another wish, reflecting even greater hubris from our point of view. He asks himself: Would it not have been "more glorious" had he himself tried to do the same thing as Kačić had done with the collected texts? But, continues Martić, he as well as Karadžić and others are "only collectors."

The continuation of Martić's argument is very important. Martić clearly acknowledges that he had consistently changed the original texts he and Jukić collected.[8] Martić admits to having made the following corrections: He had changed all the "awkward" provincialisms, and he changed the dialect in which the songs had been dictated (from the so-called *ikavica* into *ijeka-*

vica). Martić stated that anyone had the right to question the way in which he edited the texts; yet he felt that, based on his own experience, his method was the best. Finally, Martić stresses that he did not purge the texts of Turkish words that had penetrated the language of Bosnians, although, according to Martić, we all have the right to "scold and pity" the "impure" language of Bosnian songs.

Martić expressed what he felt was his right to do. Collectors before him, including Karadžić, and most collectors after him also changed the texts and had the same feeling that such was their right.[9]

Marijan Šunjić (1798–1860) was an extremely well-educated person. He studied in Vienna and in Bologna (with Mezzofanti). A true polyglot, he knew many Western languages, as well as Greek, Latin, Turkish, Arabic and Persian. Although known as a rebel in his youth (he was twice imprisoned by the Turkish authorities), in 1855 he became a bishop.

Šunjić collected songs in the same area and during the same period as Jukić and Martić. Unfortunately, his collection was only published long after his death (in 1915 and in 1925).[10] Some of the songs he collected were published in the Jukić-Martić collection and in Jukić's magazine, *Bosanski prijatelj*.

Šunjić was a significant collector. His linguistic abilities gave him a deep understanding and appreciation for the language of the traditional songs. He did not change the dialect in the texts he collected, nor has anyone ever claimed, to the best of my knowledge, that he had edited the songs in an improper way. Thanks to Šunjić, we know at least something about the singers from whom the Franciscans collected.

Martić admitted only once that he had obtained one of his songs from a Hercegovinian "Turk." In his manuscripts, however, Šunjić listed the names of his singers. Among them are two Muslims, Šaban "Turčin" (the Turk) and Salko from Foča. It seems that the rest of Šunjić's singers were all Christians. But one of them said to Šunjić that he had learned his song from a Muslim singer. Some of Šunjić's other singers also sang Muslim songs.

The best among all of the Franciscan's singers was Petar Raničić from Kupres, called Đole. This famous singer sang for Šunjić the longest South Slavic epic song recorded up to that time (1482 lines).[11] According to Eugen Matić, the editor of the Šunjić collection, Petar was the best Christian singer in the area of Kupres. He was a *professional singer,* who earned his living by entertaining rich Muslim beys with his songs. It is obvious that his repertory consisted primarily of Muslim epic songs.

Stjepan Banović, a well-known collector and connoisseur of the tradition in the region called Završje (where the Franciscans collected), believes that all of the "pro-Muslim" songs from the Martić-Jukić collection were sung

by Raničić.[12] To that already long list of Raničić's songs Banović adds songs
from Šunjić's collection and four excellent epic songs collected by Đuro
Margetić.[13]

Banović suggests that the Franciscan collecting activity assembled the
finest epic material ever gathered among South Slavic Christians. Banović
also believes that many of Karadžić's haiduk songs have their origins and
even were collected in the area of Završje.

I find it hard to agree with Banović. It seems to me that there are two
comments that should be made about the collecting activity of the Franciscans. First, *the Franciscans consciously misrepresented the tradition as a
whole.* The best material they collected consisted in reality of Muslim rather
than Christian epic songs, although perhaps sung primarily by Christian
singers. The fact that the songs were collected mainly from Christians only
confirms the fact that traditional Muslim oral epic singing was the main and
the only truly developed epic tradition, even in this predominantly Christian
area. I am convinced that the content of some of the songs was changed,
both by the singers and by the collectors, in order to make them more
acceptable to the Christian population. Second, *the Franciscans Jukić and
Martić freely edited the texts they collected.* There is no doubt that they
introduced products of their own poetic inspiration into the texts without
acknowledging the fact and that they changed the dialect of the songs, thus
depriving the texts of their authentic and aesthetic quality.

The Great Collections of Muslim Epic Poetry

The Franciscans collected in the middle of the nineteenth century
(approximately from 1840 to 1860).[14] Since many of the Muslim songs from
their collections were published only in literary magazines, those songs were
neglected and nearly forgotten.[15]

The famous ethnographer Friedrich Salomo Krauss, born in Slavonia in
1857, was the next to continue collecting Muslim epic songs on a large scale.
In 1885 and 1886, he made an excellent collection and published six epic
songs.[16]

Krauss was an extraordinarily good collector. He published the texts of
songs exactly as he had written them down, and he always noted from
whom and where he collected. Although Krauss claimed as early as 1889
that his collection amounted to 190,000 lines, he never published it as a
whole. If it was indeed that large, then it would have represented the first
great collection of Muslim epic songs. Krauss published many epics individually, together with the necessary critical apparatus and a translation into

German.[17] It is to Krauss's credit that the South Slavic Muslim epics were translated and published at this early date in a Western language.[18]

The goal of a long-term project, carefully planned and executed by writers and scholars belonging to the academic society Matica Hrvatska, was to preserve the songs sung in all of the regions where the Croatian language is spoken. In 1886 the Croatian Luka Marjanović started to collect for Matica Hrvatska Muslim epic songs in the Bosnian region of Bihać; his work was to become one of the largest collections of the national epic and lyric heritage. About the same time, in 1887, Kosta Hörmann started to build his own collection of Muslim epic songs, covering other areas of Bosnia. Both of these two enormous collections were completed by 1890.

Kosta (Konstantin) Hörmann (1850–1921), born in Bjelovar (Croatia) and descended from Bavarian immigrants, served as representative for cultural affairs of the Austro-Hungarian Empire in occupied Bosnia and was a well-known literary editor.[19] He was the director of the Zemaljski Muzej Bosne i Hercegovine; he founded the well-known literary magazine *Nada* and was its managing editor; and he was a councillor of the Zemaljska vlada (the local government) of Bosnia and Hercegovina. After the First World War, he fled to Austria, where he died.

Hörmann created and published his collection in the short period of only three years. It is still disputed whether Hörmann collected any of the songs himself (although he claimed to have done so), or whether he only organized the collecting activity and later worked together with his helpers on editing and preparing the texts for publication.

The published part of the Hörmann collection consists of seventy-five epic texts, with fifteen more added later from his manuscripts.[20] The epic songs were recorded in many different regions of Bosnia (a chart of localities can be found in Buturović's book; see note 19). Some of Hörmann's scribes or aides (possibly the real collectors), coped satisfactorily with the task of writing down the songs; others had less success. All of them worked with enthusiasm, but they were not accustomed to such work, nor were they trained or even informed about how it should be done. Thus the quality of the collected texts is the result not only of the singer's dictation, but also of the relative ability of the various collectors.

According to Hörmann, he and his assisting editors did not substantially change the collected texts for publication. In his introduction to the first volume of the collection, Hörmann admitted "only" the following interventions: 1) he changed the dialect of the songs to the established literary norm; 2) he shortened lines that were "too long"; and 3) he excluded "non-aesthetic" expressions from the texts (perhaps he meant vulgarities, awkward lines, and so forth).[21]

After the first volume of the Hörmann collection was published, Luka Marjanović criticized it in detail in a long series of articles.[22] Hörmann had employed incompetent collectors for the purpose of writing down the songs, according to Marjanović, and the songs were poorly edited. Further, Marjanović claimed, Hörmann neither provided the names of the singers nor did he note who collected which song.[23]

The famous Slavist Vatroslav Jagić was more temperate in his criticism. His primary objections were: 1) Hörmann had no right to change the dialect in the songs; and 2) he should have provided necessary information about the singers and about the actual collectors of their songs.

In his introduction to the second volume of the collection Hörmann admitted that Jagić's criticism was justified. He indicated his intention not to change the dialect of the songs in the proposed third volume of his collection and declared his willingness to provide information about the singers and the collectors of the songs. However, he rejected Marjanović's criticism. Although Hörmann did work on the third volume of his collection, it was never published.

The conclusion of Hörmann's introduction is significant. He stated that he had prepared the publication of his collection in order to present traditional lore to a large readership.[24] Concerning the scholars and their special interests, Hörmann promised that he would preserve the manuscripts of his collection for scholarly use. Hörmann kept his promise. Today the manuscripts are kept in the Zemaljski muzej Bosne i Hercegovine.

In 1976, the third edition of Hörmann's collection was published.[25] It was edited by Đenana Buturović, who compared the manuscripts of the Hörmann collection with the published epics and noted all alterations of the original texts.[26]

Hörmann's collection of Muslim epics became one of the most popular books ever published in Bosnia, and its influence on the Muslim population may properly be compared with the influence which Kačić's and Karadžić's collections had on Catholic and Orthodox readers, respectively. The influence had its tragic side: it undermined the traditional art of creating epics, for singers started to learn songs from this book, and other published sources as well, rather than from other singers. In my opinion, a song learned by a singer from a published source is not traditional. Fortunately, many of the Muslim singers, while learning their songs from published sources, also continued learning them in the natural and traditional way from other singers. Both the length of the songs in their tradition and the high level of artistry required by a good singer prevented them from memorizing texts of published songs.

It is ironic that the great number of Muslim singers who had heard or seen published songs firmly believed that these songs were more genuine than the songs of their fellow singers. Muslim singers consider their songs true history. There was a widespread legend among them that at some point in history all of the songs had been written down in order to preserve the truth about important historical events. Many singers therefore longed to get hold of the published collections. An excellent singer whose songs I have transcribed and edited, although a rather poor man, gave two sheep in order to obtain the collection of Kosta Hörmann.

Luka Marjanović (1844–1922), professor of church law and dean of the Faculty of Law at the University of Zagreb, is the compiler of the largest collection of South Slavic Muslim epic songs. Marjanović was well acquainted with traditional singing from his early youth. His grandfather was a Christian singer. He made his own collection of epic and lyric songs amounting to 25,000 lines even before he decided to start collecting Muslim epics for the project of Matica Hrvatska mentioned above.

Marjanović was the embodiment of many of the qualities needed for a collector. He was enthusiastic, energetic, and diligent; and he knew how to organize in detail collecting on a professional scale. Experienced in working in the field, he was also familiar with previously published collections and with many of the unpublished ones in the possession of the Matica Hrvatska.

In 1888 Marjanović and his assistants completed their collection. However, he continued editing the relevant texts for almost two years. In his opinion, collecting was the easiest part of the complex task of representing the tradition in published form. In 1898 and 1899 two volumes of Marjanović's phenomenal collection were published.[27]

In the introduction to the first volume, Marjanović describes the process of collecting Muslim epic songs, the singers themselves, the songs and the way the texts were edited.

From 1886 to 1888 Marjanović and his assistants wrote down 290 Muslim epic songs and 30 Muslim lyric songs, amounting to a total of 255,000 lines. All of the songs were recorded from only twelve singers. The greatest number of songs were taken from the best singers. From two of them Marjanović collected all the songs in their repertoire; from the other singers he wrote down only selected songs. Marjanović's introduction contains a vivid description of the singers. He notes the number of songs collected from each of them; he describes their singing and repertoire, the way they learned their songs and from whom; he provides their biographies and even tells how they were recompensed for their work. There are also photographs of the main singers.

Marjanović continues the introduction with his own classification of the types of Muslim epic songs. He notes the exceptional length of the Muslim epics as compared with the shorter songs in the Christian epic tradition. Marjanović also describes the singers' performances and writes about the contents of the songs and the image of the world they represent.

Both volumes contain fifty epic songs. In appendices Marjanović provided the contents of sixty-eight additional epic songs related to the ones published. In those appendices sixty-three unpublished epic songs are also mentioned. Unfortunately, no table of contents of the collection is provided.

Marjanović's introduction also contains an important contribution to the understanding of the nature of traditional epic singing. He noticed that *the texts of the songs are not fixed* and that *the texts of the songs, even those sung by the same singer, change from one performance to another*. He clearly understood that *the contents of the songs change after a lapse of time*. Marjanović was also interested in the metrical characteristics of the songs. He asserted that in their performance the Muslim singers from northwestern Bosnia (where he collected) sometimes added one or two syllables to individual decasyllabic lines.

Marjanović's discoveries were later corroborated by Matthias Murko,[28] when the era of collecting with sound recorders started. It became obvious to many scholars that the texts of songs, and even the contents of the stories told in the epic and lyric songs, change and are not fixed, both in the Muslim and in the Christian tradition. It awakened scholarly interest in studying and collecting "variants" of songs, which had been ignored for so long, and it finally turned the attention of scholars to the singers as the creators of songs.

For over fifty years the publication of the Marjanović collection was considered the best and the first critical edition of South Slavic epics. In 1947 Branislav Krstić came to Zagreb and made a request to examine the manuscripts of the songs. He was surprised to find that Marjanović had freely changed the original texts of songs while editing them for publication.[29]

Krstić provided many examples of Marjanović's alterations of his texts. In fact, Marjanović's interventions were so numerous that Krstić was able to classify them into eight groups: 1) correcting of irregular lines; 2) merging of two or more lines into one; 3) expanding one line into two or more; 4) changing the order of lines; 5) omitting lines; 6) inserting new lines; 7) correcting the language of songs; 8) correcting regular lines.

I also had an opportunity to study a microfilmed copy of Marjanović's manuscripts kept in the Milman Parry Collection at Harvard and saw alterations of the texts. Whole passages of songs are crossed out. Fortunately, either the editors of the volume did not fully accept Marjanović's way of editing, or perhaps he himself changed his mind about editing, since the songs are apparently not shortened substantially in their published form.

It is naïve to consider the texts of oral epic and lyric songs that have already been written down true products of the tradition. Marjanović stated that he advised his assistants about how to write the songs down, and the singers how to dictate them. According to Marjanović, a good collector is one who is able to train the singer how to dictate his songs "correctly"; he should also be able to catch the singer's mistakes and warn him about them. Marjanović considered topographic and historical confusion in the contents of songs mistakes of the singer. The repetitions and duplications that are common features of traditional Muslim epic singing irritated Marjanović. He explained that it was sometimes hard to teach singers to avoid repetitions and "irregular" lines and not to make their songs too long. It is obvious that he forced the singers to dictate the songs in a way that suited his own personal taste.

Marjanović made all the alterations of his texts very conscientiously and in the firm belief that the singers themselves would approve of his manner of editing. Marjanović felt that *it was unjust to the singer as an artist to represent his song in its unedited form*, since such a published text would appear awkward from an aesthetic point of view to a reader unfamiliar with original epic singing and ignorant of the singer's creation of epic in the course of a rapid performance. Marjanović was the last, and perhaps the greatest, of all the collectors who believed that they were capable of reconciling the poetics of written and oral literature.

The Milman Parry Collection

Milman Parry (1902–35), the discoverer of a possible solution to the "Homeric question," is the founder of the best modern collection of south Slavic Muslim and Christian epic and lyric songs.[30]

Milman Parry studied the works of the famous Slovene ethnographer Matthias Murko. Murko provided important proof that the text of the South Slavic epic song is not fixed;[31] he was also the first scholar to begin collecting South Slavic traditional poetry with a sound-recorder.[32] Parry followed Murko in his collecting, as Murko had followed in Marjanović's footsteps more than twenty years earlier.[33]

Parry expressed his indebtedness to Murko in the foreword to his unfinished study *Ćor Huso: A Study of South Slavic Heroic Song*: "It was the writings of Professor Murko more than those of any other which in the following years led me to the study of oral poetry in itself and to the heroic poems of the South Slavs" (*The Making of Homeric Verse*, p. 439).

Parry was also well acquainted with Friedrich Krauss's work and with Gerhard Gesemann's research on the structure of South Slavic epics.[34] Moreover, he was familiar with the collections of Karadžić, Hörmann, and Marjanović.

According to Il'ja Nikolaevič Goleniščev-Kutuzov (1904–69), the Russian scholar who helped Parry in the beginning of his collecting and taught him Serbo-Croatian, Parry first came to Yugoslavia in 1932.[35] In the summer of 1933 Parry started to collect South Slavic epic songs. This period of Parry's field work is described by Goleniščev-Kutuzov and in Parry's unpublished field notes titled *Ćor Huso*. Parry's assistant was Nikola Vujnović, who wrote down songs dictated by singers. Literate singers wrote down their songs themselves.

In 1934 Parry became aware that this way of collecting was not satisfactory for a close study of traditional singing. He therefore purchased a special sound-recorder, which enabled him to record long epic songs for the first time.[36] The way Parry and Vujnović collected with the sound-recorder from the summer of 1934 until September 1935 is described by Albert Bates Lord, who accompanied Parry on that trip.[37] Suffice it to say here that no one had ever collected South Slavic epic songs in such a scholarly, rigorous, and methodical way as Parry did. Parry was also privileged to record the songs of Avdo Međedović, one of the best singers among South Slavic Muslims.

The field notes of Milman Parry, his translation of the beginning of the song *The Wedding of Smailagić Meho*, and the first pages of his projected book *The Singer of Tales*, clearly indicate that Parry was undertaking a comprehensive and theoretical work on traditional epic poetry.

Albert Bates Lord (1912–91), late honorary curator of the Milman Parry Collection, undertook the preservation and publication of the materials Parry had gathered after Parry's premature death.[38]

In 1937 Lord collected Albanian epics (presumably aided by someone who knew Albanian). These epics are closely related to South Slavic Muslim epics. In 1950–51 Lord and his native-speaker assistant Miloš Velimirović collected South Slavic epics from some of the singers of Milman Parry, but they also encountered new ones. In 1960–65 Lord and David Bynum again collected Muslim epic songs (see Appendix I) and microfilmed the materials of Croatian and Serbian archives containing unpublished Christian and Muslim songs collected mostly during the nineteenth century.

Lord's collecting in the same area formerly explored by Milman Parry added a diachronic dimension to the Milman Parry Collection. The recordings have fine sound quality, since Lord and Bynum used more advanced sound-recorders than the ones available in the thirties. Bynum's contribution to the quality of the collected materials is his conversations with the singers about the contents of their songs.

In 1953 Lord published the first two volumes of *Serbo-Croatian Heroic Songs,* containing epics collected in the area of Novi Pazar. The goal of that publication was to represent traditional epic singing in unaltered form. This publication illustrated Parry's experiments in collecting in the field.

In 1974 Lord and Bynum published volumes three and four of the series mentioned above, containing the text and translation of the epic song *The Wedding of Smailagić Meho (Ženidba Smailagina sina),* dictated by Avdo Međedović to Nikola Vujnović.[39] This epic is not traditional, strictly speaking, because the singer learned it from a published source.

David Eliab Bynum (born in 1936), former curator of the Milman Parry Collection, collected together with Lord in the sixties and edited the texts of most of the publications of the Milman Parry Collection.

In 1979 Bynum edited volume fourteen of *Serbo-Croatian Heroic Songs,* containing seven epics collected by Milman Parry in the area of Bihaćka Krajina and one song collected in 1963 by Lord and Bynum.[40]

In 1980, Bynum edited volume six of *Serbo-Croatian Heroic Songs,* containing Međedović's dictated and sung version of the epic *The Wedding of Alija, the Son of a Vlah Woman* and Međedović's epic *Osmanbey Delibegović and Pavićević Luka,* the longest song ever recorded among South Slavic Muslims (13,326 lines).[41]

Partial Verification of the Transcription and Editions of the Milman Parry Collection

The purpose of the publications of the Milman Parry Collection was to prepare editions of the collected epics which would not differ from the singer's dictated or sung text. The intention was thus to provide a reliable tool for research.

Most of the recordings of the Muslim epic songs collected by Milman Parry in the thirties were transcribed by Nikola Vujnović. I have read all of Vujnović's published transcriptions and several of the unpublished ones, but

I have never had the opportunity to compare them with the sound-recordings. They seem to be reliable, but each of the texts I have seen requires careful checking and editing before it can be published. All of the recorded texts collected by Albert Lord in the fifties were transcribed by Miloš Velimirović. In the course of my research I have checked many of them.[42] Velimirović's transcriptions are not reliable and should therefore not be used for publication without additional checking and correction. All of the recorded texts collected by Lord and Bynum in the sixties were transcribed and in great part edited by myself (except one single epic text, transcribed and edited by David Bynum).

I have compared the original recordings of the songs with the published texts of the Milman Parry Collection. The following section reports on some of the results of my verification.

In 1979 volume fourteen of *Serbo-Croatian Heroic Songs* was published with Albert Lord as general editor and David Bynum as managing editor. As indicated, the book contains eight epic songs collected primarily in the region of Bihaćka Krajina. Two of the songs were written down by the singer, two other songs were dictated to Nikola Vujnović. There remain four epic songs. Three of them were recorded in 1935 (Parry texts 1920a, 6423, 1971), and the fourth was recorded in 1963. The editor does not mention who transcribed the songs from 1935. If it was Vujnović who transcribed them, and if Lord and Bynum used Vujnović's transcription in editing the volume, this should have been mentioned. However, Bynum edited all the texts. I have checked the epic song recorded in 1963, which was transcribed by Bynum. The song was sung by the extraordinarily good singer Ibrahim Nuhanović from Cazin.

As it turns out, the published text contains numerous mistakes. I have classified them in three groups: A) meaningless lines; B) editor's misunderstandings; and C) awkward lines. I have provided translations for both the editor's transcriptions and mine; when a word or phrase is incomprehensible I mark it "senseless."

	A. *Meaningless lines in published*	*What the singer sang*
line	*text*	
17	Jer valajbeg zavrgove si'	Jer valajbeg zavrg'o vese(lje),
	Al' s Taslidže dovjelo divoj',	A iz Taslidže dovjeo divoj(ku),
	A oda grana Taslidžkog dizdara,	A od akrana taslidžkog dizdara,
17	Since alajbey (2nd hemist. senseless)	Since alajbey made a celebration [wedding-feast],
	But from Taslidža it brought the girl,	And brought the girl from Taslidža

(1st hemist. senseless) the dizdar of Taslidža,	From his friend the dizdar of Taslidža,

In his textual notes the editor did not provide an explanation of the lines. He heard "od akrana" (from [his] friend) as "oda grana" (senseless); and he heard the perfectly sensible 2nd hemistich "zavrg'o vese(lje)" (made a celebration) as "zavrgove si' " (senseless).

23	Jej, jä et*e* . . . , jä je '*v*o *v*ahar*o* bilu,	Ej, a ihtijari u aharu bilu,
23	(senseless) . . . , in the white guest-room,	Hey, and the old men [were gathered] in the white guest-room,

The editor notes: "a bad line. The bride is the subject, and Nuhanović should have said: Jej, jä je evo (v)u (v)aharu bilu." (Hey, here she comes to the white guest-room). Here the editor is mistaken: 1) It is not a bad line; the editor simply did not understand its meaning. 2) The bride cannot be the subject, since in this situation, according to folk custom, the bride's place is in the house and not in the guest-room. In line 21, the singer placed the bride exactly where she belongs in the common traditional setting. Samo je mlada dvore naselil' = Only the bride was in the house. 3) It is unfortunate when an editor tries to guess what the singer should have said. Instead of hearing the words "a ihtijari u" (and the old men in) the editor heard only "jä et*e* . . . , jä je '*v*o" (senseless).

36	Hej, jä neg' kad se je bliže preko t*j*eju,	Hej, al*j*' kad se je bliže pr*e*ko*ć*ijo
36	Hey, but when has nearer (senseless)	Hey, but when he came closer,

The verb "prikućiti se" (to come closer) the editor misunderstood as "preko" and "t*j*eju." "Preko" means "over," and "t*j*eju" is senseless, although the editor believes it is the genitive (dual) of "tlo" = ground, soil. Even if we accept the editor's understanding, this line is meaningless.

58	Još mi je s licu *v*u životu glav'	Još mi je stricu *v*u životu glava.
58	It is still from face in life my head.	My uncle still lives. (Literally: The head of my uncle still lives.)

The editor did not provide a note to this line. He heard the word "stricu" (dative of the word "stric" = uncle) as "s licu" (from face). The editor thought perhaps that the phrase might mean "it seems." But this is not the case; "s licu" does not have that meaning. The editor missed the sense of this line, since the hero said that it is his uncle, not he himself, who is still alive.

77	Beg se dva mu ninut učinej',	Beg fermanu ninut učini(o),
	A rukom mlapi pa ga poljubij',	A rukom lapi, pa ga poljubi(o),
77	The bey did obeisance twice,	The bey did obeisance to the fir-man [letter]
	And with hand (senseless), and kissed it.	And took it in his hand, and kissed it.

The editor notes that the verb "mlapi" is a deformation of mlati (= to thrash) or (h)lapi, or a fusion of the two. The editor, again, is mistaken. The hero would never thrash a sultan's edict; there is a very common colloquial verb, lapiti (= to take something in hand, to take something without hesitation). The word "fermanu" (the dative of the word "ferman") the editor heard as "se dva mu" (word for word it means: [he] has two [times] to it; I translated it as "twice").

106	Pa su mi hodehani s' otvorej',	Pa su mi hodže hadis otvoril',
	A 'lebhadije čečve razavej',	A levhadžije fečve razavil',
106	And then my campaign stores were opened	And then my priests opened the "hadis,"
	And the bakers scattered the win-nowed grain,	And the carriers of the well-writ scripts unfolded the prophetic texts,

This example demonstrates very well what a difference in the sense of the story may be caused by wrong transcription. The editor invented three non-existent words: "hodehani," "'lebhadije," and "čečve." The first means, according to the editor, "campaign stores," and the second "the bakers," and the third, "winnowed grain." The editor heard the words "hodže hadis" as "hodehani," and the word "levhadžije" as "'lebhadije," and the word "fečve" as "čečve." The verb "razaviti," to unfold, he understood as "to scatter."

Those two lines represent part of the letter written by the sultan to the Bosnian hero. The sultan describes to the hero his unsuccessful seven-year-long siege of the enemy city. The sultan says:

And then my priests (hodže) *have opened the hadis* (= the sacred book containing Mohammed's words) / *And the carriers of well-writ scripts* (levhadžije; from levha = citations from the Koran calligraphically written) *unfolded* (razavil') *the prophetic texts* (fečve; from fetva = the book containing the right answers).

The sultan continues:

Pa mi 'vako jesu govorili: / Da brez Bosne osvajanja nema! 108/109
And this is what they (the priests) told me: That there is no way to conquer (the enemy city) without the Bosnians! 108/109

This important segment of the epic song, containing the prophecy, does not appear in the published text because of the editor's misunderstanding. Instead, he introduced several new words, suggesting a riot among the sultan's soldiers.

110	Hej, ev' od ovog' drugog nemam povozanja,	Hej, u ovo drugog nemam pouzdanja,
110	Hey, I don't have of this other (senseless)	Hey, I don't have confidence in the others,

The editor explains the senseless word "povozanje" as "way of proceeding" (with the military campaign). But the word "povozanje" does not exist. The editor heard the senseless word "povozanje" instead of the well-attested "pouzdanje" (confidence).

135	Bujurola, na konak ve!"	Bujurola, na konak meneka!"
	"Neka tebe, beže. Fala, Osmanbeže:	"Tebi beže, fala, Osmanbeže!
135	Please be so kind as to sleep at my house!"	
	"I am grateful to you, oh bey Osmanbey!	

It is difficult to indicate this editor's mistake in translation. The hero politely invites the sultan's messenger to sleep at his home (line 135). In the same courteous way the messenger thanks him (line 136). The editor did not understand the common colloquial form of the possessive pronoun "mene" (meneka) and transcribed it wrongly as "ve" and "neka." Thus he broke two fine and sensible decasyllabic lines into an octosyllabic and a duodecasyllabic line, both awkward. The sense of those perfectly clear lines becomes blurred.

272	Tad stigoše *vu* Travnica heli.	Tad stigoše *vu* Travnik carevi.
272	Then they came to Travnika (senseless)	Then they came to the imperial town Travnik.

The editor marks the senseless word "heli" with "sic!" and suggests an equally senseless word, "hele." What is meant remains unclear. The editor obviously did not understand the singer, and the common word "carevi" (imperial) has become "-ca heli." The glorious town of Travnik has become non-existent Travnica.

287 A valja viš' ter svojoj kući nej'."	A da ja viš' ter svojoj kući neć'."
287 (Senseless) to my house (sense-less)	And that I will not go back to my house."
290 Jer ʃim svijo po Bosni Bošnjake.	Vezir svijo po Bosni Bošnjake.
290 Because he assembled to them Bosnians.	The vezier had assembled Bosnians.

In the editor's text a perfectly clear line became awkward and hard to understand. The word "vezir" he misunderstood as "jer" (because) and "ʃim" (to them). Thus the published line lacks a subject.

301 Svi imejete na carevu vojsku.	Svi idete na carevu vojsku.
301 You are all (senseless) in imperial army.	You are all going to (join) the imperial army.

The editor uses non-existent words, such as "imejete," without any explanation.

359 Je! a jam sam svojim babom voje-vaᵥo A svojim babom, ᵥOmer alajbe-gom.	Ehe, o ja sam s tvojim babom vojevaᵥo, A s tvojim babom, ᵥOmer alaj-begom.
359 Yeah, and I fought along with my father, With my father Omer the Alajbey.	Yeah, and I fought along with your father, With your father Omer the Alaj-bey.

Those words are uttered by the hero's faithful helper. He reminds the young hero that he has great experience in fighting, since he fought along with *the hero's own father*.

417 "Haj'mo, što no k'o se o' sultana traži,	"Haj', muštuluk kod sultana traži,
417 "Let's go, as it is required by the sultan,	"Go, ask the sultan for a gift as a messenger of good news,

The order is given *to the messenger*, who immediately rides to the sultan's palace. The editor's misunderstanding rendered the whole passage senseless. It is perfectly apparent that he did not understand the singer's word "muštu-luk," and heard it as "-mo što no k'."

423 A od ologa četiri sahata,	A od dolova četiri sahata,
423 And of (senseless) four hours,	And four hours [of riding] over the valley,

The editor did not provide any note to this line. If he thought that the word "ologa" should be understood as "ovoga" (this), then he should have so indicated. Yet even that would be incorrect.

437 Al' no care lakrdiju daje: A odma' care lakrdiju daje:
     "Rateni Bosni mistro napravi!   Rad'te ni, Bosni misto napra-vi(te)

437 But the sultan utters a word: And the sultan instantly uttered a word:

     "(Senseless) make a place for Bosnia [the Bosnian army]!   "Work, make a place for Bosnia [the Bosnian army],

The editor did not explain the meaning of the word "rateni." To be sure, it has none.

451 Mehmed hodža, od careva viša,   Mehmed hodža, od careva Bišća,
451 Mehmed the priest, a member of the sultan's council,   Mehmed the priest, from the imperial town Bihać,

The editor thinks that the word "viša," which might also be spelled "viša" = veća, makes sense. I disagree. A few lines later the singer speaks about how the priest longed for his homeland, Bosnia. The town Bihać is in Bosnia, the genitive of Bihać is Bišća. The editor heard the word "Bišća" as "viša" (senseless).

494 Jej, vaš je refeta od dragog kamena,   Ej, a šerefeta od dragog kamena,
494 (1st hemist. senseless) of precious stone,   Hey, and the fence around the minaret [is built] of precious stone,

The editor heard the word "šerefeta" as "vaš je refeta" (senseless) and did not provide any explanation.

534 Jej! "Ja vas ne hranim, beže Osmanbeže,   "Ej, a vas ne hrani beže uOsmanbeže,
     Vi ne mi njega nositi nećet'!   Dine mi, njega nositi nećet'!
     A, beže, Ibro hrani bajraktar,   A beže Ibru hrani bajraktar',

534 Hey!, "I do not feed you, bey Osmanbey,   "Hey, the bey Osmanbey is not providing food for you,
     You will not carry him!   I swear by faith, you will not carry him!

     And, oh bey, Ibro the standard-bearer provides food,   The bey provides food for Ibro the standard-bearer,

The sultan's high officials came to carry Osmanbey in their arms into the mosque. The standard-bearer did not allow them to carry him, saying that the bey was providing his food; that is the reason why he himself must carry the bey. The editor heard "a vas ne hrani" (is not providing food for you)

as "ja vas ne hranim" (I do not feed you); "Dine mi" ([I swear] by my faith) as "Vi ne mi" (You will not). The editor's rendering of line 536 is incorrect. According to him, the standard-bearer provides food for his own master.

560	Je, silimo ti Bogu i ferman',	Jesi li multim Bogu i ferman',
560	We are forcing to God and to fir-man (letter),	Are you the favored one by God and by the firman (letter),

The editor heard "Jesi li multim" (Are you the one who is favored) as "Je, silimo ti" (We are forcing).

582	To sva je zlatit carev' begog'lar.	To, svoje svlači, careve obla(či).
582	She is entirely the golden sultan's begoglar.	He takes his [clothes] off, and puts the sultan's on.

The editor has heard "svoje" (his) as "sva je" (she is entirely, all of her is); "svlači" (takes off) as "zlatit" (golden); and "careve oblač(i)" (puts on the sultan's [cloths]) as "carev' begog'lar" (the sultan's begoglar). He provides the meaning of this non-existent word as follows: "A conflated word from Turkish *bey* and *agalar*. The Serbocroatian loan-word *agalar* is singular (plural: *agalari*) despite the plurality of the Turkish original *alagar*." The line makes no sense even if the reader agreed with the editor's explanation.

593	E, parmaljade dva para kićeni,	E, pa mu dade dva para gičermi,
593	Eh, (1st. hemist. senseless) two beautiful pairs,	Eh, then he gave him two pairs of gičerma,

Gičerma is a vest-like garment. The editor heard "pa mu dade" (then he gave him) as "parmaljade" (senseless); "gičermi" (vests) as "kićeni" (beautiful, ornamented).

606	vOd pripodne pa do' si se lig'.	vOd pripone pa do sise li(ve).
606	From the morning 'til you lay down.	From the groin up to the left breast.

The editor heard the word "pripone" (the groin) as "pripodne" (the morning); "sise li(ve)" (the left breast) as "si se lig'" (you lay down).

line	B. *Editor's misunderstandings*	*What the singer sang*
2	Ej, al'—a udara more u dugoli,	Ej, al'—a udara more od obali,
2	Hey, is the ocean striking (senseless)	Hey, is the ocean striking the shore,

The editor explains the meaningless word "dugola" as "a Serbocroatian augmentative formation from Hungarian *duga*, 'embankment, breakwater'." The same formulaic expression occurs once again in line 8, and I hear it again as "obala" (shore). This is the beginning of the song, and the expression represents a part of the famous Slavic antithesis. For example, the epic song dictated by the excellent Muslim singer Salko Vojniković (no. 5 in the publication of the Marjanović collection) begins as follows:

> Al grm grmi, al se zemlja trese,
> Al pucaju po gori kudreti,
> Ili more od *obale* lupa?
> Nit grmi grmi, nit se zemlja trese,
> Niti more lup od *obale*,

If the editor believed that he was correct, he should have provided more examples of the occurrence of what he perceived as "dugola."

66	Otklen je bio beže Osmanbeže?	Otklen bi bio beže Osmanbeže?
	Luda glava nausnice nema!	Luda je glava, nausnice nema,
	Da za njega sultan care znade,	Da za njega sultan care znade!"
	Pašalija ferman izvadio.	Pašalija ferman izvadio.
	Where was bey Osmanbey from?	How could he be the bey Osmanbey?
66	The crazy head has no mustaches!"	He is crazy-headed, he has no mustaches,
	In order that the sultan know about him	How could the sultan know about him!"
	The messenger took out the firman.	The messenger took out the firman.

The scene is well-known. The messenger comes with the sultan's letter. He has an order to hand it to the famous hero. He finds a young man who does not yet have a mustache. The messenger doubts that the young man is the hero he is looking for and puts him to the test. The editor's mistakes have rendered this scene incomprehensible. He heard "Otklen bi bio" (How could he be, i.e., Is it possible that he is) as "Otklen je bio" (Where was he from); "Luda je glava" (He is crazy-headed, implying that he is too young) as "Luda glava" (The crazy head). Since the editor misunderstood lines 66/67, he also misinterpreted the next two lines.

| 90 | De nije hrana za sav asker bila. | De mi je hrana za sav asker bila. |
| 90 | Where there was not food for the whole army. | Where I had food for the whole army. |

The editor heard the words "mi je" (I have) as "nije" (is not).

| 134 | *V*a nešavlju mladu ostaviti. | *v*A ne žalim mladu ostaviti. |
| 134 | And (senseless) leave the bride. | And I do not regret leaving my bride. |

The editor invented the word "nešavlja," which is, according to him, "an adjectival formation from *neša* (a hypocoristic derivative from *nevjesta*)." He thus heard the words "ne žalim" (I do not regret) as "nešavlju" (senseless).

149	Eh, hodža skoči u hubavi odaj':	Eh, hodža skoči, u avliju do(đe).
149	Eh, the priest leaped up in beauti-ful(?) room:	Eh, the priest leaped up, he came to the courtyard.

The editor heard the common formula "u avliju do(đe)" (he came to the courtyard) as "hubavi odaj" (beautiful[?] room). The word "hubavi" might mean "beautiful" or "good-looking" (= ubavi), but I have never encountered this Old Croatian word in a Muslim epic song. The editor misplaced the action, since it takes place in the courtyard.

176	Ej, vazdan plaka mlada Taslidžki-nja:	Ej, a zaplaka mlada Taslidž-kinja:
176	Hey, the young woman from Tasli-dža was crying all the time:	Hey, the young woman from Taslidža started to cry:

The editor heard "a zaplaka" as "vazdan plaka." Thus he misinterpreted the tragic scene describing a *sudden unhappy moment* in which the young just-married bride finds out that her husband is going to leave her.

222	Hajde, draga, privodi mi majku.	Hajde, draga, prÍbudi mi majku!
222	Go, my dear, bring me my mother.	Go, my dear, wake up my mother!

The editor heard the word "prÍbudi" (probudi = wake up) twice (lines 222 and 224) as "privodi" (= bring).

241	"Ta nemoj, beže, urok ti je Bog'.	"Ta nemoj, beže, u ruke te lju-b(im).
241	"Do not (talk in that way), oh bey, your spell is God.	"Do not (talk in that way), oh bey, I kiss your hands.

I have quoted forty-three senseless or misunderstood lines in the first six hundred lines of the published song. I will now quote the same number of *awkward* lines also to be found in the first six hundred lies of the published text. I have also provided the singer's words as I have heard them. An awkward line I define as a line which has not completely lost its sense, but is difficult to understand because of the poor transcription. Senseless and misunderstood lines destroy the sense of passages in the epic. An abundance of awkward lines, on the other hand, destroys the artistic value of the song as a poetic work.

line	C. *Awkward lines in published text*	*What the singer sang*
4	Jeh, jä *v*al' s*j*e straža po granica tuči,	Ej, al' s*j*e straža po granicam' tuče,
10	Da ne tuči se na granici stra*r*'	A ne tuče se na granici straž(a),
13	Ven pucaju bojni se lubardi,	Ven pucaju bojnice lumbarde,
48	Ej, *đ*e je Glasinac, na kojoj je stranu,	Ej, *đ*e je Glasinac, na koju je stranu.
51	Jej, bih ja mog'o do njegaka doći,	E, bi l' ja mogo do njegaka doći,
54	Jej, jä no smija se beže Osman-beže:	E, a nasmija se beže Osmanbeže:
62	"Ala ti mene ne bi prevare'?"	"A da ti mene ne bi prevarij'?"
72	"Ako će bide beže prigod*e*jo,	"Ako se bide beže prigodijo,
73	Sanćim mu se ferman otvoriti.	Sam će mu se ferman otvoriti.
88	Ta kilerhanu carsku zavoze'	Ta kiljerhanu carsku zauzeli,
89	A Rumenliju zemlju prefate,	O, Rumenliju zemlju prefatili,
91	Jä oduzeše Hotim po temelju,	Ej, oduzeše Hotin po temelju,
95	Jej, jä Angleja, i š njim Francuz-lija,	Ej, Englezlija, i š njim Francuz-lija,
96	Moskoviću, jej i' zemlje Rusije.	Moskoviću, *h*iz zemlje Rusije,
100	*V*a pod Hotim glavom nasili'.	v*A* pod Hotin glavom naseli'.
103	a. Hotim tučem svakog evo dan-	a. Hotin tučem svakog bijelog dan-
113	Gle de mi kupi po Bosni Bošnjake.	Dede mi kupi po Bosni Bošnjake.
182	E! Ti zdravijo, ona ti umrila,	E! Ti zdrav bijo, ona ti umrila,
206	Pa s' udaj, e, *đ*e je tebi drago,	Pa s' udaji *đ*e je tebi drago
211	"A ne cipaj mi srca u prs*e*!	"A ne cipaj mi srca u prsim'!

214	Jer se kurbani za bajrama hranil'	Jer se kurbani za bajrama hrane
221	Dug' je đogu konja sigurao.	Dok je đogu konja sigurao.
260	Ej! Onda je Ibro konja pojahavo.	Ej, a dok je Ibro konja pojahavo.
262	A i gospoja Ibro halalij'.	A i gospoja Ibru halalil'.
268	E, nek' mi Bosnu potegne u svijet."	E, neg' mi Bosnu po temelju sve(de).
284	A jerbo sam se s dragom rastavij',	A jedvo sam se s dragom rastavij',
293	E, sve dan po dan a val' misec dana	E, sve dan po dan ravan misec dana.
309	Je! a dave vezir tembih od sebeka	Ej, a dade vezir tembih od sebeka
381	Je, jä l' Osmanbeže stazu izgubijo.	Ej, Osmanbeg je stazu izgubijo,
388	Tamam magla na dolovid bila.	Taman magla na dolovi bila,
394	Biva' je glava vonog fermandžije,	Bila je glava vonog fermandžije
403	Jej, a sa živa kožu ogolit'."	E, a sa živa kožu ogulit'."
411	E, dovle odpade, turski salam viknu,	E, dok dopade, turski salam viknu,
415	Hej, Hotin na kojoj je stranu?"	Gđe je Hotin, na koju je stranu?"
429	Jer je njegova ostanula glava.	Neg njegova ostanula glava.
454	Svojej se je Bosni zaželijo.	Svoje se je Bosne zaželijo.
458	"Jej, a đe si, đeco, Bošnjaci junaci?	"Ej, a đe ste, đeco, Bošnjaci junaci?
575	E, nara nemam za osmu godinu.	Emera nejmam za osmu godinu.
590	O, dva mu krila došla do koli',	Oba mu krila došla do kolin',
604	A sve je zlatna i konje srebre'.	A sve je zlatna i konj je srebren.

Conclusion

The earliest historical documents concerning South Slavic Muslim epic songs date from the beginning of the sixteenth century.[43] We can only guess what forms of epic singing existed in northern Bosnia and Lika before the Turkish conquest of thoses areas, where the South Slavic Muslim epics presumably originated and from whence they spread all over Bosnia and beyond. Some of the earliest recordings of South Slavic Muslim epic and lyric songs, gathered in the beginning of the eighteenth century, have been found in the Erlangen manuscript.[44]

The core of the Franciscan collection was the South Slavic Muslim epics. Many of the manuscripts of that collection have been lost. It is to be hoped that some of them may still be found in the archives of the Franciscans. The Šunjić collection, many epics published in literary magazines, and the manuscripts of texts recorded in the period of the 1840s (yet to be found) should be added to that collection. The main value of the Franciscan collection is that it represents both Muslim and Christian traditional epic singing in a single region.

The ethnographer Friedrich Salomo Krauss published only a small part of his collection and translated it into German. It is not known if the manuscripts of his collection are preserved.[45]

Kosta Hörmann and his assistant collectors made the best-known collection of South Slavic Muslim epic songs. Forty-six unpublished epics from that collection have been found. The texts of the Hörmann collection were not gathered in a proper manner. However, its publication influenced both the epic singing and the traditional beliefs of the Bosnian village. It represents the tradition of the kind of epic singing which was accompanied by the musical instrument *gusle* as found throughout the region of Bosnia.

The published part of Luka Marjanović's impressive collection contains approximately one sixth of all the materials he recorded. His manuscripts of unpublished epics have been preserved. The published Marjanović collection represents traditional epic singing accompanied by the musical instrument *tambura,* as found in the region of northern Bosnia. Marjanović edited the texts inadequately from a contemporary point of view (see above). The texts of his collection should be published again in unaltered form, as found in the original manuscripts. Nevertheless, this collection even in its present form has proven of value for scholarly research. Thus, it was studied by Vatroslav Jagić, Matthias Murko, Gerhard Gesemann, and above all, Alois Schmaus.[46]

The modern collection of sound-recordings and texts taken down by dictation was made by Milman Parry. Only a small part of the materials of the Parry collection has been published. It is unfortunate that the publications of the Milman Parry collection could not be accompanied by the original recordings of the songs because of financial considerations. Only through close analysis of the recordings may the scholars concerned be able to comprehend the art of Muslim epic singing in its original form. The transcription of the texts alone lacks the musical component and the rhythm of the actual performance. The recordings also provide the necessary tool for checking the reliability of the published texts. My verification of one of them has proven that it differs considerably from the text of the original recording.

Manuscripts of the old collections and of all texts taken by dictation should be published in unaltered form. It is the best way of checking the quality of the actual collector. Special attention should be paid to the investigation of unpublished materials (Vrčević,[47] Luburić, etc.). The publication of the texts made by sound-recorder should be accompanied by the recording itself. Matthias Murko, Gerhard Gesemann and Milman Parry collected with the aid of a sound-recorder and were fully aware that the study of the traditional epics and lyrics has to be based on such—and improved—sound-recordings.

The collecting of South Slavic Muslim epic songs must be continued. Collectors should naturally use better equipment for recording than has been available so far (video-cameras and high-quality sound-recorders).

From Grgo Martić, alias "A Hercegovinian Who-Loves-Homer" to Milman Parry, Albert Lord, and David Bynum, the collectors of South Slavic Muslim epics gathered and recorded them for their own purposes and according to their own special interests. Likewise, the materials they published also served those purposes and interests.

The time has now come to turn our attention away from the collectors and their interpretation of the tradition and to focus all efforts on a close scrutiny of the singers and their songs. The singers are the creators and sometimes the masters of the tradition. What we now need is further and better work on the aesthetics of the art of epic singing.

Appendix I: The Recordings of the Epic Texts in the Milman Parry Collection collected in the Sixties

(by Albert B. Lord and David E. Bynum, 1962–66; transcribed and edited by Zlatan Čolaković, 1984–87)

In 1954, for the first and, to date, last time, a partial list of the contents of the South Slavic epic texts in the Milman Parry Collection was published. It was volume one of the series *Serbo-Croatian Heroic Songs* that contained *A Digest of Serbo-Croatian Epic Songs in the Milman Parry Collection of South Slavic Texts.*[48]

In that "digest" Lord listed the titles of epics and the recordings of conversations with singers of epic songs. To the impressive list of the original Parry Collection of epic texts recorded in the thirties, Lord added a list of his own recordings made in the early fifties.

Unfortunately, Lord's digest is not satisfactory. It provides only the differentiation between sound-recordings and texts collected in some other way. It does not provide information about the length of the songs; also, it does not describe the way the songs listed were collected (for example, the list does not differentiate between texts taken by dictation and texts written down by the singers themselves). Although more than thirty years have passed, that "digest" is still the only available reference for the contents of the Milman Parry Collection as a whole.

The "digest" covered as indicated, Milman Parry's collection from the thirties as well as Lord's collection from 1950–51. The list of materials collected by Lord and Bynum in the sixties has never been published.

Since I, as a Fulbright scholar, devoted several years to the study of the songs collected in the sixties, and since I transcribed and edited them for the first time, I decided to publish here such a list for the benefit of all those scholars interested in the field of South Slavic and oral epic literature in general.

1962

1.   Ramo Babić: Ženidba Smailagić Meha. *The Wedding of Smailagić Meho.* 2054 lines. Novi Pazar.

2.   Džemail Zogić: Bojičić Alija izbavlja Eminu. *Bojičić Alija Rescues Emina.* 1328 lines. Novi Pazar.

3.   Džemail Zogić: Omer Hrnjica izbavlja Fatimu, Muja i Halila. *Omer Hrnjica Rescues Fatima, Mujo and Halil.* 1249 lines. Novi Pazar.

4.   Šefko Ibrović: Ženidba Ajanović Meha. *The Wedding of Ajanović Meho.* 1353 lines. Duga Poljana.

5. Šefko Ibrović: Ropstvo kićene Fatime. *The Captivity of Fatima the Fair*. 1102 lines. Duga Poljana.

6. Hamdo Džondić: Razgovor. Conversation. Sopoćani.

7. Hamdo Džondić: Katal-ferman na Muja Hrnjicu. *The Firman of Execution on Mujo Hrnjica*.[49] 1293 lines. Sopoćani.

8. Hamdo Džondić: Kajtaz bajraktar zauzima Badgad. *Kajtaz the Standard-Bearer Takes Bagdad*. 652 lines. Sopoćani.

9. Ašir Ćorović: Smrt Marije Grujića. *The Death of Marija Grujić*. 42 lines. Rožaje.

10. Ašir Ćorović: Ropstvo pašine Emine. *The Captivity of Pasha's Emina*. 1021 lines. Rožaje.

11. Murat Kurtagić: Katal-ferman na Đerđelez Aliju. *The Firman of Execution on Đerđelez Alija*. 2075 lines. Rožaje.

12. Ramo Toković: Halil na košiji izbavi Ahmetbegove kćeri. *Halil Rescues Ahmetbey's Daughters in A Horse Race*. 542 lines. Sjenica.

13. Ramo Toković: Smrt Sirotan Alije (Nahod Simeun i nahod Husein). The Death of Alija the Orphan (The Foundling Simeun and the Foundling Husein). 556 lines. Sjenica.

14. Hamid Latović: Vilić Husein i Matija od Kapije. *Vilić Husein and Matija of Kapija*. 786 lines. Sjenica.

15. Sinan Gudžević: Smrt Halilova. *The Death of Halil* (+ Conversation). 179 lines. Sjenica.

16. Ivan Mrvić: Mali Marijan. *Marijan the Little*. 270 lines. Sjenica.

1963

1. Bejto Smakić: Ženidba Smailagić Meha. *The Wedding of Smailagić Meho*. 2245 lines. Karajukići Bunari.

2. Ahmed Turković: Senjanin Ivan i Suljaić Ibro. *Senjanin Ivan and Suljagić Ibro*. 993 lines. Karajukići Bunari.

3. Bejto Smakić: Budimska Fatima zauzima Bagdad. *Fatima of Budim Takes Bagdad*. 976 lines. Karajukići Bunari.

4. Ahmed Turković Katal-ferman na Bojković Aliju. *The Firman of Execution on Bojković Alija*. 764 lines. Karajukići Bunari.

5. Bejto Smakić: Ropstvo Ličkog Mustajbega (+ Razgovor). *The Captivity of Mustajbey of the Lika* (+ Conversation). 2258 lines. Karajukići Bunari.

6. Šaban Seferović: Budimska Fatima zauzima Bagdad. *Fatima of Budim Takes Bagdad*. 455 lines. Karajukići Bunari.

7. Rašid Hamidović: Ženidba malog Marijana. *The Wedding of Marijan the Little*. 620 lines. Karajukići Bunari.

8. Jusuf Makić: Mujo Hrnjica brani Udbinu. *Mujo Hrnjica Defends Udbina*. 1294 lines. Sjenica.

9. Jusuf Makić: Pašina Fatima i Novljanin Alija zauzimaju Bagdad. *The Pasha's Fatima and Novljanin Alija Take Bagdad.* 2058 lines. Sjenica.

10. Jusuf Makić: Ibrić bajraktar izbavlja sestru i brata iz ropstva u Janoku. *Ibrić the Standard-Bearer Rescues His Sister and Brother from Captivity in Janok.* 2349 lines. Sjenica.

11. Jusuf Makić: Velagić Ibro u ropstvu (+ Razgovor). *The Captivity of Velagić Ibro* (+ Conversation). 2046 lines. Sjenica.

12. Jusuf Makić: Sirotan Alija u Timoku. *Alija the Orphan in Timok.* 1119 lines. Sjenica.

13. Jusuf Makić: Katal-ferman na Đerđelez Aliju. *The Firman of Execution on Đerđelez Alija.* 1987 lines. Sjenica.

14. Jusuf Makić: Halil Hrnjica i Ćirko od Džiljita (+ Razgovor). *Halil Hrnjica and Ćirko of Džiljit* (+ Conversation). 915 lines. Sjenica.

15. Himo Ibrović: Pašić Husein i Tokalija ban. *Pašić Husein and the Ban of Tokalija.* 2091 lines. Duga Poljana.

16. Bejto Smakić: Ženidba Kurtagić Hasana. *The Wedding of Kurtagić Hasan.* 1732 lines. Karajukići Bunari.

17. Bejto Smakić: Smail bajraktar. *Smail the Standard-Bearer.* 2805 lines. Karajukići Bunari.

18. Bejto Smakić: Goljo serhatlija, Mujo i Halil nabavljaju konje u Kormanu. *Goljo the Border-Man, Mujo and Halil Get Their Horses in Korman.* 1271 lines. Karajukići Bunari.

19. Bejto Smakić: Halil izbavlja Glamočkog Rama i Glamočane iz ropstva u Primorju. *Halil Rescues Ramo of Glamoč and Other Men of Glamoč from Captivity in Primorje.* 2747 lines. Karajukići Bunari.

20. Himo Ibrović: Vilić Husein i ban od Jegeta. *Vilić Husein and the Ban of Jeget.* 1491 lines. Duga Poljana.

21. Himo Ibrović: Sirotan Alija izbavlja sestru (+ Razgovor). *Sirotan Alija Rescues His Sister* (+ Conversation). 1898 lines. Duga Poljana.

22. Himo Ibrović: Ženidba Ajanević Meha (+ Razgovor). *The Wedding of Ajanević Meho* (+ Conversation). 2000 lines. Duga Poljana.

23. Ćamil Kulenović: Ćustović Osman izbavlja Zlatu. *Ćustović Osman Rescues Zlata.* 757 lines. Bihać.

24. Murat Kolaković: Ženidba Ograšović Ala. *The Wedding of Ograšović Ale.* 1741 lines. Bihać.

25. Ibrahim Nuhanović: Robovanje Osmanbey Omerbegovića. *The Captivity of Osmanbey Omerbegović..* 1479 lines (transcribed, edited, and published by David Bynum). Cazin.

Note: Song no. 25 is the only one already published (see *Serbo-Croatian Heroic Songs,* vol. 14). I revised and improved Bynum's transcription, after careful consideration of the original recording. The copy containing my corrections is kept in the Milman Parry Collection.

1964

1. Zahir Ahmetović: Omer Hrnjica izbavlja Muja i Halila iz ropstva u Lenđeru. *Omer Hrnjica Rescues Mujo and Halil from Captivity in Lenđer.* 2457 lines. Vrhovina.

2. Fikret Ahmetović: Kurtagić Hasan i Filip Mađarin (+ Razgovor). *Kurtagić Hasan and Filip Mađarin.* (+ Conversation). 142 lines. Vrhovina.

3. Mladen Luketa: Ženidba Janković Stojana. *The Wedding of Janković Stojan.* 378 lines. Kifino Selo.

4. Božo Gušić: Ženidba Janković Stojana. *The Wedding of Janković Stojan.* 234 lines. Kifino Selo.

5. Božo Gušić: Ženidba bega Milanbega. *The Wedding of Bey Milanbey.* 120 lines. Kifino Selo.

6. Marko Gušić: Nikac od Rovina (+ Razgovor). *Nikac of Rovin* (+ Conversation). 196 lines. Kifino Selo.

7. Marko Gušić: Ženidba bega Ljubovića. *The Wedding of Bey Ljubović.* 349 lines. Kifino Selo.

8. Božo Gušić: Pohod Dušana na Carigrad. *Dušan's Attack on Constantinople.* 63 lines. Kifino Selo.

9. Avdo Kevelj: Ženidba Smailagić Meha. *The Wedding of Smailagić Meho.* 1770 lines. Odžak.

10. Gavro Lalović: Mitrović Stojan. *Mitrović Stojan.* 237 lines. Odžak.

11. Avdo Kevelj: Mujo i Halil u Janoku. *Mujo and Halil in Janok.* 708 lines. Odžak.

12. Avdo Kevelj: Marko i Musa (kazivana + dva razgovora). *Marko and Musa* (spoken + two conversations). Odžak.

13. Avdo Kevelj: Kurtagić Hasan (kazivana + dva razgovora). *Kurtagić Hasan* (spoken + two conversations). Odžak.

14. Smail Aličić: Ropstvo Hrnjičine kule. *The Capture of the Tower of the Brothers Hrnjica.* 1007 lines. Kljuna.

15. Smail Aličić: Ćustović Osman. *Ćustović Osman.* 695 lines. Kljuna.

16. Avdo Kevelj: Halil na košiji izbavlja dvije kćeri Osman Alibega. *Halil in a Horse-Race Rescues Two Daughters of Osman Alibey.* 1434 lines. Odžak.

17. Adem Ćustović: Katal-ferman na Muja i Halila. *The Firman of Execution on Mujo and Halil* (+ Conversation). 1156 lines. Gacko.

18. Sajto Bašić: Bolest Đerđelez Alije (+ Razgovor). *The Illness of Đerđelez Alija* (+ Conversation). 1156 lines. Gacko.

19. Osmer Đeko: Ropstvo Tanković Osmana. *The Captivity of Tanković Osman.* 255 lines. Drugovići.

20. Halil Bajgorić: Omer izbavlja Muja, Halilia i Osmana iz ropstva u Lenđeru (+ Razgovor). *Omer Rescues Mujo, Halil and Osman from Captivity in Lenđer* (+ Conversation). 1120 lines Dabrica.

21. Pero Papac: Anđelija, sestra hercega Stjepana, na mejdanu. *Anđelija, the Sister of Stjepan the Duke, in a Duel.* 70 lines. Burmazi.

22. Bećo Idriz: Boj na Temišvaru. *The Battle of Temišvar.* 1081 lines. Stolac.

23. Halil Bajgorić. Krnjević Alija (+ Razgovor). *Krnjević Alija* (+ Conversation). 744 lines. Dabrica.

24. Ilija Medan: Miloš i vila. *Miloš and the Vila.* 213 lines. Žegulja.

25. Halil Bajgorić: Mujo dobavi konja (+ Razgovor). *Mujo Finds His Horse* (+ Conversation). 538 lines. Dabrica.

1965

1. Himo Ibrović: Sestra izbavlja Bojičić Aliju iz ropstva. *The Sister of Bojičić Alija Rescues Him from Captivity.* 1605 lines. Rasno.

2. Himo Ibrović: Ajkuna izbavlja braću Hrnjice iz ropstva u Ćorfezu. *Ajkuna Rescues the Brothers Hrnjica from Captivity in Ćorfez.* 1117 lines. Rasno.

3. Hazir Čolaković: Nahod Husein i nahod Radovan, sinovi Alijini. *The Foundling Husein and the Foundling Radovan, the Sons of Alija.* 707 lines. Kladnica.

4. Tahir Jusović: Katal-ferman na Muja (kazivana). *The Firman of Execution on Mujo* (spoken). 888 lines. Prijepolje.

5. Tahir Jusović: Katal-ferman na Muja. *The Firman of Execution on Mujo.* 900 lines Prijepolje.

6. Hazir Čolaković: Dvije sultanije. *Two Sultanas.* 558 lines. Kladnica.

7. Hazir Čolaković: Murat bajraktar u Indiji (+ Razgovor). *Murat the Standard-Bearer in India* (+ Conversation). 754 lines. Kladnica.

1966

1. Slavoljub Stevanović: Pjesma o heroju Ratku Pavloviću. *The Song of the Hero Ratko Pavlović.* 89 lines. Lukovo.

2. Slavoljub Stevanović: Banović Sekul i Mujo. *Sekul the Duke and Mujo.* 194 lines. Lukovo.

3. Ognjan Dimić: Razgovor. Conversation. Bijelo Polje.

4. Borisav Stević: Razgovor. Conversation. Vlajkovci.

5. Jeremija Tomić: Dušanova ženidba. *The Wedding of Dušan.* 470 lines. Gornja Pološca. (Varda).

6. Sreten Marjanović: Kraljević Marko i Arapin. *Kraljević Marko and the Arab.* 589 lines. Varda.

7. Veljko Spasojević: Zmaj od ognja Vuče i Porča od Avale. *Vuk the Fiery Dragon and Porča of Avala.* 195 lines. Brnjica.

8. Veljko Spasojević: Kraljević Marko i Filip Madžarin. *Marko Kraljević and Filip Madžarin.* 252 lines. Brnjica.

9. Veljko Spasojević: Miloš Obilić i Crni Arapin. *Miloš Obilić and the Black Arab.* 291 lines. Brnjica.

10. Ilija Vranić: Pivljanin Bajo i beg Ljubović. *Pivljanin Bajo and the Bey Ljubović.* 134 lines. Čedovo.

11. Nićifor Ristović: Miloš izbavlja Kraljevića Marka (kazivana + Razgovor). *Miloš Rescues Kraljević Marko* (spoken + Conversation). 175 lines. Panevica.

12. Dragomir Stanki: Stari Vujadin. *Old Vujadin.* 73 lines. Beotime.

13. Dragomir Stanki: Rusko-japanski rat. *The Russo-Japanese War.* 47 lines. Beotime.

14. Slavoljub Stevanović: Ženidba Senjanin Tadije. *The Wedding of Senjanin Tadija.* 157 lines. Lukovo.

15. Vasilije Milićević: Novaković Grujo i paša od Zagorja. *Novaković Grujo and the Pasha of Zagorje.* 253 lines. Mrče.

16. Radoje Lazić: Pogibija Miloša Obilića. *The Death of Miloš Obilić.* 110 lines. Trebinje.

17. Radoje Lazić: Šaljiva pesma. *A Humorous Song.* 51 lines. Trebinje.

18. Radoje Lazić: Pesma o heroju Ratku Pavloviću. *The Song of the Hero Ratko Pavlović.* 71 lines. Trebinje.

Note: All of the texts listed are available in typescript.

Appendix II: Texts of the Milman Parry Collection Inputted into Computer by Zlatan Čolaković

Contents of the disk "KATAL"

1. Tahir Jusović: Katal-ferman na Muja Hrnjicu (kazivana). *The Firman of Execution on Mujo Hrnjica* (spoken). 888 lines. Prijepolje.

2. Tahir Jusović: Katal-ferman na Muja Hrnjicu *The Firman of Execution on Mujo Hrnjica.* 900 lines. Prijepolje.

3. Hamdo Džondić: Katal-ferman na Muja Hrnjicu. *The Firman of Execution on Mujo Hrnjica.* 1293 lines. Sopoćani.

4. Ahmend Turković: Katal-ferman na Bojković Aliju. *The Firman of Execution on Bojković Alija.* 764 lines. Karajukići Bunari.

5. Adem Ćustović: Katal-ferman na Muja i Halila (+ Razgovor). *The Firman of Execution on Mujo and Halil* (+ Conversation). 1226 lines. Gacko.

6. Ragib Gojaković: Katal-ferman na Đerđelez Aliju (diktirana + Razgovor). *The Firman of Execution on Đerđelez Alija* (dictated + Conversation). 3094 lines. Komarane. (Parry texts nos. 12407 and 12425.)

Contents of the disk, "BAGDAD"

1. Hamdo Džondić: Kajtaz bajraktar zauzima Bagdad. *Kajtaz the Standard-Bearer Takes Bagdad.* 652 lines. Sopoćani.

2. Šaban Seferović: Budimska Fatima zauzima Bagdad. *Fatima of Budim Takes Bagdad.* 455 lines. Karajukići Bunari.

3. Jusuf Makić: Mujo Hrnjica brani Udbinu. *Mujo Hrnjica Defends Udbina.* 1294 lines. Karajukići bunari.

4. Džemail Zogić: Omer Hrnjica izbavlja Fatimu, Muja i Halila. *Omer Hrnjica Rescues Fatima, Mujo and Halil.* 1244 lines. Novi Pazar.

5. Šefko Ibrović: Ženidba Ajanović Meha. *The Wedding of Ajanović Meho.* 1353 lines. Duga Poljana.

6. Ramo Babić: Ženidba Smailagić Meha. *The Wedding of Smailagić Meho.* 2054 lines. Novi Pazar.

7. Ašir Ćorović: Ropstvo pašine Emine. *The Captivity of the Pasha's Emina.* 1021 lines. Rožaje.

8. Rašid Hamidović: Ženidba malog Marijana. *The Wedding of Marijan the Little.* 620 lines. Karajukići Bunari.

Notes

1. The published collections represent only a *small number* of the Muslim epic songs which have been collected. There are still hundreds of unpublished, and thus unknown, Muslim epic songs preserved in Yugoslav archives. The same may be said for the contents of the Milman Parry Collection. Moreover, there are some excellent epic singers still living in Yugoslavia. It is to be hoped that collecting activities will continue.

2. Among Jukić's several biographers, the most distinguished was Tugomir Alaupović. See his *Ivan Frano Jukić (1818–57)* (Sarajevo, 1907). There is also a biography written by the Franciscans J. Markušić and B. Skarica on the basis of Augustin Ćorić's manuscript *Život i rad Ivana Frane Jukića* (Sarajevo, 1908). See also Ilija Kecmanović, *Ivo Franjo Jukić* (Belgrade, 1963). Jukić's documents and selected correspondence were published in Ivan Franjo Jukić, *Dokumentarna građa*, (Sarajevo, 1970). A complete bibliography of Jukić and further critical literature about him and his work can be found in Ivan Frano Jukić, *Sabrana djela*, ed. B. Ćorić (Sarajevo, 1973, 3 vols.).

3. *Bosanski prijatelj, Časopis saderžavajući potriebite koristne i zabavne stvari*, ed. I. F. Jukić Banjalučanin (Zagreb, 1850). Volumes 2 and 3 were published in 1851 and 1861.

4. The first Martić biography was written by the Croatian scholar Josip Milaković, *Fra Grgo Martić (Spomen knjiga)* (Sarajevo, 1906). There is also a useful biography written by A. Čičić, *Monografija o Fra Grgi Martiću:*

24.1.1822 - + 30.VIII.1905 (Zagreb, 1930). Martić's selected works, edited by Ilija Kecmanović, appeared in Fra Grgo Martić, *Izbrani spisi* (Sarajevo, 1956).

5. *Narodne piesme bosanske i hercegovačke*, comp. Ivan Franjo Jukić Banjalučanin and Ljubomir Hercegovac (Fr. Gr. Martić), ed. O. F. Kunić Kuprješanin, Svezak pervi: Piesme junačke (Osijek, 1858). The second edition of this collection was published in 1892. In that edition not only was the orthography changed by the editors, but they also freely edited the texts of songs from the first edition. According to Josip Milaković, the changes were not introduced by Martić (see Josip Milaković, *Bibliografija hrvatske i srpske narodne pjesme; Građa I* (Sarajevo, 1919), 214–15. In the introduction to the second edition Martić says that Jukić, Šunjić, and he collected many more songs during 1840–52, but the manuscripts have been lost.

6. Among those Muslim songs there is the first recorded version of the song *Ženidba Smailagić Meha (The Wedding of Smailagić Meho)* under the title *Mali Mehinaga*. Avdo Međedović, Parry's famous singer, dictated that song to Nikola Vujnović in July 1935.

7. In the nineteenth century the "Homeric question" had a strong impact on the studying and collecting of South Slavic epic songs. The evident kinship between Homeric and South Slavic epics still has not been explained satisfactorily. In his book *Naša narodna epika* (1st ed., Zagreb, 1909; 2nd ed., Belgrade, 1966), Tomo Maretić attempted to prove that Homeric epics could not, directly or indirectly, have influenced the South Slavic epics. Being also a translator of the *Iliad* and the *Odyssey*, he was well acquainted with the problem. Although there have been attempts to refute Maretić's view, it still holds up well.

8. Jukić obviously used to change the texts he collected, as did Martić. This was proved long ago by Milaković, Banović, and other competent scholars.

9. Among collectors, the only exception to this rule was Simo Milutinović Sarajlija (1791–1848). In 1833 Milutinović published the first volume of epic songs he collected in Montenegro and Hercegovina under the title *Pevaniia Cernogorska i Hercegovačka, sobrana Čubrom Čoikovićem Cernogorcem; izdana Josifom Milovukom. Čast perva (Volkslieder der Montenegriner und Herzegowinaer Serben)* (Budim, Kral. Sveučilište Ugarsko, 1833). One of the earliest of Karadžić's rivals, in 1837 Milutinović published the second book of his collection under the title *Pievaniia cernogorska i hercegovačka, sabrana Čubrom Čoikovićem Cernogorcem, pa i njim izdana istim. Volkslieder der Montenegriner und Herzegowinaer Serben,* (Leipzig, 1837). Milutinović was the first among all collectors to note the names of his singers. Also, he published the texts of the songs exactly as he wrote them down. Vuk Karadžić successfully but unjustly discredited Milutinović and his collection in the eyes of Jacob Grimm, L. v. Ranke and I. I. Sreznevskij; see *Sabrana*

dela Vuka Karadžića, knjiga sedma, ed. Lj. Zuković (Belgrade, 1986). On Jacob Grimm's relations with South Slavic lyric and epic poetry, see Miljan Mojašević, *Jakob Grimm i srpska narodna književnost: Književnoistorijske i poetološke osnove.* SANU, Posebna izdanja, knjiga DLIII; Odeljenje jezika i književnosti, knjiga 34 (Belgrade, 1983).

10. Marijan Šunjić, *Narodne junačke pjesme iz Bosne i Hercegovine,* 2nd ed. (Sarajevo, 1925).

11. This song was published, under the title *Mejdani i ženidba Ahmet bega iz Varada (The Duels and the Wedding of Ahmet, Bey of Varad),* in the 2nd volume of the magazine *Bosanski prijatelj,* published in Zagreb in 1851.

12. Stjepan Banović, "Martićevo ispravljanje narodnih pjesama i završka guslarska zona," *Zbornik za narodni život i običaje Južnih Slavena* (Zagreb, JAZU, knj, XXVIII, sv. 2, 64–87).

13. Those four songs, considered by Martić as of the highest quality, were published in *Vienac uzdarja narodnoga O. Andriji Kačić-Miošiću na stolietni dan preminutja,* ed. I. Danilof and B. Petranović (Zadar, 1861).

14. Although Šunjić's collecting activity falls into the same period, his collection of Muslim songs was still in the process of publication as late as during World War I, in 1915. Thus Šunjić's collection was unknown in the nineteenth century.

15. In his survey of the history of collecting and publishing Muslim epics, Albert Lord does not mention the collecting activity of the Franciscans (see Albert B. Lord, "The Effect of the Turkish Conquest on Balkan Epic Tradition," *Aspects of the Balkans: Continuity and Change.* ed. H. Birnbaum and S. Vryonis, Jr. (The Hague and Paris, 1972, 298–318). Lord believes that the oldest collection of Muslim songs are the unpublished materials gathered in the 1860s by Vuk Vrčević and that the first Muslim epic song was published as late as 1886 (ibid., 303–4).

16. *Tri riječi Hercegovca,* ed. Dr. Friedrich S. Krauss (Mostar, 1885). *Pandžić Huso i Pavečić Luka: Pobra. Pjesan naših muhamedovaca,* ed. Dr. Friedrich S. Krauss (Mostar, 1885). *Naše doba* (literary magazine) (Novi Sad, 1885, nos. 44, 46, 47). *Smailagić Meho; Pjesan naših muhamedovaca* (Dubrovnik, 1886). A German translation of this famous song, over two thousand lines long, appeared in 1890 under the title *Mehmed's Brautfart (Smailagić Meho); Ein Volksepos der südslavischen Mohammedaner,* ed. Friedrich S. Krauss, trans. Carl Gröber (Vienna, 1890).

17. See Krauss's main work in the area of South Slavic Muslim epics, *Slavische Volksforschungen: Abhandlungen über Glauben, Gewohnheitrechte, Sitten, Bräuche und die Guslarenlieder der Südslaven* (Leipzig, 1908). It contains four excellent Muslim epic songs collected by Krauss. In addition, Krauss also published the texts of two more songs, together with a German translation; see Friedrich S. Krauss, *Orlović, der Burggraf von Raab; Ein mohammedanisch-slavisches Goslarenlied aus der Hercegovina* (Freiburg im

Breisgau, 1889); F. S. Krauss and T. Dragičević, *Gesühnte Grabschändung: Ein mohammedanisch-slavisches Guslarenlied aus Herceg-Bosna* (Leipzig, n.d.).

18. Krauss's collecting activity and his publications of Muslim epic songs were unjustly criticized by Luka Marjanović; see *Vienac zabavi i pouci* (Zagreb, 1890, no. 11, 168–70; no. 12, 186–88).

19. See Ilija Kecmanović, "O jednoj neobičnoj činovničkoj karijeri u Sarajevu 1878–1919 godine," *Prilozi za proučavanje istorije Sarajeva* (Sarajevo, Muzej grada Sarajeva, god. 1, knj, 1, 183–95). See also Tomislav Kraljačić, *Kalajev režim u Bosni i Hercegovini (1882–1903)* (Sarajevo, 1987).

20. The first edition of the collection was published under the title *Narodne pjesme Muhamedovaca u Bosni i Hercegovini*, comp. Kosta Hörmann (Sarajevo, vols. 1–2, 1888–89). The second edition was printed under the title *Narodne pjesme Muslimana u Bosni i Hercegovini* (Sarajevo, 1933). On the basis of the manuscripts of the Hörmann collection, in 1966 Đenana Buturović published fifteen more epic songs, as well as a synopsis and description of the other, as yet unpublished, songs, under the title *Narodne pjesme Muslimana u Bosni i Hercegovini; Iz rukopisne ostavštine Koste Hörmanna* (Sarajevo, 1966).

21. Alija Nametak, the collector of Muslim epics and tales, wrote about Hörmann's redaction of epic texts in his article "O Hörmannovoj zbirci narodnih pjesama u Bosni i Hercegovini." *Narodno stvaralaštvo* (Sarajevo, sv. 6, april 1963, 447–55).

22. See *Vienac zabavi i pouci*, no. 30, 478–79; no. 31, 488–92; no. 32, 508–11; no. 33, 523–27; no. 34, 541–43; no. 35, 557–59; no. 36, 572–75; no. 37, 588–91 (Zagreb, 1888).

23. On page ten Hörmann acknowledged his indebtedness to exactly thirty-five persons for their assistance in collecting and editing the texts. But Hörmann "forgot" to provide information as to whether *he himself* had collected any of the songs in the publication, and, if indeed he had, which ones.

24. The second volume of Hörmann's collection was received well even among scholars. In the same magazine where Marjanović's attack had appeared previously, Tomo Maretić published a eulogy of Hörmann in a very influential article dealing with the relation between Muslim and Serbo-Croatian epics (see *Vienac zabavi i pouci*, no. 41, 650–62; no. 42, 666–67 (Zagreb, 1889).

25. See *Narodne pjesme Muslimana u Bosni i Hercegovini. Sabrao Kosta Hörmann 1888–1889*, 2 vols. ed., Đenana Buturović (Sarajevo, 1976).

26. See Đenana Buturović: *Studija o Hörmannovoj zbirci muslimanskih narodnih pjesama* (Sarajevo, 1976). This study contains a list of important works written about the epics of the Hörmann collection.

27. See *Hrvatske narodne pjesme; Matica Hrvatska, Odio prvi: Junačke pjesme (muhamedovske)*, ed. L. Marjanović, knjiga treća, knjiga četvrta (Zagreb, 1898–99).

28. See the following section on Milman Parry.

29. See Krstić's article "Luka Marjanović i Nikola Andrić kao izdavači narodnih pesama," *Prilozi za književnost, jezik, istoriju i folklor*. Knj. 22, sv. 3–4 (Belgrade, 1956).

30. The only biography of Milman Parry, as well as the most useful introduction to Parry's work and thought in the area of Homerology, was written by his son, Adam Parry; see *The Making of Homeric Verse: The Collected Papers of Milman Parry*, ed., Adam Parry (Oxford, 1971, pp. ix—lxii). This edition contains all the published and unpublished works of Milman Parry except the field notes titled *Ćor Huso* (now kept in the Milman Parry Collection). Adam Parry published from those notes only passages that have direct bearing on Homeric scholarship.

31. In 1885, Vasilij V. Radlov published the results of his investigation of Kara-Kirghiz oral epics; see *Proben der Volkslitteratur der nördlichen türkischen Stämme* (St. Petersburg, 1885). Radlov noted that the texts of the Kara-Kirghiz epics are not fixed and believed that the same was true of the Homeric epics in ancient Greece. Parry studied Radlov's work as well.

32. The main work of Matthias Murko in the field of Serbo-Croatian epic songs, originally written in Czech, was published for the first time in Yugoslavia: *Tragom srpsko-hrvatske narodne epike: Putovanja u godinama 1930–1932*. Đela JAZU, knj. 41–42 (Zagreb, 1951). Murko's selected works were published in Slovenian: Matija Murko, *Izbrano delo*, ed. A. Slodnjak (Ljubljana, 1962). The single work of Matthias Murko that influenced Parry the most, one which Parry often quotes, was *La poésie populaire épique en Yougoslavie au début du XXe siècle. Travaux publiés par l'Institut d'études slaves*, 10 (Paris, 1929). Murko's other important works are listed in John Miles Foley's bibliography, *Oral-Formulaic Theory and Research: An Introduction and Annotated Bibliography* (New York, London, 1985).

33. Murko collcted from Marjanović's famous singer Bećir Islamović; Parry recorded the songs of Salih Ugljanin, from whom Murko and Schmaus had previously collected.

34. See Gerhard Gesemann, *Studien zur südslavischen Volksepik*. (Reichenberg, 1926).

35. Goleniščev-Kutuzov, the well-known specialist in the area of Slavic and Romance medieval literature and the editor of the Russian edition of the Chanson de Roland, assisted Parry in his collecting venture in the summers of 1933 and 1934. Goleniščev-Kutuzov did not agree with Parry's views, yet he gave Parry credit for employing a much more rigorous method of collecting than anyone before him (see his *Èpos serbskogo naroda* (Moscow, 1963). See also Il'ja N. Goleniščeva-Kutuzova, *Slavjanskie literatury: stat'i i issledovanija*, ed. I. V. Goleniščev-Kutuzov, esp. the chapter: "Èpos narodov Jugoslavii," 220–359 (Moscow, 1973).

36. In the beginning of his projected book, *The Singer of Tales*, Parry

admitted that the work of scholars before him (presumably Murko and Gesemann) "tended ever more and more towards this [i.e., his own—Z.Č.] method, until the time had come for someone to attempt a rigid formulation and use of it. It is even more than likely that someone else would have done this before had it not been for the lack of mechanical means; it has only been in the last few years that the science of electrical sound recording has given us an apparatus of such a sort that it can record songs of any length and in the large numbers needed before one can draw conclusions, and finally which can make records which are so good that the words on them can be accurately written down for the purpose of close study" (*The Making of Homeric Verse*, 470).

37. See Lord's "General Introduction" to volumes one and two of *Serbo-Croatian Heroic Songs*, comp. Milman Parry, ed. and trans. Albert Bates Lord (Cambridge, Mass. and Belgrade, 1953–54); see also Lord's "Homer, Parry and Huso," *American Journal of Archaelogy*, 52 (1948), 33–44, reprinted in *The Making of Homeric Verse*. See further Lord's "Nasljeđe Milmana Parryja" [The Heritage of Milman Parry], trans. Zlatan Čolaković, *Latina et Graeca* 26 (Zagreb, 1986), 3–16.

38. A comprehensive bibliography of Albert Lord is provided in Foley.

39. See *Serbo-Croatian Heroic Songs*, comp. Milman Parry, trans., with introduction, notes and commentary by Albert B. Lord, ed. David. E. Bynum with Albert B. Lord (Cambridge, Mass., 1974).

40. See *Serbo-Croatian Heroic Songs*, comp. Milman Parry, Albert B. Lord, and David E. Bynum, vol. 14: *Bihaćka Krajina: Epics from Bihać, Cazin, and Kulen Vakuf*; ed., with prolegomena and notes, by David E. Bynum (Cambridge, Mass., 1979).

41. See *Serbo-Croatian Heroic Songs*, comp. Milman Parry, vol. 6: *Ženidba Vlahinjić Alije; Osmanbeg Delibegović i Pavićević Luka; Kazivao i pjevao Avdo Međedović*, ed., with prolegomena and notes, by David E. Bynum (Cambridge, Mass., 1980).

42. I have checked the following transcriptions by Velimirović: L.12, L.14, L.15, L.33 (partly), L.200.

43. See the articles written by A. Olesnicki, "Tko je zapravo bio Đerđelez Alija" and "Još o ličnosti Đerđelez Alije," *Zbornik za narodni život i običaje južnih Slavena*, knj. XXIX, sv. 1, 18–37; knj. XXIX, sv. 2, 21–55 (Zagreb, 1933). See also Đenana Buturović, "Najstarija svjedočanstva o narodnim pjesmama bosanskohercegovačkih muslimana," *Narodna književnost Srba, Hrvata, Muslimana i Crnogoraca. Izbor kritika*, ed. Đ. Buturović and V. Palavestra (Sarajevo, 1974).

44. See *Erlangenski rukopis starih srpskohrvatskih narodnih pesama*, ed. Gerhard Gesemann, Srpska Kraljevska akademija, *Zbornik za istoriju, jezik i književnost srpskog naroda*, I. odel., *Spomenici na srpskom jeziku* 12 (Sr. Karlovci, 1925).

45. I was recently informed that some of Krauss's manuscripts, presumably written in Serbo-Croatian, are kept at UCLA.

46. See Alois Schmaus's (1901–70) collected works in the field of Slavic studies, *Gesammelte slavistische und balkanologische Abhandlungen*, 4 vols., ed. P. Rehder (Munich, 1971–79).

47. Vuk Stepan Vrčević (1811–82) was one of the most diligent of Karadžić's helpers. His collection of Muslim songs was published in *Hercegovačke narodne pjesme (koje samo Srbi muhamedove vjere pjevaju* (Dubrovnik, 1890).

48. See *Serbo-Croatian Heroic Songs*, comp. Milman Parry, ed. and trans. by Albert Bates Lord, vol. 1: Novi Pazar; English translations, with musical transcription by Béla Bartók and prefaces by John H. Finley, Jr. and Roman Jakobson (Cambridge, Mass. and Belgrade, 1954), 21–45.

49. The firman of execution refers to the sultan's written order for the execution of the hero; it can also be translated as the letter of execution.

A LITERARY AND SPIRITUAL PROFILE
OF RUĐER J. BOŠKOVIĆ

On The Occasion of the 200th Anniversary of His Death

ANTE KADIĆ

Just as, long ago, seven Greek cities quarreled about where Homer was born, so several nations now claim Bošković. One can understand the dispute about Homer, for it is not certain whether Homer even existed as a person, still less where he was born; but there is no doubt that Ruđer Bošković was born on May 18, 1711, in Dubrovnik, and died on February 13, 1787, in Milan. We also know what his native tongue was, which schools he attended, and his family's national and religious allegiances.

If the French consider him their own, it is understandable, because he became a French citizen; if some Italians even today claim him as their countryman, there is some basis for the claim, because it was in Rome that he acquired his higher education, he wrote treatises and books in Italian, and it was in Milan that he died.[1] However, there is no single reason why the Serbs should think of him as their son; nevertheless, there are some among them who do. Thus, for example, in the foreword to the English translation of Bošković's *Theory of Natural Philosophy*, Branislav Petronijević contends that Bošković was of "purely Serbian origin."[2] When Croatian scholars reacted against this appropriation, Serbs began to say that it was not important whether Bošković was a Serb or a Croat, that this question did not enter his mind, for he was above these national disputes; he considered himself a Slav and consequently belonged to all "brotherly" nations.[3]

At least in Yugoslavia, Bošković is now accepted as one of the brightest sons of the Croatian nation. Some foreign encyclopedias and manuals, however, continue to assign him to other neighboring nations and even to some distant ones.

This is not a petty skirmish. The Croats justly ask: How would their compatriots feel if, for example, Galileo were considered Spanish, or Descartes Portuguese, or Newton Dutch, or Leibniz Polish, or Copernicus Russian, and so on?

Several specialists have already written about the many, nearly always successful, enterprises undertaken by Bošković on behalf of his native city-republic when it became entangled in difficulties with the English, French, Austrian, or Russian authorities. I will not, therefore, tackle this aspect of his diplomatic activity.

Though Bošković readily assisted many of his countrymen, especially young clerics during their student years in the Eternal City, his relations with Stay, Kunić, and Džamanjić were the most cordial and helpful. They loved and respected him as an elder brother and famous scholar, and he was a powerful stimulus to their literary and other achievements.

Of these three priests, closest to him was his relative Benedikt (Beno) *Stay* (1714–1801). Finishing his humanistic studies in Dubrovnik at the local Jesuit college, Stay wrote a description of Descartes's philosophy in Latin verses.[4] He became popular and was called a "new Lucretius." He soon left for Rome, where he studied theology, became a priest, professor of rhetoric and, thanks to the energetic intervention of Bošković, head canon of the Croatian Confraternity of St. Jerome. During his rectorship, the Confraternity gave monetary aid to, among others, Ruđer Bošković and his brother Bartol (Baro), also a Jesuit.[5]

Under Bošković's influence and with his help, Stay presented in Latin verse the whole of Newton's natural philosophy, in three volumes published at Rome in 1755, 1760, and 1792.[6]

In the foreward to this *New Philosophy,* Bošković tells the "zealous reader" that Stay has not merely "popularized" Newton's philosophy, as Algarotti and Voltaire had done before him, but has everywhere plumbed its depths and gotten to the very essence of it (*ad intimam ubique medullam usque se insinuat*). Bošković affirms that Stay's work will be pleasing and useful to all those who enjoy the beauty of the Latin language, who have penetrated the most abstruse secrets of nature, who are accustomed to the investigation of natural phenomena.[7]

Stay knew how much he owed to Bošković. At the end of the third volume of his *New Philosophy,* published after Bošković's death, he told Dubrovnik to be proud, since, because of Bošković, it would one day be ranked among the leading cities of the world:

> Tu quoque tolle caput felix Epidauria Cive
> Terra tuo, primis teque urbibus insere clarum (III, 1320–21)[8]

Rajmund Kunić (1719–94) completed his schooling at the Jesuit College in Rome, where Bošković was his mathematics professor; later he too became a professor (of Greek) at the Collegium Romanum. When the Jesuit order was disbanded in 1773, Kunić remained in Rome as a secular priest.

As a poet, Kunić early found acceptance in the Roman academies and associated with well-known representatives of the Italian settecento. Kunić's satirical epigrams are very neat; with a few strokes, he presents striking portraits of well-to-do Romans. While the Italians hail Monti's translation of the *Iliad* (1810), Monti himself readily admitted that Kunić's translation of Homer's epic in 1776 helped him greatly. (Some experts have said that Kunić's translation of the *Iliad* reads like an original work.) From Bošković's letters it is evident how much he himself appreciated Kunić as a man and as a poet.

During Bošković's long sojourn (1758–63) in Paris, London, Constantinople, and Vienna, Kunić missed his friendly and erudite conversation; when Bošković returned from this prolonged trip, Kunić wrote an "Elegy," in which he said that his own brother was not dearer to him than Bošković; he was delighted that he was walking again on the banks of the Tiber and looking at the Capitoline; to live among the Romans, he believed, must be more enjoyable than with the "gloomy British, ugly Ottomans, and barbaric Orientals."[9]

When Bošković died, Lukša Sorkočević, a nobleman from Dubrovnik, knowing how intimate Kunić had been with Bošković, begged the poet to compose a lament in his memory. Kunić at first gladly accepted this suggestion, but later claimed that (at least for the moment) he was unable to praise adequately this great man:

> . . . Nunc plorat meus hic tantum; post tempore lungo
> Foris erit, ut fundat verba diserta dolor.[10]

Brno Džamanjić (or Zamanja, 1735–1820) studied under the Jesuits in Dubrovnik and Rome, where his teachers were Bošković and Kunić, the former in mathematics, the latter in Greek. Before translating Homer's *Odyssey* into Latin (Siena, 1777), he wrote two short poems ("Echo," Rome 1764; "Navis aerea" — "Air Ship," Rome 1768): in the first he treated the theory of echoes as he had learned it from Bošković, while in the second, in his imagination, he reached into the lofty heights of the sky and saw different continents below him.

At that time a rumor spread that Bošković would travel to California to observe Venus as it passed before the sun. Džamanjić eagerly begged his countryman and teacher to go to America, because, whatever the result of his observation, he would return triumphantly:

> I, decus o nostrum: non tu sine laude redibis,
> Quo res cumque cedat![11]

Four years after Džamanjić returned to Dubrovnik in 1783, he heard that Bošković had died. He was invited by the Great Council of the Republic to deliver Bošković's funeral oration in the cathedral. He gladly accepted and extolled the virtues and merits of the deceased. He began his panegyric, "If ever there existed a citizen of Dubrovnik who is entitled to be honored and thanked by us, it is Bošković." He eulogized the sharpness of his intellect, the depth and clarity of his thought, and the high reputation which he enjoyed abroad, from Rome to Milan, from London to Vienna, from Paris to Istanbul.[12]

Džamanjić's speech pleased Bošković's sister Anica so much that she responded to him with verses of her own. Džamanjić, however, did more than deliver his oration, for soon afterwards he composed an epigram in honor of Bošković. In it he addressed the city of Dubrovnik and said that, though it was small, it was not insignificant; it stood above other republics:

> Is it possible, you ask? Are you not the homeland of the man who had no
> equal elsewhere and whose like will not be born? As Ruđer is superior to
> other humans, so you too surely surpass all realms.

> . . . Homines idcirco quam anteit omnes
> Rogerius, tam regna omnia tute supra es.[13]

In 1986 I examined at Berkeley, in the Bancroft Library, the vast correspondence of Bošković in manuscript, bought by the University of California from Nikola Sorgo-Mirošević.[14] While Bošković usually kept letters from his correspondents, those he wrote are largely lost. This correspondence, now at Berkeley, has to a great extent already been published by such Croatian scholars as F. Rački, V. Varićak, V. Radatović, and Br. Truhelka. It is without doubt a solid reference source for Bošković's biography and extremely valuable for ascertaining his basic ideas. Here I will discuss the content of some letters addressed to him by three foreigners.

The first is the Englishman Joseph Priestley (1733–1804), who infuriated Bošković by implying that his materialistic doctrine was based on Boškovic's writings.

Bošković was not the first physicist or philosopher whose theories and beliefs were misunderstood. Certain scholars were impressed by his "magnum opus," namely his *Theory of Natural Philosophy* (*Theoria philosophiae naturalis,*[15] [Vienna, 1758; Venice, 1763; Cambridge, Mass., 1922 and 1966; Zagreb, 1974]), but from it they wrongly interpreted his weltanschauung. As if he had anticipated all this, at the end of his *Theory* Bošković included an Appendix on Metaphysics, concerning the soul and God,[16] in which he categorically stressed the dual principle, namely the existence of body and soul as separate entities. In the same context he eloquently spoke of God, who not only created human beings but also revealed Himself to them. While in the main body of his *Theory,* explaining atomic energy, Bošković is often (at least to laymen) difficult to follow, in his Appendix he becomes very clear, personal, and even aggressive toward those who do not share his views.

Though in general temperamental, Bošković was seldom so pugnacious as in the exchange of letters with Priestley, the English theologian and chemist, who had acquired a certain reputation for having first described the properties of oxygen.[17] Bošković and Priestley had met in Paris in 1774; during their conversations, Priestley conveyed to Bošković that he fully agreed with the basic tenets of his *Theory.* Three years later Priestley published his most significant work, *Disquisitions Relating to Matter and Spirit* (London, 1777). Some friends from the French Academy informed Bošković that Priestley, claiming that he was following Bošković's theory of the structure of matter, had propagated a materialistic doctrine. Bošković, afraid that his followers and enemies would accuse him of duplicity and lack of clarity, was convinced that he must react. He wrote to Lord W. Shelburne, with whom he had corresponded previously and in whose service Priestley was. He begged Shelburne to intervene and convince Priestley to state publicly that he had misinterpreted Bošković.[18]

Priestley, though financially dependent on Shelburne and aware that his writings had in England likewise been severely cirticized for containing arbitrary utterances (the reason he later moved to Philadelphia, where he died)—had one of those characters which rarely accepts any objection. As soon as he was informed by Shelburne of Bošković's complaint, he wrote a virulent response to the latter on August 19, 1778, saying at the outset that he was disgusted by his behavior: first, if he had any serious objections to his, Priestley's, writings, he should have written directly to him and not to his "patron"; second, he had never indicated that his materialistic conclusions were accepted by Bošković; he himself deduced from Bošković's theory of the nature of matter what he thought to be its logical consequences. Further, he proudly declared that his materialistic doctrine was "the only one consonant with the genuine system of revelation . . . and not that of the Church of Rome" [of which Bošković was a member], which he considered *anti-Christian,* and "a system of abomination little better than heathenism."[19]

Bošković, who did not read or write English, waited until someone translated to him exactly what Priestley had said, and then, on October 17, 1778, sent a letter no less ferocious than that of his British correspondent. Not only did he not apologize for writing to Shelburne, but he continued to label

Priestley's writing "abominable, detestable and impious" and demanded a retraction, since Priestley had put in doubt his personal honor and had called the head of his Church an Antichrist. He excused himself for the expressions he used in his letter, but he considered them none too strong, when his religion and honor were questioned and slandered. He could be a friend only "up to the altar" (*amicus usque ad aras*).[20]

Not only in the Appendix to his *Theory* and in his correspondence, but also on many other occasions, Bošković proved that he did not become a Jesuit out of economic necessity; he remained an abbé when his Order was abolished, and all his life he stayed firm in the religious beliefs which he had received in his family and which were those of the Roman Catholic Church. This was also the reason why several popes entrusted him with many important missions.

The second of Bošković's correspondents I shall discuss is Jérôme L. de Lalande (1732–1807), a famous French astronomer. Already as a young man Lalande excelled so much in science that, not yet thirty years old, he became professor of astronomy in the Collège de France, and in 1768 he was appointed director of the Paris Observatory.

Lalande early became acquainted with Bošković, read his "dissertations," valued his ideas, and soon began to correspond with him. During a trip to Italy he became fond of Bošković for his cordiality and erudition. Later, in France, he popularized Bošković's discoveries and wrote during three decades about him in the *Journal des sçavans,* where in February, 1792, he published an interesting and detailed obituary of Bošković. In it he stressed the virtues and merits of the deceased, but also pointed out his well-known foible, namely his "irascibility" even with his friends.

In Varićak's second "Fragment" of Bošković's correspondence (containing, besides letters from Anica Bošković, only those of foreigners), Lalande's letters predominate. There are thirty (nos. 21–50).

The first letter is from September, 1764. He writes that he has learned through Charles la Condamine, their mutual friend, that Bošković has moved from Rome to Pavia to teach at the university there. Congratulating Bošković on this appointment, he declares that he is happy for personal reasons also, since when he comes the next year to Italy, he will be able to visit Bošković.[21]

Bošković accompanied Lalande during his journey through the central parts of Italy. Soon after his departure (November 30, 1765), Lalande compliments Bošković, saying that when he recalls his enjoyable stay in Italy, he immediately thinks of him who brought him all "delices." He lacks appropriate words to thank him and therefore he hopes that Bošković will find "in his beautiful soul" the "agreeable reward" for all his troubles and pains.[22]

In a letter dated June 16, 1766, Lalande writes ironically about d'Alembert, who had said that Bošković was an Italian who was known as a mathematician. Lalande affirms that Bošković is for him one of the greatest men whom he knows and says he loves him more than anyone else (*et celui de tous que j'aime le plus*).[23]

Bošković had intended to go to England and from thence to California to observe the passage of Venus in front of the sun. Lalande asks Bošković to stop on his way in Paris. In the letter containing the request (written April 29, 1767) he calls Bošković "his dear and illustrious teacher, his guardian angel, his protector and benefactor."[24]

In other letters Lalande informs Bošković of what is happening in the French Academy, of how d'Alembert (whom Lalande calls "a despot") has become Bošković's resolute enemy, of Lalande's plans for translating Bošković's works, and of what he likes most in his studies; he solicitously warns Bošković to take care of his health and not to be bothered by trifles because his enemies (e.g. La Place and Rochon, Frisi and Luino) would be jubilant if they learned that he was annoyed by their remarks and writings. They are not worthy of his attention (*"guarda e passa"*). Though we must take into consideration the fact that in the eighteenth century scholars often praised each other excessively, nevertheless, as Varićak says, "the charm of Bošković's personality was without doubt great."[25]

We now turn to G. I. Le Sage (1724–1803), a Swiss in his time famous as a mathematician and physicist; he was intelligent, inventive and industrious, but extremely scrupulous, and therefore published very little. Those traits of Le Sage were noted by his first biographer, Pierre Prévost, who taught the same subjects in Geneva.[26]

In the age of the Enlightenment scientists eagerly corresponded, even when they could not meet personally. Thus we have three of Bošković's letters to Le Sage and two from the Swiss professor to the reverend abbot.

In Bošković's letters, which Varićak also published, there are autobiographical details known from other sources.[27] Le Sage wrote to Bošković in French, and he responded in Latin, excusing himself on the grounds that he speaks French better than he writes it. In his second letter (May 7, 1767) Bošković returns to the question of language: "It is a pity that among scholars, in our time, the custom has prevailed that everyone writes in his own language. How much easier it would be if Latin, which used to be common to all, but nowadays does not belong to anyone, were kept for mutual exchange in the domain of science."[28]

In the first preserved letter (June 22, 1771), Le Sage tells how for several years he has been trying to reestablish his connection with Bošković. In his second letter (written May 8, 1772, also from Geneva) he explains his views, different from those of Bošković, concerning molecules in the structure of matter (which he calls "corpuscules ultramondains"). I shall not discuss this scientific dispute, but will rather quote a tribute paid to Bošković by Le Sage, just at the moment when the Dalmatian was bitterly disappointed that Lagrange had been appointed in his stead as director of the Observatory at Brera:

> Because of your generous expenditures (in building the Observatory) and your ingenious discoveries, allow me, O great man, to express to you, however feebly, the admiration which you have inspired in me. What a consoling and ravishing spectacle for those who cherish science to see, especially in this century when men of letters are preoccupied with their own interests, a scholar who is unselfish and industrious, original and profound, who combines to the highest degree different talents which seem incompatible.[29]

Bošković had been sent earlier (in 1761) to Constantinople by the British Royal Society to observe the passage of Venus in front of the sun. In Venice he took a ship, but near the island of Tenedos, in the vicinity of Troy, the ship was overtaken by a storm. Bošković took the advantage of this misfortune to visit and examine what were considered to be the ruins of Troy (later he published a study "Relazione delle rovine de Troia"). However, he did not reach the Ottoman capital in time to observe the astronomical phenomenon. After spending seven months in Istanbul, where he had become ill, he traveled, in the company of the British ambassor, J. Porter, through Bulgaria, Moldavia, Poland, and Austria. He returned to Rome in 1763.

This difficult journey through the Eastern Balkans, which had been ruled by the Turks for several centuries, is described in his travelogue *Giornale de un viaggio da Constantinopoli in Polonia,* which was published in Bassano (Italy) only in 1784; a translation into French (Lausanne, 1772) and another into German (Leipzig, 1779) had appeared earlier. Elizabeth Hill states: "Boscovich was a keen observer and on his journey kept a revealing and sensible record. His diary presents great interest, for it is one of the few travel records of the eighteenth century that cover that area of Turkey, Bulgaria and Moldavia. Small wonder that it aroused great interest when it was subsequently published."[30]

I do not intend to discuss this travelogue in its entirety; on another occasion I hope to devote to it a well-deserved and long-awaited study, since in this *Giornale* there is plenty of interesting and useful information about the beautiful Balkan countryside; the ruling class and its subjects; the common people and their dress, houses, and commerce; the religious beliefs and utter ignorance of the inhabitants. Here, I will limit my remarks to Bošković's first impressions of Bulgaria and its inhabitants (June 1–3, 1762). The author, being an acute observer, depicts in a few sentences the terrible poverty and lack of education but also the good quality of the Bulgarian peasants; he further refers to the corruption and tyranny of the Ottoman ruling class.

Although the countryside was enchanting, with green fields and blossoming flowers, the villagers of Kanara lived in houses made of wood and mud. There were doors but no windows, and through the chimney the rain would fall into the fireplace. Apart from blankets and kitchen utensils, the rooms were almost empty. In front of their dwellings and throughout the entire village there was so much mud that egress was difficult from these places, which therefore were like a jail.

These people, doing their best to keep clean in their shanties, were utterly ignorant. From their religion they knew something about fasting, the holy days, the sign of the cross and the veneration of saintly pictures. They had not learned the creed or the basic tenets of their faith. They told Bošković that their priest did not teach either themselves or their children.[31] The priest was under the authority of a bishop, who recognized the patriarch in Constantinople. He paid the bishop a certain sum to perform his duties ("come in affitto"). This priest was a young married man with children. He was dressed like other peasants and was paid by the villagers when he performed funeral services, baptisms, and weddings. He read the liturgy in Greek, but was otherwise as ignorant as his flock.[32]

The villagers were obliged to provide food and lodging for the ambassador's entourage. Considering their poverty, this was a great burden upon them. The Turkish official, moreover, with the aid of the janissaries, robbed them in every possible way.

Male inhabitants were supposed to pull the carriage out of the mud or push it over the more difficult mountain tracks. To avoid this, they had escaped to the woods; and so only women could be seen. The Turks then forced the village priest and an old man to perform the arduous task.

At the end of this brief but revealing sketch of Kanara, a typical Bulgarian village, Bošković emphasizes the following point: "The language of this region is a dialect of the Slavic language, which is also my mother tongue (naturale) in Dubrovnik; they understood me, and I was able to grasp something (qualche cosa) of what they were saying."[33]

Upon the arrival of the ambassadorial escort at the village of Faki, many girls swarmed around the carriage; they held in their hands a sieve filled with barley, which they threw into the carriage, and the officials began putting money in the same sieve. As they departed, the peasant women sang and danced on the muddy ground. Bošković comments: "I do not know whether it could be called a dance, this slow movement, which they accomplish holding each other by the hand and moving a few steps forward and then backward."[34]

Bošković cheerfully wrote poems in honor of various women, and also in honor of those who held power, including some popes. Though claiming he did not know how to flatter the mighty, he eagerly sought their company and protection. At that time all power was in the hands of a few, and Bošković was no exception among the scientists and men of letters who "burned incense" to those who loved adulation.

Bošković's Latin has been much praised for its grammatical correctness and fluency. Some of his poems excel in their musicality and meditative quality, and they frequently include personal digressions. Bošković, however, was not endowed with a special artistic gift. Many of his poems would certainly have remained buried in archives had their author not been a famous scientist.

Bošković's best-known poetic work is his *De Solis ac Lunae defectibus*— On Eclipses of the Sun and the Moon, first published in London in 1760 and later reprinted in Venice and Graz; a decade afterwards it was translated into French (*Les Eclipses,* 1770).

As a student in 1735, Bošković had written a poem of three hundred verses about eclipses of the sun and moon. He continued to enlarge and improve it and had completed its five cantos at the beginning of the fifties, but he waited an entire decade before publishing it. Although many reasons have been suggested for this postponement, we do not know the real cause.[35]

Bošković was influenced as a Latinist by the works of Horace, Ovid, and Virgil, but especially by Lucretius's *De rerum natura*. Not only his vocabulary, but also certain similes and, at times, his thoughts closely follow those of these classical authors.

The poet used mythology abundantly: the earth, sun, moon, and planets are all designated by mythological names; the modern reader would need a handbook of mythology to know what he is referring to. But to him a greater deity than those ancient gods and godesses was Isaac Newton, who had opened up to him so many new ideas:

> Tu decus Angligenum atque humanae gloria gentis,
> Tu majus mihi numen eris, Newtone, repostos
> Cui primo penetrare aditus penitusque latentes
> Sponte dedit vires Natura arcanaque jura
> Discere et attonitum late vulgare per Orbem (V, 9–13)

You pride of Englishmen and glory of the human race,
Newton, you are for me greater divinity, since
Nature has allowed you to be the first who penetrated
unexplored currents and learned Nature's hidden forces
and divulged them everywhere to an astonished mankind . . .

Bošković was not the only one who wrote polished hexameters about
scientific matters. Trying to remain within the limits of his métier (astronomy), he was prevented from giving free rein to his poetic imagination. His
Muse was thus the "handmaid" (ancilla) of science. Moreover, his determination to write correct and chiseled verses at times impaired the clarity of
his text. Just as he had provided notes to Stay's *New Philosophy,* so he
accompanied his *Eclipses* with abundant commentary; these notes are valuable for the help they give the common reader in grasping what Bošković
had often written in condensed and symbolic form.[36]

After the Jesuit Order was abolished in 1773, Bošković moved to Paris,
where he became a French citizen; he was well paid as Director of Optics for
the Navy, and he had many friends in important positions.

He convinced his old friend, the Jesuit A. de Barruel, to translate his
Eclipses into French, often helping him render difficult passages. Barruel's
translation is often too ornate, but it excels in a polished style.[37]

The first edition of *Eclipses,* published in London, was dedicated by
Bošković to the British Royal Society and its president, Lord Macclesfield.
When he moved to France, where he enjoyed special privileges, he dedicated
its new edition (with a French translation) to Louis XVI.[38] He obsequiously
predicted that this "illustrious" king would have a successor who would
happily and gloriously reign over France. Bošković claimed that he saw all
this in the stars. As it turned out, for Bošković as for others, astrology was
not a reliable guide to the future.

In the third canto of the London edition, mentioning the Paris Observatory, Bošković celebrated the French capital through which flows the majestic river Seine:

Est locus Europae in medio, qua regius altis
Ingreditur ripis dominamque interluit urbem
Sequana. Dives opum et duro fortissima bello
Gens tenet, at simul et placidae studiosa Minervae. (III, 681–84)[39]

In the middle of Europe is a place where the royal Seine
flows between high banks and passes through the metropolis.
A race possesses it that is rich in resources and very brave
in cruel war, yet also devoted to peaceful Minerva . . .

Now, in the *Dedicatory Epistle* to the king of France, he not only glorified the benevolent king and several of his secretaries (ministers) who were well disposed toward him, but he was also deeply thankful for their friendly attitude towards his homeland, Dubrovnik, with which they had concluded a treaty that was much more advantageous than Dubrovnik's noblemen had feared it might be. Bošković did not forget, even on this occasion, to mention that this republic, though small in territory, was supported by its resources, its ancient nobility, its ingenious talents, and its long-standing liberty (libertate perenni), and enjoyed wide-ranging maritime commerce.

Charles de Vergennes, the Secretary of Foreign Affairs, was Bošković's friend; they had become acquainted in the early sixties, when de Vergennes was French ambassador to Istanbul. As an influential diplomat at the French court he helped the American colonies free themselves from the British. Bošković had met Benjamin Franklin in London; both now being in Paris, they met in high circles, where Franklin was advancing the American cause. Further, as a citizen of Dubrovnik, Bošković appreciated freedom and therefore sided with those who fought for their independence. For these and perhaps other reasons Bošković followed with great interest events in North America. When he heard that the British had been defeated and American independence proclaimed, he enthusiastically welcomed this turning point in the history of mankind.[40] In his *Dedicatory Epistle* to Louis XVI, Bošković writes that previously oppressed nations had risen for "beautiful freedom" (*in bellum pulchra pro libertate ruebant oppressi nuper populi*); liberated Philadelphia was happy as the enemy forces were fleeing; and the great new empire was growing safely (*Imperiique novi surgit tutissime moles*).[41]

Though *Eclipses* cannot be considered a great literary work, it helps us to understand Bošković as a scientist and an artist through its numerous digressions about contemporary events and personalities and through its meticulous commentary on the interrelationship of all planets. We must remember that at the time he was writing his *Eclipses* the distinction between the man of science and the man of letters was not as clearly perceived as it is today.

Bošković was loyal not only to the faith of his ancestors and to his Jesuit Order but also to Dubrovnik, in favor of which he intervened at important European courts; to the members of his family, for whom he cared very much and with whom he entertained a regular correspondence; and to his countrymen and friends, to whom he revealed his thoughts and torments at critical moments of his life. He was always truthful (except when indulging in courtly flattery); he did not resort to duplicity, so common among those who moved in foreign and influential circles, for he was totally sincere, and for this reason sometimes created difficulties for himself; moreover, he was not always able to control his emotions and his Dalmatian temperament.

All his biographers, especially the earliest (J. de Lalande and Fr. Ricca),[42] agree that Bošković was irascible and touchy, and that as he gradually became aware of his intellectual superiority and achievements in science, he did not tolerate being downgraded and denied recognition. He was easily chagrined, as when his colleagues did not recognize that his *Theory of Natural Philosophy,* though having much in common with the writings of Leibniz and Newton, nevertheless was different from and, he felt, in some respects superior to them (*ab utrique discrepat et vero utrique praestat*).[43]

Professor M. D. Grmek writes that Bošković had "strong erotic inclinations," which he was able to overcome and sublimate.[44] He sought the company of women, particularly those of higher social status, and wrote poems in their praise. However, nobody reproached him for going too far, or for doing or saying anything improper or unfitting to his calling and position. Bošković succeeded in keeping his good moral reputation.

Slander and gossip were frequent among Bošković's contemporaries; in their conversations, letters, and pamphlets, wicked and envious people often pointed out supposed blemishes in order to diminish the moral standing of certain individuals. About Bošković, however, we do not find anything opprobrious. He was very controversial in the field of science, and had many competitors and enemies, some even denying the primacy or importance of his discoveries; but from all accessible documents his spiritual and moral profile comes out unsullied.

This brilliant scholar became insane in his old age. How and for what reason? Some say that he suffered from hereditary melancholy, that one of his brothers committed suicide (the family maintained that in a fit of fever he had jumped from a window), but better informed sources assert that his tragic sickness, accompanied by senility, was caused by an acute arteriosclerosis to which certain persons succumb at an advanced age. We do not know if this was a consequence of the abundant food which he enjoyed when younger or of excessive and strenuous work (he had prepared in a rather short time five volumes of his significant work on optics and astronomy—*Opera pertinentia ad opticam et astronomiam,* [Bassano, 1785]). Perhaps his illness was caused by the severe discipline to which he submitted himself: as a member of a religious order renowned for its rigorous discipline, he may have found it hard to contain his explosive temper.

He began to fantasize that he was surrounded by enemies who watched what he was saying, and he feared that he would starve, that his books were filled with mistakes, that he would die alone in a foreign country, and that soon after his death he would be forgotten. Grmek and other pathologists mention all these symptoms of his mental disturbance but reject the concept of a relationship between genius and insanity.[45]

Desperate, crazy, thoroughly sick physically as well as mentally, Bošković died of pneumonia. Witness to his death was his faithful companion, Luigi Tomagnini. His funeral was modest, attended by a few friends and acquaintances. He was buried in the Church of Santa Maria Podone in Milan, but soon all traces of his tomb were lost. Several eulogies were written about him, then silence followed. It seemed for a while that Bošković belonged to the mass of men, the memory of whom gradually fades, that he had not succeeded in erecting to himself a durable monument. Some decades after Bošković's death, however, it became clear that he was one of those whose seed bears abundant fruit. Even present-day scholars are still indebted to him.

Bošković has been praised by well-known philosophers, physicists and historians. For example, Nietzsche considered Copernicus's heliocentric theory and Bošković's idea that matter cannot be extended "the greatest triumph over the senses which mankind has achieved."[46] Niels Bohr and Werner Heisenberg stated that Bošković's conceptions had a far-reaching influence on the generations of physicists who followed him,[47] and Elizabeth Hill asserts that the author of the *Theory* "stands in line with Leibniz and Newton."[48]

Numerous are the fellow countrymen of Bošković who have written about him. Among those of recent years I will mention only three whose opinions are highly valued: Mihovil Kombol called Bošković "the greatest Croat of the eighteenth century,"[49] Veljko Gortan emphasized that only recently has it been established that Bošković was a precursor of many new scientific achievements,[50] and Vladimir Filipović insisted that Bošković was the inventor of a system which forms the basis of modern quantum physics, the theory of relativity, and our modern philosophy of nature.[51]

Notes

1. G. Carducci remarked that Bošković, Stay, Kunić, and Džamanjić did not pretend to be Croatians: *"Allora non affettavano d'esser Croati" (Opere,* vol. 8, 1944, 13). From Carducci's time to the present many Italians have considered them their own.

2. Theory of Natural Philosophy (Cambridge, Mass., 1966), p. vii; Elisabeth Hill, in her otherwise excellent essay on Bošković's life [*Roger J. Boscovich,* ed. L. L. Whyte (New York, 1961), 17 and 24] asserted without foundation that Bošković's father was a Serb.

3. Dušan Nedeljković, *Ruđer Bošković u svom vremenu i danas* (Belgrade, 1961), 91 and 132.

4. *Philosophiae versibus traditae libri VI* (Venice, 1744).

5. J. Burić, "Kanonici hrvatskog kaptola sv. Jeronima u Rimu," *Radovi Hrvatskog povijesnog Instituta u Rimu,* III–IV (1971), 126–28.

6. *Philosophiae recentioris versibus traditae libri X,* 3 vols. (Rome, 1755, 1760, 1792).

7. *Hrvatski latinisti,* II (Zagreb 1970), 326.

8. Ž. Marković, *Ruđe Bošković,* I (Zagreb, 1968), 326.

9. Ž. Marković, *Ruđe Bošković,* II (Zagreb, 1969), 637.

10. *Hrvatski latinisti,* II, 518.

11. *Hrvatski latinisti,* II, 593.

12. Ž. Marković, *Ruđe Bošković,* II, 1047–48.

13. *Hrvatski latinisti,* II, 568.

14. See Roger Hahn, "The Boscovich Archives at Berkeley," *ISIS* (Brussels), vol. 56 (1962), no. 183, 70–78.

15. Its first full title was *Philosophiae naturalis theoria redacta ad unicam legem virium in Natura existentium,* which was changed in the Venetian edition to *Theoria philosophiae naturalis.*

16. "Appendix ad metaphysicam pertinens de Anima et Deo," in the Zagreb edition of *Theory* (1974), 248–63; in the English translation (Cambridge, 1966), 187–96.

17. See R. E. Schofield, *A Scientific Autobiography of Joseph Priestley* (Cambridge, Mass.), 1966.

18. Ž. Marković, *Ruđe Bošković,* II, 884–85.

19. This letter was first published by Varićak in "Drugi ulomak Boškovićeve korespondencije," *Rad* 193 (1912), 206–7; Varićak and Nedeljković (*Bošković u svome vremenu i danas,* 82) instead of "heathenism" read wrongly "atheism." See Schofield, 166–68.

20. *Rad* 193 (1912), 208–10.

21. *Rad* 193, 224.

22. *Rad* 193, 227.

23. *Rad* 193, 234–35.

24. *Rad* 193, 240.

25. *Rad* 193, 179.

26. Pierre Prévost, *Deux traités de physique mécanique* (Geneva, 1818), pp. xxxiii–xxxvii.

27. V. Varićak, "Nekoliko pisama Boškovićevih," *Rad* 241 (1931), 211–28; P. Costabel, "Correspondence Le Sage–Boscovich," *Atti del convegno internazionale celebrativo del 250 annversario della nascità di R. G. Boscovich* (Milano, 1963), 205–16.

28. "Quanto commodius fuisset illud, si latinam, uti olim in more fuerat positum, null nunc quidem propriam, pro communi scientiarum commercio retinuissent" (*Rad* 241, 215).

29. "Un savant désintéressé et laborieux, original et profond, le quel réunit au plus haut degré, tous les talents les plus differents, et qui sont presque incompatibles!" (*Rad* 193, 213).

30. Elisabeth Hill, "Biographical Essay" (in L. L. Whyte, R. J. Boscovich), p. 76.

31. Boscovich, *Giornale di un viaggio . . .*, 29–31.

32. Ibid. 31–32.

33. Ibid. 31.

34. Ibid. 34–35.

35. See Divina Ježić, "R. J. Bošković—poète des Éclipses," in *Ruđer Bošović*, ed. G. Vidan (Zagreb, 1983), 256–57.

36. *Hrvatski latinisti*, II, 326.

37. I do not agree with Divina Ježić who writes that Barruel "a réalisé une de ces rares traductions qui sont à la fois artistiques et *fidèles*" ("Bošković—poète des Éclipses," *Ruđer Bošković*, [Zagreb, 1983], 263).

38 *Les éclipses*. Poème en six chants, dédié à sa Majesté par l'abbé Boscovich, traduit en français par l'abbé de Barruel (Paris, 1779).

39. Barruel, however, has reinforced these verses: "Une nation puissante, enrichie des dons de la fortune, terrible et redoutable dans l'art de la guerre, mais en même temps dévouée aux arts paisibles de Minerve, y tient son empire" (Ch. IV, 293–95).

40. A. Kadić, "Ruđer Bošković on American independence," *Journal of Croatian Studies*, XVII (1976), 10–13.

41. *Les éclipses* (Paris, 1779), p. vi.

42. Francesco Ricca, *Elogio storico dell' abbate Ruggiero Giuseppe Boscovich* (Milano, 1789).

43. *Theoria philosopiae naturalis—Teorija prirodne filozofije* (Zagreb, 1974), p. xvii.

44. "Il est facile de deviner dans son naturel des tendances érotiques très fortes, mais elles paraissent maîtrisées, réprimeés. Il est possible que la sublimation de cette forte sexualité se trouve à la source d' une partie de son énergie créatrice" (Essai medico-psychologique sur la personalité de Boškovíć," *Ruđer Bošković*, ed. G. Vidan [Zagreb, 1983], 229–30).

45. M. D. Grmek, "Le malattie di Ruggiero Boscovich," *Physis, Rivista di Storia della Scienza*, III, no. 3 (Firenze, 1961), 195–204.

46. F. W. Nietzsche, *Beyond Good and Evil* (New York, 1907), 19.

47. See the Epilogue by Vl. Filipović to Bošković's *Theoria* (Zagreb, 1974).

48. In her essay on Bošković, p. 98.

49. M. Kombol, *Povijest hrvatske knijiževnosti* (2nd edition, Zagreb, 1961), 239.

50. V. Gortan, *Hrvatski latinisti,* II, 313.

51. Vl. Filipović in the Epilogue to the *Theoria,* p. 4.

THE PROSODIC POSSIBILITIES
OF MODERN STANDARD SLOVENE
AND SLOVENE DIALECTS*

MARC L. GREENBERG

Prosodic phonological features are perhaps among the most rapidly changing systems in language. As a way to understand how prosodic features behave within a language in time and space, it might prove useful to analyze a linguistic area by quantifying the prosodic systems of its regional variants in order to hold it up for external comparison. The Slovene dialects comprise a particularly interesting linguistic territory, as they preserve in a relatively wide variety of patterns the tone, quantity and stress distinctions inherited from Common Slavic.

The first part of this study will provide a sketch—based on a standard reconstruction—of the historical developments in prosody from the Late Common Slavic period to the present relevant to determining the prosodic possibilities of the two codified prosodic varieties of Modern Standard Slovene (hereafter MSS) and the Slovene dialects. The historical discussion will be divided into two parameters: 1. *metatony,* by which we mean prosodic changes within the syllable, and 2. *metataxis,* by which we shall denote the movement of prosodic units among syllables. The second part of the study will present a typology of the functional load of prosodic features in MSS and the Slovene dialects.

Preliminaries

Before proceeding to the body of the study, we shall first outline our method of determining the functional load of prosodic features at the level of word phonology.[1] We may express the functional load in terms of a mathematical equation of the prosodic possibilities for a given linguistic system (e.g., a standard language, village dialect).

The functional load of a given domain may be formulated as an equation of the potential number of combinatory possibilities, or, in other words, the inventory of distinctive prosodic oppositions and their distributional constraints. Accordingly, we may calculate the number of distinctive prosodic word shapes for {1, 2, 3 . . . n} syllables (S) and determine the equation that will generate the series of possibilities {P1, P2, P3 . . . Pn}. To illustrate this procedure, let us examine the prosodic possibilities of some non-Slavic languages. For example, Finnish has fixed (i.e., non-distinctive) stress in the prima and quantitative oppositions in any syllable without distributional constraints upon them. The possible distinctive word shapes in Finnish may thus be schematized as follows (where *o* represents a syllable):

one-syllable words—*o o:* (= 2 possibilities)
two-syllable words—*oo o:o oo: o:o:* (= 4 possibilities)
three-syllable words—*ooo o:oo oo:o ooo: o:o:o o:oo: o:oo: o:o:o:* (= 8 possibilities)

This configuration gives the series {2, 4, 8 . . . n} which is generated by the equation $P = 2^S$, i.e., the number of prosodic possibilities in Finnish is equal to two to the number of syllables in the word. This geometric progression represents a relatively high functional load in prosody (see Ivić 1961: 303–04). On the other end of the spectrum, a language such as Turkish, which has fixed word stress on the ultima and non-distinctive oppositions (such as tone or quantity), would yield identical prosodic shapes for every word, regardless of the number of syllables. Thus the functional load for Turkish prosody yields the equation $P = 0$, i.e., no distinctive prosodic possibilities.

The utility of this type of analysis has been elucidated by P. Ivić, whose work is applied primarily to standard Serbo-Croatian and its dialects (see esp. Ivić 1961, 1961–62, 1970, 1973). To briefly summarize the potential applications of such a study: we may characterize the relative differences in prosodic patterns throughout a dialect area (as will be attempted in the present study), we may contribute to the study of universals by measuring the limits and averages of prosodic systems, and in general linguistic theory analyze the relative share of prosodic versus inherent phonological features. A diachronic approach would calculate the change in functional load through time by comparing earlier and modern stages of prosodic patterns.

Our analysis of the prosodic pattern of Slovene may be most easily juxtaposed as a type with that of neighboring Serbo-Croatian. It will be seen that the functional load of prosodic features in Slovene dialects (and Croatian Kajkavian dialects; see Ivšić 1936, Lončarić 1979) is characterized by arithmetical progressions, i.e., multiplicative and additive equations, while in Serbo-Croatian dialects, primarily Štokavian and Čakavian dialects, the range may reach geometrical dimensions, i.e., it may be expressed in terms of exponential equations. This difference is due to the well-known facts that distinctive prosodic features (tone and quantity) are limited to the tonemic syllable (with some exceptions, e.g., the village dialect of Žiri, which will be discussed further) in Slovene, while in many Serbo-Croatian dialects distinctive quantity may also occur in unstressed syllables. One can find also transitional dialects, such as the Kajkavian and Torlak dialects, which display only traces or complete loss of quantitative distinctions outside of the stressed syllable.

Diachrony

Our study of the prosodic possibilities of MSS and the Slovene dialects must necessarily rest upon an understanding of the temporal and geographical progress of prosodic innovations. We shall not attempt a new or exhaustive treatment of the history of Slovene accent, but rather we shall sketch the principal developments that are relevant for determining the prosodic possibilities of the systems under analysis. The facts of reconstruction adduced here agree, along general lines, with a standard reconstruction as found in Valjavec 1897; Ramovš 1929, 1950; Jakobson 1963; Jaksche 1965.[2] The discussion will, for heuristic reasons, separate two lines of development, *metatony* (intra-syllabic change) and *metataxis* (inter-syllabic change). While these two processes may and do occur concurrently and co-territorially, the division between them is made here on the assumption that it is useful to separate different types of changes.

Metatony

Two of the earliest changes in South Slavic were the shortening of the old acute accent, e.g., **brá:trъ, **brá:tra > *b'ratr(ə), *b'ratra 'brother (nom., gen./acc. sg.),' and the lengthening of the short circumflex, e.g., **bògъ, **bòga > *bò:gə, *bò:ga 'god (nom., gen./acc. sg.)'.[3] The shortening of the old acute accent appears to have been earlier—according to Ramovš, completed by the end of the 8th c. (1950:21)—as it is common to both Serbo-Croatian and Slovene, cf., Štokavian bràt, bràta. The lengthening of the short circumflex is dated to the 10th c. (Ramovš: op. cit.). Thus at an early stage of Slovene the opposition between the old acute and circumflex was translated into a purely quantitative distinction. Tonemicity in the system was apparently never lost, however, as a new rising tone (the "neo-acute") developed, as a result of retraction from final short and reduced vowels, concurrently with the prosodic innovations just mentioned. Long neo-acute accents remained in opposition to the long circumflex, thus retaining tonemicity, e.g., **kl'u:č'ъ > *kl'ū:č(ə) (=kl'ú:č(ə)) 'key,' while short neo-acutes were identified with short stress from the shortened old acutes, e.g., **ko'n'ъ > *kõn'(ə) (= 'kon'(ə)) 'horse.'

The number and distribution of long acute and circumflex accents were increased by contraction, e.g., **stojá:lъ > *stá:l(ə) 'stand (l-pcpl., masc. sg.),' **konъčá:je(tъ) > *kon(ə)čà: 'finishes.' The number of long circumflex accents was further increased by the development of the neo-circumflex, a two-part change involving the loss of post-tonic length (a general Slovene and Croatian Kajkavian innovation) and concomitant compensatory lengthening of the short accented vowel (from shortened old acute) with the preservation of tonal peak in the first mora of the new two-morae syllable, e.g., *'děla:š > (MSS) dè:laš 'work (2 sg.)'.

Non-final short syllables that did not undergo the neo-circumflex development were lengthened as long acute. Thus *b'rata 'brother (gen. sg.)' > MSS brá:ta, but *b'rat(ə) (nom. sg.) remained short, cf., MSS > br'at. This development relegated the opposition of quantity to the ultimate (and monosyllables), while other stressed syllables maintained the distinction in tone only. The result of the changes described so far established the basic prosodic inventory of the present-day tonemic dialects, and is reflected in the tonemic variant of MSS, as will be discussed further.

The prosodic developments underlying the tonemic dialects were translated into quantity in the Styrian dialect of Mostec. In this village dialect long acute accents are reflected as length, e.g., 'mi:za (MSS mí:za) 'table,' 'dü:ša (MSS dú:ša) 'soul,' including also new acutes from retraction (see discussion below), e.g., 'žɛ:na (MSS žě:na) 'wife.' Short stress remained and long circumflex became short stress, e.g., 'krœx (MSS 'kruh) 'bread,' 'nuč (MSS nọ̀č) 'night,' 'vidim (MSS vì:dim) 'I see,' nu'gɛ 'legs' (material from Toporišič 1961, 1962).

The complete loss of tone and quantity is evident in a number of Slovene dialects, e.g., Rezija, the Southern Coastal dialects and Eastern Styria. It is worth noting that such dialects tend to be grouped around the periphery of the Slovene dialect area, and one might speculate that this has something to do with contact with languages that do not have phonemic pitch or quantity.[4]

Metataxis

Two tendencies in the history of Slovene accent may be discerned. The first of these is the maximization of prosodic distinctions in the ultima (and thus also the monosyllable). The result of this tendency mirrors the Common Slavic pattern, which maintained the maximum number of distinctions in the prima. Early Common Slavic distinguished three accents in the prima, i.e., acute *brá:trъ 'brother,' circumflex *mę̑:so 'meat,' and short stress *'nebo 'sky.' Non-prima stressed syllables could receive the acute accent, e.g., *želě:zo 'iron,' while short syllables could carry short stress, e.g., *pъ'sъ 'dog.' Ultima stresses were short in all instances, e.g., *vъdo'va 'widow.'

This set of relationships was translated in Slovene into a system of maximal contrasts in the ultima. The developments underlying MSS which led to this situation were the following: (1) the rise of the neo-acute, e.g., **gospoda:'r'ъ > *gospodā:r(ə), MSS gospodá:r 'master'; (2) contraction, e.g., *gospo'ja > MSS gospá: 'mistress'; (3) the shift of the inherited circumflex to the second syllable and concomitant lengthening of the newly accented syllable, e.g., *mę̑:so > MSS mesò:; (4) lengthening of short acute stress outside of the ultima, e.g., *želězo > MSS želé:zo but *bogát(ə) > MSS bo'gat 'rich.'

As a result of these developments, from a synchronic point of view, MSS distinguishes three prosodic oppositions in monosyllables and the ultima of polysyllables, e.g., acute kljú:č 'key,' zidá:r 'builder'; nò:č 'night,' mesò:; and short stress k'ruh 'bread,' bo'gat 'rich.' In syllables other than the ultima, stressed syllables may be differentiated by the binary opposition of tone only, e.g., acute šȋ:ba 'switch, rod,' circumflex šȋ:ba 'hurries'.

Consequently, the syntagmatic relationship of prosodic oppositions of MSS gives a mirror image of that in Common Slavic. In Common Slavic the acute tone was lexically assigned to any syllable (if it fell on a short syllable, then it yielded phonetically acute short stress), while the circumflex fell automatically on the prima (including enclitics) of words lacking this lexical stress assignment (see Jakobson 1963). Similarly, in MSS, the acute and circumflex (redundantly long, except on /ə/, which is inherently short) accents are lexically assigned, while short stress is assigned to the ultima by default in the absence of a long stressed syllable.

The second and more recent tendency in the Slovene dialects is the ongoing process of unburdening the ultima syllable as the locus of prosodic oppositions. In some areas this development is borne out by the neutralization of contrasts in the ultima, e.g., the change of final acute to circumflex in part of the Lower Carniolan dialect: po zobà:ix (cf. MSS po zobẹ̄:x) 'on one's teeth (loc. pl.)' (for details see Rigler 1980b:220–21). A much more widespread process in the dialects is that of unburdening the ultima by accent retraction onto the penultima or (more rarely) further towards the beginning of the word.

The dialectal Slovene accent retractions appear to occur in a clear hierarchy (as suggested in Ramovš 1929), which may be illustrated in the chart below.[5] Retraction types that occur dialectally in Slovene are enclosed by the box, while the remaining types are retractions common to all Slovene dialects.

	Non-retracted form	Retracted form
0.1	*kl'uːč'ə, *gospodaː'r'ə	kljúːč, gospodár (MSS)
0.2	*kl'uːč'a (gen. sg.)	kljúːča (MSS)
1.1	že'na 'wife'	žéːna (MSS)
1.2	məg'la 'fog'	mə̑gla (MSS)
1.3	okọ̀ː 'eye'	óko (dial.)

The first retraction (0.1), known as the "rise of the neo-acute," occurred in all Slavic dialects, owing to the reduction and ultimate loss of jers in weak positions. The second retraction (0.2) is general to Slovene; oxytone forms are known elsewhere in Slavic, cf., Russian koro'l'a 'king,' zvez'da 'star.' To the extent that these retractions are due to phonetic change, the hierarchy rests upon competing syntagmatic variables: the quantity of the pretonic and tonic vowels. To the above chart we might also wish to add word forms with closed ultima syllables. It is not quite clear where these types fit in the hierarchy, if they fit at all. For example, in MSS the types bo'gat and ot'rok 'child' are normally unretracted, which one might assign to the fact that the stressed syllable is closed, "heavier," and therefore the stress tends to remain on the ultima. This could be the case, though it is also true that the retention may be due to analogy with the other forms of the paradigm, thus bo'gat on the model of bogàːta (nom. sg. fem.), bogáːtega (gen. sg. masc./neut.), or ot'rok on the model of otróːka (acc./gen. sg.), otróːku (dat./loc. sg.).[6]

The type gospodáːr may be subject to further retraction in dialects that have lost tonemic distinctions while the process of retraction from the ultima was still active. In such dialects this type becomes identified with the okọ̀ː type. Thus, for example, in the Lower Carniolan Kostelsko dialect, long final stresses are retracted from both long neo-acute as well as circumflex syllables, e.g., *kováːč(ə) > 'kavač 'blacksmith,' *golòːb(ə) > 'galọp 'pigeon' (Babno Polje[7]). In dialects where the circumflex retraction occurred before tonemic distinctions were lost, oxytone types are retained in acute-stressed forms, e.g., Styrian 'mi̭ɛːsə 'meat,' 'ni̭ɛːbə but (*krompíːr>) krəm'piːr 'potato,' (*mrač(ə)niːk >) mrač'niːk 'bat' (Luče[7]).

Let us now trace the hierarchy of retractions through some examples from local dialects. Accentually archaic dialects, such as the Carinthian dialect of

Rož, retain oxytones of types 1.1–1.3, e.g., *ža'na* 'woman,' *məh'u̯a* 'fog,' *bo'hat* 'rich,' *u̯əqù:* 'eye' (Breznica pri Št. Jakobu[8]). The progress of types 1.1 and 1.2 is seen in the Upper Carniolan dialects, e.g., Selca has the retraction *žé:na,* but retains oxytones in *məɣ'la, ot'rok* and *okǫ̀:;* Eastern Upper Carniola has *'ži̯ɛ:na, 'məɣla,* but retains *puɣ'rɛp* 'funeral,' *ne'bǫ* 'sky' (Moravče) (Logar 1967). Futher progress may be traced in the Styrian dialects, e.g., Southern Pohorje *'nǫ:go, s'tɛ:bər,* but *ot'rǫ:k, me'so:u̯* (Pivola[8]); and Pannonian, eg., Slovenske gorice *žɛna, 'mɛgla, 'bǫgat* (exceptional shorts from other sources are to be found here: *o'ra* 'ploughed' < **orǎl(ə)*), but *ǫ'kǫ;* (Videm ob Ščavnici[7]). The retention of oxytones from acute-stressed forms is found in Styrian Upper Savinja *'ži̯ɛ:na, 'məgla, 'u̯ɔtrak, 'ni̯ɛ:bə,* but *mrač'ni:k* 'bat' (Luče[7]); Lower Carniolan Southern Bela Krajina *žé:na, 'məgła, ví:sok* 'high,' *tɛ̣:sto* 'dough,' but (**vihá:r* >) *vihà:r* 'tempest,' (**živí:m* >) *živì:m* 'I live, dwell' (Dragatuš[7]). All the retractions are realized in the Lower Carniolan dialect in Kostel, e.g., *'ži̯ena, 'mogu̯a, 'atrak, 'mɛsu, 'kavač* (Babno Polje[7]).

The hierarchy outlined above holds for virtually all of the Slovene dialects with the exception of the Resian and Ter dialects of the Coastal group. In these areas, archaisms of types 1.1 and 1.2 are retained, e.g., Rezija *ža'na, moh'la, ǫt'rǫk* (Osojani[8]); Ter *že'na, meh'la, ot'rok, otro'ka* (acc./gen. sg.) (Bardo[8]), while type 1.3 exhibits barytone accentuation, e.g., *'ǫku* 'eye (nom./acc. sg.)' *'u̯hu̯* 'ear (nom./acc. sg.)' (Osojani[8]); *ó:ko, mɛ̣:so* (Bardo[8]). The violation of the retraction hierarchy that seems to operate so reliably in the vast majority of Slovene dialects has cast doubt on whether oxytones of the type *mesò:* ever existed in Rezija. Consequently, the shift or absence of shift of the circumflex accent has been the subject of some scholarly debate. At least two scenarios are given for these facts: (1) that the circumflex first advanced and then retracted (Bajec 1921; Ramovš 1928, 1935: 36; Rigler 1972), or (2) that the circumflex never advanced (Stankiewicz 1984–1985). Intonation and quantity have apparently been lost in Rezija and, owing to the peculiarities of the vowel system, it is difficult to judge from modern forms whether the forms reflect anomalous retraction or simply retention of the Common Slavic place of stress. The development is clearer in Ter, where retraction is reflected by acute tone in the newly accented syllable: *tɛ̣:ško* 'heavy (adv.),' *zǫ́:bje* 'teeth,' *ú:ho* 'ear' (Bardo[8]). I assume that this means the retraction took place in Ter and I think it likely that Rezija followed the same development, given the historical connections between the two local dialects. This innovation in these areas provides an exception to the retraction hierarchy.[9]

Synchrony

The Prosodic Possibilities of Modern Standard Slovene

In order to illustrate the Slovene situation in general, let us first examine the prosodic possibilities of MSS. Here we must distinguish two prosodic norms, one based upon dynamic stress with distinctive quantity, the other with both distinctive tone and quantity. These two variants correspond to the principal prosodic division of the Slovene dialects, i.e., between tonemic and non-tonemic dialects, while place of stress and distribution of tone (in the tonemic variety) and quantity reflect the system of the central dialects, Upper and Lower Carniolan.

The first of these prosodic variants, based upon distinctive quantity alone, distinguishes quantity under stress and, specifically, only in monosyllables and the ultima of (non-compounded) polysyllables. Stress in non-ultima syllables is always long, except on /ə/, which is inherently short, e.g., *'məgla* (orth. *<megla>*). Thus, place of stress is concomitant with the long vowel (and therefore the place of stress is predictable), while in the absence of a long vowel, the ultima receives short stress. We may illustrate the distinctive prosodic possibilities of this variant as follows: (1) quantity in monosyllables and the ultima of polysyllables , e.g., *b'ra:t* 'to go read (sup.),' *b'rat* 'brother,' *pos'ta:u̯* (*<postav>*) 'of figures, laws (gen. pl.),' *pos'tau̯* (*<postàl>*) 'became'; (2) length on any non-ultima of polysyllables, e.g., *'go:vori* 'speeches, local dialects,' *go'vo:ri* 'speak! (2 sg. imp.).' The functional load of prosody in this variant of MSS may be expressed as S + 1, that is, it has as many distinctive length possible as the number of syllables and one additional distinction (which is quantitative) in the ultima or monosyllable.

The tonemic variant of MSS distinguishes tone in long syllables. The tonemic opposition is realized as high (traditionally "circumflex") and low (traditionally "acute") pitch in relation to the unstressed syllables (see Toporišič 1967, 1968). The short stress carries no such tonemic opposition. The distribution of long and short stressed syllables is the same as that of the non-tonemic system. A three-way prosodic opposition may be made in monosyllables, e.g., *dá:m* 'I give,' *dà:m* 'of ladies (gen. pl.),' *brà:t* 'read (sup.),' *b'rat* 'brother'; in the ultima of polysyllables, e.g., *postá:u̯* (*<postál>*) 'stood for a while,' *postà̂u̯* (*<postâv>*) 'of figures, laws (gen. pl.),' *pos'tau̯* (*<postàl>*) 'became.' A binary opposition may be carried by non-ultima syllables, e.g., *pá:ra* 'of a pair (gen. sg.)' *pà:ra* 'steam.' Accordingly, the prosodic possibilities of the tonemic variant of MSS yield 2S + 1, signifying a binary opposition available in all syllables with an additional opposition possible in the ultima.

The Prosodic Possibilities of the Slovene Dialects

The two prosodic variants of MSS represent not only the division between tonemic and non-tonemic dialects, but also approximate mid-points of variation among the dialects. Prosodic possibilities in the dialects range from S, where place of stress is the sole distinctive prosodic feature (in a number of Coastal and Syrian dialects, for example), to 5S – 2, where quantity, place of stress, and both tonic and post-tonic pitch are relevant (in the Rovte dialect of the Žiri basin). Tone as a distinctive feature is limited to the dialect areas of Carinthian, Upper and Lower Carniola, Rovte (Horjul and Poljana) and the Coast (Soča, Ter, Nadiž and Brda). Quantity remains distinctive for the above-mentioned tonemic dialects, with the exception of a small area of Upper Carniola north of Ljubljana. Quantity is also found in the non-tonemic Coastal (e.g., Inner Carniola), Lower Carniolan (Bela Krajina), as well as several Styrian and Pannonian dialects. Accordingly, the prosodic patterns of the Slovene dialects may be typologized into six groups with the following combinations of distinctive features: (1) stress only, (2) pitch and stress, (3) quantity and stress, (4) pitch and quantity, (5) pitch, stress, and quantity and (6) pitch (under and after ictus), stress and quantity.[10]

1. Dialects with Stress Only. Dialects with the prosodic possibility of S, i.e., the choice of stress placement alone being distinctive, cover the areas of Rezija, the southern Coastal and eastern Styrian dialects.

The dialects of Rezija appear to have some degree of phonetic quantity, as the famous zasopli vokali (murmured vowels) under stress are shorter than normal glottal-state vowels under stress.[11] There are no distributional constraints on stress placement in these dialects, e.g., *k'ra·ṷa* 'cow,' *z'vįzda* 'star,' *ọt'rọk* (Osojani[8]), *smə'rẹka* 'spruce,' *urete'nọ* 'spindle' (Solbica[8]).

Southern Coastal dialects have stress only, e.g., Kras *k'rəh,* 'bread,' *'ṷotrok* 'child,' *yə'lup* 'pigeon' (Komen[7]); Istria *'pəs* 'dog,' *k'ṷäza* 'goat,' *li'pu* 'beautiful (adv.)' (Dekani pri Kopru[8]). The Istrian dialects have retracted all but certain circumflex oxytones, making them transitional to the prosodic possibilities of S – 1 (where S > 1), e.g., *'sẹno* 'hay,' *'tẹstọ* 'dough,' but *yu'loụp* 'pigeon,' *kọs'ti* 'bone (gen. sg./nom. pl)' (Pomjan[7]); *'ukụə* 'eye,' *'suhụə* 'dry (adv.)' but *mi'su* 'meat' (Dekani pri Kopru[8]).

Many villages in Styria east of the Savinja river have stress only. Some of these are without distributional constraints on the placement of stress, e.g., *'hiša* 'house,' *me'su* 'meat' (Pilštanj[8]); *mįegła, na'bu* 'sky,' (Kozje[8]); *'žiena, pe'pẹiu* 'ash' (Šmarje pri Jelšah[7]); *'visok, nọ'cọi* (Oplotnica) (Zorko 1983); *'bɛtica* 'little house,' *po'sọt* 'everywhere,' (Spodnja Ložnica[7]); *'cįesta* 'road,' *bo'gat* 'rich' (Pivola[8]); *st'rįeha* 'roof,' *ot'rọk* (Zgornja Kungota[8]). Most of these dialects have retracted all but some of the circumflex oxytones. Accordingly, such dialects must be viewed as being in transition to the type S – 1, e.g., Central Styrian *'nauga* 'leg,' *'miegla, 'vüesok* 'high,' *'sarce* 'heart,' but *u'kau* (Ratanska vas[8]); Central Savinja *k'voza* 'goat,' *s'tieza* 'path,' *b'vogat* 'rich,' but also *šer'vok, o'ko* (Vojnik[8]). In some dialects etymological neo-acutes on long syllables are retracted, e.g., *'kovač* 'blacksmith,' (Pivola[8]), though in most of these dialects the forms have remained oxytone while etymological circumflex accents have retracted, e.g., *ko'voč, gov'rei* 'speaks,' *ži'vei* 'lives, dwells,' but *'sieno* 'hay,' *'mieso* (Oplotnica) (Zorko 1983).

The dialect of Haloze may also belong to the S – 1 type, though Kolarič reports some (probably free) variation in quantity, e.g., *'leto/'le:ito* 'year,' *b'reza/b're:za* 'birch,' *k'rüh/k'rü:h* 'bread.' Accent retractions are reflected in *'no:uga, 'megla, 'o:uko,* though also *go'loup, dre'vou* 'wood.' Some fluctuation is also registered for retractions, cf., *z ro'ko:/z 'ro:ko* 'by hand (instr. sg.),' though these and other alternating forms most likely reflect the heterogeneous local dialects from which the material was gathered (see Kolarič 1964: 397–400).[12]

2. Dialects with Pitch and Stress. A small area of Upper Carniola north of Ljubljana has lost distinctive quantity but retained phonemic pitch. So far only two village dialects of this type have been described, Valburga pri Smledniku and Srednje Jarše. Here acute and circumflex accents may occur in any syllable without distributional constraints. Stressed syllables, including /ə/, are redundantly long. The number of prosodic possibilities in these dialects is, accordingly, 2S. The following examples from two essentially identical local dialects illustrate the distinctive oppositions, e.g., *mlék* 'milk (nom. sg. masc.),' *pəs* 'dog,' *žéna* 'wife,' *məsta* 'cities (nom./acc. pl.),' *zidár* 'builder,' *təmən* 'dark' (Valburga pri Smledniku,[7] Srednje Jarše[8]). Unretracted oxytones from short stress and long circumflex have become uniformly (long) circumflex, e.g., *məγwà* 'fog,' *buγàt* 'rich,' *məsọ̀* (Srednje Jarše[8]).

This prosodic configuration is somewhat rare in world languages. In this regard it is of some historiographical interest to note here Trubetzkoy's assertion that "Sprachen mit muskalischem Akzent aber ohne Quantitätsunterschiede [. . .] nirgends in der Welt vorkommen" (1925: 303–04), which is controverted by the Upper Carniolan evidence.

3. Dialects with Quantity and Stress. A number of geographically widespread dialects have lost tone but maintain the binary opposition of quantity under stress. Those without further distributional constraints have, consequently, the functional load of prosody 2S.

Rovte dialects that have lost tone have redistributed quantitative oppositions throughout the word by the process of stress retraction, resulting in new short stresses, e.g., *'žena, 'watrak* 'child,' *'moɣla* (Cerkno[7]); as well as shortening of stressed /i/ and /u/, e.g., *'sila* 'power,' *'duša* 'soul' (Podbrdo[8]). In the village dialect of Črni Vrh, where only stress retraction has given rise to new short stresses, quantity is limited to the penultima and ultima. Though all retractions are attested in this dialect, ultima stresses are found frequently, owing to paradigmatic support, e.g., *wę'sɔːk, wę'sɔːdzɣa* 'high (nom., gen. sg. masc./neut.),' *at'rɔːk, at'rɔːka* 'child (nom., acc./gen. sg.).' Consequently, the prosodic possibilities of this dialect are S + 2, which may be illustrated by the forms *'waːs* 'village,' *'daš* 'rain,' *k'raːwa* 'cow,' *'testu* 'dough,' *šę'rɔːk* 'wide,' *ab'ras* 'face,' *ra'patat* 'to make noise' (cf. MSS *ropotáːti*) (Tominec 1964). Where both retraction and shortening of diffuse vowels have taken place, any syllable may carry a quantitative opposition. In dialects with this pattern, the prosodic possibilities are 2S, e.g., *s'ljeːp* 'blind,' *'u̯oč* 'eye (nom. sg. masc.),' *k'raːwa* 'cow,' *'hiša, 'žena, ne'bu̯o* 'sky,' (Most na Soči[8]); *'daːn* 'day,' *'dɔš* 'rain,' *m'liːka* 'milk (nom. sg. fem.),' *'lipa* 'linden,' *zla'tuː* 'gold,' *kle'či* 'kneels' (Cerkno[7]).

At least one Styrian dialect maintains quantitative oppositions in any syllable, again giving 2S as the number of prosodic possibilities. The distribution of quantity in this dialect is due to the historical change of circumflex into short stress and acute into long stress, e.g., *g'rẹːh* (MSS *grẹ́ːh*) 'sin,' *'dan* (MSS *dàːn*) 'day,' *m'lẹːku* (MSS *mlẹ́ːko*) 'milk,' *'vɛsuk* 'high,' *hu'diːč* (MSS *hudíːč*) 'devil,' *u'kü* 'eye' (Mostec[13]).

2S-1 is the typical pattern for Prekmurje village dialects that have not yet lost quantitative distinctions. Here quantitative oppositions may be in any syllable but the ultima, where short stress does not occur, e.g., the village of Cankova has *k'lüːč* 'key,' *k'rü* 'bread,' *'küːpi* 'buy! (2 sg. imp.),' *'küpɛc* 'customer,' *mɛ'düː* 'of honey (gen. sg.).' The restriction on stress placement in the ultima owes to regular retraction of short ultima stress of the type *'žena, 'bogat* (Pável 1909).

The eastern Upper Carniolan dialect of Moravče differs from the remainder of Upper Carniola in the loss of tone. Here quantity is maintained in monosyllables and the ultima of polysyllables, while stressed syllables outside of the ultima are redundantly long, with the exception of stressed /ə/. This vowel is predictably short and therefore no phonemically relevant quantity obtains when it is stressed. Thus, like the non-tonemic variety of the standard language, this dialect maintains the number of prosodic oppositions S + 1, e.g., *'nɔːs* 'nose,' *p'sa* 'dog (acc./gen. sg.),' *'hiːša* 'house,' *'wəla* 'will,' *ne'bɔː* 'sky,' *pug'rɛp* (Moravče[8]).

Some dialects in southern Lower Carniola maintain quantitative oppositions in pre-ultima syllables due to both shortening under stress of /i/ and /u/ (like the Rovte dialects with which they share a relatively recent history) and retraction. Here both long (from all etymological sources) and short accents are restricted from the ultima (i.e., the ultima is not accentable), giving the prosodic functional load of 2(S - 1), e.g., 'va:s 'village,' 'luč 'light,' k'ra:va 'cow,' 'lipa 'linden,' 'vęsak 'high,' 'mɛsu 'meat,' 'kavač 'black-smith' (Babno Polje[7]); 'vu:s 'wagon,' 'nus 'nose,' žɛna, 'šərok 'wide,' 'ɔku 'eye' (Metlika[8]).

4. *Dialects with Pitch and Quantity.* Pitch and quantity oppositions are preserved in the Carinthian, Upper Carniolan, Lower Carniolan and the Coastal dialect groups (specifically the local dialects of Soča, Brda, Nadiža and Ter). With the exception of the anomalous Brda dialect, these areas have undergone the prosodic innovations described earlier for the tonemic variant of the standard language and have either preserved the same situation or modified the distribution of accentual oppositions.

Dialects with an accentual pattern like that of the standard language maintain pitch oppositions in any syllable with concomitant length and have an additional possibility of short stress on the ultima. Such dialects maintain a prosodic functional load of 2S + 1, e.g., Zilja in Carinthian čú:rč 'ear of corn,' mù:əst 'bridge,' má:tə[14] 'mother,' pù:əš'le 'afterwards,' ušệ:t 'of ears (gen. pl),' z mastjó 'with fat (instr. sg.),' Bə'soᵃk 'high' (Brdo pri Šmohorju) (Logar 1975); Nadiža kjú:č 'key,' pà:s 'belt,' zí:ma 'winter,' brì:tu 'razor,' marlí:č 'corpse,' sarcè: heart,' reb'ro 'rib' (Ošne pri Lenartu[8]); mlá:ð 'young (nom. sg. masc. def.),' mlà:ð 'young (nom. sg. masc. indef.),' 'šu 'went,' sé:Bɛ 'oneself (acc./gen.),' drù:go 'second, other (acc. sg. fem.),' Bɛsé:l 'joy,' krempì:r 'potato,' pər'šu 'came' (Drežnica pri Kobaridu) (Logar 1975); Ter prí:t 'to come,' mò:š 'husband,' 'męš 'mouse,' ú:ho 'ear,' ù:ha 'ears (nom./acc. pl.),' marjó: 'they die,' marjè: 'dies (3 sg.),' že'na (Bardo v Terski dolini); Upper Carniolan mé:hk 'soft,' mòst 'bridge,' b'rat 'brother,' sé:stra 'sister,' vètər 'wind,' žəví:š 'you live (2 sg.),' təstò 'dough,' u'sɔk 'high,' (Srednja vas v Bohinju[8]); spá:t 'to sleep,' spà:t (sup.),' 'jət 'to go,' žé:na, pù:nca 'girl,' damú: 'homeward,' okọ̀:, bo'gat (Selca) (Logar 1975); Lower Carniolan grá:ịh 'sin,' nù:s 'nose,' 'gost 'forest,' dúša 'soul,' brì:tu 'razor,' klabú:k 'hat,' mesù:, ot'rok (Ribnica[8]).

The prosodic functional load of 2S + 1 is realized with a strikingly different distribution in the Coastal dialect of Brda. Here a binary opposition of quantity occurs in any stressed syllable, while long rising tone is limited to the monosyllable and the ultima of polysyllables. This pattern arose after the dialect had already lost its inherited pitch oppositions and then gained a new rising tone due to the elision of final vowels. The prosodic oppositions in this dialect may be illustrated as follows: *krá:v* 'cow (acc./gen./dat./instr./loc. sg./ nom./acc. pl.),' *krà:u̯* 'of cows (gen. pl.),' *u̯'zau̯* 'took,' *krȁ:va* 'cow (nom. sg.),' *u̯'zəməm* 'I take,'[15] *podné:v* 'during the day-time,' *šerò:k* 'wide,' *tər'potc* 'Plantago' (Šmartno v Brdih[7]).

A further tonemic opposition in final short syllables, due to vowel short-ening in the ultima, gives the number of possibilities 2S + 2, e.g., Zilja *kljú:č* 'key,' *sù:h* 'thin,' *brȁt, mé:so, štȉ:je* 'counts,' *zɣəbí:* 'loses,' *šérwò:k* 'wide,' *ərčę̇* 'of things (gen. pl.),' *вəsę̇* 'of the village (gen. sg.)' (Potoče[7]).[16]

In the Carinthian dialect of Rož, further distributional restrictions on pitch and quantity give the prosodic possibilities 2S. Here tonemic opposi-tions in the long ultima and monosyllable are neutralized and become phonetically acute. Thus this pattern restricts the binary oppositions of pitch to pre-ultima syllables and of quantity to monosyllables and the ultima of polysyllables, e.g., *mú:əst* 'bridge,' *'boß* 'bean,' *hu̯á:u̯a* 'head,' *nù:əsəm* 'I carry,' *mesú, čo'u̯ak* 'person' (Konstanje nad Vrbskim Jezerom) (Logar 1967).

5. Dialects with Pitch, Quantity, and Stress. A few territorially disparate dialects maintain tonemic and quantitative distinctions where quantity is not restricted to a particular syllable of the word. In such dialects place of stress cannot be determined by the placement of quantity.

In the Carinthian dialect of Podjuna, long acute and circumflex accents may occur in any syllable, while short stress is limited to the penultima and ultima of polysyllables and the monosyllable. New short stress in the penultima is a result of accent retraction from both final shorts and long circumflex from the ultima, e.g., (**ko'za* >) *ʔȯza* 'goat,' (**bo'gat* >) *'boɸat,* (**stə'za* >) *s'təzda* 'path,' (**okò:* >) *'oʔə* 'eye.' Circumflex accents are some-times retained in the ultima due to analogical support, e.g., *ɦau̯ò:f* 'pigeon.' New short stresses in the ultima are the result of vowel abridgement in final syllables, e.g., *um'rit* 'to die (inf.).' Thus, this dialect maintains the functional prosodic load of 2S + 2, e.g., *pó:š* 'snail,' *zò:f* 'tooth,' *ʔlat* 'to swear (inf.),' *sédm̥* 'seven,' *žȁ:tu̯a* 'harvest,' *'tą̊žaʔ* 'heavy,' *zɦubí:* 'loses' (Kneža[7]).

In part of the Carinthian dialect in Rož, long acute and circumflex accents may occur in any syllable, while short acute and circumflex accents may in principle occur in all but monosyllables and the ultima of polysyllables. This last restriction is due to the neutralization of pitch in the ultima. It is not clear whether short circumflex may occur in the penultima. In the material available, only etymological oxytones of the type **bere'mo* 'we read (pres.)' give rise to new short circumflexes when shifted onto the prima, e.g., *bȁʀamo* 'we read,' *zȁlano* 'green (adv.).' The functional load of prosody may thus be posited as 4S − 1, where S > 1, though this may be demonstrated, for the moment, only in monosyllables and disyllables, e.g., *ʔúːč* 'key,' *mùːst* 'bridge,' *ʔʀẹ̣i* 'edge,' *zwíːzda* 'star,' *lìːtas* 'this year,' *žʀámo* 'we eat greedily,' *šwíːgartọ̀hter* 'daughter-in-law,' *sːastró:* with one's sister (instr. sg.),' *wəʔù:* 'eye,' *stézˈda* 'path' (Breznica pri Št. Jakobu v Rožu[7]). The phonemic status of pitch in short syllables to the left of the penultima is somewhat dubious. J. Rigler reports that "in syllables further than two towards the beginning of the word, quantity is frequently indeterminate (particularly in the type *dáwatə* 'to do [inf.]') [. . .] in certain instances (particularly in the type *zàlano, doʀoje* 'dobro je' 'it is good'), the toneme is uncertain and difficult to determine" (*Fonološki opisi . . .* : 194). As a result, in the words of more than two syllables, the functional load must be estimated more conservatively, on the order of 2S + 5.

The Rovte dialect of Horjul distinguishes four pitch and quantity accents, short and long circumflex and short and long acute. The long accents may occur in any syllable, while the short accents are restricted to the penultima and ultima of polysyllables. The short acute occurs in the penultima when shifted from the ultima, e.g., *bógat,* (**miže'te* >) *məžéte* 'you squint (2 pl.),' and in the ultima as a result of vowel elision, e.g., (**prineˈsi* >) *pərnə̀s* 'bring! (2 sg. imp.).' Short circumflex in the penultima is due to analogical leveling, e.g., *umrète* 'you die (2 pl.)' on the model of *umrè* 'dies.' The functional load of the Horjul dialect is thus 2S + 4, where S > 1: *stráːšt* 'to frighten (inf.),' *vràːt* 'neck,' *vrát* 'to/on one's neck (dat./loc. sg.),' *brát* 'brother,' *kóːᵃžuh* 'pelt,' *mìːslim* 'I think,' *nésen* 'I carry,' *nàma* 'to/with us two (dat./loc./instr. du.),' *dihúːr* 'skunk,' *mesù:* 'meat,' *watràk* 'child' (Breznik 1909).

The Lower Carniolan southern Bela Krajina dialect of Dragatuš[7] maintains the opposition of long acute and circumflex and short stress in all syllables but the ultima of polysyllables, where only long circumflex may stand. Only long circumflex and short stress may occur in monosyllables. This pattern arose due to the loss of inherited tonemic distinctions giving way to quantitative and the rise of new acutes from more recent retraction. Thus circumflex oxytones are reflexes of acutes, e.g., (**viháːr* >) *vihàːr* 'tempest,' *dəsàːk* 'of boards (gen. pl.),' while other original oxytones result in new long acutes, e.g., (**testò:* >) *téːsto* 'dough,' (**hudọ̀:* >) *húːdo* 'bad (adv.),' or short, e.g., 'mẹso (**golò:p* >) 'goɫop 'pigeon.' Short stress outside of the ultima occurs also as a result of the non-lengthening of inherited short vowels (e, o, ə), e.g., 'mɛlem 'I grind, mill,' 'nòsim 'I carry,' *maša* 'Mass.' The functional load of prosody in the dialect of Dragatuš is thus 3S – 2, where S > 1, e.g., *klùːč* 'key,' 'miš 'mouse,' *lẹ̄ːpo* 'beautiful (adv.),' *krùːha* 'of bread (gen. sg.),' 'kolo 'wheel, 'vihàːr 'tempest.'

6. A Dialect with Pitch (Under and After the Ictus), Quantity, and Stress.
At least one microdialect, the Rovte dialect of Poljana in the Žiri basin, exhibits phonemic pitch in both stressed and unstressed syllables. Such a phenomenon is so far unknown elsewhere in the Slovene dialects.[17] In this dialect long acute and circumflex may occur in the penultima and ultima of polysyllables as well as in monosyllables. In polysyllables tone may or may not be concomitant with stress. Short stress may occur in any of the three final syllables of a word and may be followed by a long syllable.

A significant redistribution of pitch and quantity due to both metatony and metataxis has taken place in Žiri. Acute occurs as a result of retraction, e.g., *sé:stra* 'sister,' *žé:na,* contraction, e.g., (**jàblko >*) *i̯á:pk* 'apple,' and from circumflex (**sl̥:nce >*) *só:nce* 'sun.' Circumflex may be from acute, e.g., (**krá:l'*) > *krà:l* 'king,' (**člové:ka >*) *člavè:ka* 'of a person (gen. sg.)'; circumflex in monosyllables, e.g., *nọ̀:č* 'night'; or contraction of the suffix *-әc,* e.g., (**studé:nәc >*) *stadè:nc* 'well, spring.' Retractions of the *že'na* type create new pre-ultima shorts, e.g., *'maɣla* 'fog,' *'baɣat* 'rich.' When stress has retracted from long syllables, the pitch of the previously stressed syllable remains in place, e.g., (**otró:ku >*) *'atru̯ó:k* 'to a child (dat. sg.),' *imi̯é:na* 'of a name (gen. sg.).' Pitch is neutralized from the antepenultima and further towards the beginning of the word, so that long stresses are phonetically realized as acute. Thus, for monosyllables and disyllables, the functional load of prosody is 5S – 2, while no more than (S – 3) + 13 may be (in theory, at least) realized in trisyllables and beyond, e.g., *i̯á:pk, krà:l, 'krah* 'bread,' *só:nce, mà:ter* 'of one's mother (gen. sg.),' *'šerak* 'wide,' *'atra:c* 'children,' *ževè̀:t* 'to live (inf.),' *z:ab'mi* 'with one's teeth (instr. pl.),' *'kakọ̣:š* 'hen (gen. sg./nom./acc. pl.),' *'kakò:š* 'hen (nom. sg.)' (Stanonik 1977[8]).

Conclusion

The majority of Slovene dialects surveyed exhibit a functional load in word prosody that does not exceed that of the tonemic variant of MSS, that is, 2S + 1. This formula represents the end point of a historical development that maximized the prosodic distinctions in the ultima. A general tendency in the dialects is to unburden the ultima, a process which in the majority of instances reduces the number of prosodic possibilities (for example, Cankova 2S – 1, Babno Polje 2(S – 1)), while in a few instances it increases the number of distinctive oppositions (e.g., Kneža 2S + 2, Dragatuš 3S – 2). Reductions in prosodic opposition are accounted for also by the loss of quantity (Srednje Jarše 2S), pitch (Videm ob Ščavnici 2S – 1), and both quantity and pitch (Komen S).

Some local dialects have maintained equilibrium by transferring the function of pitch to quantity (Mostec 2S), or by regaining pitch distinctions (Šmartno v Brdih 2S + 1).

The upper limits of the functional load of prosody in Slovene dialects occur in isolated village dialects. These appear to severely limit the realization of the potential number of prosodic oppositions, while in theory generating functional loads much greater than the average for Slovene (e.g., Breznica pri Št. Jakobu v Rožu 4S - 1, Žiri 5S - 2).

Summary

This study examines the prosodic variation in Modern Standard Slovene and the Slovene dialects by expressing in mathematical terms the number of potential phonemic prosodic oppositions in accentogenic words. Though typological in intent, the study to some extent analyzes the linguistic geography of prosodic features in that it utilizes a representative sample of dialects distributed over the entire Slovene linguistic area. A historical sketch discussing the changes relevant to the development of modern Slovene prosodic oppositions is given. This discussion delineates two processes, metatony and metataxis. A synchronic account gives concrete examples of the prosodic possibilities of Modern Standard Slovene and compares them with those of local dialects. It is found that most dialects fall roughly within the range of the potential possibilities of the standard language, while many dialects are in the process of reducing phonemic prosodic oppositions. Increases in prosodic oppositions are anomalous and appear to occur in geographically isolated local dialects.

References

Abbreviations: *JAZU* = *Jugoslavenska akademija znanosti i umjetnosti;* *SAZU* = *Slovenska akademija znanosti in umjetnosti; SR* = *Slavistična revija.*

Bajec, Anton. 1921. O prvotnem naglasu v rezijanskem narečju. *Časopis za slovenski jezik, književnost in zgodovino* 3:40–42.

Boduèn de Kurtenè, I. [= J. Baudouin de Courtenay]. 1875. *Opyt fonetiki rez'janskix govorov.* Warsaw-Petersburg.

Breznik, Anton. 1909. *Westkrainerdialekte: Postojna, Horjulj und Poljane nad Škofjo Loko* [Unpublished seminar thesis].

Isačenko, Alexander V. 1939. *Narečje vasi Sele na Rožu.* Ljubljana: Znanstveno društvo.

Ivić, Pavle. 1958. *Die serbokroatischen Dialekte: Ihre Struktur und Entwicklung*, 1: *Allgemeines und die štokavische dialektgruppe.* The Hague: Mouton.

―――. 1961. The Functional Yield of Prosodic Features in the Patterns of Serbocroatian Dialects. *Word* 17/3:293-308.

―――. 1961-62. Broj prozodijskih mogućnosti u reči kao karakteristika fonoloških sistema slovenskih jezika. *Južnoslovenski filolog* 25:75-113.

―――. 1970. Prosodic Possibilities in Phonology and Morphology. *Studies in General and Oriental Linguistics,* ed. by Roman Jakobson and Shigeo Kawamoto: 287-301.

―――. 1973. The Place of Prosodic Phenomena in Language Structure. *Sciences of Language,* ed. by Roman Jakobson and Shirô Hattori: 109-138.

Ivić, Pavle, ed. 1981. *Fonološki opisi srpskohrvatskih/hrvatskosrpskih slovenačkih i makedonskih govora obuhvaćenih opšteslovenskim lingvističkim atlasom* (= *Posebna izdanja Odjeljenja društvenih nauka* 55/9), 1981. Sarajevo: ANU BiH.

Ivšić, Stjepan. 1936. Jezik Hrvata kajkavaca. *Ljetopis JAZU* 148:47-89.

Jakobson, Roman. 1963. Opyt fonologičeskogo podxoda k istoričeskim voprosam slavjanskoj akcentologii (Pozdnij period slavjanskoj jazykovoj praistorii). *American Contributions to the Fifth International Congress of Slavists* (Sofia). The Hague: Mouton.

Jaksche, Harald. 1965. *Slavische Akzentuation II: Slovenisch.* Wiesbaden: Otto Harrassowitz.

Kalnyn', L. E. 1981. Review of Fonološki opisi . . . *Obščeslavjanskij lingvističeskij atlas: materialy i issledovanija:* 339-46.

Kolarič, Rudolf. 1964. Haloški govor. *Prace filologiczne* 18/2:395-401.

―――. 1968. Prleško narečje. *Svet med Muro in Dravo,* ed. by Viktor Vrbnjak: 630-50.

Ladefoged, Peter. 1973[2]. *Preliminaries to Linguistic Phonetics.* Chicago: University of Chicago Press.

Logar, Tine. 1957, Dialektološke študije X. Belokranjski govori. *SR* 10:145-55.

―――. 1967. Dialektološke študije XIII. Govori vasi Kostanje nad Vrbskim jezerom; XIV. Vokalizem moravškega govora. *SR* 15: 1-27.

―――. 1975. *Slovenska narečja: besedila.* Ljubljana: Mladinska knjiga.

Logar, Tine and Jakob Rigler, eds. 1983. *Karta slovenskih narečij.* Ljubljana: Univerzum.

Lončarić, Mijo. 1979. Naglasni tipovi u kajkavskom narječju. *Rasprave Zavoda za jezik* 4-5:109-17.

Neweklowsky, Gerhard. 1973. Slowenische Akzentstudien: Akustische und linguistische Untersuchungen am Material slowenischer Mundarten aus Kärnten (= *Schriften der Balkankommission, Linguistische Abteilung* 21). Vienna: Verlag der Österreichischen Akademie der Wissenschaften.

Pável, Ágost [= Avgust Pavel]. 1909. *A vashidegkúti szlovén nyelvjárás hangtana* (= *A Magyar szláv nyelvjárások* 1, ed. by Oszkár Asbóth). Budapest: A Magyar Tudományos Akadémia.

Pintar, Luka. 1895. Slovarski in besedoslovni paberki. *Letopis Matice slovenske:* 1-52.

Ramovš, Fran. 1950. Relativna kronologija slovenskih akcentskih pojavov. *SR* 3/1-2:16-23.

Rigler, Jakob. 1963. Pregled osnovnih razvojnih etap v slovenskem vokalizmu. *SR* 14/1-4:25-78.

―――. 1967. Pripombe k Pregledu osnovnih razvojnih etap v slovenskem vokalizmu. *SR* 15/1-2:129-152.

―――. 1972. O rezijanskem naglasu. *SR* 20/1:115-26.

―――. 1973: Smeri glasovnega razvoja v panonskih govorih. *Študije o jeziku in slovstvu:* 113-28.

―――. 1977. K problematiki daljšanja starega aduta. *SR* 25: (= *Zbornik prispevkov za VII. mednarodni slavistični kongres v Zagrebu [Ljubljana] 1978):* 83-99.

―――. 1980a. Nekaj pripomb o glasovnih značilnostih gornjesavinjskih govorov. *SR* 28/1:21-34.

―――. 1980b. Nekaj opažanj pri akutu na zadnjem zlogu v slovenščini. *SR* 28/2:219-22.

Slovar slovenskega knjižnega jezika I (A-H) 1970, 2 (I-Na) 1975, 3 (Ne-Pren) 1979, 4 (Preo-Š) 1985. Ljubljana: Državna založba Slovenije.

Stang, Christian S. 1957. *Slavonic Accentuation* (= *Norske Videnskaps-Akademi i Oslo I. Hist.-Fil. Klasse* 3). Oslo: W. Nygaard.

Stankiewicz, Edward. 1979a The Common Slavic Posodic Pattern and its Evolution in Slovenian. Edward Stankiewicz, *Studies in Morphophonemics and Accentology:* 32-41. Ann Arbor: Michigan Slavic Publications.

―――. 1979b. The Prosodic Features of Modern Standard Slovenian. Edward Stankiewicz, *Studies in Morphophonemics and Accentology:* 127-32. Ann Arbor: Michigan Slavic Publications.

————. 1984–85. The Dialect of Resia and the "Common Slovenian" Accentual Pattern. *Zbornik za filologiju i lingvistiku* 27–28:719–25.

Stanonik, Marija. 1977. Govor Žirovske kotline in njenega obrobja. *SR* 25/2–3:293–309.

Tominec, Ivan. 1964. *Črnovrški dialekt.* Ljubljana: SAZU.

Toporišič, Jože. [1961] 1978. Vokalizem moščanskega govora v brežiškem Posavju. Jože Toporišič, *Glasovna in naglasna podoba slovenskega jezika:* 141–163. Maribor: Obzorja.

————. 1962. Ablösung des relevanten Wortintonationssystems durch den Quantitätsunterschied in einer slovenischen Mundart. *Scando-Slavica:* 239–254.

————. 1967. Pojmovanje tonemičnosti slovenskega jezika. *SR* 15/1–2: 64–108.

————. 1968. Liki slovenskih tonemov. *SR* 16:1–79.

————. 1978. Razločevalna obremenitev slovenskih prozodičnih parametrov. *Slavica Pragensia* 21, *Acta Universitatis Carolinae-Philologica* 3–5:89–96.

Trubetzkoy, Nikolaj S. 1925. Einiges über die russische Lautentwicklung und die Auflösung der gemeinrussischen Spracheinheit. *Zeitschrift für slavische Philologie* 1:287–319.

Valjavec, Matija. 1897. Glavne točke o naglasu kñiževne slovenštine. *Rad JAZU* 132:116–213.

Zorko, Zinka. 1983. Oplotniški govor. *Zbornik občine Slovenska Bistrica* 1:293–310.

Notes

* This study was funded in part by a travel and research grant from the Center for Russian and East European Studies at UCLA. The work began as a term paper assigned by Professor Pavle Ivić (Serbian Academy of Arts and Sciences, Belgrade) during his seminar as a visiting scholar at UCLA in the winter quarter 1986. I am indebted to Professor Ivić for his guidance in the initial stages of the work. I am also grateful to Professors Jože Toporišič (Ljubljana University), Ronelle Alexander (UCB), Henrik Birnbaum (UCLA) and Alan Timberlake (UCLA) for their time spent in consultation on the paper. Thanks are also due to Academic and Professor Tine Logar and the Dialectological Section of the Slovene Academy of Arts and Sciences for permitting me to use unpublished dialect data. [The manuscript was completed in September 1986. It was first published in

Slovene in 1987 as Prozodične možnosti v slovenskem knjižnem jeziku in slovenskih narečjih, *Slavistična revija* 35(2):171–86.]

1. In order to simplify the discussion, we shall consider only *accentogenic* words (thus, we shall exclude clitics and unstressed words in syntagms, e.g., *dober dà:n* 'good day'), and only words with one accent (i.e., with one prominent syllable). While the parameter of accentability is an essential part of a complete description of Slovene prosody, its inclusion would only burden our description by uniformly adding a unit to each functional load formula. For a thorough treatment of a single Slovene system (MSS), see Toporišič 1978.

2. It is acknowledged that many of the elements of this reconstruction (or more properly, reconstructions) are controversial. An attempt has been made to stay with a neutral approach to the extent possible; at any rate, a discussion of the history of South Slavic accent with full justification is outside the scope of this paper.

3. In this paper we shall employ the transcriptional conventions used in the Obščeslavjanskij dialektologičeskij atlas: <'> denotes place of (dynamic) stress and is placed before the consonant preceding the accented vowel; <:> denotes a long vowel and follows the vowel in question; tone is represented in the vowel by <´> for "rising" or "acute" and <`> for "falling" or "circumflex" accent. (The terms acute and circumflex will be used in this paper in the meaning just cited; their use here as cover terms is intended to distance the metalanguage from stating too precisely the properties of the prosodemes, which would be impossible to obtain for all of the microdialects included in the study.) Another type of acute accent, known in Slavic studies as the neo-acute, is marked with the sign <~>. Forms quoted in Modern Standard Slovene are from the *Slovar slovenskega knjižnega jezika*. Apart from the modifications for suprasegmental features just mentioned, segmental features will be transcribed identically to the source material. To prevent misunderstandings, it should be understood that this approach very likely results in a heterogeneous presentation of the segments of local dialects (e.g., sometimes a sign will represent a phoneme, sometimes a phone). As a rule, however, transcriptions are phonetic.

4. It is difficult to find language-internal explanations for the loss; in some areas language contact seems to have played a role. For example, the loss of both tone and quantity in Rezija may owe to Italian and Friulian influence and the loss of tone in some Rovte dialects may owe to German influence (Toporišič 1984:654). The loss of tonemic opposition in the Pannonian dialects may be explained internally, as has been suggested above. Here one might also entertain the possible effect of contact with Hungarian.

It seems plausible that the influence of Hungarian word prosody (a quantity-distinguishing system) supported the retention of sensitivity to length that was lost in other dialects in non-ultima syllables. Such statements are, of course, purely speculative and deserve further investigation.

5. Here one should compare the similar hierarchy found in the Neošto-kavian dialects of Serbo-Croatian (Ivić 1958:105ff). In these dialects retraction may occur from any non-prima syllable.

6. The list of retraction types is limited to those given in the questionnaire for the Slovene Linguistic Atlas project, as conceived by F. Ramovš. The corpus of tokens is small and does not allow us to follow the geographic distribution of other salient word forms, nor does it provide paradigmatic information in most instances.

7. The material is taken from *Fonološki opis* . . . under the corresponding village name.

8. The material is taken from the database of the *Slovene Linguistic Atlas* project, housed in the Dialectological Section of the Slovene Academy of Arts and Sciences.

9. Although the reversal of the expected retraction hierarchy is disturbing (cf. Stankiewicz 1984–1985:722), some evidence speaks for the shift of the circumflex and its subsequent retraction: (1) the raised articulation of the ultima vowel, e.g., 'ǫku̯ (< *ǫ́ko), 'u̯hu̯ (< *ū́:ho) (Osojani[8]); (2) the appearance of murmured vowels in retracted forms, e.g., 'nǫga 'leg,' versus their absence in unretracted oxytones, e.g., ža'na 'wife,' ko'za 'goat' (Osojani[8]). Comparative evidence from the Ter dialect indicates that the early retraction of circumflex from the ultima is plausible. [Since this manuscript was completed, the opposite view, that the retraction never occurred in Rezija, has been argued for quite convincingly by W. Vermeer, 1987, "The Treatment of the Proto-Slavic Falling Tone in the Resian Dialects of Slovene" in *Dutch Studies in South Slavic and Balkan Linguistics* (= *Studies in Slavic and General Linguistics* 10, ed. by A. A. Barentsen, B. M. Groen, and R. Sprenger), pp. 275–98; Amsterdam: Rodopi.]

10. This typology agrees in principle with that of Stankiewicz 1979a:39. His breakdown of dialect areas leaves out the entire Pannonian group (where stress and quantity are relevant), the existence of quantity in Styrian dialects (e.g., Prlekija, Mostec). Since this article, at least one other village dialect with pitch as the sole distinctive prosodic feature in addition to Smlednik has been recorded, that of Srednje Jarše.

11. The term *zasopli vokali* has remained enigmatic to the uninitiated in Slovene dialectology (see Kalnyn' 1981:345). This state of affairs is understandable as, to my knowledge, they do not occur in other European lan-

guages. Descriptions of *zasopli vokali* (de Courtenay 1875:5; Ramovš 1935: 36) and my own impression from tape recordings of a Rezija dialect suggest that the term corresponds to *murmured vowels* in American phonetic terminology. Ladefoged has described the phenomenon for Gujarati and other Indian languages (1973:12).

12. To the best of my knowledge, there are no other published or unpublished reports on Haloze village dialects besides Kolarič 1964.

13. Material is taken from *Fonološki opisi* . . . and the *Slovene Linguistic Atlas* database. See also Toporišič 1961, 1962.

14. The prosodic shape of this word is actually *má:tә*. Characteristic of several Carinthian dialects is the realization of pitch at the word rather than the syllable level. According to Logar, intensity is realized in long syllables while the tonal peak is reached in the ultima of polysyllables (*Fonološki opisi* . . . 184). (See also Ramovš 1935: 14ff; Isačenko 1939: 19ff; Logar 1967:1–19; Neweklowsky 1973.) This potentially distracting phonetic detail has no importance for our analysis, as we are concerned only with the pitch oppositions in the long syllable.

15. /ә/ in this dialect appears to permit a distinction of quantity, cf. *bә:ha* 'flea.'

16. No evidence was found for short acute in monosyllables in the material available. Therefore it is uncertain whether the number of possibilities exceeds 2S + 1 for monosyllables.

17. Cf. Pintar 1895, Ramovš 1935:95; Stanonik 1977:296. Ramovš shows post-tonic length in the Kostel dialect of Lower Carniola. This is supported by a more recent investigation of the dialect of Banja Loka by a student researcher who records *'uku:* 'eye,' *'vihu:* 'ear,' *'mesu:* 'meat,' and *'lipu:* 'beautiful.' Too little material is given for this microdialect, however, to determine the phonemic status of this new variation.

CONTRIBUTORS

Henrik Birnbaum is Professor of Slavic Languages and Literatures and Chairman of the Slavic Department, University of California, Los Angeles. He is the author of more than 300 publications in the fields of Slavic and general linguistics, early Slavic civilization, and Russian literature. From 1968 to 1978 he was Director of the UCLA Center for Russian and East European Studies. Birnbaum is a member of the Swedish, Yugoslav, and Polish Academies of Science, and in 1985 he was the UCLA Faculty Research Lecturer.

Zlatan Čolaković, formerly administrative secretary of the Institute for Literature of the Yugoslav Academy, was also a Fulbright Fellow at Harvard. His book *Tri orla Tragičkoga Svijeta* (1989) and other essays deal with the origins of ancient Greek tragedy. He has transcribed and edited over 80,000 lines of sound recordings of Yugoslav epics belonging to the Milman Parry collection, and in 1989 he made a collection of video and sound recordings of South Slavic Muslim epics.

Leighton Brett Cooke is Assistant Professor of Russian at Texas A & M University; he has also taught at the University of Alberta and the University of California, Riverside. He has recently completed a book manuscript on Puškin's psychology of creativity, and he plans sociobiological studies of other Russian authors, notably Pasternak.

Thomas Eekman taught Russian and other Slavic literatures at the University of Amsterdam from 1948 to 1966 and at UCLA from 1966 to 1990, where he is now Professor Emeritus. His publications include, among others, *A. Čexov, 1860–1960* (ed., 1960); *The Realm of Rime* (1974); *Thirty Years of Yugoslav Literature, 1945–1975* (1978). He is working in the area of comparative Slavic prose and poetry.

Terence Emmons teaches Russian history at Stanford University. He is the author of *The Formation of Political Parties and the First National Elections in Russia* and a former editor of *The Russian Review*.

Marc L. Greenberg studied Slavic languages and literatures at the University of California, Los Angeles (B.A., 1983; Ph.D., 1990) and the University of Chicago (M.A., 1984). In 1988–89 he held a Fulbright fellowship to conduct research on Slovene dialects in Yugoslavia. He is the author of several research papers on

Slovene, Slovak, and general Slavic linguistics. Since 1990 he has been Assistant Professor of Slavic Linguistics at the University of Kansas, Lawrence.

Jerry T. Heil holds an interdisciplinary doctorate in Modern Russian Literature and Film Theory and Criticism from the University of California, Berkeley. He has taught at the University of California, Irvine, and at Indiana University. His publications on Russian or Soviet literature and the cinema (on Babel', Tynjanov, Oleša, and others) have appeared in *Russian Literature, Slavistische Beiträge, Avant-Garde,* and *Griffithiana.*

Ante Kadić is Professor Emeritus of South Slavic literature at Indiana University. Among his recent books are *The Tradition of Freedom in Croatian Literature* (1983) and *Essays in South Slavic Literature* (1988). He has contributed articles and reviews to numerous scholarly journals both in Europe and America.

Paul A. Karpuk is Assistant Professor of Russian at the University of the Pacific and co-editor of the *Gogol Bulletin*, the annual publication of the Gogol Society. A Ph.D. from the University of California, Berkeley, he is currently working on several articles and a book dealing with Gogol's use of Ukrainian history.

John M. Kopper is Assistant Professor of Russian and Comparative Literature at Dartmouth College. His most recent work has been on Andrej Belyj's novels and their place in the early twentieth century's reassessment of the uses of metaphor.

Bernice Glatzer Rosenthal is Professor of History at Fordham University. Her publications include *D. S. Merezhkovsky and the Silver Age* (1975); *A Revolution of the Spirit: Crisis of Values in Russia* (with Martha Bohachevsky-Chomiak, 1982; new edition in press); *Nietzsche in Russia* (1986); and numerous articles and reviews.

Walter Schamschula, who holds a doctorate from the University of Frankfurt, is currently Professor of Slavic Languages and Literatures at the University of California, Berkeley. His publications on Czech and Russian literatures include books on the Russian historical novel and on the Czech national and cultural revival in the eighteenth century. He has edited a volume of essays on Jaroslav Hašek, 1883–1983, and an anthology of Old Czech literature. His two-volume *History of Czech Literature* is forthcoming.